# TABLE OF CONTENTS

**PERLY'S INC.**

TEL: 416-785-6277 (MAPS)  -  WWW.PERLYS.COM

**Copyright © Perly's Inc. 2002 Edition**        **ISBN 1-894720-13-X**

All rights reserved. No part of this book may be reproduced or transmitted in any form or by any means, electronic or mechanical, including photocopying, recording, or by any information storage and retrieval system, without permission in writing from the publisher. The publisher and distributors of this publication disclaim from any liability for damages of any nature arising from any error or omission.

**Published by Perly's Inc.**

# Belper Ct?

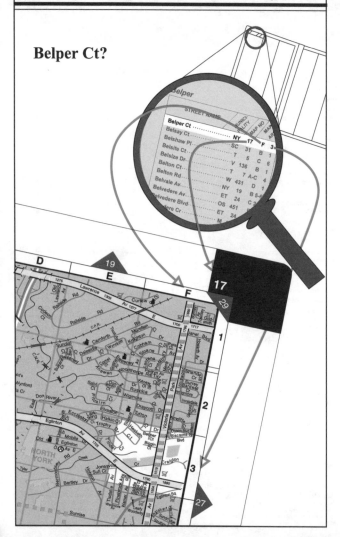

# HOW TO USE THE BOOK

Perly's Map book is designed for you, the user. It is very easy to use, and constructed to withstand heavy use. Before you start, please take a few minutes to read the following instructions:

**HOW TO FIND A STREET:** Our instructions on page 4 tell you the contents of our maps and index.
**HOW TO READ THE INDEX:** Street Designation Abbreviation & Municipality Abbreviations on this page will help you understand the information listed in our index.
**HOW TO LOCATE MAPS:** "GTA-Plus" Key Map on pages 2-4, and the fold-out map at the back help you quickly spot the map locations - our area of coverage is in white and map numbers are in blue.
**MAP PAGES:** Numbers at the corner of each map (inside the black box) are map numbers not page numbers. Most of our maps consist of 2 sides: left and right.

# STREET DESIGNATIONS ABBREVIATIONS

| | | |
|---|---|---|
| AV . . . . . . . . .Avenue | GDNS . . . . . .Gardens | PR . . . . . . . . .Promenade |
| BLVD . . . . . . .Boulevard | GR . . . . . . . .Grove | PT . . . . . . . .Point |
| CIR . . . . . . . .Circle | GT . . . . . . . .Gate | PTWY . . . . . . .Pathway |
| CL . . . . . . . . .Close | HTS . . . . . . .Heights | RD . . . . . . . .Road |
| CR . . . . . . . .Crescent | HWY . . . . . . .Highway | SQ . . . . . . . .Square |
| CRCT . . . . . . .Circuit | LA . . . . . . . . .Lane | ST . . . . . . . .Street |
| CT . . . . . . . .Court | PL . . . . . . . . .Place | TERR . . . . . . .Terrace |
| DR . . . . . . . . .Drive | PLZ . . . . . . .Plaza | TR . . . . . . . .Trail |
| EXPWY . . . . . .Expressway | PK . . . . . . . .Park | |
| FRWY . . . . . .Freeway | PKWY . . . . . .Parkway | |

# MUNICIPALITY ABBREVIATIONS

| | |
|---|---|
| AJ . . . . . .AJAX, Town of | NY . . . . . . .NORTH YORK, Community of (incl. Don Mills, Downsview, Weston, Willowdale) |
| AU . . . . . .AURORA, Town of | OS . . . . . .OSHAWA. Town of |
| BA . . . . . .BARRIE, City of | OK . . . . . .OAKVILLE, Town of |
| BG . . . . . .BRADFORD-WEST GWILLIMBURY, Town of | OV . . . . . .ORANGEVILLE, Town of |
| BR . . . . . .BRAMPTON, City of (incl. Bramalea) | PK . . . . . .PICKERING, City of (incl. Bay Ridges, Frenchman's Bay, Liverpool Community, Rouge Valley) |
| BU . . . . . .BURLINGTON, City of | |
| CA . . . . . .CALEDON, Town of | RH . . . . . .RICHMOND HILL, Town of (incl. Oak Ridges, Wilcox Lake) |
| CL . . . . . .CLARINGTON, Municipality of | |
| EG . . . . . .EAST GWILLIMBURY, Town of | SC . . . . . .SCARBOROUGH, Community of (incl. Agincourt, Malvern, West Hill) |
| ES . . . . . .ESSA, Township of | |
| ET . . . . . .ETOBICOKE, Community of (incl. Islington, Long Branch, Mimico, New Toronto, Rexdale, Weston) | SG . . . . . .SCUGOG, Township of |
| | SW . . . . . .SPRINGWATER, Township of |
| | T . . . . . .TORONTO, Community of |
| EY . . . . . .EAST YORK, Community of (incl. Leaside) | UX . . . . . .UXBRIDGE, Town of |
| FL . . . . . .FLAMBOROUGH, Township of | V . . . . . .VAUGHAN, City of (incl. Concord, Kleinburg, Maple, Pine Grove, Thornhill, Woodbridge) |
| GE . . . . . .GEORGINA, Township of | |
| HH . . . . . .HALTON HILLS, Town of | W . . . . . .WHITBY, Town of |
| IN . . . . . .INNISFIL, Town of | WS . . . . . .WHITCHURCH-STOUFFVILLE, Town of |
| M . . . . . .MISSISSAUGA, City of (incl. Clarkson, Erindale, Erin Mills, Lorne Park, Malton, Meadowvale, Port Credit, Streetsville) | Y . . . . . .YORK, Community of (incl. Weston) |
| MA . . . . . .MARKHAM, Town of (incl. Buttonville, Thornhill, Unionville) | The **MEGACITY** (East York, Etobicoke, North York, Scarborough, Toronto, York) : Despite the amalgamation of the new City of Toronto, we kept the former Municipal boundaries for the sake of clarity. |
| MI . . . . . .MILTON, Town of | |
| NM . . . . . .NEWMARKET, Town of | |

# LEGEND

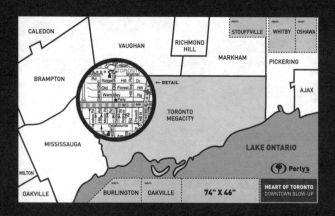

## A

| Street | | Map | | |
|---|---|---|---|---|
| Abbeville Rd | SC | 39 | C | 5-6 |
| Abbey La | T | 3 | B | 1 |
| Abbeywood Tr | NY | 9 | E-F | 4 |
| Abbotsfield Gt | SC | 29 | B | 1 |
| Abbotsford Rd | NY | 10 | E | 4-5 |
| Abbott Av | T | 14 | D-E | 3 |
| Abbottswood Rd | SC | 29 | F | 4 |
| Abbs St | T | 14 | F | 6 |
| Abell St | T | 2 | A | 1 |
| Aberdeen Av | T | 3 | B | 5 |
| Aberfoyle Cr | ET | 24 | B | 3 |
| Aberlady Rd | ET | 24 | B | 5 |
| Abigail Pl | ET | 36 | E | 1 |
| Abilene Ct | ET | 26 | A-B | 4-5 |
| Abinger Cr | ET | 36 | F | 4-5 |
| Abitibi Av | NY | 11 | A-B | 1 |
| Abner Pl | ET | 36 | F | 1 |
| Abrams Pl | NY | 9 | E | 3 |
| Acacia Av | NY | 28 | C | 3 |
| Acacia Rd | T | 7 | A | 4-5 |
| Academy Rd | NY | 28 | E | 4 |
| Access Rd | ET | 38 | B-C | 2 |
| Ace La | T | 4 | D | 6 |
| Acheson Blvd | SC | 49 | E | 5 |
| Ackroft Ct | ET | 36 | A-B | 1 |
| Acland Cr | SC | 49 | D | 4 |
| Acme Cr | ET | 26 | A | 1 |
| Acores Av | T | 4 | B | 2-5 |
| Acorn Av | ET | 34 | F | 3-4 |
| Acre Heights Cr | SC | 39 | B | 4 |
| Acton Av | NY | 10 | A-B | 5 |
| Ada Cr | SC | 39 | A | 4-5 |
| Adair Rd | EY | 17 | F | 6 |
| Adair Rd | EY | 27 | F | 6 |
| Adamede Cr | NY | 11 | F | 3 |
| Adams Dr | SC | 39 | F | 1-2 |
| Adam's Park Gt | SC | 49 | F | 4 |
| Adanac Dr | SC | 37 | B-C | 4 |
| Addington Av | NY | 10 | E | 6 |
| Addington Pl | NY | 10 | E | 6 |
| Addison Cr | NY | 19 | A | 5 |
| Adelaide Pl | T | 2 | D | 1 |
| Adelaide St E | T | 3 | A-C | 1 |
| Adelaide St W | T | 2 | B-F | 1 |
| Adelaide St W | T | 3 | A | 1 |
| Adele Av | NY | 28 | F | 3 |
| Adeline Ct | ET | 40 | E | 4 |
| Adelpha Dr | ET | 24 | B | 4 |
| Adencliff Rd | SC | 31 | A | 4-5 |
| Adenmore Rd | SC | 47 | D | 6 |
| Ademo Ct | ET | 26 | C | 3 |
| Adirondack Gt | SC | 31 | D | 4 |
| Adler St | SC | 37 | B | 3 |
| Administration Rd | SC | 29 | E | 3 |
| Admiral Rd | T | 4 | E | 2-3 |
| Adonis Ct | ET | 26 | E | 3 |
| Adra Villaway | NY | 11 | F | 4 |
| Adrian Av | T | 14 | E | 2 |
| Adriatic Rd | ET | 28 | B | 5 |
| Advance Rd | ET | 24 | A-B | 4 |
| Afton Av | T | 4 | A | 6 |
| Agate Rd | NY | 18 | C | 3-4 |
| Agatha Rd | ET | 36 | E | 5 |
| Agincourt Dr | SC | 29 | E | 1 |
| Agincourt Dr | SC | 29 | E | 5-6 |
| Aikenhead Rd | ET | 26 | B | 1-2 |
| Aileen Av | Y | 16 | D-E | 4-5 |
| Ailsa Craig Ct | NY | 10 | C | 3 |
| Ainsdale Rd | SC | 27 | E | 5 |
| Ainsdale Rd | SC | 29 | B | 5-6 |
| Ainsley Gdns | ET | 24 | B | 1 |
| Ainsley Gdns | ET | 26 | B | 6 |
| Ainsworth Rd | T | 5 | E | 6 |
| Aintree Ct | ET | 32 | B | 3 |
| Airdrie Rd | EY | 7 | D | 4-5 |
| Airley Cr | EY | 15 | A | 1 |
| Airmont Dr | SC | 37 | C | 6 |
| Airview Rd | ET | 38 | F | 2 |
| Aitken Pl | T | 3 | B | 2-3 |
| Akasha Ct | SC | 49 | C | 6 |
| Akron Rd | ET | 32 | D-E | 4 |
| Alabaster Rd | ET | 40 | E | 1 |
| Alameda Av | Y | 6 | B | 4-5 |
| Alamosa Dr | NY | 11 | E-F | 5 |
| Alan Av | T | 22 | C | 1-2 |
| Alanbull Sq | SC | 41 | A | 2 |
| Alanbury Cr | SC | 41 | C | 2-3 |
| Alba Pl | ET | 40 | C | 4 |
| Albacore Cr | SC | 39 | C | 4-5 |
| Albani St | ET | 22 | C | 4 |
| Albany Av | T | 4 | D | 2-3 |
| Albany Rd | NY | 20 | D | 1 |
| Albemarle Av | T | 5 | E | 4 |
| Albert Av | ET | 22 | D-E | 3 |
| Albert Franck Pl | T | 3 | A | 3 |
| Albert St | T | 4 | F | 6 |
| Alberta Av | T | 4 | B | 1 |
| Alberta Cir | T | 2 | A | 2 |
| Alberta Ct | T | 12 | C | 2 |
| Albertus Av | T | 6 | F | 2 |
| Albion Av | SC | 25 | A | 3 |
| Albion Rd | ET | 28 | C | 1-3 |
| Albion Rd | ET | 30 | A-B | 4-6 |
| Albion Rd | ET | 40 | A-F | 1-4 |
| Albright Av | ET | 32 | C | 3 |
| Alcan Av | ET | 32 | C | 4 |
| Alcester Ct | NY | 8 | A | 5 |
| Alcide St | ET | 40 | A | 1 |
| Alcina Av | T | 4 | C | 1 |
| Acorn Av | T | 4 | F | 2 |
| Aldburn Rd | T | 6 | B | 3 |
| Aldbury Gdns | T | 7 | A | 2 |
| Alden Av | ET | 22 | B-C | 2 |
| Aldenham Cr | NY | 19 | D-E | 4-5 |
| Alder Cr | ET | 32 | E-F | 4-5 |
| Alder Rd | EY | 17 | C | 6 |
| Alderbrae Av | ET | 32 | D | 2-3 |
| Alderbrook Dr | NY | 9 | E | 5-6 |
| Aldercrest Rd | ET | 32 | D | 2-3 |
| Alderdale Ct | NY | 9 | F | 4 |
| Aldergrove Av | T | 15 | C | 4 |
| Aldershot Cr | NY | 9 | B | 2 |
| Alderton Ct | ET | 26 | C | 6 |
| Aldgate Av | ET | 24 | E | 6 |
| Aldridge Av | T | 15 | C | 3-4 |
| Aldwych Av | EY | 5 | E-F | 3 |
| Alex Mews | T | 4 | F | 2 |
| Alexander Muir Rd | T | 7 | A | 1-2 |
| Alexander Pl | T | 5 | A | 4-5 |
| Alexander St | T | 4 | F | 5 |
| Alexander St | T | 5 | A | 5 |
| Alexander St | ET | 22 | E | 2 |
| Alexandra Blvd | T | 6 | E-F | 2 |
| Alexandra Wood | NY | 6 | D | 2 |
| Alexdon Rd | NY | 20 | E | 4 |
| Alexis Blvd | NY | 8 | B-D | 1 |
| Alexmuir Blvd | SC | 31 | E-F | 3-4 |
| Alford Cr | SC | 51 | A | 4 |
| Alfred Av | NY | 11 | A-B | 6 |
| Alfresco Lawn | NY | 11 | E | 6 |
| Algie Av | ET | 32 | E | 1 |
| Algie St | ET | 34 | E | 6 |
| Algo Ct | NY | 11 | C | 2 |
| Algoma St | ET | 22 | D-E | 2 |
| Algonquin Av | T | 14 | D | 5 |
| Algonquin Bridge Rd | T | 3 | B | 5 |
| Alhambra Av | T | 14 | D | 3 |
| Alhart Dr | ET | 30 | B-C | 5-6 |
| Alhena Av | ET | 32 | E | 3 |
| Alice Cr | SC | 29 | A | 4 |
| Alicewood Ct | ET | 40 | D-E | 5 |
| Alladin Av | NY | 18 | A-B | 5 |
| Allan Park Rd | T | 24 | C | 4 |
| Allanbrooke Dr | ET | 24 | B-C | 2 |
| Allanford Rd | SC | 29 | D | 1-2 |
| Allangrove Cr | SC | 31 | B | 5 |
| Allanhurst Dr | ET | 26 | C-D | 4 |
| Allard Av | NY | 8 | D | 4 |
| Allcroft Dr | ET | 30 | B | 5-6 |
| Allen Av | T | 5 | D-E | 6 |
| Allen Dr | T | 22 | D | 3 |
| Allenbury Gdns | NY | 21 | C-D | 5 |
| Allenby Av | ET | 28 | B-C | 4 |
| Allenvale Av | Y | 6 | A | 4 |
| Allenwood Cr | NY | 11 | F | 4 |
| Allerton Rd | ET | 24 | A | 3-4 |
| Alliance Av | Y | 16 | A-B | 5 |
| Allingham Gdns | NY | 8 | B-C | 3 |
| Allison Dr | ET | 24 | C | 5 |
| Allister Av | SC | 37 | A | 5-6 |
| Allonsius Dr | ET | 34 | B | 1-2 |
| Alloy Ct | NY | 30 | E | 6 |
| Allview Cr | NY | 11 | F | 4 |
| Alma Av | T | 4 | A | 6 |
| Alma Av | T | 14 | F | 6 |
| Alma Dr | ET | 26 | D-E | 2 |
| Almayo Cr | ET | 40 | E | 2 |
| Almington St | NY | 8 | C | 2-3 |
| Almont Rd | NY | 8 | C | 3 |
| Almore Av | NY | 8 | B-C | 2 |
| Alness St | NY | 20 | F | 1-3 |
| Alonzo Rd | NY | 10 | D | 5 |
| Alpaca Dr | SC | 37 | C | 2 |
| Alpine Av | T | 14 | E | 2 |
| Alrita Cr | SC | 29 | A | 3 |
| Altair Av | SC | 31 | A | 5 |
| Altamont Rd | NY | 10 | E | 2-3 |
| Althea Rd | SC | 49 | A | 5 |
| Alton Av | T | 15 | A | 5-6 |
| Alton Towers Cir | SC | 41 | A-B | 2 |
| Altonby Rd | SC | 49 | E | 3-4 |
| Alvarado Pl | NY | 19 | C-D | 4 |
| Alvin Av | T | 7 | A | 4 |
| Alvinston Rd | SC | 27 | A | 4 |
| Alyward St | Y | 16 | D | 3 |
| Amanda Dr | SC | 41 | A | 3 |
| Amaranth Ct | NY | 8 | A | 5 |
| Amarillo Dr | SC | 37 | B | 2-3 |
| Amaron Av | ET | 30 | A | 4 |
| Ambassador Pl | NY | 8 | B | 2 |
| Amber Cr | NY | 18 | B | 5 |
| Ambercroft Blvd | SC | 31 | C | 2 |
| Amberdale Cr | SC | 39 | A | 4-5 |
| Amberglen Ct | NY | 16 | C | 1-2 |
| Amberjack Blvd | SC | 39 | B-C | 4-5 |
| Amberley St | SC | 29 | A | 3 |
| Amberwood Rd | ET | 36 | D | 5 |
| Ambleside Av | ET | 24 | B-C | 5 |
| Amboy Rd | SC | 29 | F | 6 |
| Ambrose Rd | NY | 9 | F | 1 |
| Ambrose Rd | NY | 11 | E | 6 |
| Ameer Av | NY | 8 | B | 5 |
| Amelia St | T | 5 | B-C | 4 |
| Ames Cir | NY | 9 | E-F | 4 |
| Ames St | NY | 9 | E | 4 |
| Amesbury Dr | NY | 16 | C | 1-2 |
| Amethyst Rd | SC | 29 | C | 1 |
| Amherst Av | Y | 6 | A | 4 |
| Amiens Rd | SC | 49 | B | 5-6 |
| Amoro Ct | ET | 38 | E-F | 1 |
| Amoro Dr | ET | 40 | F | 6 |
| Amos Cr | NY | 10 | A-B | 6 |
| Ampleford Pl | SC | 31 | E | 1 |
| Amroth Av | T | 15 | D | 3-4 |
| Amsterdam Av | EY | 17 | F | 5 |
| Amulet St | SC | 29 | C | 1 |
| Anaconda Av | SC | 27 | C | 5-6 |
| Ancaster Rd | NY | 18 | F | 2-3 |
| Anchor Dr | NY | 20 | B | 6 |
| Ancona St | NY | 10 | D | 3-4 |
| Ancroft Pl | T | 5 | B | 3 |
| Anderson Av | T | 6 | E-F | 4 |
| Andes Rd | SC | 31 | D | 4 |
| Andona Cr | SC | 49 | C | 4 |
| Andover Cr | SC | 51 | A | 1 |
| Andrew Av | SC | 25 | F | 1 |
| Andrew Av | SC | 29 | F | 5-6 |
| Andrews Av | T | 4 | C | 6 |
| Aneta Cir | NY | 11 | B | 2 |
| Anewen Dr | NY | 17 | E-F | 2 |
| Angel Ct | ET | 36 | C | 5 |
| Anglesey Blvd | ET | 26 | B-C | 6 |
| Angora St | SC | 37 | E | 1-2 |
| Angus Dr | NY | 21 | A | 3-4 |
| Angus Pl | T | 2 | D | 2 |
| Ann Arbour Rd | NY | 28 | D-E | 3-4 |
| Anna Hillard La | T | 5 | B | 6 |
| Annabelle Dr | ET | 40 | F | 2 |
| Annan Dr | SC | 25 | C | 1 |
| Annapearl Ct | NY | 11 | A-B | 4 |
| Annaree Dr | SC | 29 | A | 4 |
| Anndale Dr | NY | 9 | A-B | 1 |
| Anndale Rd | SC | 25 | A | 5 |
| Anneke Rd | SC | 25 | D | 3 |
| Annesley Av | EY | 7 | B | 4 |
| Annette St | T | 14 | A-D | 2 |
| Annette St | T | 24 | F | 2 |
| Annis Rd | SC | 37 | C | 5 |
| Anola Pl | SC | 27 | F | 4 |
| Ansell Av | ET | 32 | C | 4 |
| Ansford Av | NY | 8 | B | 3 |
| Ansley St | T | 6 | F | 1-2 |
| Anson Av | SC | 37 | A-B | 5 |
| Anthia Dr | NY | 30 | B | 1-2 |
| Anthony Rd | NY | 18 | E-F | 4 |
| Antibes Dr | NY | 10 | B-C | 2-3 |
| Anticosti Dr | SC | 37 | A | 1 |
| Antioch Dr | ET | 36 | E | 4-5 |
| Antler St | T | 14 | E | 2 |
| Antoni Pl | NY | 28 | E | 4 |
| Antrim Cr | SC | 29 | D-E | 3 |
| Anvil Millway | NY | 9 | D | 3 |
| Apache Tr | NY | 21 | E-F | 3-4 |
| Apex Rd | NY | 18 | F | 6 |
| Apollo Dr | NY | 9 | F | 4-5 |
| Appian Dr | NY | 11 | F | 4 |
| Appleby Ct | ET | 34 | E | 1 |
| Appleby Rd | ET | 34 | E | 1-2 |
| Appledale Rd | ET | 36 | F | 5-6 |
| Applefield Dr | SC | 29 | F | 4-5 |
| Applegate Cr | NY | 21 | C-E | 1 |
| Applemore Rd | SC | 41 | D | 6 |
| Appleton Av | Y | 6 | A | 6 |
| Appletree Ct | NY | 18 | C | 1 |
| Apricot La | T | 13 | E | 5 |
| Apricot La | T | 15 | E | 6 |
| Apsco Av | SC | 37 | F | 2 |
| Apsley Rd | NY | 8 | E-F | 4 |

| STREET NAME | MUNICIPALITY | MAP NO | MAP AREA |
|---|---|---|---|
| Apted Av | NY | 30 | A 4 |
| Aquatic Dr | T | 12 | B-C 2-3 |
| Aquila Ct | ET | 38 | E 1-2 |
| Aragon Av | SC | 29 | B-C 1-2 |
| Aragon Av | SC | 31 | B 6 |
| Araman Dr | SC | 29 | D 1-2 |
| Araz Pl | NY | 7 | E 1 |
| Arbor Dell Rd | ET | 28 | A 1 |
| Arbor Low Gt | SC | 41 | B 4 |
| Arboretum La | NY | 20 | B-C 2 |
| Arborview Cr | ET | 40 | A 4 |
| Arborwood Dr | ET | 40 | A-B 5-6 |
| Arbroath Cr | SC | 29 | D 4 |
| Arbutus Ct | SC | 29 | D 4 |
| Arcade Dr | ET | 26 | D-E 3 |
| Arcadian Cir | ET | 32 | E 5 |
| Archer Rd | T | 6 | D 4 |
| Archer St | T | 14 | F 4 |
| Archerhill Dr | ET | 36 | B 6 |
| Archway Cr | NY | 30 | B 4 |
| Archwood Cr | SC | 29 | D 4-5 |
| Arcot Blvd | ET | 28 | C 1-2 |
| Ardagh St | T | 14 | A-B 3 |
| Ardell Av | SC | 35 | B 3 |
| Arden Cr | SC | 27 | B 4 |
| Arden Thorpe Rd | SC | 37 | A 4 |
| Ardgowan Ct | SC | 41 | A 3 |
| Ardmore Rd | T | 6 | C-D 5 |
| Ardrossan Pl | T | 3 | A 2 |
| Ardtree Av | NY | 17 | E-F 2-3 |
| Ardua St | ET | 36 | B-C 6 |
| Ardwick Blvd | NY | 30 | B-C 6 |
| Ardwold Gt | T | 4 | E 1-2 |
| Arena St | NY | 16 | A 4 |
| Ares Ct | SC | 37 | F 2 |
| Argate Pl | SC | 27 | D 4 |
| Argo Pl | SC | 37 | C 4 |
| Argonaut Dr | SC | 31 | A 5 |
| Argonne Cr | NY | 11 | D-E 2 |
| Argyle Pl | T | 4 | A-B 3 |
| Argyle St | T | 4 | A-B 3 |
| Arjay Cr | NY | 5 | C 5 |
| Arkley Cr | ET | 36 | E 1 |
| Arkona Dr | SC | 29 | B 2 |
| Arkwright St | NY | 18 | B 6 |
| Arlene Ct | SC | 29 | F 5 |
| Arleta Av | NY | 20 | B 5-6 |
| Arlington Av | T | 4 | B 1 |
| Arlington Av | Y | 6 | B 4-6 |
| Aristan Dr | NY | 10 | A 4 |
| Armada Ct | SC | 39 | D 5 |
| Armadale Av | T | 14 | A 2-4 |
| Armadale Av | T | 24 | C 2 |
| Armel Ct | ET | 28 | C 2 |
| Armitage Dr | SC | 29 | B 3 |
| Armour Blvd | NY | 8 | D-E 2-3 |
| Armoury St | T | 5 | F 6 |
| Armstrong Av | T | 14 | F 3 |
| Arnall Av | SC | 31 | A 2 |
| Arncliffe Cr | SC | 27 | A 4 |
| Arnham Rd | SC | 27 | B 4 |
| Arnold Av | T | 5 | B 4 |
| Arnold Av | Y | 16 | B 4 |
| Arnold St | ET | 22 | A 1-2 |
| Arnott Av | NY | 10 | C 4 |
| Arnott St | SC | 27 | E 2 |
| Arnprior Rd | SC | 27 | F 1 |
| Arran Cr | NY | 11 | B-C 1 |
| Arrow Rd | NY | 30 | B 4-6 |
| Arrowdale Av | NY | 18 | B 4-5 |
| Arrowsmith Av | NY | 16 | C 1-2 |
| Arrowstock Rd | NY | 11 | E 5 |
| Artech Ct | NY | 20 | A 3 |
| Arthur Griffith Dr | NY | 20 | A-B 5-6 |
| Arthur St | Y | 26 | F 2 |
| Artillery St | SC | 31 | E-F 2 |
| Artinger Ct | NY | 9 | E 5 |
| Artisan Pl | NY | 21 | B 3 |
| Artreeva Dr | NY | 10 | B 4-5 |
| Arundel Av | EY | 5 | E 2-3 |
| Arundel Av | T | 5 | E 2-3 |
| Ascolda Blvd | SC | 30 | D 2 |
| Ascot Av | T | 6 | A 4 |
| Ascot Av | T | 16 | E-F 6 |
| Ash Cr | SC | 32 | E 4 |
| Ashall Blvd | EY | 17 | D 6 |
| Ashbourne Dr | ET | 34 | F 2-3 |
| Ashburnham Rd | T | 14 | F 1 |
| Ashbury Av | Y | 6 | A 3 |
| Ashby Pl | T | 3 | C 1 |
| Ashcott St | SC | 31 | F 1 |
| Ashdale Av | T | 15 | B 4-6 |
| Ashdean Dr | SC | 27 | B 1-2 |
| Ashfield Dr | ET | 36 | B 4 |
| Ashford Dr | ET | 36 | F 4 |
| Ashgrove Pl | NY | 19 | B 5-6 |
| Ashland Av | T | 15 | B 6 |
| Ashley Pk Rd | ET | 26 | D 6 |
| Ashley Cr | ET | 26 | C 6 |
| Ashmill Ct | ET | 26 | D 4 |
| Ashmore Av | ET | 24 | B 3 |
| Ashmount Cr | ET | 26 | A-B 2 |
| Ashridge Dr | SC | 41 | B 3 |
| Ashtead Pl | NY | 21 | B 4 |
| Ashton Av | NY | 18 | B 4 |
| Ashton Manor | ET | 24 | D 3 |
| Ashtonbee Rd | SC | 27 | A-C 3 |
| Ashwarren Rd | NY | 20 | D-E 5 |
| Ashwick Dr | SC | 27 | D 4 |
| Ashwood Cr | ET | 26 | A 4 |
| Ashworth Av | T | 4 | B-C 2 |
| Aspen Av | EY | 17 | B 6 |
| Aspendale Dr | SC | 39 | A 4 |
| Aspenwood Dr | NY | 21 | B 1 |
| Asquith Av | T | 5 | A 3 |
| Assiniboine Rd | NY | 20 | C 3 |
| Astley Av | T | 15 | F 1 |
| Aston Rd | ET | 26 | C 5 |
| Astor Av | EY | 7 | D 5-6 |
| Astoria Av | Y | 16 | A 4 |
| Astral St | NY | 18 | F 5 |
| Athenia Ct | SC | 37 | F 2 |
| Atherton Ct | ET | 32 | E 4-5 |
| Athletic Av | T | 15 | A 5 |
| Athlone Cr | ET | 24 | D 4 |
| Athlone Rd | EY | 15 | A 1-2 |
| Athol Av | ET | 24 | B-C 6 |
| Atkins Av | T | 14 | F 5 |
| Atkinson Av | SC | 49 | D 6 |
| Atkinson Rd | T | 24 | A 1-2 |
| Atlantic Av | T | 2 | A 4 |
| Atlas Av | T | 4 | B 1 |
| Atlas Av | Y | 6 | B 4-5 |
| Atlee St | SC | 25 | E 1-2 |
| Atomic Av | ET | 34 | E 6 |
| Atrium La | SC | 49 | F 3 |
| Attercliff Ct | ET | 30 | C 4 |
| Attila Ct | ET | 40 | E 4 |
| Attwell Dr | ET | 38 | A-C 3-6 |
| Atwood Pl | ET | 30 | C 5 |
| Auburn Av | T | 14 | F 1 |
| Auburn Av | T | 14 | A 1 |
| Auburndale Ct | ET | 28 | B 3 |
| Audley Av | T | 5 | E-F 6 |
| Audley Ct | ET | 22 | D 2 |
| Audley St | ET | 22 | D 2 |
| Audrelane Ct | SC | 31 | F 1 |
| Audrey Av | SC | 25 | B 4-5 |
| Audubon Ct | NY | 10 | D 5 |
| Augusta Av | T | 2 | D 1 |
| Augusta Av | T | 4 | D 5-6 |
| Auld Croft Rd | ET | 40 | C 4 |
| Aura Lea Blvd | NY | 28 | D 2 |
| Aurora Ct | SC | 31 | B 4 |
| Austin Av | T | 5 | E-F 5 |
| Austin Cr | T | 4 | D 1-2 |
| Austin Terr | T | 4 | D-E 1-2 |
| Austrey Ct | NY | 18 | A-B 2 |
| Auto Mall Dr | SC | 49 | B 1-2 |
| Autumn Av | SC | 27 | E 5 |
| Autumn Glen Cir | ET | 40 | C 4 |
| Ava Cr | T | 6 | D 4 |
| Ava Rd | Y | 6 | B-D 4 |
| Avalon Av | Y | 26 | F 4 |
| Avalon Blvd | SC | 35 | C 3 |
| Avalon Rd | ET | 32 | C 3 |
| Avanti La | SC | 29 | D 3-4 |
| Aveline Cr | SC | 39 | B 4 |
| Avenal Dr | Y | 6 | B-D 4 |
| Avening Dr | ET | 40 | D-E 3-4 |
| Avenue of the Island | T | 2 | E-F 5-6 |
| Avenue Rd | T | 4 | E 1-3 |
| Avenue Rd | NY | 6 | E 1 |
| Avenue Rd | Y | 6 | E 1-6 |
| Avenue Rd | T | 16 | E 3-6 |
| Averdon Cr | NY | 19 | E 5 |
| Averill Cr | NY | 11 | A 3 |
| Avery Av | NY | 34 | C 3 |
| Aviemore Dr | NY | 30 | B 2-3 |
| Avion Av | T | 13 | E 6 |
| Avis Cr | EY | 15 | E 2 |
| Avoca Av | T | 5 | A 1 |
| Avoca Av | T | 7 | A 6 |
| Avon Av | Y | 16 | B 5-6 |
| Avon Cr | Y | 16 | B 3 |
| Avon Rd | Y | 16 | C 4 |
| Avon Park Dr | ET | 24 | C 6 |
| Avondale Av | NY | 9 | A-B 1 |
| Avondale Rd | T | 5 | A 3 |
| Avonhill Ct | NY | 10 | E 2 |
| Avonhurst Rd | ET | 24 | A 2-3 |
| Avonlea Blvd | EY | 15 | F 3 |
| Avonlea Blvd | T | 15 | F 3 |
| Avonmore Sq | SC | 37 | E 4 |
| Avonwick Gt | NY | 19 | E 4-5 |
| Awde St | T | 14 | F 4-5 |
| Axmith Cr | NY | 21 | B 4 |
| Axum Pl | SC | 27 | D 2 |
| Aylesbury Rd | ET | 26 | B 5 |
| Aylesford Dr | SC | 25 | E 3 |
| Aylesworth Av | SC | 25 | E 4 |
| Aylmer Av | T | 5 | A 3 |
| Aymarn Ct | ET | 34 | B 3 |
| Ayr Cr | NY | 30 | B 2 |
| Ayre Point Rd | SC | 35 | F 4 |
| Azalea Cr | NY | 30 | C 5 |
| Aziel St | T | 14 | C 2 |
| Azrock Rd | NY | 18 | B 5 |
| Azzarello La | T | 15 | B 4 |

**B**

| STREET NAME | MUNICIPALITY | MAP NO | MAP AREA |
|---|---|---|---|
| Babcock Rd | SC | 27 | B 1-2 |
| Babington Ct | ET | 24 | B 2 |
| Babson Rd | SC | 29 | A 5 |
| Baby Point Cr | Y | 24 | E-F 2-3 |
| Baby Point Rd | Y | 24 | E-F 2 |
| Baby Point Terr | Y | 24 | E-F 2 |
| Bachelor Pl | NY | 9 | B 3 |
| Baden St | T | 4 | B 3 |
| Badger Dr | ET | 24 | B-C 5 |
| Badgerow Av | T | 5 | E-F 5 |
| Baffin Ct | SC | 51 | A 4 |
| Bagot Ct | NY | 8 | B 5 |
| Bagwell Ct | ET | 40 | E 4 |
| Bailey Cr | SC | 39 | D 4-5 |
| Bain Av | T | 5 | D-F 4 |
| Bainbridge Av | NY | 8 | B-D 1 |
| Bainhart Cr | SC | 39 | B 4-5 |
| Baintree Ct | NY | 10 | B 4 |
| Baintree E St | NY | 10 | B 4 |
| Baird Av | T | 5 | F 4 |
| Bairstow Cr | ET | 38 | E 1-2 |
| Baker Av | T | 5 | F 5-6 |
| Bakersfield St | NY | 20 | E 5 |
| Bakerton Dr | SC | 37 | C 4 |
| Bala Av | Y | 16 | A 3 |
| Balaby Cr | NY | 17 | A 3 |
| Balaclava Dr | SC | 27 | D 1-2 |
| Balcarra Av | SC | 37 | B 6 |
| Balding Ct | NY | 9 | B 2-3 |
| Baldoon Rd | SC | 41 | A 4 |
| Baldwin St | T | 4 | D-E 5 |
| Baleberry Cr | EY | 26 | B 2 |
| Bales Av | NY | 9 | A 1 |
| Balfour Av | T | 15 | E 3 |
| Ballacaine Dr | ET | 24 | E 4-5 |
| Ballantyne Ct | ET | 26 | A 5 |
| Ballater Ct | ET | 40 | E 2 |
| Balliol St | T | 7 | A-D 5 |
| Ballyconnor Ct | NY | 11 | E 1-2 |
| Ballymena St | NY | 17 | A 1-2 |
| Ballyronan Rd | NY | 9 | F 4 |
| Ballyronan Rd | NY | 19 | A 4 |
| Balmoral Av | T | 4 | E-F 1 |
| Balmuto St | T | 4 | F 3-4 |
| Balmy Av | T | 15 | F 4 |
| Balsam Av | T | 15 | E-F 5-6 |
| Balsam Ave | T | 13 | E 5-6 |
| Baltic Av | T | 5 | F 4 |
| Baltic Av | T | 15 | A 3 |
| Baltray Cr | NY | 19 | F 2-3 |
| Bamber Ct | NY | 19 | E 6 |
| Bamboo Gr | NY | 9 | E 5 |
| Bamburgh Cir | SC | 31 | B 2 |
| Bamford Ct | NY | 30 | F 2 |
| Banbury Rd | NY | 9 | E-F 2-6 |
| Banda Sq | ET | 40 | E 1 |
| Banff Rd | T | 7 | B 3-4 |
| Bangor Rd | NY | 10 | F 6 |
| Banigan Dr | EY | 7 | E-F 5 |
| Bank St | T | 14 | F 5 |
| Bankfield Dr | ET | 30 | B 5-6 |
| Bankview Cir | ET | 40 | B 3-4 |
| Bankwell Av | SC | 39 | D 4 |
| Banmoor Rd | SC | 37 | B-C 2 |
| Bannatyne Dr | NY | 9 | E-F 1-3 |
| Bannatyne Dr | NY | 19 | A 3 |
| Bannerman St | NY | 18 | C 5 |

| Street | Muni | Page | Grid | No. |
|---|---|---|---|---|
| Bannockburn Av | NY | 8 | D-E | 4 |
| Bannon Av | ET | 24 | E | 2 |
| Bansley Av | Y | 6 | A | 4 |
| Banstock Dr | NY | 11 | E | 3 |
| Banting Av | NY | 8 | A | 1 |
| Banton Rd | NY | 8 | C | 2 |
| Bantry Av | T | 6 | D | 6 |
| Bar Harbour Sq | SC | 47 | F | 1 |
| Barbados Blvd | SC | 37 | A | 4 |
| Barbara Cr | EY | 15 | B | 1 |
| Barber Greene Rd | NY | 17 | A-B | 1-2 |
| Barberry Pl | NY | 9 | D | 1 |
| Barclay Rd | NY | 8 | C | 3 |
| Bards Walkway | NY | 21 | E | 6 |
| Bardsea Ct | SC | 37 | A | 2 |
| Bardwell Cr | SC | 27 | A | 2 |
| Bare Rock Dr | SC | 38 | B | 4 |
| Barfield Av | EY | 15 | A | 2 |
| Barford Rd | ET | 28 | A-B | 1 |
| Barford Rd | SC | 30 | A | 5-6 |
| Barkdene Hills | SC | 25 | E | 5 |
| Barker Av | EY | 15 | B-D | 2 |
| Barker Av | ET | 30 | B | 6 |
| Barksdale Av | NY | 10 | A | 5 |
| Barkin Dr | ET | 30 | B | 5 |
| Barkwood Cr | NY | 21 | B | 2 |
| Barkworth Pl | SC | 37 | C | 3 |
| Barlow Rd | SC | 39 | D | 3 |
| Barmac Dr | NY | 30 | D | 2 |
| Barnaby Pl | T | 4 | F | 5-6 |
| Barnes Cr | SC | 39 | D | 5-6 |
| Barnsley Ct | SC | 29 | B | 4 |
| Barnwell Rd | SC | 41 | A | 2 |
| Barnwood Ct | NY | 19 | C-D | 1 |
| Barolo Rd | ET | 40 | E | 1-2 |
| Baroness Cr | NY | 21 | C-E | 4 |
| Baronial Ct | SC | 47 | D-E | 5 |
| Barr Av | Y | 16 | B | 4 |
| Barrett Rd | EY | 17 | E | 6 |
| Barrhead Cr | ET | 28 | A | 2 |
| Barrie Av | Y | 6 | B | 6 |
| Barrington Av | EY | 15 | E | 2-3 |
| Barrington Av | T | 15 | E | 3 |
| Barron Rd | EY | 17 | F | 5-6 |
| Barrowcliffe Dr | SC | 41 | A | 1 |
| Barrydale Cr | NY | 9 | E-F | 4 |
| Barrymore Rd | SC | 37 | A | 1-2 |
| Barse St | NY | 8 | D | 5-6 |
| Bartel Dr | NY | 30 | F | 6 |
| Bartlett Av | T | 4 | A | 2-3 |
| Bartlett Av N | T | 4 | A | 2 |
| Bartley Dr | NY | 17 | E-F | 4 |
| Barton Av | T | 4 | B-D | 3 |
| Bartonville Av | Y | 16 | A | 3 |
| Bartor Rd | NY | 28 | E | 1-3 |
| Barvale Ct | ET | 36 | B | 1 |
| Barwell Cr | ET | 28 | A-B | 1 |
| Barwell Cr | ET | 30 | A | 6 |
| Barwick Dr | NY | 8 | E | 3 |
| Basil Hall Ct | NY | 10 | F | 5 |
| Basildon Cr | SC | 25 | F | 1 |
| Basin St | T | 3 | E | 2 |
| Baskerville Cr | ET | 34 | C | 3 |
| Basking Ridge | ET | 24 | E | 5 |
| Bassano Rd | NY | 8 | F | 1-2 |
| Bassett Av | SC | 24 | A | 5 |
| Basswood Rd | NY | 10 | F | 4-5 |
| Bastedo Av | T | 15 | B | 3 |
| Batavia Av | Y | 16 | A | 4 |
| Batawa Ct | ET | 30 | B | 5 |
| Bater Av | EY | 5 | E | 2 |
| Bathford Cr | NY | 17 | F | 4 |
| Bathford La | NY | 11 | F | 4 |
| Bathgate Dr | SC | 49 | E | 5-6 |
| Bathurst St | T | 2 | C | 1-3 |
| Bathurst St | T | 4 | C-D | 1-6 |
| Bathurst St | T | 6 | C-D | 1-2 |
| Bathurst St | NY | 6 | C-D | 2-4 |
| Bathurst St | NY | 8 | C-D | 1-6 |
| Bathurst St | NY | 10 | C-D | 1-6 |
| Battenberg Av | T | 15 | B | 6 |
| Battersea Av | NY | 18 | C | 6 |
| Batterswood Dr | SC | 31 | A-B | 6 |
| Battinger Gt | SC | 41 | A | 1 |
| Baudina Cr | SC | 29 | D | 3 |
| Bauty Pl | SC | 27 | D | 1 |
| Baxter St | T | 5 | A | 3 |
| Bay Mills Blvd | SC | 31 | B-C | 6 |
| Bay St | T | 2 | F | 1-2 |
| Bay St | T | 4 | F | 3-6 |
| Bayard Av | SC | 29 | B-C | 6 |
| Bayberry Cr | NY | 11 | D | 5-6 |
| Baybrook Av | SC | 39 | B | 4-5 |
| Baycrest Av | NY | 8 | B-C | 5 |
| Bayfield Cr | T | 5 | D | 3 |
| Bayford Av | NY | 18 | E | 3 |
| Bayhampton Ct | NY | 10 | B | 4 |
| Baylawn Dr | SC | 31 | E | 4 |
| Bayliss Av | Y | 16 | A | 4 |
| Bayshill Dr | ET | 24 | E | 5 |
| Bayside La | ET | 24 | E | 5 |
| Baytree Cr | NY | 9 | C | 3 |
| Bayview Av | AU | 5 | C | 1-6 |
| Bayview Av | T | 5 | C | 2-6 |
| Bayview Av | EY | 5 | D | 1-2 |
| Bayview Av | NY | 7 | C-D | 1-6 |
| Bayview Av | NY | 7 | C-D | 1-3 |
| Bayview Av | T | 7 | C-D | 3-6 |
| Bayview Av | NY | 9 | C-D | 1-6 |
| Bayview Av | NY | 11 | C | 1-6 |
| Bayview Heights Dr | EY | 5 | C | 1 |
| Bayview Heights Dr | EY | 7 | C | 6 |
| Bayview Mews La | NY | 11 | D | 6 |
| Bayview Ridge | NY | 9 | B-C | 4 |
| Bayview Ridge Cr | NY | 9 | C | 4 |
| Bayview Wood | NY | 7 | C | 1 |
| Baywood Rd | ET | 40 | D | 2 |
| Beach Av | T | 13 | F | 5-6 |
| Beach View Cr | T | 15 | D | 4 |
| Beacham Cr | SC | 29 | A-B | 2 |
| Beachdale Av | SC | 15 | F | 5 |
| Beachdale Av | SC | 25 | A | 5 |
| Beachell St | SC | 37 | C | 3-4 |
| Beachview Av | SC | 29 | D | 6 |
| Beaconhill Rd | ET | 40 | F | 2 |
| Beaconsfield Av | T | 2 | A | 1 |
| Beaconsfield Av | T | 4 | A | 5-6 |
| Bead Fernway | NY | 21 | B | 3 |
| Beaman Rd | NY | 8 | F | 1 |
| Beamish Dr | ET | 34 | F | 3 |
| Beamsville Dr | SC | 31 | A | 6 |
| Bearbury Dr | ET | 34 | B | 3 |
| Beardmore Cr | NY | 11 | E | 2 |
| Beare Rd | SC | 51 | E | 1-4 |
| Beaumond Dr | ET | 26 | D | 5 |
| Beath St | SC | 49 | B | 5 |
| Beaton Av | T | 15 | B | 6 |
| Beaton Dr | NY | 20 | F | 6 |
| Beatrice St | T | 4 | B | 4-5 |
| Beattie Av | ET | 28 | C | 2 |
| Beaty Av | T | 12 | B | 1 |
| Beaucourt Rd | ET | 24 | D | 5 |
| Beaufield Av | EY | 7 | D | 3 |
| Beaufort Rd | T | 15 | E | 5 |
| Beaumaris Cr | ET | 26 | B | 1 |
| Beaumonde Heights Dr | ET | 30 | A-B | 4 |
| Beaumont Rd | T | 5 | B | 2-3 |
| Beaver Av | T | 14 | F | 2 |
| Beaver Bend Cr | ET | 36 | D | 4-5 |
| Beaver Terr | T | 14 | F | 1-2 |
| Beaver Valley Rd | NY | 10 | B | 1 |
| Beaverbrook Av | ET | 36 | E-F | 6 |
| Beaverdale Rd | ET | 22 | E | 1 |
| Beaverhall Dr | NY | 9 | E-F | 2-3 |
| Becca Hall Tr | SC | 31 | E-F | 2 |
| Beck Av | T | 15 | D | 4 |
| Beckenham Ct | ET | 34 | B-C | 1 |
| Beckett Av | NY | 18 | A-B | 5 |
| Beckwith Rd | ET | 36 | C | 5 |
| Bedford Park Av | NY | 8 | D-E | 6 |
| Bedford Park Av | T | 8 | E | 6 |
| Bedford Rd | T | 4 | E | 2-3 |
| Bedle Av | NY | 21 | B | 2-3 |
| Beech Av | T | 15 | F | 5-6 |
| Beechborough Av | Y | 16 | D | 3 |
| Beechgrove Av | SC | 47 | D-E | 1-3 |
| Beechgrove Dr | SC | 49 | C-D | 6 |
| Beechwood Av | NY | 9 | B-C | 4 |
| Beechwood Av | Y | 16 | A | 4-5 |
| Beechwood Cr | EY | 5 | E | 1 |
| Beechwood Dr | EY | 7 | E | 1 |
| Beecroft Rd | NY | 10 | F | 5-6 |
| Beethoven Ct | NY | 21 | A | 3 |
| Beffort Rd | NY | 8 | A | 2-3 |
| Beffort Rd | NY | 18 | F | 2-3 |
| Belcourt Rd | T | 7 | B | 4 |
| Belfield Rd | ET | 38 | C-F | 4 |
| Belfry Av | ET | 24 | B-C | 5 |
| Belgate Pl | ET | 36 | B-C | 5 |
| Belgrave Av | NY | 8 | E | 3 |
| Belgravia Av | Y | 6 | A-B | 3 |
| Belgravia Av | Y | 16 | F | 3 |
| Belgreen Av | SC | 31 | E | 5 |
| Belgrove Dr | ET | 34 | E | 2-3 |
| Belinda Sq | SC | 31 | B | 1 |
| Bell Manor Rd | ET | 24 | E | 6 |
| Bell Royal Ct | ET | 26 | D | 5 |
| Bella Ct | NY | 28 | D | 2 |
| Bella Vista Dr | SC | 47 | F | 4 |
| Bella Vista Way | NY | 18 | C | 1 |
| Bellair St | T | 4 | F | 3 |
| Bellamy Rd N | SC | 37 | B | 1-3 |
| Bellamy Rd N | SC | 39 | B-C | 3-6 |
| Bellamy Rd S | SC | 37 | B | 4-5 |
| Bellbrook Rd | SC | 31 | E | 1 |
| Bellbury Cr | NY | 21 | A-B | 4-5 |
| Belle Ayre Blvd | T | 7 | B | 5 |
| Bellechasse St | SC | 39 | B | 5 |
| Bellefair Av | T | 13 | D | 5 |
| Bellefair Av | T | 15 | D | 5-6 |
| Bellefontaine St | SC | 31 | E | 4-5 |
| Bellegrade Ct | NY | 30 | C | 6 |
| Bellehaven Cr | SC | 37 | B-C | 5 |
| Bellemeade La | NY | 21 | B | 4-5 |
| Bellevue Av | T | 4 | D | 5 |
| Bellevue Cr | Y | 26 | E | 1 |
| Bellhaven Rd | T | 15 | C | 4-5 |
| Bellman Av | ET | 32 | E | 1-2 |
| Bellrock Dr | SC | 31 | E-F | 2 |
| Bellvare Cr | SC | 29 | A | 6 |
| Bellwoods Av | T | 2 | B | 1 |
| Bellwoods Av | T | 4 | B | 5-6 |
| Bellwoods Pl | T | 4 | B-C | 6 |
| Belmont St | T | 4 | F | 3 |
| Belmore Av | SC | 19 | F | 6 |
| Belmore Av | SC | 29 | A | 6 |
| Belmuir Pl | SC | 37 | B | 4 |
| Belper Ct | NY | 17 | F | 3 |
| Belsay Cr | SC | 31 | B | 1 |
| Belshaw Pl | T | 5 | B-C | 6 |
| Belsize Dr | T | 7 | A-D | 4 |
| Belton Rd | NY | 19 | B | 5-6 |
| Belvale Av | ET | 24 | C | 2 |
| Belvedere Blvd | ET | 24 | B-C | 2-3 |
| Belvia Rd | ET | 32 | E | 3 |
| Belvidere Av | Y | 6 | A-B | 4 |
| Belyea Cr | SC | 37 | A | 1 |
| Bemberg Ct | ET | 28 | C | 2 |
| Bemersyde Dr | ET | 26 | A-B | 3-4 |
| Bemerton Ct | SC | 31 | F | 1 |
| Ben Alder Dr | SC | 39 | B | 6 |
| Ben Doran Blvd | SC | 39 | B | 6 |
| Ben Nevis Dr | SC | 39 | B | 5 |
| Ben Stanton Blvd | SC | 37 | B | 1 |
| Ben Stanton Blvd | SC | 39 | B | 6 |
| Benadair Ct | SC | 39 | B | 6 |
| Benalto Rd | NY | 8 | A | 6 |
| Benary Cr | SC | 39 | B | 6 |
| Benbow Rd | ET | 26 | B-C | 1-2 |
| Bendale Blvd | SC | 37 | B | 2 |
| Benedict Rd | ET | 26 | B | 5 |
| Benfrisco Cr | SC | 39 | B | 6 |
| Bengal Ct | NY | 18 | C | 1 |
| Benhur Cr | SC | 39 | B | 6 |
| Benjamin Blvd | ET | 27 | C | 4 |
| Benjamin Boake Tr | NY | 20 | C | 6 |
| Benlamond Av | T | 15 | E | 4-5 |
| Benleigh Dr | SC | 39 | B | 5-6 |
| Benlight Cr | SC | 39 | B | 6 |
| Benner Av | NY | 6 | B | 2 |
| Bennett Rd | SC | 47 | C-D | 1-2 |
| Bennington Heights Dr | EY | 7 | C | 6 |
| Benorama Cr | SC | 39 | B | 6 |
| Benprice Ct | SC | 39 | B | 6 |
| Benroyal Cr | SC | 39 | B | 5-6 |
| Benrubin Dr | NY | 30 | B | 3 |
| Benshire Dr | SC | 39 | B | 5-6 |
| Benson Av | T | 4 | B-C | 1 |
| Benstrow Av | ET | 30 | A | 4-5 |
| Bentley Dr | ET | 24 | C | 5-6 |
| Benton Rd | NY | 16 | E | 1 |
| Bentwick Cr | ET | 30 | B | 5 |
| Bentworth Av | NY | 18 | E-F | 5 |
| Benvenuto Pl | T | 4 | E | 1 |
| Benway Dr | ET | 28 | A | 3 |
| Beran Dr | SC | 37 | D | 2 |
| Beresford Ct | T | 14 | A-B | 2-4 |
| Beresford Av | T | 14 | A-B | 1-2 |
| Bergamot Av | ET | 28 | A-B | 3 |
| Bergen Rd | SC | 29 | D | 5-6 |
| Bering Av | ET | 24 | A-B | 4 |
| Berkel Rd | M | 34 | A | 5 |
| Berkeley St | T | 3 | B | 1-3 |
| Berkeley St | T | 5 | B | 5 |
| Berkham Rd | SC | 39 | B | 4 |
| Berkindale Cr | NY | 9 | D | 2-3 |
| Berkindale Dr | NY | 9 | D-E | 2-3 |
| Berkinshaw Cr | NY | 19 | A-B | 5 |
| Berkshire Av | T | 3 | F | 1 |
| Berl Av | ET | 24 | A | 6 |
| Bermondsey Rd | EY | 17 | E | 4-5 |
| Bermondsey Rd | NY | 17 | E | 3-4 |
| Bermuda Av | ET | 24 | D | 3 |

**B**

| STREET NAME | MUNIC-PALITY | MAP NO | MAP AREA |
|---|---|---|---|
| Bernadine St | SC | 39 A | 4 |
| Bernard Av | T | 4 D-E | 4 |
| Berner Tr | SC | 41 E-F | 6 |
| Berney Cr | EY | 7 D | 5 |
| Bernice Av | ET | 24 D-E | 5 |
| Bernice Cr | Y | 26 E-F | 6 |
| Bernick Rd | NY | 11 F | 1 |
| Berry Creek Dr | ET | 28 A | 2 |
| Berry Rd | ET | 24 D-F | 5 |
| Berryman St | | 4 F | 3 |
| Berryton Av | NY | 18 B | 5 |
| Bertal Rd | Y | 16 B | 3 |
| Bertha Av | SC | 25 A | 1-2 |
| Berti St | T | 3 A | 1 |
| Bertmount Av | T | 5 F | 6 |
| Bertram St | T | 16 D | 3 |
| Bertrand Av | SC | 27 B-E | 1 |
| Berwick Av | T | 6 F | 4 |
| Bessarion Rd | NY | 9 E | 1 |
| Bessborough Dr | EY | 7 D | 3-6 |
| Bestobell La | ET | 32 E | 1 |
| Bestobell Rd | ET | 32 E | 1-2 |
| Bestview Dr | NY | 11 E | 1 |
| Beta St | ET | 32 E | 2-3 |
| Beth Nealson Dr | EY | 7 F | 4-5 |
| Beth Nealson Dr | EY | 17 A | 4-5 |
| Beth St | Y | 15 F | 1 |
| Bethany Leigh Dr | SC | 41 B | 3-4 |
| Bethley Dr | SC | 47 D | 2 |
| Bethnal Av | ET | 24 D-E | 5 |
| Bethridge Rd | ET | 38 D-F | 3-4 |
| Bethune Blvd | SC | 37 D | 4-5 |
| Bethwin Pl | SC | 36 E-F | 1 |
| Betteridge La | ET | 40 E | 4 |
| Betty Ann Dr | NY | 10 D-F | 5 |
| Betty Frank Gt | SC | 47 A | 2 |
| Beulah St | ET | 40 E | 1 |
| Bevdale Rd | NY | 10 D-E | 4 |
| Beveridge Dr | NY | 19 E | 5 |
| Beverley St | T | 4 E | 5-6 |
| Beverly Glen Blvd | SC | 31 A-B | 3 |
| Beverly Hills Dr | NY | 28 F | 4 |
| Bewdley Pl | ET | 26 D | 4 |
| Bexhill Av | SC | 25 A | 1-2 |
| Bexhill Ct | ET | 26 C | 6 |
| Bexley Cr | Y | 26 F | 4-5 |
| Bickerton Cr | NY | 21 E-F | 4 |
| Bicknell Av | Y | 16 C | 4-5 |
| Bideford Av | NY | 8 E | 2-3 |
| Bidewell Av | NY | 8 E | 2-3 |
| Big Pine Rd | NY | 7 F | 4 |
| Big Red Av | T | 41 A-B | 3 |
| Biggar Av | T | 4 A-B | 1 |
| Biggin Ct | NY | 17 F | 3 |
| Bigham Cr | ET | 36 B | 4 |
| Bigwood Ct | SC | 39 C | 5 |
| Billcar Rd | ET | 38 E | 1-2 |
| Billingham Rd | ET | 34 E | 4 |
| Billings Av | T | 15 A | 5-6 |
| Billington Cr | NY | 19 E | 2 |
| Bilston Ct | ET | 36 F | 5 |
| Biltmore Ct | SC | 37 A | 1 |
| Bimbrok Rd | SC | 27 F | 3-4 |
| Bimini Cr | NY | 30 F | |
| Bingham Av | T | 15 F | 4-5 |
| Bingley Rd | SC | 51 B | 4 |
| Bin-Scarth Rd | T | 5 B-C | 2 |
| Binswood Av | EY | 15 B | 1-3 |
| Birch Av | T | 4 F | 2 |
| Birch Tree Cr | NY | 26 F | 2 |
| Birchard St | SC | 29 B-C | 2 |
| Birchbank La | NY | 19 B | 5-6 |
| Birchcliff Av | SC | 25 C | 3-4 |
| Birchcroft Rd | ET | 24 B | 1 |
| Birchcroft Rd | ET | 26 B | 6 |
| Birchlawn Av | SC | 25 E | 3 |
| Birchlea Av | ET | 32 E | 5 |
| Birchleaf Cr | ET | 36 E | 2-3 |
| Birchmount Rd | SC | 25 C-D | 1-4 |
| Birchmount Rd | SC | 27 C-D | 1-6 |
| Birchmount Rd | SC | 29 C-D | 1-6 |
| Birchmount Rd | SC | 31 C-D | 1-6 |
| Birchview Blvd | ET | 24 C | 3 |
| Birchview Cr | T | 14 B | 3 |
| Birchwood Av | NY | 19 B | 3-4 |
| Birdsall Av | T | 6 F | 2-3 |
| Birdsilver Gdns | SC | 47 E | 4 |
| Birchwood Ct | SC | 31 C | 2 |
| Birgitta Cr | ET | 36 C | 5 |
| Birkdale Rd | SC | 29 F | 4-6 |

| STREET NAME | MUNIC-PALITY | MAP NO | MAP AREA |
|---|---|---|---|
| Birmingham St | ET | 22 A-C | 4 |
| Birmingham St | ET | 32 F | 4 |
| Birrell Av | SC | 51 B | 4 |
| Biscayne Blvd | SC | 27 A | 3 |
| Bishop Av | NY | 11 A-B | 3 |
| Bishop St | T | 4 F | 3 |
| Bishop Tutu Blvd | T | 2 C | 2-3 |
| Bison Dr | NY | 10 D | 1 |
| Bisset Av | ET | 32 B-C | 2 |
| Bittercot Rd | NY | 10 B-C | 5 |
| Bixby Ct | NY | 9 E | 5 |
| Black Creek Blvd | Y | 26 E-F | 5 |
| Black Creek Dr | NY | 16 B | 1-2 |
| Black Creek Dr | Y | 16 B | 3-4 |
| Black Creek Dr | NY | 18 A-B | 5-6 |
| Black Hawkway | NY | 10 B-C | 1 |
| Black Villaway | NY | 11 F | 5 |
| Blackburn St | T | 5 D | 5 |
| Blackbush Dr | ET | 40 E | 2 |
| Blackdown Dr | ET | 36 F | 4 |
| Blackfriar Av | ET | 38 F | 5-6 |
| Blackhurst Ct | SC | 51 B | 4 |
| Blackmore St | T | 4 F | 3 |
| Blacksmith Ct | NY | 20 A | 1-2 |
| Blacksmith Cr | NY | 30 F | 1-2 |
| Blackthorn Av | T | 16 E | 5-6 |
| Blackthorn Av | Y | 16 E | 4-5 |
| Blacktoft Dr | SC | 49 D | 1-2 |
| Blackwater Cr | SC | 41 F | 6 |
| Blackwell Av | SC | 41 F | 5-6 |
| Blaine Dr | NY | 7 F | 1 |
| Blaine Dr | NY | 9 E | 6 |
| Blair Athol Cr | ET | 26 A | 5 |
| Blair St | NY | 17 F | 5 |
| Blairville Rd | NY | 10 B | 6 |
| Blairwood Terr | SC | 31 A | 3 |
| Blaisdale Rd | SC | 29 D | 5-6 |
| Blake Av | NY | 16 E-F | 3 |
| Blake St | T | 5 F | 4-5 |
| Blakeley Rd | NY | 10 F | 4 |
| Blakemanor Blvd | SC | 37 C-D | 2-3 |
| Blaketon Rd | ET | 34 D | 2 |
| Blakley Av | NY | 16 B | 6 |
| Blanchard Rd | NY | 7 B-C | 2 |
| Blanche Av | SC | 25 D-E | 1 |
| Blandford St | NY | 6 A | 5 |
| Blandorman Rd | NY | 18 D | 4-5 |
| Blaney Cr | NY | 30 F | 4 |
| Blantyre Av | SC | 25 A | 4-6 |
| Blaydon Av | NY | 18 C | 2 |
| Bledlow Manor Dr | SC | 37 E | 4 |
| Bleecker St | T | 5 C | 4 |
| Blenheim St | NY | 10 E | 5 |
| Blevins Pl | T | 5 C | 5 |
| Blithfield Av | NY | 11 D | 5 |
| Blong Av | T | 5 E-F | 6 |
| Bloem Av | Y | 16 F | 5 |
| Bloomington Cr | NY | 30 F | 3 |
| Bloor St E | T | 5 A-C | 3-4 |
| Bloor St W | T | 4 A-F | 3-4 |
| Bloor St W | T | 14 A-F | 3-4 |
| Bloor St W | ET | 24 A-F | 3 |
| Bloor St W | T | 24 F | 3-4 |
| Bloor St W | ET | 34 A-F | 3-4 |
| Bloorlea Cr | ET | 34 D-E | 3 |
| Blossom Cr | NY | 30 F | 4-5 |
| Blossomfield Dr | NY | 8 A | 6 |
| Blue Eagle Tr | SC | 31 E-F | 3-4 |
| Blue Flag Gt | NY | 10 C | 4 |
| Blue Forest Dr | NY | 10 A-B | 4 |
| Blue Goose St | T | 22 D | 2 |
| Blue Grassway | NY | 30 F | 1 |
| Blue Haven Cr | NY | 30 B-C | 4 |
| Blue Jays Way | T | 2 E | 1-2 |
| Blue Lagoon Ct | SC | 37 B | 3 |
| Blue Pond Pl | SC | 41 A | 2 |
| Blue Ridge Rd | NY | 9 E | 1 |
| Blue Ridge Rd | NY | 11 E | 6 |
| Blue Springs Rd | NY | 18 C | 4-5 |
| Bluebell Gt | NY | 18 B | 6 |
| Blueberry Dr | SC | 41 A | 5 |
| Bluefin Cr | SC | 39 C | 4 |
| Bluejay Pl | NY | 9 D | 3-4 |
| Blueking Cr | SC | 47 E | 4-5 |
| Bluenose Dr | SC | 49 E | 3 |
| Bluewater Av | SC | 25 E | 5 |
| Bluewater Ct | ET | 22 E | 2 |
| Bluffwood Dr | NY | 11 F | 1 |
| Blyth Dale Rd | NY | 7 C | 2 |
| Blyth Hill Rd | NY | 7 B-C | 2 |
| Blythwood Cr | T | 7 A | 3 |
| Blythwood Gdns | T | 7 A | 2 |
| Blythwood Rd | T | 7 A-B | 2 |
| Blythwood Rd | NY | 7 B-C | 2 |
| Blywood Dr | ET | 26 A | 6 |

| STREET NAME | MUNIC-PALITY | MAP NO | MAP AREA |
|---|---|---|---|
| Boardwalk Dr | T | 13 D | 6 |
| Boardwalk Dr | T | 13 F | 1 |
| Boarhill Dr | SC | 31 E-F | 4 |
| Bobmar Rd | SC | 49 C | 4-5 |
| Bobwhite Cr | NY | 9 E-F | 2-3 |
| Bocastle Av | T | 9 A | 5-6 |
| Bodwin Av | T | 14 D | 2 |
| Boem Av | SC | 29 B-C | 6 |
| Bogart Av | NY | 8 E-F | 1 |
| Bogert Av | NY | 9 A | 1 |
| Boland La | T | 14 F | 5 |
| Boldmere Cr | NY | 11 F | 4 |
| Boler St | T | 14 B | 1 |
| Bolger Pl | ET | 38 F | 1 |
| Bolger Pl | ET | 40 F | 6 |
| Bolingbroke Rd | NY | 6 A | 1 |
| Bolster Av | SC | 25 A | 1 |
| Bomarc Rd | NY | 11 D | 5 |
| Bombay Av | NY | 8 D-E | 3 |
| Bonacres Av | SC | 49 D | 5-6 |
| Bonar Pl | T | 14 F | 5 |
| Boncer Dr | ET | 34 B | 6 |
| Bond Av | NY | 9 F | 5 |
| Bond Av | NY | 19 A-B | 5 |
| Bond St | T | 5 A | 5-6 |
| Bondgate Ct | SC | 41 E | 6 |
| Bondhead Pl | ET | 30 C | 5 |
| Boneset Rd | NY | 21 E | 6 |
| Bonfield Av | T | 13 E | 6 |
| Boniface Av | ET | 28 B | 3-4 |
| Bonis Av | SC | 31 C-E | 6 |
| Bonnacord Dr | NY | 8 B | 2 |
| Bonnechere La | SC | 27 F | 2 |
| Bonnie Brae Blvd | EY | 15 B | 2-3 |
| Bonniewood Rd | SC | 27 D | 4 |
| Bonnington Pl | NY | 9 B | 1 |
| Bonny Lynn Ct | SC | 27 D | 3 |
| Bonnycastle St | T | 3 B | 2 |
| Bonnydon Cr | SC | 49 E | 2-3 |
| Bonnyview Dr | ET | 24 E | 5-6 |
| Boon Av | T | 16 F | 5-6 |
| Boon Av | Y | 16 F | 5 |
| Booth Av | T | 3 E | 1-2 |
| Booth Av | T | 5 E | 6 |
| Boothroyd Av | T | 5 F | 4-5 |
| Bordeaux Crct | ET | 40 E | 1 |
| Borden St | T | 4 D | 4-5 |
| Boreal Rd | ET | 34 B | 2 |
| Bornholm Dr | SC | 47 E | 4-5 |
| Borough Approach E | SC | 39 A | 3-4 |
| Borough Approach W | SC | 39 A | 3-4 |
| Borough Dr | SC | 39 A-B | 3 |
| Boston Av | T | 5 E | 5 |
| Boswell Av | T | 4 E | 3 |
| Bosworth Av | ET | 26 D | 4 |
| Botany Hill Rd | SC | 39 E-F | 5 |
| Botfield Av | ET | 34 F | 2-3 |
| Botham Rd | NY | 8 F | 1-2 |
| Botley Rd | ET | 34 B | 1 |
| Bouchette St | T | 3 E | 2 |
| Boultbee Av | T | 5 F | 5 |
| Boulton Av | T | 3 E | 1 |
| Boulton Av | T | 5 E | 5-6 |
| Boulton Dr | T | 4 E | 1-2 |
| Boundy Cr | SC | 31 B-C | 3 |
| Bourdon Av | NY | 18 B | 5 |
| Bournemouth Rd | ET | 26 A | 3 |
| Bournville Dr | SC | 37 E | 4 |
| Boustead Av | T | 14 D-E | 4 |
| Bow Valley Dr | SC | 39 F | 5 |
| Bowan Ct | NY | 11 D-E | 2 |
| Bowater Dr | SC | 31 B | 6 |
| Bowden St | T | 5 D | 3-4 |
| Bowerbank Dr | NY | 11 A-B | 3 |
| Bowhill Cr | NY | 21 E-F | 5 |
| Bowie Av | Y | 16 E-F | 3 |
| Bowman St | T | 5 B | 5 |
| Bowmore Rd | T | 15 C | 4-5 |
| Bowness Ct | ET | 36 F | 4 |
| Bowood Av | T | 9 A | 6 |
| Bowring Walk Blvd | NY | 9 B | 1-2 |
| Bowspirit Av | ET | 28 D | 6 |
| Boxbury Rd | ET | 34 B | 3 |
| Boxdene Av | SC | 41 B | 2 |
| Boxhill Dr | SC | 49 E | 6 |
| Boxwood Rd | ET | 34 A-B | 2-3 |
| Boxwood Way | M | 32 A-B | 2-3 |
| Boyce Av | SC | 37 A | 4 |
| Boyd Av | Y | 28 F | 6 |
| Boydwood La | SC | 49 E | 1-2 |
| Boylen St | NY | 28 F | 5 |
| Boyton Rd | T | 7 B | 4 |
| Bracebridge Av | EY | 15 C-D | 2 |

**B**

| Street | Type | Page | Col | Row |
|---|---|---|---|---|
| Bracken Av | T | 15 | F | 5 |
| Bracken Av | T | 25 | A | 5 |
| Bracken Fernway | NY | 21 | B | 4 |
| Bracondale Hill Rd | T | 4 | B | 1-2 |
| Brad St | T | 14 | D | 2 |
| Bradbrook Rd | ET | 24 | B | 6 |
| Bradbury Cr | ET | 36 | C | 4 |
| Braddock Rd | ET | 38 | E | 1-2 |
| Bradenton Dr | NY | 21 | B | 2 |
| Bradfield Av | ET | 24 | A-B | 6 |
| Bradgate Rd | NY | 19 | A | 5 |
| Bradham Path | ET | 22 | B | 4 |
| Bradley Av | ET | 24 | F | 1 |
| Bradmore Av | NY | 28 | D | 2 |
| Bradpenn Rd | ET | 32 | F | 1 |
| Bradshaw Av | ET | 30 | B | 6 |
| Bradstock Rd | NY | 30 | D-E | 4 |
| Bradstone Sq | SC | 41 | E | 4 |
| Bradworthy Ct | SC | 51 | A-B | 6 |
| Brady Cr | NY | 20 | A-B | 6 |
| Braeburn Av | ET | 28 | D | 6 |
| Braeburn Blvd | ET | 37 | B | 2 |
| Braecrest Av | ET | 26 | C-D | 1 |
| Braemar Dr | T | 6 | E | 3-4 |
| Braemore Gdns | T | 4 | B-C | 1-2 |
| Braeside Cr | NY | 9 | B | 6 |
| Braeside Rd | T | 9 | A-B | 6 |
| Brahms Av | NY | 21 | B | 2-3 |
| Bralorme Cr | ET | 24 | E | 1-2 |
| Bramber Rd | SC | 49 | D | 4 |
| Bramble Dr | NY | 9 | E | 4 |
| Bramblebrook Av | SC | 31 | F | 2 |
| Brampton Rd | ET | 36 | E-F | 1-3 |
| Bramshott Rd | ET | 34 | E | 5 |
| Brancaster Ct | ET | 36 | E | 6 |
| Branch Av | ET | 32 | C | 4 |
| Brandon Av | T | 14 | E-F | 2 |
| Brandy Ct | NY | 9 | E | 4 |
| Branstone Rd | Y | 16 | F | 4 |
| Brant Pl | T | 2 | D | 1 |
| Brant St | T | 2 | D | 1 |
| Brantford Dr | SC | 31 | A | 4-5 |
| Brantley Cr | NY | 20 | B | 5 |
| Brantwood Dr | SC | 39 | B | 5 |
| Brassbell Millway | NY | 9 | D | 3 |
| Bratty Rd | NY | 20 | C | 4 |
| Brawley Av | ET | 24 | A | 6 |
| Braymore Blvd | SC | 49 | D | 1-2 |
| Braywin Dr | ET | 28 | B-C | 6 |
| Brazil Gt | NY | 30 | B | 1 |
| Breadalbane St | T | 4 | F | 4 |
| Breadner Dr | ET | 36 | F | 1 |
| Breanna Cr | NY | 11 | F | 1 |
| Breckon Gt | SC | 49 | A | 1 |
| Bredonhill Ct | NY | 11 | C | 2 |
| Brenham Cr | NY | 11 | C | 2 |
| Brenham Ct | ET | 28 | B | 3 |
| Brentano Blvd | M | 32 | A-B | 2-3 |
| Brentcliffe Rd | EY | 6 | E | 3-4 |
| Brentdale Dr | T | 6 | F | 5 |
| Brenthall Av | NY | 10 | D | 3 |
| Brenton St | EY | 15 | F | 2 |
| Brenton St | EY | 25 | A | 2 |
| Brentside Ct | ET | 26 | D | 2 |
| Brentwood Av | NY | 10 | E | 6 |
| Brentwood Rd N | ET | 24 | C | 2-3 |
| Brentwood Rd S | ET | 24 | C | 3 |
| Brenyon Way | SC | 41 | F | 5-6 |
| Brenyon Way | SC | 51 | A | 5-6 |
| Brett Av | NY | 18 | B | 2 |
| Bretton Ct | SC | 31 | F | 2 |
| Brewster Cr | NY | 30 | F | 6 |
| Brewton Rd | SC | 39 | D | 5-6 |
| Brian Av | SC | 29 | A-B | 6 |
| Brian Cliff Dr | NY | 9 | E | 6 |
| Brian Dr | NY | 19 | F | 1 |
| Brian Dr | NY | 21 | E | 4-5 |
| Briar Dale Blvd | SC | 25 | A | 5 |
| Briar Hill Av | Y | 6 | A-B | 2-3 |
| Briar Hill Av | T | 5 | B-F | 2-3 |
| Briarbluff Av | SC | 47 | B | 2 |
| Briarcroft Rd | T | 14 | A | 4 |
| Briarfield Dr | NY | 19 | B | 6 |
| Briarscross Blvd | SC | 41 | A | 4 |
| Briarwood Av | ET | 14 | C | 4-5 |
| Brick Ct | T | 13 | D | 1 |
| Bridesburg Dr | ET | 38 | F | 4 |
| Bridgeland Av | NY | 18 | E-F | 4 |
| Bridgend St | SC | 47 | D | 6 |
| Bridgend St | SC | 47 | D | 6 |
| Bridgend St | SC | 47 | F | 1 |
| Bridgenorth Cr | ET | 30 | C | 5 |
| Bridgeport Dr | SC | 47 | F | 1-2 |
| Bridgetown Dr | ET | 34 | B | 3 |
| Bridgeview Rd | Y | 24 | F | 2-3 |
| Bridgewater Av | ET | 24 | B-C | 1 |
| Bridgewater Rd | ET | 24 | D | 1 |
| Bridgman Av | T | 4 | D | 2 |
| Bridle Heath Gt | NY | 9 | E | 5 |
| Bridle Path, The | NY | 7 | E-F | 1-2 |
| Bridle Path, The | NY | 9 | C-E | 5-6 |
| Bridlegrove Dr | SC | 37 | B | 4 |
| Bridleholme Cir | SC | 49 | B | 3 |
| Bridletowne Cir | SC | 31 | B | 3-4 |
| Bridlewood Blvd | SC | 31 | A-B | 5-6 |
| Bridley Dr | SC | 41 | A | 3 |
| Bridlington St | SC | 39 | B-C | 4 |
| Bridport Cr | SC | 41 | A | 2 |
| Brief Rd | NY | 18 | C | 5 |
| Brigadier Pl | SC | 49 | D | 5 |
| Brigadoon Cr | SC | 31 | D | 4 |
| Brigden Pl | T | 3 | B | 1 |
| Brigham Ct | ET | 28 | B | 3 |
| Bright St | T | 3 | C | 1 |
| Brighton Av | T | 5 | E-F | 6 |
| Brighton Av | NY | 10 | A-C | 5 |
| Brightside Dr | SC | 47 | C-D | 1 |
| Brightview Cr | SC | 47 | D | 1 |
| Brightwood St | NY | 8 | C | 4 |
| Brigstock Rd | SC | 29 | D-E | 5 |
| Brill Cr | NY | 10 | D | 2 |
| Brimfrest Gt | SC | 47 | D | 6 |
| Brimley Rd | SC | 25 | F | 1-6 |
| Brimley Rd | SC | 27 | F | 1-6 |
| Brimley Rd | SC | 29 | F | 1-6 |
| Brimley Rd | SC | 31 | F | 1-6 |
| Brimley Rd | SC | 37 | A | 1-6 |
| Brimley Rd | SC | 39 | A | 1-6 |
| Brimley Rd S | SC | 25 | E | 4-6 |
| Brimley Rd S | SC | 25 | F | 1-3 |
| Brimorton Dr | SC | 39 | A-F | 5 |
| Brimstone Cr | SC | 41 | B | 3 |
| Brimwood Blvd | SC | 41 | A | 3 |
| Brimwood Blvd | SC | 41 | A | 3 |
| Brinloor Blvd | SC | 37 | D | 4-5 |
| Brisbane Rd | NY | 20 | F | 3 |
| Brisbourne Gr | SC | 41 | F | 4 |
| Bristol Av | T | 4 | A | 1-2 |
| Britain St | T | 3 | A-B | 1 |
| Britannia Av | T | 16 | B | 6 |
| British Columbia Rd | T | 12 | C | 2 |
| British Columbia Rd. | T | 2 | A | 2 |
| Brittany Ct | ET | 26 | D | 2 |
| Britwell Av | SC | 29 | F | 6 |
| Britwell Av | SC | 39 | A | 6 |
| Brixham Terr | NY | 18 | C | 2 |
| Broadbent Av | SC | 27 | E-F | 3 |
| Broadbridge Dr | SC | 47 | D-E | 4-5 |
| Broadcast La | T | 5 | B | 5 |
| Broadfield Dr | ET | 34 | A-B | 3-4 |
| Broadlands Blvd | NY | 19 | E-F | 5-6 |
| Broadleaf Rd | NY | 19 | B | 6 |
| Broadmead Av | SC | 25 | E | 5 |
| Broadoaks Dr | NY | 20 | C-D | 4 |
| Broadpath Rd | NY | 17 | A-B | 2 |
| Broadview Av | T | 3 | D | 1 |
| Broadview Av | EY | 5 | D-E | 1-6 |
| Broadview Av | T | 5 | D-E | 1-6 |
| Broadway Av | T | 7 | A-B | 3 |
| Broadway Av | NY | 7 | B-C | 3 |
| Broadway Av | EY | 7 | D-E | 3 |
| Brock Av | T | 14 | F | 3-6 |
| Brock Cr | T | 14 | F | 4 |
| Brockhouse Rd | ET | 32 | E | 1 |
| Brockington Cr | NY | 10 | B | 4-5 |
| Brockley Dr | SC | 27 | F | 1 |
| Brockley Dr | SC | 29 | F | 6 |
| Brockmount Ct | ET | 36 | F | 1 |
| Brockport Dr | ET | 38 | C | 4-5 |
| Brockton Av | T | 14 | F | 5 |
| Brome Rd | NY | 18 | C | 5 |
| Bromley Cr | ET | 24 | B | 1 |
| Bromley Dr | ET | 26 | B | 6 |
| Bromton Dr | SC | 39 | A | 4-5 |
| Brook Tree Cr | ET | 26 | B | 2-3 |
| Brookbanks Dr | NY | 19 | C-F | 3-4 |
| Brookdale Av | NY | 8 | C-E | 6 |
| Brookdale Av | T | 8 | B | 6 |
| Brooke Av | NY | 8 | D-F | 4 |
| Brookfield Rd | NY | 9 | A | 4 |
| Brookfield St | T | 4 | B | 6 |
| Brookhaven Dr | NY | 16 | B | 1-2 |
| Brooklawn Av | SC | 25 | E | 4-6 |
| Brooklawn Av | SC | 37 | A | 6 |
| Brooklyn Av | T | 5 | F | 6 |
| Brookmere Rd | ET | 28 | A | 1 |
| Brookmere Rd | ET | 30 | A | 6 |
| Brookmill Blvd | SC | 31 | B-D | 3 |
| Brookmount Rd | T | 13 | D | 5 |
| Brookmount Rd | T | 15 | C | 6 |
| Brookridge Dr | SC | 29 | F | 5 |
| Brooks Rd | SC | 39 | F | 2-3 |
| Brooks Rd | SC | 49 | A | 3-4 |
| Brookshire Blvd | SC | 31 | A | 2-3 |
| Brookside Av | Y | 24 | F | 1-2 |
| Brookside Dr | T | 15 | D | 4-5 |
| Brookview Dr | NY | 8 | B | 5-6 |
| Brookwell Dr | NY | 20 | C | 6 |
| Brookwood Ct | NY | 17 | A | 2 |
| Broomfield Dr | SC | 41 | A | 5 |
| Brougham Cr | ET | 26 | A | 2 |
| Brow Dr | ET | 32 | C | 4 |
| Brown Stone La | ET | 24 | D | 1 |
| Browning Av | T | 5 | D-E | 3 |
| Browning Av | EY | 5 | D-E | 3 |
| Brownlea Av | ET | 26 | E | 1-2 |
| Brownlow Av | T | 7 | B | 3 |
| Brownridge Cr | ET | 40 | D | 4 |
| Brown's La | T | 2 | C | 1 |
| Browns Line | ET | 32 | C | 2-4 |
| Brownspring Rd | SC | 39 | A | 1 |
| Brownville Av | Y | 16 | B | 4 |
| Browside Av | T | 6 | A | 1 |
| Brubeck Rd | NY | 30 | B-C | 4 |
| Bruce Farm Dr | NY | 11 | E-F | 2 |
| Bruce Park Av | T | 7 | C | 3 |
| Bruce St | T | 4 | B | 6 |
| Brucedale Cr | NY | 11 | D-E | 4 |
| Brucewood Cr | SC | 6 | C | 5-6 |
| Brule Cr | T | 24 | F | 4 |
| Brule Gdns | T | 24 | F | 4 |
| Brule Terr | T | 24 | F | 4 |
| Brumell Av | Y | 24 | F | 2 |
| Brumwell St | SC | 49 | F | 4-5 |
| Brunello Gt | ET | 40 | E | 1 |
| Brunner Dr | ET | 36 | D-E | 4 |
| Bruno Ct | NY | 30 | B | 1 |
| Brunswick Av | T | 4 | D | 2-5 |
| Brushwood Ct | NY | 11 | E | 4 |
| Brussels Rd | SC | 27 | E-F | 4 |
| Brussels St | ET | 22 | E | 1 |
| Bruton Rd | Y | 26 | F | 6 |
| Bryant Av | EY | 15 | F | 3 |
| Bryant Av | EY | 25 | A | 3 |
| Bryant St | NY | 10 | B | 5-6 |
| Bryce Av | T | 6 | F | 6 |
| Brydale Av | T | 5 | D | 4 |
| Brydon Dr | ET | 38 | F | 2-3 |
| Bryn Rd | NY | 18 | C | 6 |
| Brynhurst Ct | T | 7 | A | 2 |
| Brynston Rd | ET | 36 | E | 4 |
| Bucannan Rd | SC | 29 | B | 5 |
| Buchan Ct | NY | 19 | B | 1 |
| Buchan St | NY | 21 | A | 6 |
| Buckhorn Pl | ET | 30 | C | 6 |
| Buckhurst Cr | SC | 41 | B | 4 |
| Buckingham Av | T | 8 | B | 1 |
| Buckingham Av | NY | 7 | B-C | 1 |
| Buckingham St | ET | 22 | D | 2 |
| Buckland Rd | NY | 11 | B | 2 |
| Buckley Cr | ET | 36 | E | 3 |
| Bucksburn Rd | ET | 40 | D-E | 2 |
| Buddleswood Ct | SC | 41 | A | 4 |
| Bude St | Y | 6 | A-B | 4 |
| Budea Cr | SC | 29 | B | 3-4 |
| Budgell Terr | T | 14 | A | 5 |
| Budworth Dr | SC | 47 | B | 2 |
| Buena Vista Av | SC | 31 | E | 4-5 |
| Bugle Hill Rd | SC | 39 | A | 2 |
| Bulbourne Rd | ET | 40 | E | 5 |
| Buler Av | T | 13 | D | 6 |
| Bulwer St | T | 4 | E | 6 |
| Bunnell Cr | NY | 18 | C | 3 |
| Buntel La | NY | 11 | D | 5 |
| Bur Oakway | NY | 20 | A | 5-6 |
| Burbage Ct | ET | 40 | E | 2 |
| Burbank Dr | NY | 11 | D-E | 4-5 |
| Burcana Rd | SC | 29 | C | 4 |
| Burchell Rd | SC | 49 | B | 3 |
| Burdock La | ET | 17 | B | 2 |
| Burford Rd | ET | 24 | C | 4 |
| Burgess Av | T | 15 | C-D | 5 |
| Burgundy Cr | NY | 28 | D | 2 |
| Burin Ct | SC | 31 | B | 1 |
| Burke St | NY | 10 | F | 2-3 |
| Burkston Pl | ET | 36 | F | 4 |
| Burkwood Cr | SC | 41 | F | 6 |

| STREET NAME | MUNICIPALITY | MAP NO | MAP AREA |
|---|---|---|---|
| Burkwood Cr | SC | 51 | A 6 |
| Burleigh Heights Dr | NY | 11 | D 4 |
| Burley Av | EY | 5 | E 2 |
| Burlingame Rd | ET | 32 | B-C 3 |
| Burlington Cr | T | 4 | A-B 1 |
| Burlington St | ET | 22 | E 4 |
| Burma Dr | ET | 24 | E 6 |
| Burmont Rd | T | 6 | C 3 |
| Burn Hill Rd | SC | 25 | B 3 |
| Burnaby Blvd | T | 6 | E 4 |
| Burnage Ct | SC | 37 | F 3 |
| Burncrest Dr | NY | 8 | D-E 4 |
| Burndale Av | NY | 10 | E-F 6 |
| Burnelm Dr | ET | 34 | E 2 |
| Burnett Av | NY | 10 | D-F 6 |
| Burnfield Av | T | 4 | B 2 |
| Burnham Rd | EY | 7 | B 6 |
| Burnhamhall Ct | ET | 34 | F 2 |
| Burnhamill Pl | ET | 34 | A 1-2 |
| Burnhamthorpe Park Blvd | ET | 24 | A 1-2 |
| Burnhamthorpe Rd | ET | 24 | A 6 |
| Burnhamthorpe Rd | ET | 34 | A-F 2 |
| Burnley Av | SC | 29 | A 6 |
| Burnside Dr | T | 4 | C 1-2 |
| Burnt Bark Dr | SC | 31 | D 1-2 |
| Burnt Meadoway | NY | 21 | C-D 1 |
| Burntlog Cr | ET | 34 | A 3 |
| Burnview Cr | SC | 37 | B 1-2 |
| Burnwell St | NY | 10 | B 1 |
| Burr Av | NY | 18 | B 5 |
| Burrard Rd | ET | 28 | B 3-4 |
| Burrell Av | EY | 15 | D 3 |
| Burridge Rd | SC | 37 | C 2 |
| Burritt Rd | SC | 29 | B 6 |
| Burrows Av | ET | 34 | E 2 |
| Burrows Hall Blvd | SC | 39 | D-E 1 |
| Burton Rd | T | 6 | C-D 5 |
| Burtonwood Cr | ET | 40 | F 2 |
| Burwood Rd | ET | 36 | E 5 |
| Bush Dr | SC | 49 | C-D 4-5 |
| Bush Gt | SC | 49 | C-D 4-5 |
| Bushbury Dr | NY | 19 | B-D 4 |
| Bushby Dr | SC | 39 | B 3 |
| Bushcroft Gr | SC | 41 | B 4 |
| Bushell Av | T | 5 | F 5 |
| Bushey Av | T | 4 | E 5 |
| Bushmills Sq | SC | 31 | F 4 |
| Business Row | SC | 29 | E 3 |
| Busy St | T | 5 | E 6 |
| Buttercup Ct | NY | 30 | B 1-2 |
| Butterfield Dr | NY | 19 | E 5 |
| Butterick Rd | ET | 32 | F 1-2 |
| Butternut St | T | 5 | D-E 3 |
| Butterworth Av | SC | 25 | B-C 3 |
| Buttonwood Av | W | 26 | F 3 |
| Buxton Rd | NY | 18 | B 2 |
| Bychris Ct | ET | 28 | A 5 |
| Byford St | SC | 49 | E 5 |
| Bying Rd. | T | 2 | A 2 |
| Byland Rd | ET | 26 | E 4 |
| Byland Rd | ET | 36 | F 4 |
| Byng Av | NY | 11 | A-C 4 |
| Byng Av | Y | 25 | B 3-4 |
| Byng Av | ET | 28 | C 1-2 |
| Byng Rd | T | 12 | C 2 |
| Byron Dr | T | 15 | A 3-4 |
| Bywood Dr | ET | 24 | A-B 1 |
| Byworth Blvd | ET | 28 | A 5 |
| **C** | | | |
| Cabana Dr | NY | 30 | B 1-2 |
| Cabernet Cir | ET | 40 | D-E 1-2 |
| Cabot Ct | ET | 24 | A 2 |
| Cactus Av | NY | 10 | E 1-2 |
| Cadbury Ct | SC | 37 | F 3 |
| Caddy Dr | SC | 39 | E 6 |
| Cadillac Av | NY | 8 | B-C 4 |
| Cadman Ct | ET | 26 | E 4 |
| Cadmus Rd | NY | 11 | B 2 |
| Cadorna Av | EY | 15 | A 1-2 |
| Caesar Av | Y | 16 | A 5 |
| Cafon Ct | ET | 30 | A 4 |
| Caines Av | NY | 10 | D-E 2 |
| Cairn Cross | SC | 31 | F 1 |
| Cairns Av | T | 15 | B 5 |
| Cairnside Cr | NY | 21 | E-F 5-6 |
| Caithness Av | ET | 15 | A 3 |
| Calais Av | NY | 18 | B 3 |
| Calderon Cr | NY | 10 | D-E 3 |
| Calderstone Cr | SC | 47 | D 4 |
| Caldow Rd | NY | 6 | B 2 |
| Caldow Rd | T | 6 | D 2-3 |
| Caldy Ct | NY | 9 | C 2 |
| Caledon Rd | ET | 24 | D 5 |
| Caledonia Park Rd | T | 14 | E 1 |
| Caledonia Rd | NY | 16 | E 1-2 |
| Caledonia Rd | SC | 16 | E 5-6 |
| Caledonia Rd | Y | 16 | B 3-5 |
| Caledonia Rd | NY | 18 | E 4-6 |
| Caley Terr | NY | 49 | A 2 |
| Calibre Ct | SC | 49 | F 3 |
| Calico Dr | NY | 18 | B 1 |
| Callender St | T | 14 | E 6 |
| Callowhill Dr | ET | 36 | E 2-3 |
| Calm Ct | NY | 30 | D 5 |
| Calora Ct | SC | 31 | B 3 |
| Calstock Dr | ET | 30 | B-C 6 |
| Calthorpe Av | NY | 18 | C 3-4 |
| Calumet Cr | SC | 39 | C 5-6 |
| Calverley Tr | SC | 49 | C 3-4 |
| Calvin Av | NY | 9 | C 1 |
| Calvington Dr | NY | 18 | B-D 3 |
| Camaret Cr | SC | 27 | F 1-2 |
| Camberley Ct | SC | 51 | A 6 |
| Camberwell Rd | Y | 6 | C 4 |
| Camborne Av | NY | 18 | B-C 2 |
| Cambrai Av | EY | 15 | D-E 2 |
| Cambridge Av | T | 5 | D 3 |
| Camden St | T | 2 | D-E 1 |
| Camelot Ct | NY | 19 | A 6 |
| Cameo Cr | NY | 16 | A 5 |
| Cameron Av | NY | 8 | E-F 1 |
| Cameron Av | Y | 16 | D-E 4 |
| Cameron Cr | EY | 7 | D 4 |
| Cameron Glen Blvd | SC | 47 | D 4 |
| Cameron Glen Blvd | SC | 49 | F 4 |
| Cameron St | T | 2 | D 1 |
| Cameron St | T | 4 | D-E 6 |
| Camilla Cr | SC | 27 | A 5-6 |
| Camlac Pl | SC | 39 | A 4 |
| Camor Ct | SC | 49 | D 4 |
| Campania Cr | SC | 31 | F 2 |
| Campbell Av | T | 14 | E 2-3 |
| Campbell Cr | NY | 9 | A 3 |
| Camperdown Av | ET | 38 | F 5-6 |
| Campion Rd | ET | 34 | D 1 |
| Camrose Cr | SC | 27 | A-B 5 |
| Camwood Cr | NY | 19 | C-D 3 |
| Canadian Rd | SC | 29 | B-C 4 |
| Canadine Rd | SC | 29 | E-F 4 |
| Canarctic Dr | NY | 20 | D-E 2 |
| Canary Ct | NY | 11 | D 4 |
| Cancara Gt | ET | 34 | E 4 |
| Candida Gt | NY | 10 | B 5 |
| Candida Gt | NY | 11 | D-E 5 |
| Candis Dr | NY | 10 | B 4 |
| Candle Liteway | NY | 10 | C 2 |
| Candlewood Cr | NY | 20 | B-C 4-5 |
| Candy Courtway | NY | 10 | D 2 |
| Cane Grassway | NY | 30 | B 1 |
| Canerouth Dr | ET | 34 | A 1 |
| Canfield Pl | NY | 19 | A 5 |
| Canham Cr | SC | 31 | F 5 |
| Canlish Rd | SC | 27 | D 1 |
| Canlish Rd | SC | 29 | D 5-6 |
| Canmore Blvd | SC | 49 | B-C 3 |
| Canmotor Av | ET | 22 | B 1 |
| Canniff St | T | 2 | B 1 |
| Canning Av | T | 5 | E 3 |
| Cannon Rd | ET | 24 | E-F 6 |
| Cannonbury Ct | NY | 19 | F 4 |
| Canon Jackson Dr | Y | 16 | D 3 |
| Canongate Tr | SC | 31 | D 1 |
| Canso Rd | ET | 38 | E 5 |
| Canterbury Cr | NY | 24 | C 1 |
| Canterbury Pl | NY | 10 | F 4-5 |
| Canterbury Rd | NY | 24 | C 1 |
| Cantle Path | ET | 34 | D 2 |
| Canton Av | NY | 18 | B 3 |
| Canuck Av | NY | 18 | D-E 1-2 |
| Canvarco Rd | EY | 7 | E 5 |
| Canyon Av | NY | 10 | C 6 |
| Canzone Ct | SC | 27 | F 2 |
| Capella Starway | NY | 19 | D 1-2 |
| Capitol Av | NY | 6 | A 2 |
| Capstan Ct | NY | 20 | B 6 |
| Captain Hall Ct | SC | 31 | F 2 |
| Captains Way | SC | 31 | E-F 1 |
| Carabob Ct | SC | 29 | B 6 |
| Caracas Rd | NY | 9 | E 1 |
| Caravan Dr | NY | 9 | A 3 |
| Cardell Av | NY | 28 | C 4 |
| Cardiff Rd | NY | 7 | B 3 |
| Cardiff Rd | T | 7 | B 3 |
| Cardigan Rd | ET | 24 | B 4 |
| Cardinal Pl | T | 9 | A 4 |
| Cardwell Av | SC | 31 | E 6 |
| Cardy Pl | SC | 39 | D 5 |
| Carew Gt | SC | 39 | D 4-5 |
| Carey Rd | T | 7 | A 4 |
| Cariboo Av | NY | 8 | C 4 |
| Cariboo Av | T | 14 | D 2 |
| Caribou Rd | NY | 6 | C-E 1 |
| Carisbrooke Sq | SC | 51 | A 4 |
| Carl Cr | SC | 31 | B 1 |
| Carl Shepway | NY | 21 | A 6 |
| Carlaw Av | T | 3 | E 1-2 |
| Carlaw Av | T | 5 | E 2-5 |
| Carlaw Av | T | 5 | E 2-6 |
| Carletta Dr | M | 32 | A 1-2 |
| Carhall Rd | NY | 18 | E-F 4 |
| Carhall Rd | NY | 20 | D-F 5-6 |
| Carling Av | T | 4 | B 3 |
| Carlingview Dr | ET | 36 | B 1-3 |
| Carlingview Dr | ET | 38 | B 3-5 |
| Carlingwood Cr | SC | 39 | C 1 |
| Carlisle Cr | SC | 49 | F 3 |
| Carlson Ct | ET | 38 | C 6 |
| Carlton St | T | 5 | A-C 5 |
| Carluke Cr | NY | 9 | C 1-2 |
| Carlyle St | T | 4 | D 5-6 |
| Carmel Cr | NY | 11 | E-F 2 |
| Carmichael Av | NY | 8 | D-E 4 |
| Carnarvon Av | ET | 22 | C 1-2 |
| Carnarvon St | Y | 16 | E 3 |
| Carnation Av | ET | 32 | F 4 |
| Carncastle Gt | SC | 29 | C 2 |
| Carnegie Ct | NY | 10 | E 3 |
| Carney Rd | NY | 10 | E 3-4 |
| Carnforth Rd | NY | 17 | E-F 1-4 |
| Carnival Ct | NY | 10 | B 1 |
| Carnwath Cr | NY | 9 | B 3 |
| Carol Wmneway | NY | 21 | B 5-6 |
| Carolbreen Sq | SC | 31 | F 3 |
| Caroline Av | T | 3 | F 1 |
| Carondale Cr | SC | 31 | B 4-5 |
| Caronia Sq | SC | 51 | A 5 |
| Caronport Cr | NY | 19 | E 6 |
| Caronridge Cr | SC | 31 | A-B 3 |
| Carousel Ct | NY | 6 | A 1 |
| Carpenter Rd | NY | 10 | C 1 |
| Carr St | T | 4 | D 6 |
| Carrera Blvd | SC | 29 | D 3-4 |
| Carriage La | NY | 10 | B 2 |
| Carrick Av | T | 16 | E 6 |
| Carrier Dr | ET | 40 | C-D 1-3 |
| Carrington Av | Y | 16 | E-F 4 |
| Carroll St | T | 5 | D 6 |
| Carrying Pl | SC | 41 | E 5 |
| Carsbrooke Rd | ET | 34 | B 1 |
| Carscadden Dr | NY | 10 | C 4-5 |
| Carslake Cr | SC | 37 | A 2 |
| Carson Cr | NY | 8 | F 3 |
| Carson St | ET | 32 | E 3-4 |
| Carstowe Rd | T | 5 | A-B 1 |
| Carswell Pl | ET | 36 | E 2 |
| Carthage Av | SC | 29 | B 3 |
| Cartier Cr | SC | 29 | F 4-5 |
| Cartwheel Millway | NY | 9 | D 3 |
| Cartwright Av | NY | 18 | E-F 5 |
| Carus Av | T | 4 | B 2 |
| Carysfort Rd | ET | 24 | A-B 3 |
| Cascaden St | SC | 31 | F 1 |
| Casci Av | T | 15 | B 5 |
| Casebridge Ct | SC | 51 | B 6 |
| Casemore Rd | SC | 51 | A-B 3-4 |
| Cashew Ct | NY | 21 | E 6 |
| Cashman Cr | Y | 16 | B 4 |
| Casimir St | T | 4 | D 6 |
| Casino Ct | NY | 10 | B 6 |
| Cass Av | SC | 29 | B-D 1-2 |
| Cassandra Blvd | NY | 19 | D-F 4-5 |
| Cassels Av | T | 15 | C-D 4 |
| Cassidy Pl | NY | 19 | A 6 |
| Cassis Dr | ET | 40 | D-E 1-2 |
| Castille Av | SC | 27 | B 2 |
| Castle Frank Cr | T | 5 | B-C 4 |
| Castle Frank Rd | T | 5 | B 3 |
| Castle Green Cr | ET | 26 | B 1 |
| Castle Hill Dr | SC | 31 | D 4-5 |
| Castle Knock Rd | T | 6 | E 3-4 |
| Castle View Av | T | 4 | C 5 |
| Castlebar Rd | ET | 24 | B-C 5 |
| Castlebury Cr | NY | 11 | F 3 |
| Castledene Cr | SC | 31 | A-B 6 |
| Castlefield Av | Y | 6 | A-B 3 |
| Castlefield Av | T | 6 | B-F 3 |
| Castlefield Av | Y | 16 | D-F 3 |
| Castlegate Rd | ET | 36 | F 5 |
| Castlegrove Blvd | NY | 19 | E-F 5-6 |

|  | | | | |
|---|---|---|---|---|
| Castlemere Cr | SC | 31 | A-B | 5 |
| Castlethorpe Dr | SC | 37 | B | 4 |
| Castleton Av | Y | 16 | A | 6 |
| Castlewood Rd | T | 6 | E | 2-3 |
| Castor Cr | SC | 39 | D-E | 3 |
| Caswell Dr | NY | 11 | C | 1-2 |
| Catalda Ct | NY | 10 | D | 5 |
| Catalina Ct | SC | 37 | D-E | 4-5 |
| Cataraqui Cr | SC | 25 | B | 2 |
| Catford Rd | NY | 20 | D | 4 |
| Cathcart St | NY | 16 | F | 2 |
| Cathedral Bluffs Dr | SC | 25 | F | 4-5 |
| Cathedral Bluffs Dr | SC | 37 | B | 6 |
| Cather Cr | NY | 8 | B | 5 |
| Catherwood Ct | SC | 31 | B | 5 |
| Cathlo St | SC | 47 | D | 1 |
| Cathron St | ET | 22 | E | 1 |
| Cathy Jean Rd | ET | 40 | F | 1 |
| Caulfield Rd | ET | 28 | B | 3 |
| Cavehill Cr | SC | 26 | B | 3 |
| Cavell Av | T | 5 | E-F | 4 |
| Cavell Av | ET | 22 | D-E | 2 |
| Caven St | ET | 22 | A-B | 1 |
| Cavendish St | T | 8 | E | 5 |
| Caverley Dr | ET | 36 | E | 2-3 |
| Cavern Ct | NY | 16 | C | 2 |
| Cavotti Cr | NY | 10 | A | 4 |
| Cawthra Av | T | 14 | D | 1 |
| Cawthra Sq | T | 5 | A | 4 |
| Cayuga Av | Y | 16 | B-C | 5 |
| Cecil Cr | SC | 25 | E | 3 |
| Cecil Cr | SC | 25 | F | 3 |
| Cecil St | T | 4 | E | 5 |
| Cedar Av | T | 13 | F | 5 |
| Cedar Av | T | 15 | F | 6 |
| Cedar Brae Blvd | SC | 37 | B | 2-3 |
| Cedar Dr | SC | 37 | D | 3-4 |
| Cedar Springs Gr | NY | 10 | A-B | 4 |
| Cedarbank Cr | NY | 19 | B | 6 |
| Cedarcrest Blvd | NY | 15 | F | 1-2 |
| Cedarcrest Dr | ET | 24 | C | 1-2 |
| Cedarcroft Blvd | NY | 10 | C | 2 |
| Cedarland Dr | ET | 24 | A-B | 1 |
| Cedarvale Av | EY | 15 | D | 1-3 |
| Cedarvale Av | T | 15 | D | 1-3 |
| Cedarview Dr | SC | 49 | E | 4-5 |
| Cedarwood Av | NY | 9 | B | 3-4 |
| Cedric Av | Y | 16 | E | 5 |
| Celandine Rd | ET | 30 | A | 4-5 |
| Celeste Dr | ET | 36 | F | 1-2 |
| Celestine Dr | ET | 36 | F | 1-2 |
| Celt Av | NY | 8 | A | 6 |
| Centennial Park Gt | ET | 36 | B | 6 |
| Centennial Park Rd | ET | 36 | A-B | 5-6 |
| Centennial Rd | SC | 47 | E | 1 |
| Centennial Rd | SC | 49 | E-F | 4-6 |
| Centennial Rd N | SC | 49 | E | 4 |
| Central Hospital La | T | 5 | B | 5 |
| Central Pk Rdwy | ET | 24 | B | 2 |
| Central St | ET | 22 | D | 3 |
| Centre Av | T | 4 | E | 4 |
| Centre Av | NY | 11 | A-B | 2 |
| Centre Dr | ET | 26 | D | 4 |
| Centre Rd | SC | 37 | C | 3-4 |
| Centre St | SC | 37 | C | 3-4 |
| Centrepark Dr | NY | 16 | A | 2 |
| Centurion Ct | NY | 11 | D | 4 |
| Century Dr | SC | 27 | F | 4 |
| Ceramic Rd | NY | 20 | E | 4-5 |
| Cetus Starway | NY | 19 | D | 1-2 |
| Chad Cr | SC | 51 | A | 5 |
| Chadburn Rd | ET | 24 | E | 5-6 |
| Chadbury Pl | SC | 31 | A | 2 |
| Chadwick Av | T | 6 | D | 4 |
| Chaldean St | SC | 31 | C | 5 |
| Chalet Rd | NY | 21 | E | 4 |
| Chalfont Rd | ET | 28 | B | 3-4 |
| Chalkfarm Dr | NY | 7 | B | 2-3 |
| Challenger Ct | SC | 49 | B | 3 |
| Challister Av | NY | 11 | E | 5 |
| Chamberlain Av | Y | 16 | E | 4 |
| Chambers Av | T | 16 | D | 5-6 |
| Chambers Av | Y | 16 | D | 5 |
| Champagne Dr | NY | 20 | F | 4 |
| Champlain Blvd | NY | 8 | B | 3-4 |
| Chancellor Dr | SC | 39 | D | 4 |
| Chancery La | SC | 39 | F | 3-4 |
| Chandler Dr | SC | 39 | D-E | 5-6 |
| Chandos Av | T | 14 | F | 2 |
| Channel Av | T | 3 | B | 4 |
| Channel Nine Ct | SC | 39 | B | 2 |
| Channing Pl | ET | 40 | D | 4 |
| Chantilly Gdns | NY | 28 | E | 5 |
| Chantrey Ct | SC | 39 | E | 3 |
| Chapais Cr | SC | 47 | D | 5 |
| Chapais Cr | SC | 49 | E | 5-6 |
| Chapel Park Sq | SC | 31 | D | 1 |
| Chapel Rd | ET | 32 | D-E | 5 |
| Chapeltown Cr | SC | 31 | A | 2 |
| Chapleau Pl | NY | 7 | F | 2 |
| Chaplin Cr | T | 6 | D-F | 2-5 |
| Chapman Av | EY | 15 | E-F | 2 |
| Chapman Rd | ET | 26 | D-E | 2-3 |
| Chappel Hill Rd | NY | 18 | B | 3 |
| Charade Ct | SC | 31 | A | 4 |
| Charcoal Dr | SC | 49 | C | 3 |
| Charity Rd | SC | 27 | E | 4 |
| Charlemagne Dr | NY | 11 | A-B | 4 |
| Charlemont Cr | SC | 29 | A-B | 2 |
| Charles St E | T | 4 | F | 4 |
| Charles St E | T | 5 | A | 4 |
| Charles St W | T | 4 | E-F | 4 |
| Charleigh Ct | ET | 40 | E | 3 |
| Charleston Rd | NY | 19 | A | 4 |
| Charleston Rd | ET | 34 | E | 2-3 |
| Charleswood Dr | NY | 8 | B-C | 3 |
| Charlotte St | T | 2 | E | 1 |
| Charlottetown Blvd | SC | 49 | F | 5-6 |
| Charlton Blvd | NY | 10 | D-F | 3 |
| Charlton Settlement Av | Y | 7 | F | 2-3 |
| Charnleigh Ct | ET | 40 | E | 3 |
| Charnwood Rd | NY | 19 | A | 4 |
| Charrington Cr | NY | 20 | B | 6 |
| Charterhouse Rd | SC | 39 | A | 1 |
| Chartland Blvd S | SC | 31 | F | 4 |
| Chartland Blvd S | SC | 41 | A | 4-5 |
| Chartway Blvd | SC | 49 | B | 3 |
| Chartwell Rd | ET | 24 | B | 5-6 |
| Chase Av | NY | 11 | F | 4 |
| Chateau Ct | NY | 18 | B | 1-2 |
| Chater Ct | NY | 6 | B-C | 1 |
| Chatfield Dr | NY | 19 | A | 5 |
| Chatham Av | T | 5 | F | 4 |
| Chatham Av | T | 15 | A | 4 |
| Chatsmere Pl | SC | 39 | B | 5 |
| Chatsworth Dr | T | 6 | F | 1 |
| Chatterton Blvd | SC | 37 | B-C | 4 |
| Chauncey Av | ET | 24 | A-B | 4 |
| Cheatham Pl | SC | 41 | E | 6 |
| Checkendon Dr | ET | 30 | A | 5-6 |
| Checkers Ct | NY | 30 | F | 3 |
| Chedington Pl | NY | 7 | D | 1 |
| Chelford Rd | NY | 9 | E-F | 5 |
| Chelmer St | SC | 49 | B-C | 6 |
| Chelmsford Av | NY | 10 | D-E | 1-2 |
| Chelsea Av | T | 14 | D-E | 3 |
| Chelsea Dr | ET | 32 | C | 3 |
| Chelway Rd | SC | 37 | C | 3 |
| Chelwood Rd | SC | 27 | D | 4 |
| Chemical St | SC | 47 | C-D | 2-3 |
| Cheritan Av | T | 6 | F | 1 |
| Cherokee Blvd | NY | 21 | E | 3-4 |
| Cherriebell Rd | M | 32 | B | 5 |
| Cherry Nook Gdns | T | 15 | A | 6 |
| Cherry Post Cr | ET | 34 | A | 3 |
| Cherry St | T | 3 | C-D | 1-4 |
| Cherrydale Ct | SC | 49 | E | 5 |
| Cherryhill Av | SC | 47 | E | 1 |
| Cherrylawn Av | NY | 30 | B-C | 3 |
| Cherrystone Dr | NY | 21 | B | 3-4 |
| Cherrywood Av | Y | 6 | B | 5-6 |
| Cheryl Shepway | NY | 21 | A | 4 |
| Chesapeake Av | SC | 25 | C | 1 |
| Chesham Dr | NY | 18 | A-B | 3 |
| Cheshire Dr | ET | 36 | F | 5 |
| Chesley Av | T | 14 | F | 4 |
| Chesswood Dr | NY | 20 | E-F | 4-5 |
| Chester Av | T | 5 | E | 3 |
| Chester Hill Rd | T | 5 | D | 3 |
| Chester Le Blvd | SC | 31 | A | 3-4 |
| Chestergrove Ct | SC | 31 | A | 5 |
| Chestermere Blvd | SC | 37 | C | 2-3 |
| Chesterton Shores | SC | 47 | E | 6 |
| Chestnut Cr | SC | 27 | C-D | 5 |
| Chestnut Hills Av | ET | 24 | B | 2 |
| Chestnut Hills Pkwy | ET | 24 | B-C | 1-2 |
| Chestnut Pk | T | 5 | A | 3-4 |
| Cheston Rd | T | 7 | A | 4 |
| Chetta Pl | ET | 28 | A-B | 6 |
| Cheval Dr | NY | 9 | E | 4 |
| Cheviot Pl | ET | 26 | A | 3 |
| Chevron Cr | SC | 27 | E | 4 |
| Cheyenne Dr | SC | 37 | C | 2 |
| Chianti Sq | ET | 40 | D | 1 |
| Chichester Pl | SC | 31 | A | 6 |
| Chicora Av | T | 4 | E | 2 |
| Chicoutimi Av | NY | 6 | D | 1 |
| Chiefswood Sq | SC | 31 | A | 4 |
| Chieftain Cr | NY | 9 | C | 2 |
| Chilcot Av | ET | 28 | A | 5 |
| Chillery Av | SC | 27 | F | 3 |
| Chillery Av | SC | 37 | A | 3 |
| Chiltern Hill Rd | Y | 6 | C | 4-5 |
| Chilton Rd | EY | 5 | F | 1 |
| Chilton Rd | EY | 7 | F | 6 |
| Chimneystack Rd, The | NY | 20 | D | 1 |
| Chine Dr | SC | 25 | E | 1-2 |
| Chine Dr | SC | 25 | E | 1-2 |
| Chine Cr | SC | 27 | F | 6 |
| Chipper Cr | SC | 27 | F | 3 |
| Chippewa Av | T | 2 | F | 5-6 |
| Chippewa Av | T | 3 | A | 5-6 |
| Chipping Rd | NY | 19 | B | 5 |
| Chipstead Rd | NY | 9 | E | 3-4 |
| Chipwood Cr | NY | 21 | E | 4 |
| Chisholm Av | EY | 15 | E | 2-3 |
| Chisholm Av | T | 15 | E | 3 |
| Chiswell Cr | NY | 11 | C | 4 |
| Chiswick Av | NY | 16 | A | 1-2 |
| Choiceland Blvd | SC | 49 | E | 6 |
| Chopin Av | SC | 27 | D | 2-3 |
| Christie St | T | 4 | B | 1-3 |
| Christie St | T | 6 | B | 6 |
| Christina Cr | SC | 29 | A | 4 |
| Christine Cr | NY | 10 | D | 5 |
| Chryessa Av | Y | 16 | A | 4-5 |
| Chrysler Cr | SC | 29 | A | 6 |
| Chudleigh Av | T | 6 | F | 1 |
| Chudleigh Rd | Y | 16 | E-F | 4 |
| Church Av | NY | 11 | A-B | 4 |
| Church St | T | 3 | A | 1-2 |
| Church St | T | 4 | F | 3 |
| Church St | T | 5 | A | 3-6 |
| Church St | T | 28 | D-F | 5-6 |
| Churchill Av | T | 4 | A-B | 5 |
| Churchill Av | NY | 10 | D-F | 4-5 |
| Cibola Av | T | 2 | F | 5-6 |
| Cibola Av | T | 3 | A-B | 4-6 |
| Cicada Ct | NY | 9 | F | 5 |
| Cicerella Cr | SC | 27 | F | 1-2 |
| Cimmaron Ct | NY | 11 | F | 1 |
| Cinder Av | T | 4 | B | 5 |
| Cindy Nicholas Dr | SC | 49 | A | 2-3 |
| Cinnickbar Dr | ET | 40 | A-B | 5-6 |
| Circle Ridge | NY | 18 | E | 6 |
| Circuit Ct | NY | 20 | C | 5 |
| Cirillo Ct | NY | 18 | C | 5 |
| Citadel Dr | SC | 27 | F | 2-3 |
| Citation Dr | NY | 11 | D-E | 5 |
| City Rd | T | 32 | F | 5 |
| City View Dr | ET | 38 | D | 4-6 |
| Civic Centre Ct | ET | 34 | C | 2 |
| Civic Rd | SC | 27 | B-C | 4 |
| Clair Rd | NY | 30 | F | 4 |
| Claireport Cr | ET | 40 | A | 1 |
| Claireville Dr | ET | 40 | B | 2-3 |
| Clairlea Cr | SC | 27 | A | 5 |
| Clairton Cr | T | 26 | E | 5 |
| Clairtrell Rd | NY | 11 | C | 6 |
| Clancy Dr | NY | 21 | A-B | 4 |
| Clansman Blvd | NY | 21 | A-B | 2 |
| Clanton Ct | NY | 8 | B | 2 |
| Clanton Park Rd | NY | 8 | B-C | 2 |
| Clanwilliam Ct | SC | 29 | B | 4 |
| Clapperton Av | SC | 25 | C | 1 |
| Clappison Blvd | SC | 47 | D | 5 |
| Clappison Blvd | SC | 49 | F | 5-6 |
| Claremont Av | T | 4 | D | 5 |
| Claremore Av | SC | 25 | E | 1-3 |
| Clarence Sq | T | 2 | E | 1-2 |
| Clarendon Av | T | 4 | E | 1 |
| Clarendon Cr | T | 4 | E | 1 |
| Claresholme Dr | SC | 49 | D-E | 3 |
| Claret Ct | ET | 26 | E | 4 |
| Clareville Av | NY | 21 | A | 5 |
| Clarinda Dr | NY | 11 | E | 5-6 |
| Clarion Rd | ET | 36 | D-E | 2 |
| Clarke Av | T | 14 | E | 2 |
| Clark Secor Pl | SC | 47 | D-E | 4 |
| Clark St | T | 5 | D-E | 6 |
| Clarke St | EY | 7 | E | 4 |
| Clarkhill St | NY | 10 | D | 3-4 |
| Clarkson Av | Y | 16 | E | 3 |
| Claude Av | T | 14 | D | 6 |
| Clawson Rd | NY | 6 | A-B | 1 |
| Claxton Blvd | Y | 6 | C-D | 5-6 |
| Clay Ct | T | 26 | E | 4 |
| Claybrooke St | Y | 16 | D | 3 |
| Clayhall Cr | NY | 20 | B-C | 5 |
| Clayland Dr | NY | 19 | E | 3 |
| Claymore Cr | ET | 24 | B-C | 4 |
| Clayoquot Rd | NY | 28 | E | 2-4 |
| Claywood Rd | NY | 10 | E | 4 |
| Cleadon Rd | SC | 31 | F | 2-3 |
| Clearbrooke Cir | ET | 28 | A | 2 |
| Clearcrest Av | NY | 11 | C | 1 |

| STREET NAME | MUNICIPALITY | MAP NO | MAP AREA |
|---|---|---|---|
| Clearfield Gt | SC | 27 | B 2 |
| Clearlake Av | SC | 47 | E 4 |
| Clearside Pl | ET | 34 | B 3 |
| Clearview Hts | Y | 16 | B-C 3 |
| Clearwater Dr | M | 32 | B 2-3 |
| Cleethorpes Blvd | SC | 39 | A 1-2 |
| Clematis Rd | NY | 21 | E 4 |
| Clement Rd | ET | 36 | E-F 3 |
| Clementine Sq | SC | 39 | D 4 |
| Clements Av | T | 6 | D-F 3 |
| Clementvine Ct | ET | 36 | F 2 |
| Clemes Dr | SC | 49 | E 6 |
| Clendenan Av | T | 14 | B 1-3 |
| Cleo Rd | NY | 18 | C 5 |
| Cleta Dr | SC | 27 | E 5-6 |
| Clevedon St | NY | 18 | B 3 |
| Cleveland St | T | 7 | C 4-5 |
| Cliff Fernway | NY | 21 | B 3 |
| Cliff St | Y | 16 | B 4-5 |
| Cliffcrest Cr | SC | 25 | F 2 |
| Cliffcrest Dr | SC | 25 | F 2-3 |
| Clifford Ct | SC | 29 | B 4 |
| Cliffside Dr | SC | 25 | C 3 |
| Cliffwood Rd | NY | 21 | B-E 1-2 |
| Clifton Av | NY | 10 | A-B 5 |
| Clifton Rd | T | 5 | B 1 |
| Climans Rd | NY | 19 | E 3 |
| Clinton Pl | T | 4 | B-C 4 |
| Clinton St | T | 4 | C 2-5 |
| Clintwood Dr | NY | 19 | F 5 |
| Clipper Rd | NY | 21 | F 4-5 |
| Clissold Rd | ET | 24 | B 3 |
| Clive St | ET | 24 | C 6 |
| Cliveden Av | ET | 24 | C 6 |
| Cloebury Ct | NY | 10 | D 4 |
| Clonmore Dr | SC | 25 | A 4-5 |
| Close Av | T | 12 | B 1-2 |
| Closson Dr | SC | 49 | E 4-5 |
| Cloud Dr | NY | 30 | A 2 |
| Clouston Av | Y | 26 | F 2 |
| Clovelly Av | T | 6 | A-B 4 |
| Clovercrest Rd | NY | 21 | A 5 |
| Cloverdale Rd | T | 16 | D 6 |
| Cloverdale Rd | ET | 24 | B 3-4 |
| Cloverhill Rd | ET | 24 | E-F 5 |
| Cloverlawn Av | Y | 6 | A 6 |
| Cloverleaf Gt | SC | 29 | B 4 |
| Clovis La | NY | 8 | A 5 |
| Club Golfway | NY | 17 | D 4 |
| Clubhouse Ct | NY | 20 | B 6 |
| Clubhouse Rd | ET | 38 | A-B 1-2 |
| Clubine Av | NY | 16 | C 5 |
| Clumber Rd | ET | 36 | B 3 |
| Cluny Dr | T | 5 | A 2-3 |
| Clyde Av | NY | 8 | D 3-4 |
| Clyde Rd | SC | 49 | E 5 |
| Clydebank Blvd | SC | 31 | C 4 |
| Clydesdale Dr | NY | 21 | E-F 5 |
| Coach Liteway | NY | 10 | C 2-3 |
| Coady Av | T | 5 | F 6 |
| Coalport Dr | SC | 25 | A 4 |
| Coates Av | Y | 6 | B 5 |
| Coatsworth Cr | T | 15 | B 6 |
| Coatsworth St | T | 5 | B 6 |
| Cobalt Av | T | 16 | A 2 |
| Cobalt St | T | 16 | A 2 |
| Cobb Av | NY | 20 | A 6 |
| Cobble Hills | ET | 26 | C 5 |
| Cobbler Ct | NY | 20 | B 3 |
| Cobblestone Dr | NY | 21 | A 4 |
| Cobden St | NY | 10 | C 4-5 |
| Cobham Cr | NY | 10 | C 4 |
| Cobourg Av | T | 14 | F 4 |
| Cobourg Pl | Y | 16 | A 4 |
| Cochrane Ct | ET | 24 | C 6 |
| Cochrane Dr | ET | 24 | C 6 |
| Cockburn Dr | SC | 49 | F 5-6 |
| Cocksfield Av | NY | 10 | A-C 6 |
| Codeco Ct | NY | 10 | D 1-2 |
| Codlin Cr | ET | 40 | A 1 |
| Codsell Av | NY | 10 | A-C 6 |
| Coe Hill Dr | T | 14 | A-B 5-6 |
| Colt St | ET | 22 | B 4 |
| Colbeck St | T | 14 | A-B 6 |
| Colborne Lodge Dr | T | 14 | B-C 4-5 |
| Colborne St | T | 2 | A 4 |
| Colborne St | T | 3 | A 1 |
| Colchester Ct | ET | 26 | E 4 |
| Coldstream Av | NY | 6 | B-E 1-2 |
| Coldstream Av | T | 6 | E 1-2 |
| Coldwater Rd | NY | 19 | A 3 |
| Cole Millway | NY | 9 | A 4 |
| Coleman Av | T | 15 | E-F 3 |
| Coleman Av | EY | 15 | F 3 |
| Coleridge Av | EY | 15 | D 2-3 |
| Colfax St | Y | 16 | D-E 3 |
| Colgate Av | T | 5 | E 6 |
| Colin Av | T | 6 | F 3-4 |
| Colinayre Cr | SC | 31 | D 4-5 |
| Colinroy St | SC | 47 | D 6 |
| Collahie St | T | 4 | A 5 |
| Collanus Ct | ET | 40 | B 4 |
| College Pl | T | 4 | C 5 |
| College St | T | 14 | E-F 5 |
| College St | T | 30 | B 6 |
| College View Av | T | 6 | E 4 |
| College St | T | 4 | F 3 |
| Collier St | T | 5 | A 3 |
| Collingdale Rd | ET | 40 | E-F 5 |
| Collingsbrook Blvd | SC | 31 | A-B 4-5 |
| Collingwood St | SC | 29 | E 1 |
| Collingrove Rd | SC | 49 | B 6 |
| Collinson Blvd | NY | 8 | C 2-3 |
| Colonel Danforth Tr | SC | 49 | C-D 6 |
| Colonial Av | SC | 37 | B 4 |
| Colonnade Rd | NY | 11 | E 3 |
| Colony Rd | SC | 29 | B 6 |
| Coltbridge Ct | NY | 10 | A-B 5 |
| Coltman Cr | NY | 20 | D 3 |
| Columbia Gt | NY | 9 | A 4 |
| Columbine Av | T | 13 | D 5 |
| Columbine Av | T | 15 | C-D 6 |
| Columbus Av | T | 14 | E 5 |
| Colvestone Rd | NY | 9 | E 3 |
| Colville Rd | NY | 19 | D-E 1 |
| Colwick Dr | NY | 11 | D 3 |
| Colwood Rd | ET | 26 | D 6 |
| Colwyn Rd | ET | 24 | C 4 |
| Comay Rd | NY | 16 | B-C 2 |
| Combe Av | NY | 10 | A-B 5 |
| Combermere Dr | NY | 19 | F 4 |
| Comet Ct | NY | 17 | E 2 |
| Commander Blvd | SC | 41 | A-B 5-6 |
| Commerce Blvd | M | 36 | A 4 |
| Commercial Rd | EY | 7 | E-F 4 |
| Commissioners St | T | 3 | C-F 2-3 |
| Commodore Av | Y | 16 | D-E 4 |
| Commons Rd | SC | 29 | A 1-2 |
| Commonwealth Av | SC | 27 | F 4-5 |
| Community Cir | NY | 10 | D 4-5 |
| Compass Ct | SC | 41 | B 5 |
| Compton Cr | NY | 18 | C 3 |
| Compton Dr | SC | 29 | B 5-6 |
| Comrie Terr | SC | 27 | F 5-6 |
| Comrie Terr | SC | 37 | A 5-6 |
| Comstock Rd | SC | 27 | A-C 5 |
| Conacher Dr | NY | 11 | C 1-2 |
| Conamore Cr | NY | 20 | B-C 4 |
| Conan Rd | ET | 28 | B 4 |
| Concord Av | T | 4 | B 2-4 |
| Concorde St | NY | 17 | D 2 |
| Concorde Pl | NY | 17 | D 2-3 |
| Condor Av | T | 5 | E 6 |
| Condor Av | T | 15 | A 4-5 |
| Coney Rd | ET | 24 | B-C 5 |
| Confederation Dr | SC | 37 | D-E 1-2 |
| Conference Blvd | SC | 47 | D 6 |
| Conference Blvd | SC | 49 | E-F 5-6 |
| Conifer Dr | ET | 34 | B 3-4 |
| Coniston Rd | SC | 27 | A 4 |
| Conlan Av | NY | 8 | A 6 |
| Conlins Rd | SC | 49 | B 1-4 |
| Connable Dr | T | 4 | D 1 |
| Connaught Av | NY | 10 | D-F 2 |
| Connaught Cir | T | 13 | E 1 |
| Connaught Cir | Y | 6 | C 5 |
| Connell Ct | ET | 22 | A 2 |
| Connie St | NY | 18 | E 4-5 |
| Connolly St | T | 14 | D-E 1 |
| Connorvale Av | ET | 32 | E 3 |
| Conover Av | ET | 24 | B 6 |
| Conrad Av | T | 4 | B 1 |
| Conron Pl | Y | 28 | D 5-6 |
| Conroy Av | SC | 15 | F 2 |
| Conroy Av | SC | 25 | A 2 |
| Consilium Pl | SC | 39 | B 2-3 |
| Constance St | T | 14 | D-E 4 |
| Constellation Ct | ET | 38 | B 5 |
| Consumers Rd | NY | 19 | E-F 1-2 |
| Continental Pl | SC | 29 | B 4 |
| Convair Dr | ET | 36 | A 3 |
| Convair Dr | M | 36 | A 3 |
| Convent Ct | NY | 16 | F 1 |
| Conway Av | Y | 6 | A 6 |
| Coolhurst Dr | ET | 28 | A 2 |
| Coolhurst Dr | ET | 38 | F 2 |
| Coolmine Rd | T | 4 | A 5 |
| Cooper St | T | 3 | A 2 |
| Coopman Pathway | SC | 51 | A 4 |
| Copeland Av | T | 15 | C 4 |
| Copeland St | EY | 7 | A 4 |
| Copperfield Rd | SC | 47 | B-E 3 |
| Coppermill Dr | ET | 28 | A 2 |
| Copperwood Sq | SC | 31 | E 2 |
| Copping Rd | SC | 25 | D 3 |
| Copthorne Av | SC | 31 | F 1 |
| Coquette Rd | NY | 18 | A-B 1-2 |
| Cora Cr | SC | 39 | A 4 |
| Coral Cove Cr | NY | 19 | F 6 |
| Coral Gable Dr | NY | 30 | C-D 6 |
| Coram Av | M | 34 | A 5-6 |
| Coram Ct | M | 34 | A 6 |
| Corbett Av | Y | 16 | A 6 |
| Corbridge Ct | ET | 26 | B 3 |
| Corby Av | Y | 16 | E 5 |
| Cordella Av | T | 16 | B 4-5 |
| Cordova Av | ET | 24 | B 2-3 |
| Coraydale Ct | NY | 10 | B 4-5 |
| Corinne Cr | SC | 27 | D 3 |
| Corinth Gdns | NY | 7 | B 3 |
| Corinth Gdns | T | 7 | B 3 |
| Corinthian Blvd | SC | 31 | A 4-5 |
| Cork Av | NY | 6 | A-B 1 |
| Corktown La | T | 3 | B 1 |
| Corley Av | T | 15 | C-D 5 |
| Cormack Cr | M | 32 | A 3 |
| Cornelius Pkwy | NY | 18 | D-E 3-5 |
| Cornell Av | Y | 16 | A 3 |
| Cornell Av | SC | 25 | B 4 |
| Corner Brook Dr | NY | 19 | D-E 5-6 |
| Corning Rd | NY | 21 | A 4-5 |
| Corningham St | SC | 47 | E-F 1 |
| Cornish Rd | T | 7 | A 6 |
| Cornwall St | T | 5 | C 3 |
| Cornwallis Dr | SC | 29 | D-E 6 |
| Corona St | NY | 6 | A 1 |
| Coronado Ct | NY | 30 | D 5-6 |
| Coronation Dr | SC | 47 | A-D 2 |
| Coronet Rd | ET | 34 | D-E 5 |
| Corporate Dr | SC | 39 | A-C 2-3 |
| Corrigan Cl | T | 5 | A 3 |
| Cortland Av | T | 6 | F 1 |
| Cortleigh Blvd | NY | 6 | C-D 2 |
| Cortleigh Blvd | NY | 6 | D-F 2 |
| Cortleigh Cr | T | 6 | E 2 |
| Corton Gt | SC | 31 | A 4 |
| Corundum Cr | SC | 29 | C 2 |
| Corvette Av | SC | 27 | E 5 |
| Corvus Starway | NY | 19 | D 1 |
| Corwin Cr | NY | 8 | B-C 2-3 |
| Corylus Ct | ET | 40 | C 4 |
| Cosburn Av | EY | 5 | E-F 2 |
| Cosburn Av | EY | 15 | A-D 2 |
| Cosentino Dr | SC | 29 | F 3 |
| Cosmic Dr | NY | 9 | A 4 |
| Cosmo Rd | ET | 24 | C 3 |
| Costain Av | T | 15 | D 4 |
| Cosway Ct | ET | 34 | B 3 |
| Cotillion Ct | SC | 41 | B 4 |
| Cotman Cr | ET | 36 | E 5 |
| Cotswold Cr | NY | 9 | B 2 |
| Cotteswood Pl | SC | 39 | E 4 |
| Cottingham Rd | T | 4 | E 2 |
| Cottingham St | T | 4 | E-F 2 |
| Cotton Av | SC | 25 | D 1 |
| Cotton Ct | SC | 27 | D 6 |
| Cotton Downway | NY | 21 | E 6 |
| Cottonwood Dr | NY | 17 | B 2 |
| Cottrelle Ct | ET | 36 | D 6 |
| Cougar Ct | SC | 37 | C-D 3 |
| Coules Ct | ET | 32 | C 2 |
| Coulson Av | T | 6 | D-E 5 |
| Coulter Av | T | 28 | D-E 5 |
| Council Cr | NY | 20 | D 4 |
| Country Club Dr | NY | 26 | C 4 |
| Country La | NY | 9 | D 5 |
| Countryman Cir | ET | 40 | A 4 |
| Courage Av | NY | 20 | A 5-6 |
| Courcelette Rd | T | 13 | F 5 |
| Courcelette Rd | SC | 25 | A 5-6 |
| Court Sq | T | 3 | A 1 |
| Court St | T | 3 | A 1 |
| Courtlands Dr | SC | 51 | A 4 |
| Courton Dr | SC | 27 | A 1-2 |
| Courtsfield Cr | ET | 26 | D 4 |
| Courtwood Pl | NY | 11 | E 5 |
| Courtwright Rd | ET | 36 | B-C 3-4 |
| Courville Coachway | NY | 21 | E 6 |
| Cove Dr | ET | 28 | C 2 |
| Coventry St | SC | 25 | B 3-4 |

| Street | Type | Page | Col | Row |
|---|---|---|---|---|
| Coverdale Cr | Sc | 31 | D | 1 |
| Covewood St | NY | 11 | E | 1 |
| Covington Rd | T | 8 | B-C | 6 |
| Cowan Av | T | 12 | C | 1-2 |
| Cowdray Rd | SC | 29 | E | 2 |
| Cowley Av | ET | 34 | D-E | 1 |
| Coxwell Av | T | 15 | B | 1-3 |
| Coxwell Av | EY | 15 | B | 3-6 |
| Coxwell Av | T | 15 | B | 1 |
| Coxwell Blvd | EY | 15 | B | 1 |
| Coxworth Cr | SC | 41 | F | 6 |
| Crab Appleway | NY | 19 | F | 6 |
| Craggview Dr | SC | 49 | A | 6 |
| Cragmuir Ct | NY | 17 | E | 2 |
| Craig Cr | EY | 7 | D | 3 |
| Craighurst Av | T | 4 | F | 2 |
| Craiglee Dr | SC | 25 | D-E | 2 |
| Craigmont Dr | NY | 11 | E-F | 3 |
| Craigmore Cr | NY | 9 | B-C | 1 |
| Craigton Dr | SC | 17 | F | 3 |
| Craigton Dr | SC | 27 | A | 3 |
| Craik Rd | ET | 24 | D | 2 |
| Craketts Av | SC | 41 | B | 5 |
| Cramond Ct | ET | 36 | E | 5 |
| Cranborne Av | NY | 17 | F | 4 |
| Cranbrooke Av | T | 8 | D-E | 6 |
| Cranbrooke Av | T | 8 | E-F | 6 |
| Crane Av | ET | 26 | D-E | 2 |
| Cranfield Rd | ET | 17 | E | 5-6 |
| Crang Av | Y | 6 | A | 6 |
| Cranleigh Dr | ET | 26 | B | 5-6 |
| Cranston Manor | SC | 37 | E | 3 |
| Cranston Rd | ET | 34 | D | 3 |
| Craven Rd | T | 15 | B | 3-6 |
| Crawford St | T | 2 | B | 1 |
| Crawford St | T | 4 | B | 3-6 |
| Craydon Av | Y | 16 | A | 3 |
| Crayford Dr | SC | 31 | A | 1 |
| Credit Union Dr | NY | 17 | E | 3 |
| Crediton Ct | ET | 36 | F | 4 |
| Cree Av | NY | 37 | A-B | 5 |
| Creekside Rd | NY | 11 | C | 1 |
| Creekwood Dr | SC | 39 | E | 2-3 |
| Cremorne Av | ET | 22 | C | 1-2 |
| Crendon Dr | ET | 34 | B | 1 |
| Crescent Pl | EY | 15 | D | 3 |
| Crescent Rd | T | 5 | A-B | 2-3 |
| Crescent Town Rd | EY | 15 | F | 2-3 |
| Crescentwood Rd | SC | 25 | C | 5 |
| Cresswell Dr | SC | 39 | F | 4-5 |
| Crest Fairway | NY | 21 | A-B | 3 |
| Crest Hill Rd | SC | 37 | E | 4 |
| Cresthaven Dr | NY | 21 | A-B | 2 |
| Crestland Av | EY | 15 | B | 2 |
| Creston Dr | NY | 9 | A | 5 |
| Crestridge Heights Rd | ET | 26 | C | 3 |
| Crestview Rd | T | 6 | E | 3 |
| Crestwood Dr | SC | 37 | E | 3-4 |
| Crete Ct | NY | 7 | F | 2 |
| Crewe Av | EY | 15 | D-E | 2 |
| Cricklewood Rd | ET | 28 | A-B | 2 |
| Crimscott Rd | SC | 30 | B-C | 3 |
| Crioline Rd | NY | 9 | D | 3 |
| Crimson Millway | NY | 9 | D | 3 |
| Cripps Av | Y | 16 | B | 5 |
| Criscoe St | Y | 16 | B | 6 |
| Crispin Cr | NY | 10 | E | 1 |
| Critchley La | T | 4 | F | 3 |
| Crittenden Sq | SC | 41 | E | 4 |
| Croach Cr | SC | 41 | B | 4 |
| Croatia St | T | 14 | F | 4 |
| Crockarnhill Dr | SC | 31 | F | 4-5 |
| Crocker Av | SC | 27 | C | 1-3 |
| Crockford Blvd | SC | 27 | C | 1-3 |
| Crocus Dr | SC | 29 | B | 3-4 |
| Croft St | T | 4 | D | 4 |
| Crofton Rd | EY | 7 | D-E | 4 |
| Croham Rd | Y | 16 | E | 3-4 |
| Cromarty Dr | ET | 28 | A-B | 2 |
| Cromer Pl | ET | 36 | A-B | 1 |
| Cromwell Rd | SC | 37 | E | 3 |
| Cronin Dr | ET | 34 | E | 2-3 |
| Crosby Av | Y | 24 | E | 1 |
| Crosland Dr | SC | 29 | A | 3-4 |
| Cross Hill Rd | SC | 31 | D | 4 |
| Cross St | T | 4 | A | 5 |
| Cross St | NY | 28 | E | 5-6 |
| Crossbow Dr | NY | 21 | A | 5 |
| Crossburn Dr | NY | 19 | B | 5 |
| Crossen Dr | NY | 10 | E-F | 1 |
| Crouse Rd | SC | 27 | C | 2 |
| Crow Tr | SC | 41 | E | 4-5 |
| Crowfoot Pl | SC | 31 | A | 2 |
| Crowland Dr | ET | 28 | A | 1-2 |
| Crown Acres Ct | SC | 39 | C | 1 |
| Crown Ct | ET | 24 | B | 6 |
| Crown Hill Pl | ET | 24 | E | 5 |
| Crown Park | T | 13 | E | 5 |
| Crown Park Rd | T | 15 | E | 6 |
| Crowns La | T | 4 | F | 2 |
| Croydon Rd | Y | 6 | C-D | 5 |
| Cruikshank Av | T | 5 | E | 3 |
| Crusader St | SC | 37 | B-C | 1 |
| Crystal Arts Sq | T | 5 | F | 4-5 |
| Crystal Cr | ET | 32 | E | 5 |
| Cudham Dr | SC | 41 | A | 4 |
| Cudia Cr | SC | 25 | F | 4 |
| Cudia Cr | SC | 37 | B | 6 |
| Cudworth Pl | ET | 24 | B | 1 |
| Cuffley Cr N | NY | 18 | D-E | 2-3 |
| Cuffley Cr S | NY | 18 | D-E | 3 |
| Culford Rd | NY | 16 | B | 1-3 |
| Culford Rd | NY | 18 | B | 4-6 |
| Culloden Ct | ET | 24 | A | 6 |
| Cultra Sq | SC | 47 | A | 2 |
| Cumber Av | SC | 47 | A-B | 3 |
| Cumberland St | T | 4 | E-F | 2 |
| Cummer Av | NY | 11 | A-E | 2 |
| Cummings St | T | 5 | E | 6 |
| Cunard St | SC | 37 | B | 3 |
| Cunningham Av | T | 14 | F | 6 |
| Curity Av | EY | 17 | D-E | 6 |
| Curlew Dr | NY | 19 | E-F | 6 |
| Curly Vineway | NY | 11 | F | 1 |
| Curran Dr | EY | 15 | E | 1 |
| Currie Av | T | 15 | B | 4 |
| Curtis Av | SC | 49 | A | 1 |
| Curzon St | T | 15 | F | 5-6 |
| Cusack Ct | NY | 9 | F | 1 |
| Cushendale Dr | NY | 11 | A | 3 |
| Cushendun Rd | SC | 47 | B | 3 |
| Cuthbert Cr | T | 7 | A | 4 |
| Cutler Cr | ET | 32 | C | 2 |
| Cynthia Rd | Y | 26 | E-F | 4-5 |
| Cypress St | T | 3 | C-D | 1 |

## D

| Street | Type | Page | Col | Row |
|---|---|---|---|---|
| Dacotah Av | T | 3 | A-B | 5 |
| Dacre Cr | T | 14 | B | 4 |
| Dagmar Av | T | 5 | F | 6 |
| Dailing Gt | SC | 39 | D | 1-2 |
| Daisy Av | ET | 32 | E-F | 4 |
| Dalbeattie Av | NY | 28 | F | 5 |
| D'Albret Cr | SC | 31 | D | 5 |
| Dalcourt Dr | SC | 47 | B | 2 |
| Dale Av | T | 5 | B | 3 |
| Dale Av | SC | 37 | E | 3 |
| Daleberry Pl | NY | 9 | D-E | 4 |
| Dalecliff Cr | SC | 29 | B | 4 |
| Dalecrest Dr | EY | 17 | E | 6 |
| Daleena Dr | NY | 19 | E | 5 |
| Dalegrove Cr | ET | 36 | E | 3-4 |
| Dalegrove Dr | NY | 16 | A | 5 |
| Dalemount Av | NY | 6 | C | 1-2 |
| Dalesford Rd | ET | 22 | D-E | 1 |
| Daleside Cr | NY | 17 | E | 2 |
| Dalewood Rd | T | 7 | B | 2 |
| Dalhousie St | T | 5 | A | 5-6 |
| Dalkeith Dr | NY | 9 | B | 4-5 |
| Dallas Rd | NY | 10 | D-E | 5 |
| Dallington Dr | NY | 21 | B | 5 |
| Dallner Rd | NY | 28 | F | 3-4 |
| Dallyn Cr | SC | 27 | F | 3 |
| Dalmatian Cr | SC | 49 | D | 4 |
| Dalraith Rd | NY | 18 | C | 2-3 |
| Dalrymple Dr | Y | 16 | A | 5 |
| Dalsby Rd | NY | 18 | B | 2-3 |
| Dalston Rd | ET | 32 | C | 3 |
| Dalton Rd | T | 4 | D | 3 |
| Damascus Dr | ET | 40 | D | 4 |
| Damask Av | NY | 30 | D | 5 |
| Danby Av | NY | 8 | C | 2 |
| Dancy Av | SC | 31 | D | 3 |
| Dane Av | NY | 8 | A | 6 |
| Danesbury Av | NY | 6 | A | 2 |
| Danesbury Av | Y | 6 | A | 2-3 |
| Daneswood Rd | NY | 7 | C | 2 |
| Danforth Av | T | 5 | D-F | 3 |
| Danforth Av | T | 15 | A-F | 3 |
| Danforth Av | EY | 15 | F | 3 |
| Danforth Av | SC | 25 | A | 3 |
| Danforth Av | SC | 25 | D-E | 1-2 |
| Danforth Av | SC | 27 | E-F | 4-2 |
| Danforth Rd | SC | 37 | A-C | 1-4 |
| Daniels St | T | 24 | D-E | 6 |
| Danilack Ct | SC | 41 | A | 2 |
| Danish Cr | ET | 36 | B | 4 |
| Danjohn Cr | SC | 31 | F | 3 |
| Danmary Rd | SC | 37 | B | 3 |
| Danrose Cr | NY | 9 | E | 5-6 |
| Dansk Ct | ET | 40 | B-C | 2 |
| Dante Rd | NY | 18 | B | 6 |
| Danube Dr | SC | 27 | B | 1 |
| Danville Dr | NY | 9 | B | 3 |
| Danzig St | SC | 47 | A-B | 2 |
| Daphne Rd | SC | 37 | C | 1 |
| Darby Ct | SC | 51 | A-B | 4 |
| D'Arcy Magee Cr | SC | 49 | E-F | 5 |
| D'Arcy St | T | 4 | E | 5 |
| Darien Ct | NY | 16 | B | 1 |
| Darlingbrook Cr | ET | 26 | C | 5 |
| Darlingside Dr | SC | 47 | B | 2-3 |
| Darlington Dr | ET | 24 | C | 5 |
| Darnborough Way | SC | 31 | B-C | 3 |
| Darrell Av | T | 15 | D | 4 |
| Dartford Rd | T | 5 | D | 3 |
| Dartmoor Dr | SC | 49 | A | 2-3 |
| Dartmouth Ct | T | 22 | D | 4 |
| Dartnell Av | T | 4 | D | 2 |
| Darwin Rd | T | 6 | D | 3 |
| Dashwood Cr | ET | 30 | B-C | 5 |
| Datchet Rd | NY | 18 | A-B | 3 |
| Dault Rd | SC | 25 | C | 6 |
| Davean Dr | NY | 9 | F | 2 |
| Davelayne Rd | NY | 30 | C | 4 |
| Davenport Rd | T | 4 | A-F | 1-3 |
| Davenport Rd | T | 14 | D-F | 1 |
| Daventry Rd | SC | 39 | C | 5 |
| David Dr | SC | 49 | A | 2 |
| Davidson Av | SC | 25 | D | 1 |
| Davies Av | T | 3 | C-D | 1 |
| Davies Av | T | 5 | D | 6 |
| Davies Cr | EY | 15 | A | 1 |
| Davis Downs Rd | SC | 47 | C | 1 |
| Davisbrook Blvd | SC | 31 | B | 5-6 |
| Davistow Cr | ET | 40 | E-F | 4 |
| Davisville Av | T | 7 | A-C | 5 |
| Dawes Ct | T | 15 | E | 4 |
| Dawes Rd | EY | 15 | E-F | 1-3 |
| Dawes Rd | SC | 25 | A | 1 |
| Dawlish Av | T | 7 | A-B | 1-2 |
| Dawlish Av | NY | 7 | B-C | 1-2 |
| Dawnmist Cr | SC | 41 | A | 1 |
| Dawson Av | T | 5 | F | 4 |
| Dawson Av | T | 15 | A | 4 |
| Day Av | T | 16 | F | 5-6 |
| Day Av | Y | 16 | F | 5 |
| Daysland Rd | ET | 28 | A | 2 |
| Daystrom Dr | NY | 30 | C | 4 |
| Dayton Av | ET | 22 | C | 1 |
| De Grassi St | T | 5 | E | 5-6 |
| De Marco Blvd | NY | 18 | B | 6 |
| De Quincy Blvd | NY | 8 | B-C | 3 |
| De Savery Cr | T | 7 | A-B | 4 |
| De Vere Gdns | NY | 8 | F | 3-4 |
| Deaconwood Rd | NY | 10 | C | 3 |
| Deaconwood Rd | NY | 11 | F | 3 |
| Deakin Av | T | 16 | A | 5 |
| Deal Av | T | 9 | A | 6 |
| Dean Park Rd | SC | 49 | C | 1-2 |
| Dean Park Rd | SC | 49 | C-E | 1-2 |
| Deanecourt Rd | ET | 36 | D | 4 |
| Deanecrest Rd | ET | 36 | D | 4-5 |
| Deanefield Cr | ET | 36 | D | 4 |
| Deanewood Cr | ET | 36 | D | 4-5 |
| Deanlea Ct | ET | 30 | B | 5 |
| Deanscroft Sq | SC | 47 | B | 2 |
| Deanvar Av | T | 19 | F | 6 |
| Deanvar Av | SC | 29 | A | 5-6 |
| Dear Gt | SC | 47 | D | 4 |
| Dear Gt | SC | 49 | E | 4 |
| Dearbourne Av | T | 5 | D | 4 |
| Dearham Wood | SC | 37 | F | 3 |
| Dearham Wood | SC | 37 | A | 3 |
| Deauville La | NY | 17 | C | 4 |
| Debby Ct | NY | 28 | D-E | 5 |
| Debell La | NY | 11 | C | 1 |
| Deblyn Dr | SC | 31 | E | 4 |
| Deborah Dr | SC | 39 | B | 5 |
| Decarie Cir | ET | 36 | D-E | 3-4 |
| Decimal Pl | SC | 47 | D | 4 |
| Dee Av | NY | 28 | C | 4 |
| Dee Cr | NY | 28 | C | 4 |
| Deekshill Dr | SC | 47 | B | 1-2 |
| Deep Dene Dr | SC | 49 | B | 3 |
| Deepdale Dr | SC | 31 | F | 4 |
| Deegglade Cr | NY | 19 | B | 1-2 |
| Deepwood Cr | NY | 17 | C | 1 |
| Deer Park Cr | T | 7 | F | 6 |
| Deer Pen Rd | T | 14 | C | 5 |
| Deerbrook Tr | SC | 31 | A | 3 |
| Deerfield Pl | SC | 47 | F | 2 |
| Deerfield Rd | SC | 27 | F | 2 |
| Deerfoot Rd | SC | 31 | F | 3 |
| Deerford Rd | NY | 21 | B | 4-6 |
| Deerhide Cr | NY | 30 | E | 4-5 |

C

D

| STREET NAME | MUNICIPALITY | MAP NO | MAP AREA |
|---|---|---|---|
| Deerhurst Av | NY | 28 | E 5 |
| Deering Cr | NY | 11 | A 3 |
| Deerpath Rd | NY | 19 | E-F 5 |
| Deeth Dr | ET | 26 | C 1 |
| Deevale Rd | NY | 18 | B-C 3 |
| Deforest Rd | T | 14 | A-B 4 |
| Defries St | T | 5 | C 6 |
| Degrey Ct | SC | 37 | E 1 |
| Dehaviland Dr | NY | 18 | E 1-2 |
| Dehaviland Dr | NY | 20 | E 6 |
| DeHaviland St | NY | 8 | B 1 |
| Del Ria Dr | NY | 18 | B-C 6 |
| Delabra Rd | ET | 30 | C 5 |
| Delahaye St | NY | 8 | B 3-4 |
| Delaney Cr | T | 14 | F 5 |
| Delano Pl | SC | 25 | E 3 |
| Delavan Av | T | 6 | D 5 |
| Delawana Dr | SC | 39 | D 5 |
| Delaware Av | T | 4 | A-B 2-5 |
| Delaware Av N | T | 4 | A 1-2 |
| Delbasso Ct | ET | 28 | B 5 |
| Delbeatrice Cr | SC | 49 | E 5 |
| Delbert Dr | SC | 29 | D 4 |
| Delburn Dr | SC | 41 | A 3 |
| Delemere Av | Y | 26 | E-F 5 |
| Delfield Rd | SC | 29 | A 4 |
| Delhi Av | NY | 8 | C-E 3 |
| Delia Ct | NY | 8 | C 2 |
| DeLisle Av | T | 6 | F 6 |
| Dell Park Av | NY | 6 | B-D 1 |
| Dellbank Rd | NY | 10 | B 5 |
| Dellbrook Cr | NY | 30 | A-B 2 |
| Delma Dr | ET | 32 | C 2-3 |
| Delo Rd | NY | 16 | E 1 |
| Deloraine Av | NY | 8 | C-E 5 |
| Deloraine Av | T | 8 | E-F 5 |
| Delrosa Ct | ET | 40 | F 4-5 |
| Delroy Dr | SC | 24 | D-E 6 |
| Delsing Dr | ET | 38 | C 1 |
| Delsing Dr | ET | 40 | E 6 |
| Delta St | ET | 32 | E 2-3 |
| Delverton Pl | NY | 21 | B 6 |
| Delwood Dr | SC | 27 | A 5-6 |
| Demaris Av | NY | 20 | B 4 |
| Dempsey Cr | T | 9 | E 3 |
| Dempster St | SC | 29 | D 4 |
| Denarda St | Y | 16 | A 3 |
| Denewood Cr | NY | 9 | E 5 |
| Denfield St | ET | 36 | F 4 |
| Dengate Rd | T | 15 | F 4 |
| Denham Rd | SC | 29 | D 6 |
| Denise Rd | M | 32 | A 2 |
| Denison Av | T | 2 | D 1 |
| Denison Rd W | Y | 16 | A 2 |
| Denison Rd W | Y | 26 | F 2 |
| Denison Sq | T | 4 | D 5 |
| Denlow Blvd | NY | 9 | E-F 4-5 |
| Denmark Ct | NY | 10 | C 4 |
| Dennett Dr | SC | 31 | F 6 |
| Dennis Av | Y | 16 | A-B 4 |
| Denny Cr | SC | 47 | B 3 |
| Denrock Dr | NY | 11 | E 6 |
| Densgrove Rd | SC | 39 | D-E 5 |
| Dension Rd E | NY | 26 | F 2 |
| Densley Av | NY | 16 | D-E 2 |
| Densmore Av | ET | 32 | B 3 |
| Denton Av | SC | 25 | A-B 3 |
| Dentonia Park Av | EY | 15 | E-F 5 |
| Denvale Rd | EY | 17 | D 6 |
| Denver Cr | NY | 18 | B 1 |
| Denver Pl | T | 4 | A 2 |
| Derby St | T | 3 | B 1 |
| Derbyshire Pl | SC | 49 | E 2 |
| Derek Dr | SC | 49 | D 2 |
| Dermott Pl | T | 3 | B 5 |
| Derry Rd E | M | 38 | A 1 |
| Derrydown Rd | NY | 20 | B-C 4-5 |
| Dervock Cr | NY | 9 | E 1 |
| Derwent Ct | NY | 11 | B 3 |
| Derwyn Rd | EY | 15 | B 1-2 |
| Desmond Rd | NY | 28 | F 3 |
| Deta Rd | M | 32 | B 5 |
| Detling Ct | ET | 38 | E 1 |
| Detling Dr | ET | 40 | F 6 |
| Deverell Cr | NY | 18 | E 4 |
| Devon Rd | T | 15 | D 4 |
| Devondale Av | NY | 10 | D-E 3 |
| Devonian Sq | T | 5 | A 6 |
| Devonridge Cr | SC | 49 | D 3 |
| Devonshire Pl | T | 4 | E 4 |
| Dewbourne Av | Y | 6 | B-C 4 |
| Dewbourne Av | T | 6 | C-D 4 |
| Dewey Dr | SC | 29 | A-B 4-5 |
| Dewhurst Blvd | EY | 5 | F 3 |
| Dewhurst Blvd | T | 5 | F 3 |
| Dewhurst Blvd N | EY | 5 | F 2-3 |
| Dewitt Rd | ET | 36 | E 4 |
| Dewlane Dr | NY | 10 | D 2 |
| Dewsbury Cr | ET | 36 | D 4 |
| Dewson St | T | 4 | A-B 4 |
| Dexter Blvd | NY | 21 | A 2 |
| Diagonal Rd | NY | 10 | E 5 |
| Diana Dr | NY | 18 | C 1 |
| Dibble St | T | 3 | E 1 |
| Dibgate Blvd | SC | 41 | A 4-5 |
| Dickens St | T | 5 | E 6 |
| Didrickson Dr | NY | 9 | B 3 |
| Dieppe Rd | EY | 15 | A 2 |
| Diesel Dr | ET | 32 | E 1 |
| Digby Ct | NY | 10 | D 2 |
| Dignam Ct | SC | 37 | B 1 |
| Dilworth Cr | EY | 5 | E 2-3 |
| Dimplefield Pl | ET | 36 | C 4-5 |
| Dinan St | ET | 8 | D 5 |
| Dingwall Av | T | 5 | E-F 4 |
| Dinnick Cr | T | 7 | A-B 1 |
| Disan Ct | ET | 30 | B 5 |
| Disco Rd | ET | 38 | A-C 3-4 |
| Distin Av | ET | 22 | C 1-2 |
| Dittmer Cr | ET | 38 | E 1-2 |
| Divadale Dr | EY | 7 | D-E 3 |
| Dixfield Dr | ET | 36 | B-C 5-6 |
| Dixiana Ct | NY | 18 | C 1 |
| Dixie Rd | BR | 32 | A-B 1-5 |
| Dixington Cr | ET | 26 | B-C 1 |
| Dixon Av | T | 15 | C-D 6 |
| Dixon Ave | T | 13 | D 5 |
| Dixon Rd | ET | 26 | A-D 1 |
| Dixon Rd | ET | 28 | A-D 6 |
| Dixon Rd | ET | 36 | B-F 1 |
| Dixon Rd | ET | 38 | A 2 |
| Dobbin Rd | SC | 29 | A 2 |
| Doddington Dr | ET | 24 | E 5 |
| Dodge Rd | SC | 25 | B 4 |
| Dods Av | T | 14 | C 1 |
| Doerr Rd | SC | 39 | A 4 |
| Dogleg Ct | NY | 20 | C 6 |
| Dogwood Ct | SC | 29 | F 4 |
| Dolme Av | EY | 17 | E 5-6 |
| Dolan Gt | T | 21 | A 4 |
| Dollery Ct | NY | 10 | B 3 |
| Dolly Varden Blvd | SC | 39 | C 4-5 |
| Dolomite Dr | NY | 10 | A 2 |
| Dolomite Dr | NY | 20 | F 2 |
| Dolores Rd | NY | 20 | A-B 5-6 |
| Dolphin Dr | SC | 25 | A 2 |
| Dombey Rd | NY | 18 | B 1 |
| Dominion Rd | ET | 32 | D-E 5 |
| Don Avon Dr | T | 7 | E 3 |
| Don Jail Rdwy | T | 5 | D 5 |
| Don Mills Rd | EY | 15 | A-B 1 |
| Don Mills Rd | NY | 17 | A-B 5-6 |
| Don Mills Rd | NY | 17 | B 1-5 |
| Don Mills Rd | NY | 19 | B-D 1-6 |
| Don Mills Rd | NY | 21 | B-D 1-6 |
| Don Mills Rd E | NY | 21 | A 5 |
| Don Mills Rd W | NY | 21 | B 4-5 |
| Don River Blvd | NY | 10 | D 6 |
| Don Roadway | T | 5 | D 2 |
| Don Valley Dr | T | 5 | D-E 2 |
| Don Valley Pkwy | T | 3 | C-D 1-2 |
| Don Valley Pkwy | T | 5 | C-D 3-6 |
| Don Valley Pkwy | EY | 5 | D-F 1-3 |
| Don Valley Pkwy | EY | 7 | A-B 5-6 |
| Don Valley Pkwy | T | 17 | C-D 1-5 |
| Don Valley Pkwy | T | 19 | C-D 2-6 |
| Donald Av | Y | 16 | D-E 4 |
| Donalda Cr | SC | 31 | E 5-6 |
| Doncaster Av | EY | 15 | D-E 3 |
| Doncliffe Dr | NY | 9 | A 5 |
| Doncliffe Dr | T | 9 | A 5 |
| Doncliffe Pl | NY | 9 | A 5 |
| Doncrest Rd | T | 5 | D 3 |
| Donegal Path | ET | 34 | C 1 |
| Donegall Dr | EY | 7 | D 4-5 |
| Donewen Ct | NY | 17 | E 2 |
| Donino Av | NY | 9 | A 4-5 |
| Donino Ct | NY | 9 | A 4 |
| Donlands Av | EY | 5 | F 1-2 |
| Donlands Av | T | 5 | F 3 |
| Donlands Av | EY | 15 | A 1-3 |
| Donlands Av | T | 15 | A 3 |
| Donlea Dr | EY | 7 | D-E 3 |
| Donmac Dr | NY | 19 | A 5 |
| Donmore Av | EY | 15 | A 2 |
| Donna Ct | NY | 11 | B 3 |
| Donnacona Dr | SC | 47 | B 2 |
| Donnalyn Dr | NY | 10 | D-E 1 |
| Donnybrook La | ET | 24 | B 2 |
| Donofree Rd | NY | 18 | C 5-6 |
| Donora Dr | EY | 15 | F 2 |
| Donora Dr | EY | 25 | F 2 |
| Donridge Dr | NY | 9 | A 3 |
| Donside Dr | SC | 15 | F 2 |
| Donside Dr | SC | 25 | A 2 |
| Donwoods Dr | NY | 9 | A 4-5 |
| Donwoods Gr | NY | 9 | A 4-5 |
| Donwoods La | NY | 9 | A 5 |
| Doog Murless Sq | SC | 49 | F 2 |
| Doon Rd | NY | 9 | B 4 |
| Doonaree Dr | NY | 19 | D-E 5 |
| Dora Av | T | 14 | E 4 |
| Dora Spencer Rd | Y | 26 | F 2-3 |
| Doran Av | Y | 24 | E-F 1 |
| Dorchester Av | ET | 22 | B 1 |
| Dorchester Dr | NY | 8 | C 2 |
| Dorcot Av | SC | 29 | E-F 5 |
| Dorine Cr | SC | 27 | A 6 |
| Doris Av | NY | 11 | A 4-5 |
| Doris Dr | EY | 17 | D 6 |
| Dorking Cr | NY | 18 | C 3 |
| Dormington Dr | SC | 39 | D 3-4 |
| Dorney Ct | NY | 8 | B 6 |
| Dornfell St | NY | 10 | D 3 |
| Dornoch Dr | ET | 36 | B 5 |
| Dorothy Bullen Pl | T | 15 | B 6 |
| Dorothy St | T | 15 | B 6 |
| Dorset | SC | 25 | E 4-5 |
| Dorset Rd | SC | 37 | A 5-6 |
| Dorsey Ct | NY | 18 | C 5 |
| Dorsey Dr | NY | 18 | C 5 |
| Dorval Rd | T | 14 | D 3 |
| Dorward Dr | ET | 40 | E-F 2 |
| Dosco Rd | ET | 38 | E 6 |
| Doubletree Rd | NY | 21 | E 6 |
| Doucett Pl | SC | 39 | F 4 |
| Douglas Av | NY | 8 | D-E 6 |
| Douglas Av | T | 8 | E-F 6 |
| Douglas Blvd | ET | 22 | B 3 |
| Douglas Cr | EY | 5 | C 1 |
| Douglas Dr | T | 5 | A-C 1-2 |
| Douglas Dr | T | 2 | B 1 |
| Douville Ct | T | 3 | B 2-3 |
| Dovedale Ct | SC | 41 | C 6 |
| Dovehaven Ct | NY | 30 | F 2 |
| Dovehouse Av | NY | 20 | C-D 6 |
| Dover Dr | ET | 32 | C 4 |
| Dovercourt Rd | T | 2 | A 1 |
| Dovercourt Rd | T | 4 | A 1-6 |
| Doverwood Ct | NY | 11 | A 4 |
| Dowling Av | T | 12 | B 1-2 |
| Downing St | ET | 34 | E 4 |
| Downpatrick Cr | ET | 26 | B 2 |
| Downsview Av | NY | 18 | A-B 4 |
| Dowry St | SC | 31 | E 6 |
| Dowsell Dr | SC | 39 | E 1 |
| Dragoon Cr | SC | 41 | B 3 |
| Drake Cr | SC | 25 | F 3 |
| Draper St | T | 2 | D 1-2 |
| Draycott Dr | NY | 17 | F 3 |
| Drayton Av | T | 15 | B 3-4 |
| Dresden Rd | NY | 8 | B 2 |
| Drewry Av | NY | 10 | E-F 2 |
| Driftwood Av | NY | 20 | A-B 2-5 |
| Driftwood Ct | NY | 20 | B 2 |
| Dromore Cr | NY | 10 | D 3 |
| Droxford Av | SC | 27 | A 1-2 |
| Druid Ct | EY | 15 | E 1-2 |
| Drumheller Rd | ET | 28 | A 2 |
| Drummond Pl | T | 2 | B 2 |
| Drummond St | ET | 22 | C 3 |
| Drumoak Rd | ET | 24 | B 1 |
| Drumoak Rd | ET | 26 | B 6 |
| Drumsnab Rd | T | 5 | B-C 3 |
| Drury La | ET | 26 | D 2 |
| Drysdale Cr | NY | 21 | A 2 |
| Du Maurier Blvd | T | 9 | A 6 |
| Duart Park | T | 13 | E 5 |
| Duart Park Rd | T | 15 | E 6 |
| Dubarry Av | SC | 47 | B 2 |
| Dublin St | T | 14 | E 4 |
| Dubray Av | NY | 18 | D-E 3 |
| Duck Hawkway | NY | 10 | B 1 |
| Duckworth St | NY | 11 | A 1 |

| Street | Muni | Pg | Col | Row |
|---|---|---|---|---|
| Dudley Av | NY | 9 | B | 1 |
| Dudley Av | NY | 11 | A | 3-6 |
| Duern St | Y | 26 | F | 5-6 |
| Dufferin Park Av | T | 4 | A | 4 |
| Dufferin St | T | 2 | A | 1-2 |
| Dufferin St | T | 4 | A | 1-6 |
| Dufferin St | NY | 6 | A | 1-2 |
| Dufferin St | Y | 6 | A | 2-6 |
| Dufferin St | NY | 8 | A | 1-6 |
| Dufferin St | NY | 10 | A | 1-6 |
| Dufferin St | T | 12 | C | 1-2 |
| Dufferin St | T | 14 | F | 1-6 |
| Dufferin St | NY | 16 | F | 1-2 |
| Dufferin St | T | 16 | F | 5-6 |
| Dufferin St | Y | 16 | F | 2-5 |
| Dufferin St | NY | 18 | F | 3-6 |
| Duffield Rd | ET | 26 | C | 2 |
| Dufflaw Rd | NY | 18 | F | 5-6 |
| Duffort Ct | SC | 51 | A | 5 |
| Dufresne Ct | NY | 17 | C | 4 |
| Duggan Av | T | 6 | E-F | 5 |
| Dukinfield Cr | NY | 19 | E | 3 |
| Dulverton Rd | SC | 29 | D | 6 |
| Dumas Ct | NY | 19 | F | 5 |
| Dumbarton Rd | ET | 24 | C | 5 |
| Dumfrey Rd | SC | 27 | E | 4 |
| Dumont St | NY | 11 | A | 1-2 |
| Dunbar Rd | T | 5 | B | 3 |
| Dunblaine Av | NY | 8 | D-E | 4 |
| Dunbloor Rd | ET | 24 | A | 3 |
| Dunboyne Ct | NY | 10 | C | 3 |
| Duncairn Rd | ET | 36 | E | 5-6 |
| Duncairn Rd | NY | 19 | A-B | 5-6 |
| Duncan Mill Rd | NY | 19 | A-B | 3 |
| Duncan St | T | 2 | E | 1 |
| Duncan St | T | 4 | E | 6 |
| Duncannon Dr | T | 6 | E | 4 |
| Duncanwoods Dr | NY | 30 | B-C | 3-4 |
| Duncombe Blvd | SC | 37 | D | 4-5 |
| Dundalk Dr | SC | 29 | D | 3-4 |
| Dundas Sq | T | 5 | A | 6 |
| Dundas St E | T | 5 | A-F | 6 |
| Dundas St E | T | 4 | A-C | 6 |
| Dundas St E | M | 34 | A-B | 5-6 |
| Dundas St W | T | 14 | A | 1 |
| Dundas St W | T | 14 | A-F | 1-5 |
| Dundas St W | T | 4 | A | 1-6 |
| Dundas St W | ET | 24 | A-E | 1-3 |
| Dundas St W | Y | 24 | E-F | 1 |
| Dundas St W | E | 34 | C-F | 3-4 |
| Dundee Dr | NY | 20 | B-C | 4 |
| Dundonald St | T | 4 | F | 4 |
| Dundonald St | T | 5 | A | 4 |
| Dundurn Cr | T | 5 | B | 6 |
| Dundurn Rd | T | 7 | B | 1-2 |
| Dunedin Dr | ET | 24 | B | 3 |
| Dunelm St | SC | 37 | C-E | 3 |
| Dunera Av | SC | 37 | F | 2 |
| Dunfield Av | T | 7 | A | 4 |
| Dunforest Av | NY | 11 | B-C | 4 |
| Dunhill St | SC | 47 | F | 3 |
| Dunington Dr | SC | 25 | B | 4 |
| Dunkirk Rd | EY | 15 | B-D | 2 |
| Dunlace Av | NY | 9 | E-F | 2 |
| Dunloe Rd | T | 6 | D | 4-5 |
| Dunlop Av | SC | 25 | D | 4 |
| Dunmail Dr | SC | 31 | E-F | 3-4 |
| Dunmurray Blvd | SC | 31 | B-C | 5-6 |
| Dunn Av | T | 12 | C | 1-2 |
| Dunn Cr | SC | 47 | F | 4 |
| Dunning Cr | ET | 32 | B | 2-3 |
| Dunraven Dr | NY | 16 | D-E | 4-5 |
| Dunreo Dr | NY | 28 | F | 3 |
| Dunrobin Dr | ET | 36 | E | 5 |
| Dunsany Cr | T | 36 | E | 2 |
| Dunsdale Sq | SC | 31 | F | 5 |
| Dunsfold Dr | SC | 41 | E | 4 |
| Dunsmore Gdns | NY | 8 | B | 1 |
| Dunstable Pl | ET | 26 | B | 2 |
| Dunstall Ct | SC | 47 | D | 1 |
| Dunster Av | NY | 8 | F | 4 |
| Dunthorne Ct | SC | 51 | A-B | 6 |
| Duntroon Ct | ET | 40 | D-E | 3 |
| Dunvegan Rd | T | 6 | D-E | 4-5 |
| Dunvegan Rd | T | 4 | E | 1 |
| Dunview Av | NY | 11 | B-C | 4 |
| Dunwatson Dr | SC | 49 | E | 5 |
| Duplex Av | T | 6 | F | 1-4 |
| Duplex Av | T | 8 | F | 6 |
| Duplex Av | T | 6 | F | 3-4 |
| Duplex Av | NY | 10 | F | 3-4 |
| Duplex Ct | T | 6 | F | 4 |
| Dupont St | T | 4 | A-E | 3 |
| Dupont St | T | 14 | D-F | 2 |
| Durant Av | EY | 15 | B | 1-3 |
| Durban Rd | ET | 24 | B | 3 |
| Durham St | Y | 6 | B | 4 |
| Durie St | T | 14 | A | 2-3 |
| Durie St | T | 14 | A | 1-2 |
| Durness Av | SC | 49 | E-F | 3 |
| Durnford Rd | SC | 49 | F | 3 |
| Durrington Cr | ET | 24 | A | 5 |
| Dusay Pl | SC | 31 | A | 4 |
| Dustan Cr | SC | 47 | D | 1-2 |
| Dutch Myrtleway | NY | 19 | B | 6 |
| Duthie St | SC | 47 | D | 6 |
| Duval Dr | NY | 18 | D | 6 |
| Duvernet Av | T | 15 | C-D | 5 |
| Duxbury Dr | SC | 31 | E-F | 1 |
| Dwight Av | ET | 22 | C | 3-4 |
| Dyas Rd | NY | 19 | A-B | 4 |
| Dynamic Dr | SC | 41 | D | 2-3 |
| Dynasty La | NY | 8 | A | 6 |
| Dynevor Rd | Y | 16 | F | 4 |
| Dyson Blvd | SC | 47 | A | 3 |
| Dyson Rd | SC | 47 | F | 6 |

## E

| Street | Muni | Pg | Col | Row |
|---|---|---|---|---|
| Eagle Dance Av | SC | 41 | A | 1 |
| Eagle Point Rd | SC | 31 | A | 2 |
| Eagle Rd | ET | 24 | B | 3-4 |
| Eaglestone Rd | SC | 31 | C | 6 |
| Eagleview Cr | SC | 31 | B | 4 |
| Eagleview Gt | SC | 39 | E | 2 |
| Ealing Dr | NY | 9 | F | 2 |
| Earl Grey Rd | T | 5 | F | 4 |
| Earl Rd | SC | 25 | E-F | 4 |
| Earl Rd | SC | 37 | A-B | 4 |
| Earl St | T | 5 | A-B | 4 |
| Earldown Dr | ET | 36 | D | 3 |
| Earlington Av | ET | 24 | E | 1 |
| Earlscourt Av | Y | 16 | F | 5-6 |
| Earlscourt Av | Y | 16 | F | 4-5 |
| Earlsdale Av | Y | 6 | A-B | 5 |
| Earlthorpe Cr | SC | 39 | B | 4 |
| Earlton Rd | SC | 29 | D | 1-2 |
| Early Appleway | NY | 19 | E | 4 |
| Earlywood Ct | NY | 11 | E | 5 |
| Earnbridge St | T | 14 | F | 6 |
| Earnscliffe Rd | Y | 6 | A | 4 |
| Earswick Dr | SC | 31 | D | 3 |
| Easson Av | T | 14 | A | 4-5 |
| East Av | T | 14 | A | 1-5 |
| East Ave | SC | 47 | D | 4-6 |
| East Don Roadway | T | 3 | C-D | 1 |
| East Don Roadway | T | 5 | D | 6 |
| East Dr | NY | 26 | E-F | 2 |
| East Dr | Y | 16 | A | 4 |
| East Haven Dr | SC | 25 | E | 2-3 |
| East Liberty St | T | 2 | A-B | 2 |
| East Lynn Av | T | 15 | C | 3-4 |
| East Mall Cr | ET | 34 | D | 4 |
| East Mall, The | ET | 32 | D | 1-2 |
| East Mall, The | ET | 34 | D | 1-6 |
| East Mall, The | ET | 34 | D | 3-6 |
| East Metro av | SC | 51 | C | 6 |
| East Rd | SC | 25 | B | 4 |
| East Willow Ga | SC | 47 | D | 5 |
| Eastbourne Av | T | 6 | E | 5 |
| Eastbourne Ct | ET | 22 | D | 4 |
| Eastdale Av | EY | 15 | E | 2-3 |
| Eastern Av | T | 3 | B-F | 1 |
| Eastern Av | T | 15 | A-C | 6 |
| Eastern Av | T | 13 | D-F | 1 |
| Eastgate Cr | SC | 27 | E | 4 |
| Eastglen Cr | ET | 34 | E | 1 |
| Easthampton Dr | ET | 26 | E | 3 |
| Eastlea Cr | SC | 31 | D | 4 |
| Eastmoor Cr | SC | 25 | E | 3 |
| Eastmount Av | T | 5 | D | 5 |
| Easton Rd | NY | 8 | E | 1 |
| Eastpark Blvd | SC | 37 | B-D | 1-2 |
| Eastport Dr | SC | 47 | D | 6 |
| Eastport Dr | SC | 47 | F | 1-2 |
| Eastside Dr | ET | 34 | D | 5-6 |
| Eastview Cr | NY | 8 | E | 2 |
| Eastville Av | SC | 25 | E | 4-6 |
| Eastwick Rd | ET | 26 | B | 1-2 |
| Eastwood Av | SC | 25 | C | 3-4 |
| Eastwood Rd | T | 15 | B-D | 5 |
| Eaton Av | EY | 5 | F | 3 |
| Eaton Av | T | 5 | F | 3 |
| Ebonywood Dr | NY | 21 | C | 1 |
| Ecclesfield Dr | SC | 31 | A | 4 |
| Eccleston Dr | NY | 11 | E | 3 |
| Echo Glen Rd | SC | 39 | E | 5 |
| Echo Valley Rd | ET | 34 | F | 1-2 |
| Echo Valley Ridge | ET | 34 | F | 1 |
| Ecker Dr | SC | 32 | C | 2 |
| Ed Evans La | T | 13 | B | 1 |
| Ed Evans La | T | 13 | B | 1 |
| Eda Ct | ET | 34 | B | 1 |
| Eddystone Av | NY | 20 | A | 5 |
| Eddystone Av | NY | 30 | F | 5 |
| Eden Park Rd | EY | 17 | D | 5 |
| Eden Pl | T | 4 | D | 6 |
| Eden Valley Dr | ET | 26 | B-C | 3-4 |
| Edenbridge Dr | ET | 26 | C-E | 4-5 |
| Edenbrook Hill | ET | 26 | C | 4-5 |
| Edengarth Ct | NY | 8 | A | 5 |
| Edenmills Dr | SC | 39 | F | 2 |
| Edenrock Ct | ET | 40 | E | 2 |
| Edenvale Cr | ET | 26 | C | 3-4 |
| Edenwood Dr | ET | 36 | F | 6 |
| Edgar Av | T | 5 | B | 2 |
| Edgar Av | T | 28 | E | 3-4 |
| Edgar Rd | T | 28 | B | 1 |
| Edgar Woods Rd | NY | 21 | B | 1 |
| Edge Park Av | SC | 27 | A | 5 |
| Edgebrook Dr | V | 30 | A | 5 |
| Edgecliff Golfway | NY | 17 | D | 4 |
| Edgecombe Av | NY | 6 | E | 1 |
| Edgecroft Rd | ET | 24 | D | 2 |
| Edgedale Rd | T | 5 | B | 4 |
| Edgehill Rd | ET | 26 | D | 5-6 |
| Edgemore Dr | ET | 24 | D | 4 |
| Edgevalley Dr | ET | 26 | D | 5-6 |
| Edgeware Dr | ET | 32 | C | 4 |
| Edgeway Gt | SC | 31 | E-F | 2 |
| Edgewood Av | T | 15 | B | 5-6 |
| Edgewood Cr | T | 5 | B | 1-2 |
| Edgewood Gdns | T | 15 | C | 5 |
| Edgewood Gr | T | 15 | B-C | 5 |
| Edilou Dr | ET | 32 | E | 2-3 |
| Edinborough Ct | Y | 26 | E | 5 |
| Edinburgh Dr | NY | 8 | D | 3 |
| Edison Cir | NY | 18 | D-E | 5 |
| Edith Av | T | 14 | E | 2 |
| Edith Dr | T | 6 | D | 3 |
| Edithvale Dr | NY | 10 | E | 4 |
| Edmonton Dr | NY | 21 | E | 4-5 |
| Edmonton Rd | NY | 21 | E | 4-5 |
| Edmund Av | T | 4 | E | 1 |
| Edmund Av | Y | 26 | F | 2 |
| Edmund Gt | T | 4 | E | 5 |
| Edna Av | T | 14 | D-E | 3 |
| Edwalter Av | ET | 24 | D | 5 |
| Edward St | T | 4 | F | 6 |
| Edward St | T | 14 | E | 2-3 |
| Edyth Ct | ET | | D | 4 |
| Egan Av | T | | F | 5 |
| Eglinton Av E | T | 7 | A-C | 3-4 |
| Eglinton Av E | EY | 7 | C-F | 3-4 |
| Eglinton Av E | NY | 17 | A-F | 3-4 |
| Eglinton Av E | SC | 27 | A-F | 4 |
| Eglinton Av E | SC | 37 | A-D | 4 |
| Eglinton Av W | Y | 6 | A-B | 4 |
| Eglinton Av W | T | 7 | B-F | 3-4 |
| Eglinton Av W | NY | 16 | A-F | 3-4 |
| Eglinton Av W | ET | 26 | A-E | 3 |
| Eglinton Av W | NY | 26 | F | 4 |
| Eglinton Sq | ET | 36 | A-F | 3-5 |
| Eglinton Sq | SC | 27 | A | 4 |
| Eighth St | ET | 22 | B | 3-4 |
| Eileen Av | Y | 24 | B | 5 |
| Eileen Av | T | 26 | E-F | 6 |
| Elana Dr | NY | 21 | A | 6 |
| Elana Dr | NY | 30 | F | 6 |
| Elba Av | SC | 25 | B | 3 |
| Elder Av | ET | 32 | E-F | 4 |
| Elder St | NY | 10 | B | 4-6 |
| Elderberry Ct | ET | 26 | B | 2 |
| Elderfield Cr | ET | 24 | C | 1-2 |
| Elderidge Av | ET | 24 | D | 5 |
| Elderwood Dr | T | 6 | C-D | 4 |
| Eldon Av | EY | 15 | F | 3 |
| Eldora Av | NY | 10 | F | 3-4 |
| Eldorado Ct | NY | 20 | C | 5-6 |
| Eleanor Av | Y | 6 | A | 4 |
| Electra Ct | M | 36 | A | 3 |
| Electra Rd | M | 36 | A | 3 |
| Electro Rd | SC | 41 | A | 3 |
| Eleventh St | ET | 22 | B | 4-5 |
| Elfindale Cr | NY | 19 | B | 1 |
| Elford Blvd | SC | 31 | C | 6 |
| Elfreda Blvd | SC | 25 | C | 1 |
| Elfreda Blvd | SC | 37 | A | 6 |
| Elgar Av | SC | 37 | A | 3 |
| Elgin Av | T | 4 | E | 1 |
| Elgin Rd | NY | 10 | E | 4 |
| Elhurst Ct | Y | 16 | A | 4 |
| Elinor Av | SC | 29 | B | 1 |
| Elinor Av | SC | 29 | B | 5-6 |
| Elise Terr | NY | 10 | D | 1 |
| Elizabeth St | T | 4 | F | 5-6 |
| Elizabeth St | ET | 22 | D | 3 |
| Elk St | SC | 29 | F | 2 |
| Elk St | SC | 39 | A | 2 |
| Elkhorn Dr | NY | 11 | D-E | 6 |
| Elkpath Av | NY | 9 | E | 3 |

D

E

| STREET NAME | MUNICIPALITY | MAP NO | MAP AREA |
|---|---|---|---|
| Elkwood Dr | SC | 47 | D 5 |
| Elkwood Dr | SC | 49 | F 5 |
| Ellen Av | T | 14 | B 1 |
| Ellendale Dr | SC | 29 | D 5-6 |
| Ellenhall Sq | SC | 31 | A 1 |
| Ellerbeck St | T | 5 | D 3 |
| Ellerslie Av | NY | 10 | D-F 5 |
| Ellesmere Rd | SC | 19 | F 4 |
| Ellesmere Rd | SC | 29 | A-F 4 |
| Ellesmere Rd | SC | 39 | A-F 3-4 |
| Ellesmere Rd | SC | 49 | A-E 4 |
| Ellie Dr | SC | 39 | E 6 |
| Ellington Dr | SC | 29 | B-C 4-6 |
| Ellins Av | Y | 26 | E-F 6 |
| Elliott Av | ET | 24 | E 1-2 |
| Elliotwood Ct | NY | 9 | F 2-3 |
| Ellis Av | T | 14 | B 4-6 |
| Ellis Av | Y | 26 | F 1 |
| Ellis Gdns | T | 14 | B 6 |
| Ellis Park Rd | T | 14 | B 4 |
| Ellison Av | NY | 14 | D 2 |
| Ellsworth Av | T | 4 | B-C 1 |
| Elm Av | T | 5 | A-B 3 |
| Elm Bank Rd | SC | 27 | A-B 2 |
| Elm Grove Av | T | 12 | C 1 |
| Elm Rd | NY | 8 | E 4 |
| Elm Ridge Cir | T | 6 | B 3 |
| Elm Ridge Dr | T | 6 | B-D 3 |
| Elm St | T | 4 | E-F 5 |
| Elm St | T | 28 | E 6 |
| Elma St | ET | 22 | D 6 |
| Elmartin Dr | SC | 31 | B-C 2 |
| Elmbrook Cr | ET | 36 | A-B 4-5 |
| Elmcliffe Ct | ET | 40 | E 2 |
| Elmcrest Rd | SC | 34 | A 1 |
| Elmcrest Rd | SC | 36 | A 5-6 |
| Elmdon Ct | SC | 37 | A 2 |
| Elmer Av | T | 13 | D 5 |
| Elmer Av | T | 15 | D 5-6 |
| Elmfield Cr | Sc | 31 | D 1 |
| Elmhurst Av | NY | 10 | E-F 6 |
| Elmhurst Dr | ET | 28 | A-C 1-2 |
| Elmhurst Dr | ET | 30 | A 6 |
| Elmira Ct | NY | 11 | D 4 |
| Elmlea Rd | ET | 28 | C 6 |
| Elmont Dr | EY | 15 | E 2 |
| Elms, The | ET | 26 | E 1 |
| Elmsdale Rd | EY | 5 | F 1 |
| Elmsley Pl | T | 4 | F 4 |
| Elmsthorpe Av | T | 6 | E 4 |
| Elmvale Cr | NY | 40 | D-E 3 |
| Elmview Dr | NY | 10 | F 4 |
| Elmview Ct | SC | 24 | C 2 |
| Elmview Dr | SC | 25 | A 4-5 |
| Elmwood Av | NY | 11 | A-C 6 |
| Elnathan Cr | NY | 30 | B 2 |
| Elora Rd | T | 14 | B 3 |
| Elrose Av | NY | 28 | E 3-4 |
| Elsa Vineway | NY | 11 | F 4 |
| Elsbury Lane | SC | 47 | D 6 |
| Elsfield Rd | ET | 24 | D 3-4 |
| Elsinore Path | ET | 22 | A-B 4 |
| Elstree Rd | Y | 28 | E 6 |
| Elstree Rd | ET | 26 | B 1 |
| Elswick Rd | EY | 17 | C 6 |
| Eltham Dr | ET | 32 | C 3 |
| Elton Cr | ET | 32 | E 5 |
| Elvaston Dr | NY | 17 | E-F 3 |
| Elvin Av | Y | 26 | F 6 |
| Elvina Gdns | SC | 25 | A 3-4 |
| Elward Blvd | SC | 31 | B 3 |
| Elway Ct | NY | 6 | B 1 |
| Elwood Blvd | T | 6 | E 3 |
| Elynhill Dr | NY | 10 | D-E 5 |
| Embers Dr | ET | 34 | B 1 |
| Embla St | NY | 17 | B 2 |
| Emblem Ct | SC | 29 | E-F 2 |
| Embro Dr | NY | 8 | A-B 1 |
| Emcarr Dr | SC | 37 | F 2 |
| Emerald Cr | ET | 22 | B 5 |
| Emerson Av | T | 14 | B 2-3 |
| Emery Cir | ET | 26 | C 1 |
| Emilion Way | ET | 40 | D 3 |
| Emily Av | NY | 30 | A 2-3 |
| Emily Av | T | 2 | F 1 |
| Emmeline Ct | SC | 31 | E 5 |
| Emmett Av | Y | 26 | F 3 |
| Emmott Av | SC | 25 | A 3-4 |
| Empire Av | T | 15 | E 5 |
| Empress Av | NY | 11 | A-C 5 |
| Empringham Dr | SC | 51 | A 5 |
| Enchanted Hills Cr | SC | 41 | A 1 |
| Endean Av | T | 5 | F 5 |
| Endean Av | T | 15 | A 5 |
| Endell St | NY | 10 | D 3-4 |
| Enderby Rd | T | 15 | E 4 |
| Endicott Av | ET | 28 | B 2 |
| Endsleigh Cr | NY | 21 | E 5 |
| Endwood Rd | ET | 34 | B 1 |
| Englehart Av | NY | 16 | B 1-2 |
| Englemount Av | NY | 6 | B 1-2 |
| English Ivyway | NY | 11 | F 1 |
| Enid Cr | NY | 6 | B 2 |
| Ennerdale Rd | Y | 16 | F 4-5 |
| Ennerdale St | NY | 16 | F 1-2 |
| Ennismore Pl | NY | 21 | A 5 |
| Ensign Pl | SC | 39 | D 4 |
| Enterprise Rd | ET | 38 | E-F 5 |
| Enverne Dr | NY | 30 | A 2 |
| Epic Lane Rd | NY | 18 | A 3-4 |
| Epping St | ET | 26 | B 2 |
| Eppleworth Rd | SC | 27 | E 4-5 |
| Epsom Av | EY | 15 | D-E 3 |
| Epsom Downs Dr | NY | 18 | A-B 3-4 |
| Equestrian Ct | NY | 11 | F 1 |
| Erica Av | NY | 8 | C 2 |
| Erie St | NY | 17 | C 4-5 |
| Eriksdale Rd | ET | 34 | B-C 3 |
| Erin St | T | 3 | B 1 |
| Erinbrook Ct | ET | 26 | E 4-5 |
| Erindale Av | T | 5 | D 3 |
| Eringate Dr | ET | 36 | B-C 5 |
| Erinlea Cr | SC | 39 | B 4 |
| Ernest Av | T | 14 | E 3 |
| Ernest Av | NY | 21 | E-F 4 |
| Ernest Av | NY | 31 | A 4 |
| Ernest Dockray | Y | 16 | A 3 |
| Errington Av | Y | 5 | B 1 |
| Erskine Av | T | 7 | A-B 3 |
| Esandar Dr | EY | 7 | E 4-5 |
| Esgore Dr | NY | 8 | E-F 3-4 |
| Esmond Cr | ET | 28 | C 3-4 |
| Esplanade, The | T | 2 | F 2-3 |
| Esplanade, The | T | 3 | A-B 2-3 |
| Esposito Cr | Y | 26 | F 6 |
| Esposito Ct | ET | 34 | A 1 |
| Esquire Cir | SC | 29 | A 1 |
| Esquire Rd | SC | 29 | A 1 |
| Essex St | T | 4 | B 3 |
| Estate Dr | SC | 39 | C 2-3 |
| Estelle Av | NY | 11 | C 4-5 |
| Esten Rd | T | 4 | D 1 |
| Esterbrooke Av | NY | 21 | B 5 |
| Esther Lorrie Dr | ET | 40 | F 5-6 |
| Ethel Av | T | 14 | B-C 1 |
| Ethelwin Av | T | 15 | D 4 |
| Etona Ct | T | 22 | B 2 |
| Ettawylie Rd | ET | 22 | B 4 |
| Ettrick Cr | ET | 28 | F 5 |
| Euclid Av | T | 2 | C 1 |
| Euclid Av | T | 4 | C 3-6 |
| Euclid Av | SC | 49 | C-E 3 |
| Euclid Pl | T | 4 | C 6 |
| Eugene St | NY | 16 | E 1 |
| Eunice Av | NY | 11 | E 6 |
| Euphrasia Dr | NY | 16 | F 1 |
| Euston Av | T | 5 | F 3-4 |
| Eva Rd | ET | 34 | C 3 |
| Evan Rd | NY | 8 | E 1 |
| Evandale Rd | SC | 27 | B 5 |
| Evangeline Ct | ET | 40 | F 1 |
| Evans Av | T | 14 | A 2-3 |
| Evans Av | ET | 32 | B-F 1-2 |
| Evans La | SC | 32 | E 2 |
| Evanston Dr | NY | 10 | A 4-5 |
| Evansville Rd | SC | 31 | E 3 |
| Evansway St | SC | 31 | E 3 |
| Evelyn Av | T | 14 | B 2-3 |
| Evelyn Cr | T | 14 | B 3 |
| Evenwood Av | SC | 49 | E 4 |
| Everden Rd | Y | 6 | B 4 |
| Everett Cr | EY | 15 | D 2 |
| Everglades Dr | NY | 18 | A 6 |
| Evergreen Av | ET | 32 | E 4 |
| Evergreen Gdns | EY | 7 | B-C 6 |
| Everingham Cr | NY | 11 | A 2 |
| Evermede Dr | NY | 19 | E 2-3 |
| Evernby Blvd | SC | 39 | A 4 |
| Eversfield Rd | Y | 16 | F 5 |
| Evesham Ct | ET | 26 | B 4 |
| Ewart Av | Y | 16 | D 4 |
| Exbury Rd | NY | 18 | A-C 3 |
| Exchequer Pl | SC | 41 | B 4 |
| Executive Ct | SC | 39 | C 2 |
| Exeter St | T | 14 | E 1 |
| Exford St | SC | 29 | C-D 5 |
| Exmoor Dr | ET | 32 | C 4 |
| Explorer Dr | M | 36 | A 4 |

## F

| STREET NAME | MUNICIPALITY | MAP NO | MAP AREA |
|---|---|---|---|
| Fabian Pl | ET | 26 | D 2 |
| Fabray Ct | SC | 31 | B 1 |
| Failsworth Av | Y | 16 | E 5 |
| Fairbank Av | Y | 16 | F 3-4 |
| Fairbourne Ct | ET | 32 | A 5 |
| Fairchild Av | NY | 10 | F 2-3 |
| Faircrest Cr | EY | 17 | B 6 |
| Faircroft Blvd | SC | 37 | B 5-6 |
| Fairfax Cr | SC | 27 | A-B 5 |
| Fairfield Av | ET | 32 | E-F 4 |
| Fairfield Rd | NY | 7 | B 3 |
| Fairfield Rd | T | 7 | B 3 |
| Fairford Av | T | 15 | B 5 |
| Fairgate Close | NY | 8 | B 2 |
| Fairglen Av | SC | 31 | A 4-6 |
| Fairglen Cr | NY | 28 | C 4-5 |
| Fairhaven Dr | ET | 28 | B-C 5 |
| Fairhill Cr | NY | 19 | E 5 |
| Fairholme Av | NY | 6 | B-D 1 |
| Fairland Rd | EY | 7 | E 3 |
| Fairlawn Av | NY | 8 | C-E 5 |
| Fairlawn Av | T | 8 | E-F 5 |
| Fairleigh Cr | T | 6 | B 3-4 |
| Fairlin Dr | ET | 34 | B 3 |
| Fairmar Av | ET | 24 | D 5 |
| Fairmeadow Av | NY | 9 | B 2 |
| Fairmount Cr | T | 15 | C 5 |
| Fairside Av | EY | 15 | B 2 |
| Fairview Av | T | 14 | B 2-3 |
| Fairview Blvd | T | 5 | C 3 |
| Fairview Mall Dr | NY | 19 | C-D 1 |
| Fairview Mall Dr | NY | 21 | B-D 5-6 |
| Fairway Dr | SC | 37 | B 2 |
| Fairway Rd | ET | 24 | B 1 |
| Fairweather Rd | NY | 16 | C 2 |
| Fairwood Cr | SC | 49 | B 5-6 |
| Faith Av | NY | 8 | B 3 |
| Falaise Rd | SC | 49 | A 5-6 |
| Falcon St | T | 7 | B 4 |
| Falkirk St | NY | 8 | D 4-5 |
| Fall St | NY | 17 | B 2 |
| Fallingbrook Cr | SC | 25 | A 6 |
| Fallingbrook Dr | SC | 25 | A-B 5-6 |
| Fallingbrook Rd | SC | 25 | A-B 5-6 |
| Fallingbrook Woods | SC | 25 | A-B 6 |
| Fallingdale Cr | NY | 20 | C 5 |
| Fallingwood Rd | ET | 28 | A-B 1 |
| Fallowfield Rd | SC | 39 | A 6 |
| Fallsview Rd | ET | 24 | E 2 |
| Falmouth Av | SC | 27 | F 4 |
| Falstaff Av | NY | 18 | A-C 4-5 |
| Faludon Ct | ET | 34 | D 4 |
| Family Cr | M | 32 | A-B 2 |
| Fanfare Av | SC | 47 | D 4 |
| Faraday Dr | SC | 39 | B 4-5 |
| Fareham Cr | SC | 37 | E 3 |
| Fargo Av | NY | 10 | F 1-2 |
| Farina Millway | NY | 9 | D 3 |
| Farley Cr | ET | 36 | E 2 |
| Farm Greenway | NY | 19 | F 3 |
| Farmbrook Rd | SC | 37 | B-C 3 |
| Farmcote Rd | NY | 19 | B 5 |
| Farmcrest Dr | SC | 29 | A 2 |
| Farmhill Ct | SC | 49 | D 2 |
| Farmingdale Rd | NY | 11 | D 4 |
| Farmington Cr | SC | 31 | E 5 |
| Farmstead Rd | NY | 9 | F 3 |
| Farmview Cr | NY | 19 | C-D 1 |
| Farnboro Rd | ET | 38 | C 5-6 |
| Farnham Av | T | 4 | E-F 4 |
| Farningham Pl | ET | 36 | F 4 |
| Farnsworth Dr | NY | 16 | E 1 |
| Farquhars La | T | 3 | A 1-2 |
| Farr Av | ET | 30 | A 4 |
| Farr Av | T | 40 | F 3 |
| Farrell Av | NY | 10 | C-D 5 |
| Farrington Dr | NY | 9 | B 2-3 |
| Fashion Roseway | NY | 9 | C 1 |
| Fasken Dr | ET | 38 | A-B 5 |
| Faulkland Rd | SC | 27 | A-B 5 |
| Faulkner Cr | NY | 30 | C 4 |
| Faversham Cr | ET | 36 | B-C 5 |
| Fawcett Tr | SC | 51 | A-B 5-6 |
| Fawndale Cr | SC | 31 | B 2 |
| Fawnhaven Ct | NY | 10 | B 3 |
| Fawnridge Tr | SC | 49 | D 3 |
| Faye Dr | NY | 21 | E 4 |
| Faywood Blvd | NY | 8 | B 1-3 |
| Feagan Dr | SC | 49 | E 6 |

| Street | Type | Pg | Col | Row |
|---|---|---|---|---|
| Featherwood Pl | ET | 26 | D | 4 |
| Federal St | T | 4 | A | 5 |
| Feeney Av | SC | 51 | A | 4 |
| Felbrigg Av | NY | 8 | E-F | 4 |
| Feldbar Ct | NY | 11 | C | 4 |
| Feldwood Rd | M | 32 | A | 2-3 |
| Felicity Dr | SC | 37 | C | 1-2 |
| Feller Rd | ET | 36 | E | 1 |
| Felstead Av | T | 15 | A-B | 4 |
| Feltham Av | Y | 16 | B | 5 |
| Fenelon Dr | NY | 19 | C-D | 3 |
| Fenley Dr | ET | 26 | A-B | 1 |
| Fenmar Dr | NY | 30 | C-E | 1-3 |
| Fenn Av | NY | 9 | B-C | 2-3 |
| Fennell St | T | 8 | F | 1 |
| Fennimore St | NY | 30 | F | 5 |
| Fennings St | T | 2 | A | 1 |
| Fennings St | T | 4 | A | 6 |
| Fenside Dr | NY | 19 | E | 2-3 |
| Fenwick Av | T | 5 | E | 3-4 |
| Fenwood Hts | SC | 35 | F | 4-5 |
| Fenwood Hts | SC | 37 | B | 6 |
| Ferbane Rd | NY | 21 | A-B | 5-6 |
| Fergalea Av | SC | 49 | C-D | 6 |
| Fergus Av | M | 32 | B | 5 |
| Fermanagh Av | T | 14 | E | 5 |
| Fermoy Rd | SC | 37 | A | 6 |
| Fern Av | T | 14 | D-E | 5 |
| Fern Av | T | 28 | E | 6 |
| Fernando Rd | NY | 30 | D | 5 |
| Fernbank Av | T | 4 | A | 3 |
| Ferncliffe Ct | EY | 15 | E | 2 |
| Ferncrest Gt | SC | 21 | F | 4 |
| Ferncrest Gt | SC | 31 | A | 4 |
| Ferncroft Dr | SC | 25 | B | 4-5 |
| Ferndale Av | T | 7 | A | 6 |
| Fernside Ct | NY | 11 | C | 5 |
| Fernwood Gdns | EY | 5 | E | 1 |
| Fernwood Pk Av | T | 13 | E | 6 |
| Fernwood Rd | T | 6 | B | 3 |
| Ferrand Dr | NY | 7 | B-C | 3-4 |
| Ferrier Av | T | 5 | E | 3 |
| Ferris Rd | EY | 15 | E | 1 |
| Ferris Rd | EY | 15 | E-F | 1-2 |
| Ferris Rd | NY | 25 | A | 1 |
| Festival Dr | NY | 10 | B | 1 |
| Fi Park Av | T | 13 | E-F | 6 |
| Fidelia Av | NY | 7 | B | 2 |
| Field Av | EY | 7 | D | 4-5 |
| Field Sparroway | NY | 11 | F | 3 |
| Fielding Av | T | 5 | F | 3 |
| Fielding Av | T | 15 | A | 3 |
| Fieldside Dr | SC | 41 | B | 3 |
| Fieldstone Rd | ET | 34 | A | 3 |
| Fieldstone RD ET | ET | 34 | A | 3 |
| Fieldway Rd | T | 24 | A-B | 3-4 |
| Fieldwood Dr | SC | 41 | B | 2 |
| Fiesta La | ET | 24 | F | 5 |
| Fife Rd | NY | 9 | D | 4 |
| Fifeshire Rd | NY | 9 | C | 2-3 |
| Fifteenth St | T | 22 | A | 4 |
| Fifth St | T | 3 | B | 4 |
| Fifth St | ET | 22 | B | 4 |
| Filbert Gt | NY | 19 | E | 6 |
| Fima Ct | ET | 32 | E-F | 3 |
| Finch Av E | NY | 11 | A-F | 4 |
| Finch Av E | SC | 11 | A-F | 4 |
| Finch Av E | NY | 21 | A-F | 3-4 |
| Finch Av E | SC | 31 | A-F | 4 |
| Finch Av E | NY | 41 | A-F | 4 |
| Finch Av E | SC | 51 | E-F | 4 |
| Finch Av W | NY | 10 | A-F | 3-4 |
| Finch Av W | NY | 20 | A-F | 4 |
| Finch Av W | ET | 30 | A-B | 4 |
| Finch Av W | NY | 30 | B-F | 4 |
| Finch Av W | ET | 40 | A-F | 3-4 |
| Finch Entry Rd | NY | 21 | B | 3 |
| Finchdene Sq | SC | 41 | E | 3-4 |
| Finchgate Ct | NY | 11 | D | 4 |
| Finchley Dr | T | 24 | B | 1 |
| Finchurst Dr | NY | 10 | D | 4 |
| Findlay Blvd | NY | 8 | A-B | 1 |
| Fine Arts Rd | NY | 20 | C | 2 |
| Fingal Pl | T | 30 | B | 5 |
| Finsbury Cr | ET | 32 | C | 3 |
| Fintona Av | SC | 47 | B | 3 |
| Firebrace Rd | SC | 31 | A | 1 |
| Firenza Dr | NY | 30 | B | 3 |
| Fireside Dr | SC | 49 | D | 1 |
| Firestone Rd | ET | 36 | C | 4 |
| Firgrove Cr | NY | 30 | F | 4-5 |
| Firmette Cr | NY | 26 | E | 4-5 |
| First Av | T | 5 | D-E | 5 |
| First St | T | 3 | B | 4 |
| First St | ET | 22 | C | 4 |
| Firstbrooke Rd | T | 15 | D | 5 |
| Firth Cr | SC | 39 | E | 5 |
| Firthway Ct | NY | 9 | F | 4 |
| Firvalley Ct | SC | 25 | B | 2 |
| Firwood Cr | ET | 36 | E-F | 5 |
| Fisher St | T | 14 | F | 5 |
| Fisher's La | ET | 24 | D-E | 2 |
| Fisherville Rd | NY | 10 | B-C | 1 |
| Fishery Rd | SC | 49 | C | 3 |
| Fishleigh Dr | SC | 25 | E | 3 |
| Fisken Av | T | 14 | B | 1-2 |
| Fitzgerald Mews | T | 15 | B-C | 6 |
| Fitzgibbon Av | SC | 27 | E | 2-3 |
| Fitzroy Terr | T | 4 | D | 5 |
| Flagler St | T | 5 | B | 5 |
| Flagstaff Rd | SC | 25 | C | 1 |
| Flagstick Ct | NY | 9 | F | 4 |
| Flagstone Terr | SC | 47 | E | 4 |
| Flamborough Dr | NY | 16 | B-C | 2 |
| Flaming Roseway | NY | 9 | C | 1 |
| Flamingo Cr | NY | 16 | C | 2 |
| Flanders Rd | Y | 6 | B | 4 |
| Flaremore Cr | NY | 11 | D-E | 5 |
| Flatwoods Dr | SC | 41 | A | 1 |
| Flavian Cr | SC | 27 | D | 6 |
| Flax Gardenway | NY | 20 | A | 4 |
| Flaxman Rd | NY | 28 | C | 3 |
| Fleecelilne Rd | ET | 22 | E | 2 |
| Fleet St | T | 2 | B-D | 2 |
| Fleetwell Ct | NY | 10 | D | 4 |
| Fleetwood Av | NY | 18 | B | 4-5 |
| Fleming Cr | EY | 7 | D | 4 |
| Fleming Dr | NY | 11 | E | 2 |
| Flemington Rd | NY | 8 | A-B | 5-6 |
| Flempton Cr | SC | 27 | D | 3 |
| Flerimac Rd | SC | 49 | C | 6 |
| Fletcher Pl | ET | 26 | B | 1 |
| Fletcherdon Cr | NY | 20 | A | 2 |
| Fletcherdon Ct | NY | 30 | F | 2 |
| Fleury Ct | NY | 17 | B | 3-4 |
| Flindon Rd | NY | 28 | C | 3 |
| Flint Rd | NY | 20 | F | 1-2 |
| Flintridge Rd | SC | 27 | D | 3 |
| Flintwick Dr | SC | 39 | A | 4 |
| Flintwood Ct | NY | 21 | E | 5 |
| Flora Dr | SC | 27 | D | 4 |
| Floral Pkwy | NY | 18 | D-E | 4 |
| Florence Av | NY | 8 | E-F | 1 |
| Florence Cr | Y | 26 | F | 6 |
| Florence St | T | 14 | F | 6 |
| Florens Av | SC | 25 | A | 1 |
| Florina Blvd | SC | 29 | D | 3 |
| Floyd Av | EY | 5 | E-F | 2 |
| Fluellen Dr | SC | 31 | C | 5 |
| Foch Av | ET | 32 | C | 3-4 |
| Folcroft Av | SC | 25 | E | 3 |
| Folkes Ct | ET | 40 | B-C | 4 |
| Folkes St | Y | 24 | F | 3 |
| Follis Av | T | 4 | B-D | 3 |
| Fondy Ct | T | 38 | F | 1 |
| Fontainbleau Dr | NY | 10 | E-F | 1 |
| Fontenay Ct | ET | 26 | E | 4 |
| Fonthill Pl | NY | 20 | C | 5-6 |
| Footbridge Rd | NY | 18 | B | 5 |
| Forbes Av | NY | 16 | C | 5 |
| Forbes Rd | SC | 29 | D-E | 5 |
| Ford St | T | 14 | D | 1 |
| Fordham Pl | NY | 10 | F | 1 |
| Fordhouse Blvd | ET | 32 | E-F | 1 |
| Fordover Dr | SC | 47 | B | 3 |
| Fordwich Cr | ET | 28 | A-B | 1 |
| Foregate Av | SC | 51 | A | 6 |
| Forest Creek | SC | 51 | A | 4 |
| Forest Glen Cr | NY | 9 | A | 5 |
| Forest Grove Dr | NY | 11 | B-C | 2 |
| Forest Heights Blvd | NY | 9 | D-E | 4 |
| Forest Hill Rd | T | 6 | D-E | 4-5 |
| Forest Laneway | NY | 11 | A | 6 |
| Forest Manor Rd | NY | 19 | C-D | 1-2 |
| Forest Path Ct | ET | 30 | C | 5 |
| Forest Ridge Dr | T | 6 | C-D | 3 |
| Forest Wood | NY | 20 | C | 4 |
| Forestbrook Cr | SC | 31 | B | 6 |
| Forestone Rd | ET | 36 | B | 6 |
| Forestview Rd | SC | 34 | B | 3 |
| Foret Av | ET | 26 | A | 4 |
| Forge Dr | NY | 20 | B | 3-4 |
| Forman Av | T | 7 | A | 4 |
| Formula Cr | T | 34 | D | 3 |
| Forsyth Cr | T | 6 | A | 1 |
| Forsyth Rd | T | 15 | C | 4 |
| Forsythia Dr | SC | 47 | A | 3-4 |
| Fort Dearborn Dr | SC | 31 | D | 3 |
| Fort Rouille Pl | T | 12 | C | 2 |
| Fort Rouille St | T | 2 | A | 2 |
| Forthbridge Cr | NY | 18 | B | 3 |
| Fortieth St | ET | 32 | C | 4-5 |
| Fortrose Cr | NY | 19 | E-F | 2-3 |
| Fortune St | SC | 39 | D | 6 |
| Forty-First St | ET | 32 | C | 4-5 |
| Forty-Second St | ET | 32 | C | 5 |
| Forty-Third St | ET | 32 | C | 4-5 |
| Foster Pl | T | 4 | F | 6 |
| Founders Rd | NY | 20 | C | 1 |
| Fountainhead Rd | NY | 20 | C | 3 |
| Four Leaf Dr | ET | 40 | E | 5 |
| Four Oaks Gt | EY | 15 | A-B | 1 |
| Four Seasons Pl | ET | 34 | D | 1 |
| Four Winds Dr | NY | 20 | C-D | 3 |
| Foursome Cr | NY | 9 | B | 3 |
| Fourteenth St | ET | 22 | A | 4 |
| Fourth St | T | 3 | B | 4 |
| Fourth St | ET | 22 | B | 4-5 |
| Fourthgreen Pl | ET | 34 | A | 3 |
| Fox Grassway | NY | 30 | F | 5 |
| Fox Pt | NY | 16 | B | 1 |
| Foxbar Rd | T | 4 | E-F | 1 |
| Foxcote Cr | ET | 36 | B | 4 |
| Foxdale Cr | NY | 11 | E | 2 |
| Foxden Rd | NY | 17 | B | 2 |
| Foxhill Rd | SC | 29 | A | 1-2 |
| Foxhound Ct | NY | 11 | F | 3 |
| Foxley Pl | T | 4 | B | 6 |
| Foxley St | T | 4 | A-B | 6 |
| Foxmeadow Rd | ET | 26 | A-B | 2 |
| Foxridge Dr | SC | 27 | D-E | 5 |
| Foxrun Av | NY | 28 | F | 2 |
| Foxwarren Dr | NY | 11 | D | 6 |
| Foxwell St | Y | 26 | E-F | 6 |
| Foxwood Gr | SC | 31 | A | 4 |
| Frame Rd | ET | 24 | C | 2 |
| Franca Cr | ET | 40 | F | 1 |
| Frances Av | ET | 24 | E | 6 |
| Frances Cr | SC | 31 | F | 4 |
| Francine Dr | NY | 21 | A-B | 2 |
| Franel Cr | NY | 30 | B | 3 |
| Frank Cr | T | 4 | B | 5 |
| Frank Faubert Dr | SC | 47 | E | 5-6 |
| Frank Rivers Dr | SC | 38 | B | 1 |
| Frankdale Av | EY | 15 | A | 2-3 |
| Frankdale Av | T | 15 | A | 3 |
| Frankfort Av | NY | 18 | B | 4 |
| Frankish Av | T | 14 | F | 5 |
| Franklin Av | NY | 8 | E-F | 1 |
| Franklin Av | T | 14 | E | 2-3 |
| Franklin Av | NY | 20 | C | 4-5 |
| Frankton Cr | NY | 20 | C | 5 |
| Frankwood Rd | ET | 24 | C | 6 |
| Franson Cr | NY | 30 | C-D | 5-6 |
| Fraser Av | T | 2 | A | 1-2 |
| Fraserton Cr | SC | 34 | A | 1-2 |
| Fraserwood Av | NY | 7 | A | 6 |
| Frater Av | EY | 15 | B-D | 3 |
| Fred Bland Cr | SC | 37 | B | 3 |
| Frederick St | T | 3 | A-B | 1-3 |
| Frederick Tisdale Cir | NY | 18 | E | 3 |
| Fredrick Mowat La | NY | 20 | C | 6 |
| Freeborn Cr | SC | 29 | F | 5 |
| Freeland St | T | 3 | A | 2 |
| Freeland St | T | 7 | F | 2 |
| Freeman Rd | NY | 16 | C | 3 |
| Freeman St | SC | 25 | B-C | 4 |
| Freemont Av | NY | 26 | D-E | 1-2 |
| Freemont Av | NY | 28 | D | 6 |
| Freeport Dr | SC | 47 | D | 6 |
| Freeport Dr | SC | 47 | F | 1-2 |
| French Av | Y | 16 | A | 6 |
| French Av | SC | 47 | A | 2 |
| Freshmeadow Dr | NY | 21 | B-E | 1 |
| Frey Cr | SC | 27 | B | 1-2 |
| Friars La | ET | 26 | B | 5-6 |
| Friary Ct | NY | 20 | A | 4 |
| Frichot Av | T | 4 | D | 4 |
| Friendly Dr | ET | 34 | D-E | 2 |
| Friendship Av | SC | 47 | F | 2 |
| Frith Rd | NY | 30 | F | 5 |
| Frivick Ct | NY | 11 | C | 4 |
| Frizzell Av | T | 5 | E-F | 4 |
| Frizzell Rd | NY | 21 | A | 5 |
| Frobisher Av | T | 6 | E-F | 5 |
| Frolick Cr | SC | 39 | E | 4 |
| Front St E | T | 3 | A-D | 1-2 |
| Front St W | T | 2 | C-F | 2 |
| Front St W | T | 3 | A | 2 |
| Frontenac Av | NY | 6 | C-E | 1 |
| Frontier Pkwy | SC | 51 | A | 5 |
| Frost St | ET | 28 | A | 3 |
| Frost St | ET | 38 | F | 3 |
| Frosty Meadoway | NY | 21 | C-D | 1 |
| Frybrook Rd | T | 6 | E | 5 |
| Fulbert Cr | SC | 31 | E | 5 |
| Fulford Pl | ET | 26 | A | 2 |
| Fulham St | ET | 32 | C | 2-3 |

F

F
G

| STREET NAME | MUNICIPALITY | MAP NO | MAP AREA |
|---|---|---|---|
| Fulham St | SC | 29 | F 1-2 |
| Fuller Av | T | 14 | E 6 |
| Fulton Av | EY | 5 | D-E 3 |
| Fulton Av | T | 5 | D-E 3 |
| Fulwell Cr | NY | 20 | B 5 |
| Fundy Bay Blvd | SC | 31 | B-C 2 |
| Furlong Ct | SC | 37 | A-B 5-6 |
| Furness Cr | ET | 40 | E 2-3 |
| Furnival Rd | EY | 17 | E-F 6 |
| Futura Dr | NY | 20 | B 5 |

## G

| STREET NAME | MUNICIPALITY | MAP NO | MAP AREA |
|---|---|---|---|
| Gabian Way | Y | 16 | D 3-4 |
| Gable Pl | SC | 39 | A 4 |
| Gablehurst Cr | SC | 31 | C 5 |
| Gade Dr | NY | 18 | C 3 |
| Gadsby Dr | SC | 27 | F 3 |
| Gage Av | SC | 37 | A 2 |
| Gageview Ct | SC | 31 | F 2 |
| Gaiety Dr | SC | 30 | B 1 |
| Gail Av | NY | 32 | E 6 |
| Gailong Ct | NY | 19 | F 4 |
| Gainsborough Rd | T | 15 | B-C 4-5 |
| Gair Dr | ET | 32 | C 2 |
| Gaitwin Pl | SC | 39 | D 4 |
| Galaxy Blvd | ET | 36 | B-C 1-2 |
| Galbraith Av | EY | 17 | F 5 |
| Galbraith Rd | T | 4 | E 5 |
| Galewood Dr | NY | 28 | E 5 |
| Galley Av | T | 14 | D-E 6 |
| Galloway Rd | SC | 37 | F 1-4 |
| Galloway Rd | SC | 39 | F 4-6 |
| Galloway Rd | SC | 47 | A 1-4 |
| Galloway Rd | SC | 49 | A 4-6 |
| Galsworthy Av | SC | 29 | A 6 |
| Galt Av | T | 5 | F 5-6 |
| Gambello Ct | NY | 20 | C 5 |
| Gamble Av | EY | 5 | E-F 2 |
| Gamma St | ET | 32 | E 2 |
| Gander Dr | SC | 39 | D 4 |
| Gange Av | T | 4 | D 2 |
| Garamond Ct | NY | 17 | C 3 |
| Garbutt Cr | ET | 26 | D 3 |
| Garden Av | SC | 29 | F 1-2 |
| Garden Av | T | 14 | D-E 5-6 |
| Garden Pl | ET | 32 | C 5 |
| Gardenia Ct | NY | 10 | E 2-3 |
| Gardens Cr | EY | 17 | E 6 |
| Gardens Cr | EY | 7 | C 6 |
| Gardentree St | SC | 47 | A-B 2 |
| Gardenvale Rd | ET | 24 | B 3 |
| Gardenview Cr | Y | 24 | F 1 |
| Gardiner Expwy | T | 12 | A-C 5 |
| Gardiner Expwy | T | 14 | C-D 6 |
| Gardiner Expwy | T | 2 | A-F 2 |
| Gardiner Expwy | T | 3 | A-D 2 |
| Gardiner Expwy | T | 6 | D 4 |
| Garfella Dr | ET | 40 | E 3 |
| Garfield Av | T | 5 | B 1 |
| Garland Av | T | 7 | B 2 |
| Garnet Av | T | 4 | B 3 |
| Garnett Janes Rd | ET | 22 | A-B 3 |
| Garnier Ct | NY | 14 | F 3 |
| Garnock Av | T | 5 | E 4 |
| Garratt Blvd | NY | 18 | E 3 |
| Garrick Rd | SC | 25 | F 1 |
| Garrison Rd | T | 2 | B-C 2 |
| Garroch Pl | ET | 22 | C 2 |
| Garrow Av | Y | 16 | B 5 |
| Garrybrook Dr | SC | 31 | B 5 |
| Garside Cr | NY | 16 | B-C 1 |
| Garston Pl | SC | 41 | B 3 |
| Garthdale Ct | NY | 10 | A 4-5 |
| Garthwood Dr | SC | 27 | D 4-5 |
| Garview Ct | ET | 24 | B 3 |
| Gary Dr | NY | 28 | E-F 5 |
| Garyray Dr | NY | 30 | C-F 1-2 |
| Gaslight Cr | SC | 49 | C 3 |
| Gaslight Ct | NY | 10 | F 3 |
| Gaspe Rd | NY | 11 | D 3-4 |
| Gateforth Dr | SC | 41 | C 2 |
| Gatehead Rd | NY | 11 | F 4-5 |
| Gates Av | T | 15 | D-E 4 |
| Gatesgill Cr | NY | 18 | A-B 3 |
| Gatesview Av | SC | 37 | D-E 3 |
| Gateway Blvd | NY | 17 | B 4-5 |
| Gatewood Cr | ET | 26 | D 4 |
| Gatwick Av | NY | 7 | C 2 |
| Gaudi Rd | SC | 49 | C 1-2 |
| Gaydon Av | NY | 28 | C 3 |
| Gaylord Av | ET | 34 | E 2 |
| Gaylord Dr | SC | 27 | A 2 |
| Geary Av | T | 14 | F 2 |
| Geary Av | T | 4 | A-B 2 |
| Geddes Ct | NY | 8 | B 2 |
| Gem Pl | ET | 28 | C 3 |
| Gemini Rd | NY | 11 | D 3 |
| Gemshaw Cr | SC | 41 | F 6 |
| Generation Blvd | SC | 49 | E 2 |
| Genesee Av | Y | 6 | A 5 |
| Geneva Av | T | 5 | C 5 |
| Gennela Sq | SC | 51 | B 5 |
| Genoa St | T | 4 | F 3 |
| Genthorn Av | ET | 28 | A 1 |
| Gentian Dr | ET | 36 | B 4 |
| Geoffrey St | T | 14 | D-E 5 |
| George Anderson Ct | NY | 16 | C 1 |
| George Anderson Dr | NY | 18 | D-E 1 |
| George Butchart Dr | NY | 18 | D-E 1 |
| George Henry Blvd | NY | 19 | B-D 1 |
| George St | ET | 22 | D 3 |
| George St | SC | 33 | A 1 |
| George St | T | 5 | A 5-6 |
| George St | Y | 28 | E 6 |
| George St S | T | 5 | A 1-2 |
| George Webster Rd | EY | 15 | E 2 |
| Georgian Ct | T | 7 | A 2 |
| Georgina Ct | SC | 25 | B 1 |
| Georgina Gt | SC | 20 | B 1 |
| Gerald St | NY | 9 | D 1-2 |
| Geraldine Ct | NY | 19 | D-E 5 |
| Geraldton Cr | NY | 11 | E-F 4 |
| Gerrard Pl | T | 5 | B 5 |
| Gerrard St E | SC | 25 | A 4 |
| Gerrard St E | SC | 5 | A-F 5 |
| Gerrard St E | T | 15 | A-F 4-5 |
| Gerrard St E | T | 25 | A 4 |
| Gerrard St E | T | 5 | A-F 5 |
| Gerrard St W | T | 5 | E-F 5 |
| Gertrude St | T | 5 | E-F 3 |
| Gervais Dr | NY | 17 | B 3 |
| Ghent Ct | SC | 27 | B 1 |
| Giardino Ct | ET | 28 | B 5 |
| Gibbs Rd | ET | 34 | D 3 |
| Gibson Av | ET | 30 | B 6 |
| Gibson Av | T | 4 | F 2 |
| Gibson Av | Y | 6 | A 4 |
| Gideon Ct | NY | 21 | B 3 |
| Gidley Rd | NY | 28 | B 3 |
| Gifford St | T | 5 | B 5 |
| Gihon Spring Dr | ET | 40 | E 1 |
| Gilbert Av | T | 16 | E 4-5 |
| Gilbert Av | Y | 16 | E 4-5 |
| Gilder Dr | SC | 27 | E-F 3-4 |
| Gildersleeve Pl | T | 5 | B-C 5 |
| Gilead Pl | T | 5 | B 5 |
| Giles Ct | ET | 40 | F 2 |
| Gilgorm Rd | T | 6 | D 3-4 |
| Gillard Av | T | 15 | B 3-4 |
| Gillbank Cr | SC | 39 | E 2 |
| Gillespie Av | T | 14 | E 1 |
| Gilley Rd | NY | 18 | E-F 3 |
| Gillingham St | SC | 49 | E 2-3 |
| Gilmour Av | T | 14 | B 1-2 |
| Gilmour Cr | T | 16 | A 3 |
| Gilpin Av | Y | 16 | C 5 |
| Gilroy Dr | SC | 29 | A 4-5 |
| Giltspur Dr | NY | 18 | A-B 1-2 |
| Gisburn Rd | NY | 19 | F 3-4 |
| Givendale Rd | SC | 27 | D 2 |
| Givins St | T | 2 | B 1 |
| Givins St | T | 4 | B 6 |
| Glade Carseway | NY | 10 | C 4 |
| Gladeside Rd | SC | 29 | D 4 |
| Gladfern Rd | ET | 24 | B 4-5 |
| Gladiola Ct | NY | 8 | B 2 |
| Gladsmore Cr | ET | 28 | A 2 |
| Gladstone Av | T | 2 | A 1 |
| Gladstone Av | T | 4 | A 2-6 |
| Gladwyn Rd | NY | 19 | A 6 |
| Gladys Allison Pl | NY | 11 | A 5-6 |
| Gladys Rd | SC | 49 | C 4 |
| Glaive Dr | SC | 29 | D 4 |
| Glamis Av | Y | 26 | F 5-6 |
| Glamorgan Av | SC | 29 | D-E 3 |
| Glanvil Cr | SC | 41 | F 4 |
| Glasgow Av | SC | 25 | D 1 |
| Glasgow St | T | 4 | E 5 |
| Glazebrook Av | NY | 7 | C 3 |
| Glebe Rd E | T | 7 | A 4 |
| Glebe Rd W | T | 7 | A 4 |
| Glebeholme Blvd | T | 15 | A-D 3 |
| Glebemount Av | T | 15 | C 1-3 |
| Glebemount Av | T | 15 | C 3 |
| Gledhill Av | EY | 15 | D 2-3 |
| Gledhill Av | T | 15 | D 3 |
| Glen Agar Dr | ET | 36 | E-F 5-6 |
| Glen Albert Dr | EY | 15 | E-F 1 |
| Glen Ames | T | 15 | E 5 |
| Glen Belle Cr | NY | 8 | A 5 |
| Glen Castle St | T | 6 | F 1-2 |
| Glen Cedar Rd | Y | 6 | B-C 5 |
| Glen Davis Cr | T | 15 | D-E 4-5 |
| Glen Echo Rd | T | 9 | A 5 |
| Glen Eden Cr | EY | 15 | E 1 |
| Glen Edyth Dr | T | 4 | E 1-2 |
| Glen Edyth Pl | T | 4 | E 2 |
| Glen Elm Av | T | 7 | A 4 |
| Glen Everest Rd | SC | 25 | D-E 3 |
| Glen Gannon Dr | EY | 15 | E 1 |
| Glen Gordon Rd | T | 14 | D 3 |
| Glen Hollow Av | ET | 40 | C 4 |
| Glen Long Av | NY | 16 | E-F 1 |
| Glen Manor Dr | T | 13 | E 6 |
| Glen Manor Dr | T | 15 | E 5-6 |
| Glen Manor Dr E | T | 15 | E 5-6 |
| Glen Manor Dr S | T | 13 | E 5 |
| Glen Manor Dr W | T | 13 | E 5 |
| Glen Manor Dr W | T | 15 | E 5-6 |
| Glen Meadow Lane | T | 34 | E 1 |
| Glen Morris St | T | 4 | E 1 |
| Glen Muir Dr | SC | 37 | B 4 |
| Glen Oak Dr | T | 15 | D-E 4 |
| Glen Park Av | NY | 16 | E-F 2 |
| Glen Park Av | NY | 6 | A-D 2 |
| Glen Rd | T | 5 | B-C 1-3 |
| Glen Rd S | T | 5 | B 4 |
| Glen Robert Dr | EY | 15 | E 1 |
| Glen Rush Blvd | NY | 6 | D 1-2 |
| Glen Scarlett Rd | T | 16 | B-C 6 |
| Glen Springs Dr | SC | 31 | B 3 |
| Glen Stewart Av | T | 15 | E 5 |
| Glen Stewart Cr | T | 15 | E 5 |
| Glen Watford Dr | SC | 31 | F 5-6 |
| Glen Willow Pl | NY | 6 | E 1 |
| Glena Von Rd | T | 12 | B 1 |
| Glenaden Av | T | 24 | D-E 4 |
| Glenaden Av W | ET | 24 | D 4 |
| Glenallan Rd | NY | 7 | B-C 2 |
| Glenanden Rd | T | 6 | B 3-4 |
| Glenashton Av | NY | 7 | C 3 |
| Glenayr Rd | T | 6 | D 4-5 |
| Glenborough Park Cr | NY | 10 | D-E 3-4 |
| Glenbrae Av | EY | 7 | B 3 |
| Glenbrook Av | NY | 6 | A 1 |
| Glenburn Av | EY | 15 | E 1 |
| Glenburn Av | EY | 17 | F 5-6 |
| Glencairn Av | NY | 16 | E-F 2 |
| Glencairn Av | NY | 6 | A-D 2 |
| Glencairn Av | T | 6 | D-F 2 |
| Glencoyne Cr | SC | 31 | A 2 |
| Glencrest Blvd | EY | 15 | E-F 1 |
| Glenda Rd | SC | 37 | C 4 |
| Glendale Av | T | 14 | D 5-6 |
| Glendarling Rd | ET | 26 | D 5 |
| Glendinning Av | SC | 31 | A 1 |
| Glendonwynne Rd | T | 14 | B-C 2-3 |
| Glendora Av | NY | 9 | A-C 5 |
| Glendower Crct | SC | 31 | D 4-5 |
| Gleneagle Av | NY | 21 | C-D 5 |
| Glenelia Av | NY | 11 | C 2 |
| Glenellen Dr E | ET | 24 | D-E 4 |
| Glenellen Dr W | ET | 24 | D 4 |
| Glenfern Av | T | 13 | F 6 |
| Glenfield Cr | T | 15 | E 1 |
| Glenforest Rd | T | 9 | A-B 5 |
| Glengarry Av | T | 8 | C-E 6 |
| Glengarry Av | Y | 6 | D 2 |
| Glengowan Rd | T | 7 | A-B 2 |
| Glengrove Av | NY | 16 | E-F 2 |
| Glengrove Av | NY | 6 | A-D 2 |
| Glengrove Av E | T | 6 | F 2 |
| Glengrove Av E | T | 7 | A 2 |
| Glengrove Av W | T | 6 | D-F 2 |
| Glenhaven St | NY | 16 | D 3-4 |
| Glenholme Av | T | 4 | A 1 |
| Glenholme Av | Y | 6 | A 4-6 |
| Glenholme Pl | T | 5 | A-B 5 |
| Glenhurst Av | Y | 6 | A-B 6 |
| Glenlake Av | T | 14 | B-C 3 |
| Glenmore Rd | T | 15 | C 4-5 |
| Glenmount Av | NY | 6 | C 2 |
| Glenmount Park Rd | T | 15 | D 4-5 |
| Glenn Arthur Dr | ET | 24 | E 5 |
| Glenn Murray Dr | ET | 24 | E 5 |
| Glenora Av | Y | 6 | A 4 |
| Glenorchy Rd | NY | 7 | E 1-2 |

| Street | Code | Map | Grid | No. |
|---|---|---|---|---|
| Glenord Rd | EY | 15 | E | 1 |
| Glenridge Av | NY | 9 | C | 4 |
| Glenridge Rd | SC | 25 | F | 2 |
| Glenrose Av | T | 5 | A-B | 1 |
| Glenroy Av | ET | 24 | D | 4 |
| Glenshaw Cr | EY | 17 | D | 5-6 |
| Glenshephard Dr | SC | 27 | F | 4-5 |
| Glenside Av | T | 15 | A | 5 |
| Glenstroke Dr | SC | 39 | B | 1 |
| Glenthorne Dr | SC | 49 | C | 4 |
| Glentworth Rd | NY | 21 | A-B | 5 |
| Glenvale Blvd | EY | 7 | D-E | 3 |
| Glenvalley Dr | Y | 16 | A | 3 |
| Glenview Av | T | 6 | E-F | 1 |
| Glenwatson Dr | M | 32 | A-B | 4 |
| Glenwood Av | T | 14 | B | 3 |
| Glenwood Cr | EY | 15 | D-E | 1 |
| Glenwood Terr | EY | 15 | D | 1 |
| Gloaming Dr | SC | 47 | A | 1-2 |
| Glory Cr | SC | 37 | F | 2 |
| Glos Av | SC | 37 | A | 4 |
| Glos Rd | ET | 34 | B-C | 1 |
| Gloucester Gr | Y | 6 | A-B | 4 |
| Gloucester St | T | 4 | A | 4 |
| Gloucester St | T | 5 | A | 4 |
| Gloxinia Cr | SC | 31 | C | 4 |
| Goa Ct | ET | 32 | E | 2 |
| Goddard Av | Y | 16 | B | 3 |
| Goddard St | NY | 10 | B | 5-6 |
| Godstone Rd | NY | 21 | B | 5-6 |
| Gold Brook St | SC | 49 | E | 3 |
| Goldberry Sq | SC | 47 | E | 1 |
| Goldberry Sq | SC | 49 | E | 6 |
| Goldcrest Blvd | NY | 18 | B | 6 |
| Golden Appleway | NY | 19 | F | 6 |
| Golden Av | T | 14 | E | 4 |
| Golden Gate Ct | SC | 29 | F | 3 |
| Goldene Way | SC | 49 | D | 2 |
| Goldenridge Rd | M | 34 | A | 6 |
| Goldenridge RD | M | 34 | A | 6 |
| Goldenwood Rd | NY | 11 | E-F | 2 |
| Golders Green Av | SC | 47 | C | 5 |
| Goldfinch Ct | NY | 10 | B | 4 |
| Goldhawk Tr | SC | 41 | A | 2 |
| Goldpine Cr | NY | 30 | C | 5 |
| Goldsboro Rd | NY | 30 | B | 3 |
| Goldsmith Av | SC | 29 | A | 4 |
| Goldthorne Av | ET | 22 | A-B | 2 |
| Goldwin Av | Y | 26 | F | 3 |
| Golf Crest Rd | ET | 24 | A-B | 1 |
| Golf Valley La | SC | 34 | A | 3 |
| Golfdale Rd | T | 8 | F | 5 |
| Golfdale Rd | T | 9 | A-B | 5 |
| Golfdown Dr | ET | 28 | B-C | 2 |
| Golfhaven Dr | SC | 39 | E | 5-6 |
| Golfview Av | T | 15 | D | 4-5 |
| Golfwood Hts | ET | 28 | B-C | 6 |
| Gondola Cr | SC | 39 | E | 5-6 |
| Gooch Av | Y | 24 | F | 1 |
| Gooch Ct | Y | 24 | F | 1 |
| Good Rd | SC | 49 | B-C | 3 |
| Good Shepherd Ct | NY | 16 | F | 1 |
| Goodall Dr | SC | 51 | B | 4 |
| Gooderham Dr | SC | 27 | A | 1 |
| Gooderham Dr | SC | 29 | A | 5-6 |
| Goodland St | SC | 29 | F | 2 |
| Goodless Ct | SC | 41 | E | 6 |
| Goodmark Pl | ET | 40 | E | 1 |
| Goodrich Rd | ET | 24 | A | 5 |
| Goodview Rd | NY | 21 | B | 4-5 |
| Goodwill Av | NY | 8 | B | 3 |
| Goodwood Av | T | 16 | F | 6 |
| Goodwood Park Ct | EY | 15 | E | 3 |
| Goodwood Park Ct | EY | 15 | E-F | 3 |
| Goodyear Ct | NY | 21 | B | 2 |
| Gorden Munson La | SC | 51 | D-E | 1 |
| Gordon Av | SC | 29 | E | 1 |
| Gordon Baker Rd | NY | 21 | E-F | 1-3 |
| Gordon Baker Rd | SC | 31 | A | 1 |
| Gordon Mackay Rd | NY | 28 | F | 4 |
| Gordon Park Dr | ET | 34 | D | 3 |
| Gordon Rd | NY | 9 | B-C | 3 |
| Gordon St | T | 14 | F | 5 |
| Gordonridge Pl | SC | 27 | F | 5 |
| Gore St | T | 4 | B-C | 5 |
| Gore Vale Av | T | 2 | B | 1 |
| Gore Vale Av | T | 4 | B | 5-6 |
| Gorman Park Rd | NY | 8 | B | 1-2 |
| Gormley Av | T | 6 | E-F | 5 |
| Gorsey Sq | SC | 41 | E | 6 |
| Gort Av | ET | 32 | C | 3-4 |
| Gosfield Gt | ET | 28 | B | 1 |
| Gosford Blvd | NY | 20 | A | 1-2 |
| Goskin Ct | SC | 39 | E | 1 |
| Gossamer Av | NY | 11 | C | 1 |
| Goswell Rd | ET | 24 | A | 2 |
| Goswell Rd | ET | 34 | E-F | 2 |
| Gotham Ct | NY | 16 | C | 2 |
| Gothic Av | T | 14 | B-C | 3 |
| Gough Av | T | 5 | E | 3-4 |
| Gould St | T | 4 | F | 5 |
| Gould St | T | 5 | A | 5 |
| Goulding Av | NY | 10 | E-F | 3 |
| Gourlay Cr | T | 14 | B | 1 |
| Government Rd | ET | 24 | D-E | 1 |
| Governors Bridge | T | 5 | C | 1 |
| Governor's Rd | EY | 5 | C | 1 |
| Gowan Av | EY | 5 | E-F | 2 |
| Gower St | EY | 15 | F | 2 |
| Gower St | EY | 25 | A | 2 |
| Goya Ct | SC | 49 | C | 2 |
| Grace St | SC | 37 | B | 3 |
| Gracedale Blvd | NY | 30 | B-C | 3-4 |
| Gracefield Av | NY | 18 | B-C | 6 |
| Gracehill Ct | ET | 40 | F | 5 |
| Graceland Ct | ET | 40 | E | 2 |
| Gracemount Cr | SC | 37 | F | 1 |
| Gracey Blvd | ET | 36 | E-F | 2 |
| Grado Villaway | NY | 11 | F | 5 |
| Gradwell Dr | SC | 25 | E | 4-6 |
| Grafton Av | T | 14 | E | 6 |
| Graham Gdns | Y | 6 | B | 6 |
| Graham Pl | T | 3 | E | 1 |
| Graham Rd | NY | 18 | D-E | 4 |
| Gramercy Sq | SC | 51 | A | 4 |
| Grampian Cr | NY | 30 | B | 3 |
| Granada Cr | SC | 49 | E | 1 |
| Granard Blvd | SC | 37 | B | 4 |
| Granby St | T | 5 | A | 5 |
| Grand Av | ET | 22 | E | 1-2 |
| Grand Marshall Dr | SC | 49 | B | 1 |
| Grand Opera La | T | 2 | F | 1 |
| Grand River Blvd | SC | 49 | E | 2 |
| Grandall Rd | ET | 7 | D | 4 |
| Grandhill Ct | SC | 47 | D | 5 |
| Grandor Ct | SC | 37 | E | 4 |
| Grandravine Dr | NY | 20 | A-D | 5 |
| Grandstand Pl | EY | 7 | F | 5 |
| Grandview Av | T | 5 | E | 4 |
| Grandview Way | NY | 11 | A | 4 |
| Granville Av | Y | 16 | A | 4-5 |
| Grange Av | T | 4 | D-E | 6 |
| Grange Pl | T | 4 | E | 6 |
| Grange Rd | T | 4 | E | 6 |
| Grangemill Cr | NY | 9 | F | 5 |
| Granger Av | SC | 27 | F | 5-6 |
| Grangeway Av | SC | 39 | B | 3 |
| Granite Ct | ET | 22 | F | 4 |
| Granite St | NY | 9 | B | 1-2 |
| Granlea Rd | NY | 9 | C | 1 |
| Grant St | T | 5 | D | 6 |
| Grantbrook St | NY | 10 | E | 2-3 |
| Grantown Av | SC | 49 | C-D | 3 |
| Graphic Ct | SC | 39 | D | 5 |
| Grass Meadoway | NY | 21 | C-D | 1 |
| Grassington Cr | SC | 39 | D | 5 |
| Grassmere Rd | T | 14 | A | 3 |
| Grasspoint Ct | ET | 34 | B | 2-3 |
| Grattan St | ET | 28 | E | 5 |
| Grattan St | Y | 28 | E | 5 |
| Gravenhurst Av | NY | 28 | F | 2 |
| Gray Av | T | 16 | A | 4-5 |
| Graybark Cr | SC | 49 | C | 2-3 |
| Graydon Hall Dr | NY | 19 | B-D | 2-3 |
| Graydon Hall Pl | NY | 19 | B-D | 2 |
| Grayford Ct | SC | 51 | A | 4 |
| Graylee Av | SC | 37 | A | 3 |
| Graymar Av | NY | 8 | C | 3 |
| Grayson Av | SC | 51 | A | 5 |
| Graystone Gdns | ET | 24 | A-B | 4 |
| Graywood Dr | ET | 26 | A-B | 6 |
| Great Oak Dr | ET | 24 | A-B | 1 |
| Great Oak Dr | ET | 26 | A-B | 6 |
| Green Belt Dr | NY | 17 | B-C | 2 |
| Green Bush Rd | NY | 10 | E-F | 1 |
| Green Lanes | ET | 24 | B | 3 |
| Green Pines, The | ET | 34 | A | 3 |
| Green Spring Dr | SC | 41 | B | 2 |
| Green Valley Rd | NY | 8 | A-B | 4-5 |
| Greenacres Rd | Y | 16 | C | 3 |
| Greenberry Pl | SC | 31 | A | 5 |
| Greenbrae Cir | SC | 39 | C | 6 |
| Greenbriar Rd | NY | 9 | F | 5 |
| Greencedar Crct | SC | 37 | C-D | 1 |
| Greencedar Crct | SC | 39 | C | 6 |
| Greencoat Rd | ET | 34 | B | 3 |
| Greencrest Crct | SC | 37 | D | 1 |
| Greencrest Crct | SC | 39 | C | 6 |
| Greendale Av | Y | 16 | A | 4-5 |
| Greendale Cr | Y | 16 | A | 4 |
| Greendowns Dr | SC | 37 | C | 4 |
| Greenfield Av | NY | 11 | A-B | 6 |
| Greenfield Dr | ET | 34 | E | 3 |
| Greenford Rd | ET | 26 | B | 5 |
| Greengate Rd | NY | 9 | E | 5-6 |
| Greengrove Cr | NY | 19 | D-E | 6 |
| Greenhedges Ct | SC | 41 | D | 6 |
| Greenholm Crct | SC | 39 | C-D | 6 |
| Greenhouse Rd | T | 14 | C | 5 |
| Greenhurst Av | M | 32 | A-B | 1-2 |
| Greening Cr | ET | 26 | A | 6 |
| Greenland Rd | NY | 17 | B-C | 1 |
| Greenland Rd | NY | 19 | B | 6 |
| Greenlaw Av | T | 14 | F | 1 |
| Greenleaf Terr | SC | 41 | F | 5 |
| Greenleaf Terr | SC | 51 | A | 5 |
| Greenmount Ct | ET | 24 | D-E | 5 |
| Greenmount Rd | ET | 24 | E | 5 |
| Greenock Av | SC | 39 | E | 4-5 |
| Greensboro Dr | ET | 28 | A | A-5 |
| Greensides Av | T | 4 | B | 1 |
| Greenspire Rd | SC | 41 | E | 5-6 |
| Greentree Ct | Y | 16 | C | 3 |
| Greenvale Terr | SC | 37 | E-F | 2 |
| Greenview Av | NY | 10 | F | 3-4 |
| Greenwin Sq | SC | 37 | B | 3 |
| Greenwin Village Rd | NY | 10 | D-E | 1 |
| Greenwood Av | EY | 15 | A | 1-3 |
| Greenwood Av | T | 15 | A | 3-6 |
| Greenyards Dr | NY | 11 | B | 1 |
| Greer Rd | NY | 8 | E-F | 4 |
| Greer Rd | T | 6 | F | 1 |
| Greer Rd | T | 8 | E | 5-6 |
| Gregory Av | T | 5 | B | 2 |
| Greig Av | T | 5 | D-E | 5 |
| Grenadier Hts | T | 14 | B | 5 |
| Grenadier Rd | T | 14 | B | 4-5 |
| Grenadier Ravine Dr | T | 14 | B | 5 |
| Grenadier Rd | T | 14 | D-E | 5 |
| Grenadine Ct | NY | 30 | B | 3-4 |
| Grenbeck Dr | SC | 31 | E-F | 1 |
| Grendon Av | ET | 26 | A | 2 |
| Grenoble Dr | NY | 17 | B-C | 4-5 |
| Grenview Blvd N | ET | 24 | D | 3-4 |
| Grenview Blvd S | ET | 24 | D | 3-4 |
| Grenville St | T | 4 | F | 5 |
| Gresham Rd | T | 5 | C | 4 |
| Greta Av | NY | 17 | E | 2 |
| Grey Rd | NY | 8 | E-F | 3 |
| Greyabbey Tr | SC | 47 | B | 3 |
| Greybeaver Tr | SC | 47 | B | 5 |
| Greyfriar Ct | NY | 30 | F | 5 |
| Greyhound Dr | NY | 11 | F | 3 |
| Greylawn Cr | SC | 29 | A | 5 |
| Greypoint Dr | SC | 41 | F | 6 |
| Greystone Ct | ET | 22 | E | 2 |
| Greystone Walk Dr | SC | 27 | E-F | 5 |
| Greyswood Ct | ET | 26 | E | 3 |
| Greyton Cr | Y | 6 | A | 4 |
| Grierson Rd | ET | 28 | C | 3-4 |
| Griffen Dr | SC | 41 | E | 6 |
| Griffith St | NY | 28 | C | 3 |
| Griggsden Av | ET | 26 | D | 2-3 |
| Grimsby Cr | ET | 26 | A | 4 |
| Grimthorpe Rd | Y | 6 | B | 6 |
| Griselda Cr | SC | 39 | D-E | 3 |
| Grittani La | SC | 29 | F | 2 |
| Grittani La | SC | 39 | A | 2 |
| Groomsport Cr | SC | 31 | B-C | 5-6 |
| Grosvenor St | T | 4 | F | 5 |
| Groton St | NY | 18 | F | 5 |
| Grove Av | T | 4 | B | 5-6 |
| Grove Hill Dr | SC | 31 | D | 4 |
| Grove Park Dr | SC | 31 | A | 3 |
| Grovedale Av | NY | 18 | C | 5 |
| Groveland Ct | NY | 19 | C-D | 4-5 |
| Groveleaf Rd | SC | 29 | F | 2 |
| Grovenest Dr | SC | 39 | F | 2 |
| Grover Dr | SC | 49 | C | 2-3 |
| Groverdale Rd | ET | 34 | B | 1 |
| Grovetree Rd | ET | 30 | A | 5-6 |
| Guard House Cr | ET | 40 | F | 3 |
| Guernsey Dr | ET | 34 | B-C | 1 |
| Guest Av | T | 15 | E | 3-4 |
| Guestville Av | Y | 16 | A | 4 |
| Guided Ct | ET | 40 | D | 1 |
| Guild Hall Ct | SC | 29 | B-C | 6 |
| Guildcrest Dr | SC | 37 | E | 3-4 |
| Guildpark Ptwy | SC | 37 | E | 2 |
| Guildwood Pkwy | SC | 37 | E-F | 3-4 |
| Guildwood Pkwy | SC | 37 | F | 3-4 |
| Guillet St | NY | 17 | F | 5 |
| Guiness Av | ET | 38 | E | 1 |
| Guiness Av | ET | 40 | E | 6 |
| Gulfstream Rd | NY | 30 | D | 6 |
| Gulliver Rd | NY | 16 | B-C | 2 |
| Gully Dr | SC | 37 | A | 2 |

G

| Street | Code | Map | Col | Row |
|---|---|---|---|---|
| Herron Av | SC | 25 | B | 1 |
| Hershelen Av | NY | 10 | B | 5 |
| Hertford Av | Y | 16 | C | 4 |
| Hertle Av | T | 15 | A-B | 5-6 |
| Hesketh Ct | NY | 17 | F | 3 |
| Heslop Dr | ET | 32 | C | 3 |
| Heward Av | T | 3 | E | 1 |
| Hewitt Av | T | 14 | D-E | 4 |
| Hexham Dr | SC | 27 | A | 2 |
| Heydon Park Rd | T | 4 | A | 5 |
| Heyworth Cr | T | 15 | C-D | 5 |
| Hi Mount Dr | NY | 11 | E | 5 |
| Hiawatha Rd | T | 15 | B | 4-6 |
| Hibberts Dr | SC | 25 | D | 1-2 |
| Hibernia Av | T | 14 | E | 1 |
| Hibiscus St | NY | 30 | C | 6 |
| Hickory St | T | 4 | D | 6 |
| Hickory Tree Rd | SC | 26 | E | 1 |
| Hickorynut Dr | NY | 21 | E | 6 |
| Hickson St | T | 14 | F | 5 |
| Hidden Tr | NY | 10 | B | 1-2 |
| Higgins Pl | SC | 31 | A | 6 |
| High Meadow Pl | NY | 30 | E | 3 |
| High Park Blvd | T | 14 | C | 2-3 |
| High Park Blvd | T | 14 | C-E | 5 |
| High Park Gdns | T | 14 | D | 4 |
| High Point Rd | NY | 9 | D-E | 5-6 |
| High Point Rd | NY | 9 | E | 6 |
| High St | ET | 24 | F | 6 |
| Highbourne Rd | T | 6 | E | 3-4 |
| Highbridge Pl | SC | 31 | E-F | 1 |
| Highbrook Dr | SC | 29 | F | 5-6 |
| Highbury Rd | NY | 28 | E | 2-3 |
| Highcastle Rd | SC | 39 | F | 2-3 |
| Highcliff Cr | SC | 25 | F | 2 |
| Highcourt Cr | SC | 39 | C | 4 |
| Highcroft Dr | T | 15 | B | 3 |
| Highfield Rd | T | 15 | B | 5-6 |
| Highgate Av | NY | 11 | B | 4-6 |
| Highgate Rd | ET | 24 | C | 2 |
| Highhill Dr | SC | 29 | A-B | 1 |
| Highland Av | T | 5 | B | 2 |
| Highland Cr | NY | 9 | B-D | 3-4 |
| Highland Cr | T | 5 | A-B | 2 |
| Highland Creek | SC | 49 | D | 5-6 |
| Highland Creek Overpass | SC | 49 | D | 5 |
| Highland Gdns | T | 5 | B | 2 |
| Highland Hill | NY | 8 | A | 5-6 |
| Highvale Rd | SC | 35 | B | 1 |
| Highview Av | NY | 18 | B | 1 |
| Highview Av | SC | 25 | D-E | 3 |
| Highview Cr | T | 4 | A | 1 |
| Highway 27 | ET | 36 | C | 1-4 |
| Highway 27 | ET | 38 | C | 1-6 |
| Highway 27 | ET | 40 | C-D | 1-6 |
| Highway 401 | ET | 36 | A-E | 1-3 |
| Highway 401 | NY | 8 | A-F | 2-4 |
| Highway 401 | SC | 29 | A-F | 2-4 |
| Highway 401 | SC | 49 | A-F | 2-4 |
| Highway 401 | SC | 39 | A-F | 2 |
| Highway 404 | NY | 19 | C-E | 1-2 |
| Highway 404 | NY | 21 | C-E | 1-6 |
| Highway 427 | ET | 34 | C-D | 1-6 |
| Highway 427 | ET | 36 | A-C | 1-6 |
| Highway 427 | ET | 40 | A | 4-6 |
| Highwood Av | SC | 27 | B | 1 |
| Hilda Av | NY | 10 | F | 1-2 |
| Hildenboro Sq | SC | 31 | B | 3 |
| Hill Cr | SC | 37 | C-E | 4-5 |
| Hill Crest Pl | T | 5 | C | 4 |
| Hill Garden La | ET | 26 | E | 1-2 |
| Hill Garden Rd | ET | 26 | D | 2 |
| Hill Heights Rd | ET | 24 | E | 2 |
| Hillary Av | Y | 16 | D | 5 |
| Hillavon Dr | ET | 36 | E | 5 |
| Hillbeck Cr | SC | 49 | D | 1 |
| Hillborn Av | T | 16 | B | 6 |
| Hillcrest Av | NY | 11 | A-C | 5 |
| Hillcrest Av | T | 5 | C | 4 |
| Hillcrest Dr | T | 4 | A | 5 |
| Hillcroft Dr | ET | 36 | F | 6 |
| Hilldale Rd | Y | 16 | B | 5-6 |
| Hilldowntree Rd | ET | 24 | B | 1 |
| Hilldowntree Rd | ET | 26 | B-C | 1 |
| Hillholm Rd | T | 6 | E | 4 |
| Hillhurst Blvd | NY | 6 | B-D | 2 |
| Hillhurst Blvd | T | 6 | E-D | 2 |
| Hilliard Rd | ET | 36 | D | 2 |
| Hillingdon Av | T | 15 | B | 3-4 |
| Hillmount Av | NY | 6 | A-D | 2 |
| Hillock Pl | SC | 37 | G | 2 |
| Hillsboro Av | T | 4 | F | 3 |
| Hillsdale Av E | T | 4 | F | 4 |
| Hillsdale Av E | T | 7 | A-D | 4 |
| Hillsdale Av W | T | 6 | E-F | 4 |
| Hillside Av | ET | 22 | C-D | 3 |
| Hillside Dr | EY | 5 | E | 1-2 |
| Hillside Rd | NY | 30 | A | 2 |
| Hillside Rd | T | 14 | B | 5 |
| Hillsview Av | T | 14 | C | 3 |
| Hilltop Rd | T | 6 | C | 3-4 |
| Hilo Rd | ET | 32 | C | 5 |
| Hilton Av | T | 4 | D | 1 |
| Hiltz Av | T | 15 | A | 6 |
| Hines Dr | NY | 21 | C | 2-3 |
| Hinton Rd | ET | 30 | D | 1 |
| Hinton Rd | T | 28 | A-B | 1 |
| Hirondelle Pl | NY | 19 | E | 4 |
| Hirons St | T | 14 | D | 1 |
| Hiscock St | SC | 39 | D-E | 5-6 |
| Hisey Cr | NY | 30 | F | 1-2 |
| Historic Terr | SC | 41 | A-B | 2 |
| Hobart Dr | NY | 21 | B | 4 |
| Hobden Pl | ET | 36 | E | 1-2 |
| Hobson Av | NY | 17 | E-F | 5 |
| Hocken Av | T | 4 | C | 1 |
| Hockley Pl | NY | 19 | E | 3-4 |
| Hodder St | EY | 15 | E | 1 |
| Hodder St | EY | 17 | E | 6 |
| Hogan Dr | SC | 39 | E | 5 |
| Hogarth Av | T | 5 | C | 1 |
| Holbeach Rd | ET | 38 | E | 1 |
| Holbeach Rd | ET | 40 | E | 6 |
| Holberg St | ET | 28 | B | 3 |
| Holborne Av | EY | 15 | C-D | 2 |
| Holbrooke Av | ET | 24 | D | 6 |
| Holcolm Rd | NY | 10 | E-F | 4 |
| Holford Cr | SC | 29 | A-B | 2 |
| Holgate St | ET | 26 | B | 2 |
| Holiday Dr | ET | 34 | C | 1 |
| Holita Rd | NY | 10 | E | 3 |
| Hollaman Rd | NY | 6 | C | 2 |
| Holland Av | ET | 36 | F | 5 |
| Holland Park Av | Y | 6 | A-B | 3 |
| Holley Av | Y | 28 | D | 5 |
| Hollinger Rd | EY | 17 | D-E | 5-6 |
| Hollington Dr | SC | 27 | D | 1 |
| Hollis Av | SC | 25 | C-D | 4 |
| Hollis Cr | EG | 40 | B | 3-4 |
| Hollis St | Y | 16 | B | 3-4 |
| Hollister Rd | ET | 36 | C | 4 |
| Holloway Rd | ET | 24 | A | 2 |
| Holly Fernway | NY | 21 | B | 4 |
| Holly St | T | 7 | A | 4 |
| Hollyberry Tr | NY | 21 | C-E | 1 |
| Hollybrook Av | NY | 21 | A | 5 |
| Hollydene Rd | SC | 27 | A-B | 5 |
| Hollyhedge Dr | SC | 37 | A-B | 1-2 |
| Hollywood Av | NY | 11 | A-C | 6 |
| Hollywood Cr | T | 15 | B-C | 4-5 |
| Holmburn Cr | SC | 31 | D | 1 |
| Holmcrest Tr | SC | 47 | E-F | 1-2 |
| Holmes Av | NY | 11 | A-C | 4 |
| Holmesdale Cr | Y | 16 | F | 4 |
| Holmesdale Rd | Y | 16 | F | 4-5 |
| Holmfirth Terr | SC | 37 | D-E | 1 |
| Holmstead Av | EY | 17 | F | 6 |
| Holswade Rd | SC | 27 | A | 4-5 |
| Holton Rd | SC | 37 | D | 2 |
| Holyoake Cr | ET | 40 | B-C | 4 |
| Holywell Dr | ET | 26 | A | 1-2 |
| Home Rd | NY | 8 | E | 3 |
| Homedale Dr | SC | 31 | F | 3 |
| Homer Av | T | 16 | A | 4 |
| Homestead Rd | SC | 47 | B | 1-2 |
| Homeview Av | NY | 26 | F | 6 |
| Homewood Av | NY | 10 | D-F | 2 |
| Homewood Av | T | 5 | A | 4-5 |
| Honbury Rd | ET | 36 | A | 4 |
| Honey Dr | SC | 29 | B | 6 |
| Honeyview Pl | ET | 40 | B | 4 |
| Honeywell Pl | NY | 9 | E | 3 |
| Honeywood Rd | NY | 30 | E-F | 6 |
| Honiton St | NY | 10 | A | 4-5 |
| Honour Ct | NY | 20 | C | 6 |
| Hood Cr | SC | 37 | B-C | 2 |
| Hook Av | T | 14 | D | 2 |
| Hookwood Dr | SC | 31 | F | 4 |
| Hoover Cr | NY | 20 | B | 3 |
| Hoover Rd | NY | 20 | B-C | 2 |
| Hope St | T | 16 | E-F | 6 |
| Hopecrest Cr | SC | 27 | D-E | 5 |
| Hopedale Av | T | 5 | A | 1 |
| Hopewell Av | Y | 6 | A-B | 3 |
| Hopperton Dr | NY | 9 | E-F | 1-2 |
| Horfield Av | SC | 37 | A-B | 5 |
| Horizon Cr | NY | 20 | C | 1 |
| Hornell St | ET | 24 | C | 6 |
| Horner Av | ET | 22 | A | 1-3 |
| Horner Av | ET | 32 | B-F | 3 |
| Hornhill Rd | SC | 41 | A | 4 |
| Horseley Hill Dr | SC | 41 | E | 5 |
| Horseshoe Cr | SC | 41 | F | 4-5 |
| Horsham Av | NY | 10 | C-F | 4 |
| Horticultural Av | T | 5 | A | 5 |
| Horton Blvd | SC | 37 | A | 4 |
| Hoseyhill Cr | SC | 41 | A | 4 |
| Hoshiega Dr | SC | 38 | E | 5 |
| Hoskin Av | T | 4 | E | 4 |
| Hotspur Rd | NY | 8 | C | 4 |
| Houndtrail Dr | SC | 49 | C | 2-3 |
| Hounslow Av | NY | 10 | D-F | 4 |
| Hounslow Heath Rd | T | 14 | E | 1 |
| Housey St | T | 2 | C-D | 2 |
| Houston Cr | NY | 21 | B-D | 4-5 |
| Hove St | NY | 10 | B-C | 5-6 |
| Howard Dr | NY | 11 | E | 6 |
| Howard Park Av | T | 14 | C-E | 4-5 |
| Howard St | T | 5 | B | 4 |
| Howarth Av | SC | 27 | A | 1-2 |
| Howbert Dr | NY | 28 | E | 1 |
| Howden Rd | SC | 27 | C | 1-5 |
| Howden Rd | SC | 29 | C | 5-6 |
| Howell Sq | SC | 41 | E | 6 |
| Howick Av | T | 16 | D-E | 6 |
| Howie Av | T | 5 | D | 6 |
| Howland Av | T | 4 | D | 2-3 |
| Howland Av | Y | 24 | E | 1 |
| Howland Rd | T | 5 | E | 5 |
| Hoyle Av | T | 7 | C | 4 |
| Hubbard Blvd | T | 13 | E | 6 |
| Hubert Av | SC | 25 | D | 1 |
| Hubert Av | SC | 27 | D | 6 |
| Hucknall Rd | NY | 20 | C | 4-5 |
| Huddersfield Rd | ET | 40 | B | 2 |
| Huddleston Ct | SC | 25 | C | 1-2 |
| Hudson Dr | T | 5 | B | 1 |
| Hudson Dr | T | 7 | B | 6 |
| Hughes Pl | SC | 27 | B | 2 |
| Hughey Cr | SC | 27 | D | 3 |
| Hugo Av | T | 14 | E | 2 |
| Hullen Dr | ET | 40 | A-B | 4 |
| Hullmar Dr | NY | 20 | A | 1-3 |
| Hullmar Dr | NY | 30 | F | 1-3 |
| Hulrick Dr | ET | 40 | A-B | 5-6 |
| Humber Bay Parkway | ET | 22 | E-F | 2-3 |
| Humber Blvd | ET | 24 | E | 1-3 |
| Humber Blvd | Y | 16 | B | 4-5 |
| Humber Blvd N | Y | 16 | B | 4-5 |
| Humber College Blvd | ET | 40 | C-E | 3-4 |
| Humber Hill Av | ET | 24 | E | 1 |
| Humber Hill Av | Y | 40 | C | 4 |
| Humber Ridge Dr | ET | 24 | E | 4-5 |
| Humber Summit La | NY | 30 | B | 1 |
| Humber Tr | Y | 24 | F | 3 |
| Humber Valley Rd | ET | 24 | E-F | 4-6 |
| Humbercrest Blvd | Y | 24 | A | 1-2 |
| Humbercrest La | Y | 24 | F | 2-3 |
| Humbercrest Pl | Y | 24 | F | 2 |
| Humberline Dr | ET | 40 | B-C | 2-4 |
| Humberside Av | T | 14 | C-E | 2 |
| Humbervale Blvd | ET | 24 | D | 3-4 |
| Humberview Cr | Y | 28 | C | 5 |
| Humberview Rd | Y | 24 | E-F | 3 |
| Humberwood Blvd | ET | 40 | A-B | 4-6 |
| Humewood Dr | Y | 6 | A-B | 4 |
| Humewood Dr | Y | 6 | B | 5-6 |
| Humewood Gdns | Y | 6 | B | 4 |
| Humheller Rd | ET | 38 | E | 1 |
| Humheller Rd | ET | 40 | E | 6 |
| Hun Cr | ET | 40 | D-E | 4 |
| Hunt Club Dr | SC | 25 | B | 4-5 |
| Huntchester Cr | SC | 37 | B | 4-5 |
| Hunter Av | T | 16 | F | 4 |
| Hunter St | T | 15 | A | 4 |
| Hunter St | T | 5 | E | 5 |
| Hunthill Ct | T | 26 | C | 5 |
| Hunting Ridge | ET | 26 | A | 3 |
| Huntingdale Blvd | SC | 31 | A-B | 4 |
| Huntington Av | SC | 27 | C | 5 |
| Huntingwood Dr | SC | 31 | A-F | 5-6 |
| Huntley St | T | 5 | A | 3 |
| Huntsmill Blvd | SC | 31 | A-B | 1-2 |
| Huntsmoor Rd | ET | 28 | D | 3-4 |
| Hupfield Tr | SC | 41 | F | 4-5 |
| Hupfield Tr | SC | 51 | A | 1-2 |
| Hurdman St | NY | 16 | C | 2 |
| Hurley Cr | SC | 39 | A-B | 4 |
| Hurlingham Cr | NY | 19 | A | 4 |
| Humdale Av | T | 5 | D-E | 3 |
| Huron Gt | SC | 39 | B | 4 |
| Huronia Gt | SC | 39 | B | 4 |
| Hursting Av | Y | 6 | B | 6 |

| STREET NAME | MUNICIPALITY | MAP NO | MAP AREA |
|---|---|---|---|
| Husband Dr | NY | 30 | B-D1-22 |
| Hush La | T | 14 | B | 4 |
| Huson Ct | ET | 40 | F | 1 |
| Hutchcroft Av | SC | 41 | A | 4 |
| Hutcherson Sq | SC | 41 | E-F | 6 |
| Hutton Av | EY | 15 | B | 1-2 |
| Huxley Rd | NY | 28 | E | 3 |
| Hycrest Rd | NY | 11 | B | 6 |
| Hyde Av | NY | 16 | B-C | 5 |
| Hyde Park Cir | NY | 9 | D | 5 |
| Hyfan Ct | NY | 10 | A | 4 |
| Hyland Av | ET | 24 | D | 2 |
| Hymus Rd | SC | 27 | B-C | 5 |
| Hysel Rd | NY | 18 | B | 5 |

**I**

| STREET NAME | MUNICIPALITY | MAP NO | MAP AREA |
|---|---|---|---|
| Ian Macdonald Blvd | NY | 20 | B-D1-22 |
| Iangrove Terr | SC | 31 | A | 3 |
| Ianhall Rd | NY | 18 | C | 3 |
| Idagrove Gt | SC | 49 | D | 1 |
| Idehill Ct | SC | 41 | A | 5 |
| Idyllwood Cr | T | 14 | B | 3 |
| Ikley Rd | NY | 20 | C | 2 |
| Ilford Rd | T | 4 | B | 1 |
| Ilfracombe Cr | SC | 29 | B | 5 |
| Imogene Av | NY | 30 | D | 5 |
| Imperial St | T | 6 | E-F | 5 |
| Imperial Way | BU | 2 | E | 6 |
| Inca Rd | NY | 21 | E | 4 |
| Inchcliffe Cr | ET | 28 | C | 6 |
| Independence Dr | SC | 27 | E | 4 |
| Index Rd | ET | 34 | C | 5-6 |
| Indian Gr | T | 14 | D | 2-4 |
| Indian Mound Cr | SC | 39 | B-C | 6 |
| Indian Rd | T | 14 | D | 2-6 |
| Indian Road Cr | T | 14 | D | 2-3 |
| Indian Tr | T | 14 | D | 4 |
| Indian Valley Cr | T | 14 | D | 4 |
| Indianola Dr | ET | 34 | B | 1 |
| Indrio Rd | NY | 30 | C | 6 |
| Industrial St | EY | 7 | E-F | 4 |
| Industry St | NY | 16 | A | 2 |
| Industry St | T | 16 | A-B | 2-3 |
| Inez Ct | NY | 10 | F | 3 |
| Ingham Av | T | 5 | D-E | 2 |
| Ingleport St | ET | 36 | E | 1 |
| Ingleside Dr | NY | 18 | D-E | 3-4 |
| Ingleton Blvd | SC | 41 | B | 4 |
| Inglewood Dr | T | 5 | A-C | 1 |
| Inglis Gt | NY | 10 | C | 1 |
| Ingram Dr | NY | 16 | D | 2 |
| Ingrid Dr | SC | 39 | E | 4-5 |
| Inkerman St | T | 4 | F | 4 |
| Innes Av | T | 16 | E | 5 |
| Inniscross Cr | SC | 31 | E | 1 |
| Innisdale Dr | SC | 27 | A | 2 |
| Innisfree Ct | T | 14 | A | 5 |
| Innislawn Rd | SC | 31 | B | 2 |
| Innismore Cr | SC | 27 | A | 2 |
| Inniswood Dr | SC | 27 | A | 2 |
| International Blvd | ET | 30 | F | 3 |
| Inverary Cr | SC | 31 | D | 5 |
| Inverdon Rd | ET | 36 | C | 4-5 |
| Invergordon Av | SC | 39 | B-C | 1 |
| Inverleigh Dr | ET | 22 | D | 1 |
| Invermarge Dr | SC | 49 | E | 5-6 |
| Invermay Av | NY | 18 | A | 2 |
| Inverness Av | ET | 24 | B | 6 |
| Inwood Av | EY | 15 | A | 2-3 |
| Inwood Av | T | 15 | A | 3 |
| Iolanta Ct | ET | 40 | B-C | 4 |
| Iona Av | T | 15 | D | 4 |
| Iondale Pl | SC | 27 | D | 3 |
| Ionic La | NY | 18 | F | 4 |
| Ionview Rd | SC | 27 | D | 2-3 |
| Ipswich Ct | NY | 21 | E | 4 |
| Ireland Ct | ET | 26 | A | 3-4 |
| Irene Av | T | 4 | B | 3 |
| Iris Rd | ET | 32 | F | 5 |
| Irmac Ct | T | 24 | F | 1 |
| Iron St | ET | 38 | D | 4-5 |
| Irondale Dr | NY | 30 | D | 1 |
| Ironside Dr | SC | 41 | D-E | 2 |
| Ironwood Rd | NY | 30 | C | 4 |
| Irvine Rd | SC | 49 | E | 4 |
| Irving Rd | T | 16 | C | 3 |
| Irvington Cr | NY | 9 | C | 1 |
| Irwin Av | T | 4 | F | 4 |
| Irwin Rd | ET | 28 | B-C | 2 |
| Isabella St | T | 4 | F | 4 |

| STREET NAME | MUNICIPALITY | MAP NO | MAP AREA |
|---|---|---|---|
| Isabella St | T | 5 | A-B | 4 |
| Islandview Blvd | ET | 22 | D | 4 |
| Islay Ct | NY | 30 | B | 1 |
| Isleworth Av | T | 13 | E | 5 |
| Isleworth Av | T | 15 | E | 6 |
| Islington Av | ET | 22 | B | 1-4 |
| Islington Av | ET | 24 | B | 1-6 |
| Islington Av | ET | 26 | B | 1-6 |
| Islington Av | ET | 28 | B | 1-6 |
| Islington Av | ET | 30 | B | 4-6 |
| Islington Av | NY | 30 | B | 1-4 |
| Ivan Nelson Dr | NY | 10 | B | 3 |
| Ivan Rd | SC | 49 | E | 5 |
| Ivanhoe Ct | SC | 29 | A | 4 |
| Ivor Rd | NY | 9 | A | 4 |
| Ivordale Cr | SC | 19 | F | 4 |
| Ivordale Cr | SC | 29 | A | 4-5 |
| Ivorwood Cr | SC | 29 | A | 4-5 |
| Ivy Av | T | 15 | A | 5 |
| Ivy Bush Av | SC | 31 | D | 2 |
| Ivy Green Cr | SC | 39 | E | 4-5 |
| Ivy Lea Cr | T | 24 | E | 4 |
| Ivybridge Dr | ET | 34 | A | 1 |
| Ixworth Rd | ET | 38 | F | 1 |
| Ixworth Rd | ET | 40 | F | 6 |

**J**

| STREET NAME | MUNICIPALITY | MAP NO | MAP AREA |
|---|---|---|---|
| Jacinta Dr | NY | 18 | B | 6 |
| Jackes Av | T | 5 | A | 1 |
| Jackman Av | EY | 5 | E | 2-3 |
| Jackman Av | T | 5 | E | 3 |
| Jackmuir Cr | SC | 39 | A | 4 |
| Jackson Pl | T | 14 | C | 2 |
| Jackson Rd | ET | 22 | A | 4 |
| Jacob Fisher Dr | SC | 41 | F | 5 |
| Jacob Fisher Dr | SC | 51 | A | 4-5 |
| Jacobs Ct | NY | 10 | B | 2 |
| Jade St | SC | 29 | D-E | 1 |
| Jainey Pl | NY | 8 | E | 4 |
| James Foxway | NY | 11 | D | 4 |
| James Gray Dr | NY | 11 | F | 2 |
| James Park Sq | SC | 31 | F | 2 |
| James St | ET | 32 | C | 5 |
| James St | T | 2 | F | 1 |
| James St | T | 4 | F | 6 |
| Jamestown Cr | ET | 40 | E-F | 5 |
| Janda Ct | ET | 40 | C | 5-6 |
| Jane Osler Blvd | NY | 18 | F | 5 |
| Jane St | NY | 16 | A | 1-2 |
| Jane St | NY | 18 | A | 1-6 |
| Jane St | NY | 20 | A-B | 1-6 |
| Jane St | T | 16 | A | 2-6 |
| Jane St | Y | 24 | F | 1-3 |
| Jane St | Y | 26 | F | 1-6 |
| Janellan Terr | SC | 47 | D | 1-2 |
| Janet Blvd | SC | 27 | A | 1 |
| Janray Dr | SC | 39 | D | 5-6 |
| Jansusie Rd | ET | 40 | F | 5-6 |
| Janus Ct | NY | 21 | A | 1 |
| Japonica Rd | SC | 29 | A-B | 4 |
| Jardin Hill Ct | NY | 21 | C-E | 2 |
| Jardine Pl | ET | 36 | F | 2 |
| Jarvis St | T | 3 | A | 3-6 |
| Jarvis St | T | 5 | A | 1 |
| Jarwick Dr | SC | 39 | B | 5 |
| Jasmine Av | ET | 32 | E | 5 |
| Jasmine Rd | NY | 28 | D | 2-3 |
| Jason Rd | ET | 28 | B | 1-2 |
| Jasper Av | Y | 16 | B | 4 |
| Javelin La | ET | 28 | A | 5 |
| Jay St | NY | 10 | D | 4-5 |
| Jaybell Gr | SC | 47 | E | 4 |
| Jayfield Rd | SC | 29 | A | 5 |
| Jaymar Pl | NY | 28 | E | 5 |
| Jayzel Dr | NY | 30 | D | 4 |
| Jean Dempsey Gt | SC | 49 | D-E | 6 |
| Jean St | T | 3 | B | 1-2 |
| Jeanette St | SC | 27 | F | 6 |
| Jeavons Av | SC | 25 | D | 2 |
| Jedburgh Rd | T | 8 | F | 5-6 |
| Jeff Dr | ET | 34 | B-C | 4 |
| Jeffcoat Dr | ET | 38 | D-F | 1-2 |
| Jefferson Av | T | 2 | A | 1-2 |
| Jeffton Cr | SC | 39 | A | 4-5 |
| Jellicoe Av | ET | 32 | C | 4 |
| Jenet Av | T | 14 | E-F | 3 |
| Jennings Av | T | 18 | B | 2 |
| Jenny Wrenway | NY | 21 | B | 1 |
| Jenoves Pl | T | 3 | A | 1 |
| Jenson Ct | ET | 38 | E | 1-2 |
| Jerome St | T | 14 | D-E | 3 |
| Jersey Av | T | 4 | F | 4 |
| Jesmond Av | Y | 6 | A-B | 5 |
| Jethro Rd | NY | 28 | F | 3-4 |
| Jill Cr | ET | 36 | E | 4 |
| Jillson Av | Y | 14 | A | 1 |

| STREET NAME | MUNICIPALITY | MAP NO | MAP AREA |
|---|---|---|---|
| Jim Samuel La | T | 15 | F | 5 |
| Joanith Dr | EY | 17 | E | 6 |
| Joanna Dr | SC | 29 | A | 3 |
| Jocada Rd | NY | 18 | E | 4-5 |
| Jocelyn Cr | NY | 19 | A | 6 |
| Jodphur Av | NY | 28 | D-E | 3-4 |
| Jody Av | NY | 30 | F | 5 |
| Joel Swirsky Blvd | NY | 8 | B | 2 |
| John Best Av | NY | 26 | F | 2 |
| John Cabotway | NY | 30 | F | 6 |
| John Drury Cr | NY | 20 | D | 6 |
| John Drury Dr | NY | 18 | E | 1-2 |
| John Drury Dr | NY | 20 | D-E | 6 |
| John Garland Blvd | ET | 40 | E-F | 4-5 |
| John Graham Cr | SC | 49 | F | 2-3 |
| John Grubb Ct | ET | 30 | A | 5 |
| John Lindsay Cr | NY | 20 | B | 6 |
| John McKenzie Gt | NY | 11 | A | 5 |
| John St | T | 2 | E | 1-2 |
| John St | T | 4 | E | 6 |
| John Stoner Dr | SC | 49 | F | 2-3 |
| John Tabor Tr | SC | 51 | A-B | 6 |
| Johnston Av | NY | 8 | E-F | 1 |
| Joicey Blvd | NY | 8 | C-F | 4 |
| Joicey Blvd | T | 8 | F | 4 |
| Jones Av | T | 5 | F | 4-6 |
| Jonesville Cr | NY | 17 | E-F | 3-4 |
| Jopling Av N | ET | 34 | F | 2-3 |
| Jopling Av S | ET | 34 | F | 3 |
| Jordan St | T | 2 | F | 1 |
| Jordanroch Ct | SC | 31 | B | 2 |
| Josali Dr | SC | 47 | D | 4 |
| Joseph Duggen Rd | T | 13 | D | 6 |
| Joseph Duggen Rd | T | 13 | F | 1 |
| Joseph Salsberg La | T | 2 | C | 1 |
| Joseph St | T | 28 | E | 6 |
| Josephine Rd | NY | 8 | B | 2 |
| Joshua Av | ET | 40 | E | 6 |
| Joy Dr | SC | 29 | B | 5 |
| Joyce Pkwy | NY | 16 | E-F | 1 |
| Jubilee Cr | NY | 28 | D-E | 2 |
| Judge Rd | ET | 24 | A | 4 |
| Judhaven Rd | NY | 30 | C | 5 |
| Judith Dr | EY | 15 | B | 1 |
| Judson St | ET | 22 | A-C | 2 |
| Julian Rd | NY | 18 | C | 3-4 |
| Juliana Ct | NY | 24 | E | 1 |
| Juliet Cr | Y | 16 | C | 4 |
| Junction Rd | T | 14 | D | 1 |
| June Av | NY | 28 | E | 3 |
| Junewood Cr | NY | 9 | E | 3 |
| Juniper Av | T | 15 | D-E | 5 |
| Jupp Ct | ET | 40 | F | 1 |
| Jutland Rd | ET | 24 | A-B | 5 |
| Jutten Ct | SC | 39 | C | 5 |

**K**

| STREET NAME | MUNICIPALITY | MAP NO | MAP AREA |
|---|---|---|---|
| Kainona Av | NY | 8 | B | 2 |
| Kalligan Ct | M | 32 | A | 2 |
| Kalmar Av | SC | 25 | C | 3-4 |
| Kames Av | NY | 28 | F | 5 |
| Kamloops Dr | NY | 21 | E | 5 |
| Kanarick Cr | NY | 18 | B | 1 |
| Kane Av | NY | 16 | E | 4-5 |
| Kanturk Gt | NY | 19 | E | 2 |
| Kappele Av | T | 9 | A-B | 6 |
| Karen Ann Cr | SC | 37 | E | 2 |
| Karen Rd | NY | 19 | C-D | 3 |
| Karina Rd | SC | 49 | E | 4 |
| Karnwood Dr | SC | 27 | A | 5-6 |
| Katherine Rd | NY | 18 | E-F | 6 |
| Kathleen Cr | ET | 17 | C | 6 |
| Kathrose Dr | NY | 21 | E-F | 5 |
| Katie Ct | NY | 18 | B-C | 5 |
| Katrina Cr | NY | 18 | A | 6 |
| Katrine Rd | ET | 30 | A | 6 |
| Kay Dr | ET | 40 | F | 1 |
| Keane Av | ET | 34 | D | 6 |
| Keanegate, The | NY | 34 | E | 1 |
| Kearney Dr | ET | 38 | D-E | 1-2 |
| Kearney Dr | ET | 40 | E | 6 |
| Kebral Av | ET | 34 | A | 4 |
| Kecala Rd | SC | 29 | D | 5 |
| Keefer Rd | NY | 18 | C | 3 |
| Keegan Cr | NY | 20 | B | 6 |
| Keele St | NY | 16 | D | 1-2 |
| Keele St | NY | 18 | D | 1-6 |
| Keele St | NY | 20 | D-B | 1-6 |
| Keele St | Y | 16 | D | 3-5 |
| Keelegate Dr | NY | 18 | D-E | 3 |
| Keeler Blvd | SC | 39 | F | 2 |
| Keeler Blvd | SC | 49 | A | 2 |
| Keelesdale Dr | Y | 16 | B | 3-4 |
| Keelesdale Rd | Y | 16 | B | 4 |
| Keewatin Av | T | 7 | A-B | 3 |

| Street | Muni | Map | Grid |
|---|---|---|---|
| Keith Av | Y | 16 | E 4 |
| Kelfield St | ET | 36 | D 1 |
| Kells St | SC | 31 | B 6 |
| Kellner Ct | T | 15 | B-C 5 |
| Kellogg St | ET | 24 | B 4 |
| Kells Av | SC | 27 | F 2 |
| Kellythorne Dr | NY | 19 | E 4-5 |
| Kellyvale Rd | SC | 25 | E-F 2 |
| Kelso Av | NY | 8 | E 3-4 |
| Kelsonia Av | SC | 25 | E-F 2 |
| Keltie Av | NY | 28 | D 4 |
| Kelvin Av | NY | 28 | D 4 |
| Kelvin Av | T | 15 | F 3-4 |
| Kelvin Grove Av | SC | 31 | D 1 |
| Kelvinway Dr | SC | 31 | A 4 |
| Kelway Blvd | T | 6 | E 3 |
| Kemp Sq | NY | 16 | A 1-2 |
| Kempford Blvd | NY | 10 | F 4 |
| Kempsell Cr | NY | 21 | B-D 5 |
| Kenaston Gdns | NY | 9 | D 1 |
| Kencliff Cr | SC | 39 | A 4 |
| Kendal Av | T | 4 | D-E 2-3 |
| Kendleton Dr | ET | 40 | E-F 4-5 |
| Kenewen Ct | NY | 17 | F 2 |
| Kenfin Av | SC | 31 | E 4 |
| Kengate Dr | SC | 31 | B 4 |
| Kenhar Dr | NY | 30 | D-E 2 |
| Kenhatch Blvd | SC | 41 | B 4-5 |
| Kenhill Dr | ET | 30 | C 5 |
| Kenilworth Av | T | 13 | D 6 |
| Kenilworth Av | T | 15 | D 5-6 |
| Kenilworth Av | T | 13 | D 5 |
| Kenmanor Blvd | SC | 31 | B 5 |
| Kenmark Blvd | SC | 27 | E 4 |
| Kenmore Av | SC | 25 | D 2 |
| Kennaley Cr | SC | 31 | F 3 |
| Kennard Av | NY | 10 | A-B 5 |
| Kennebec Cr | ET | 28 | A-B 1 |
| Kennedy Av | T | 14 | B 3-4 |
| Kennedy Park Rd | T | 14 | B 3 |
| Kennedy Rd | MA | 27 | E 1-6 |
| Kennedy Rd | SC | 25 | D-E 1-3 |
| Kennedy Rd | SC | 27 | E 1-6 |
| Kennedy Rd | SC | 29 | D-E 1-6 |
| Kennedy Rd | SC | 31 | D-E 1-6 |
| Kennerly Ct | NY | 20 | B 4 |
| Kenneth Av | NY | 11 | A 3-6 |
| Kenneth Av | T | 14 | D-E 3 |
| Kenneth Dr | M | 32 | A 3 |
| Kenning Pl | ET | 36 | F 2 |
| Kenny Av | ET | 22 | C 2 |
| Kenora Cr | Y | 16 | E 5 |
| Kenrae Rd | EY | 7 | E 5 |
| Kenridge Av | ET | 24 | D 5 |
| Kenscott Rd | SC | 49 | D 2 |
| Kensington Av | NY | 10 | F 3-4 |
| Kensington Av | T | 4 | D 5-6 |
| Kensington Pl | T | 4 | D 5-6 |
| Kent Rd | T | 15 | B 6 |
| Kentish Cr | SC | 39 | B-C 1 |
| Kentland Cr | NY | 11 | E 1 |
| Kenton Dr | NY | 10 | D 3 |
| Kentroyal Dr | ET | 28 | D 3 |
| Kentucky Av | Y | 6 | C 5-6 |
| Kenway Rd | ET | 24 | B 3 |
| Kenwood Av | Y | 6 | C 5-6 |
| Kenworthy Av | SC | 25 | A 3-4 |
| Keon Pl | SC | 51 | A 5 |
| Kerbar Rd | SC | 30 | D 3-4 |
| Kereven St | NY | 8 | D 3 |
| Kern Rd | NY | 19 | B 4 |
| Kerr Rd | T | 15 | A-B 6 |
| Kersdale Av | Y | 16 | D 5 |
| Kerwood Cr | SC | 29 | D 2 |
| Kessack Ct | SC | 41 | F 6 |
| Kesswick Rd | NY | 19 | B-D 4-5 |
| Kestell La | NY | 19 | B-D 4-5 |
| Keswick Rd | NY | 18 | F 3 |
| Kevi La | ET | 36 | E 6 |
| Kew Beach Av | T | 13 | D 6 |
| Kew Beach Cr | T | 13 | D 6 |
| Keystone Av | T | 15 | D 5 |
| Keywell Ct | ET | 24 | E 5 |
| Keywest Av | Y | 6 | A 4 |
| Keyworth Tr | SC | 39 | A-B 1 |
| Khartoum Av | SC | 27 | E 4 |
| Khedive Av | NY | 8 | C 5 |
| Kidbrooke Cr | SC | 25 | F 1 |
| Kidron Valley Dr | ET | 40 | E-F 1 |
| Kilbarry Pl | T | 6 | E 5 |
| Kilbarry Rd | T | 6 | D-F 5 |
| Kilbride Rd | SC | 37 | A 1 |
| Kilburn Pl | ET | 26 | A 2 |
| Kilburn Pl | ET | 28 | B 3 |
| Kilchurn Castle Gt | SC | 31 | E 3 |
| Kilcullen Castle Gt | SC | 31 | E 3 |
| Kildonan Dr | SC | 25 | C 4-5 |
| Kildonan Rd | T | 15 | D 4 |
| Kilgreggan Cr | SC | 37 | A 1-2 |
| Kilkenny Dr | SC | 31 | A-B 5 |
| Killarnash Dr | SC | 31 | D 5 |
| Killarney Rd | T | 6 | E 5 |
| Killdeer Cr | EY | 7 | E 3 |
| Kilmarnock Av | SC | 25 | D 1-2 |
| Kilpatrick Dr | SC | 27 | B 2 |
| Kilpatrick Pl | SC | 27 | B 2 |
| Kilsyth Dr | SC | 47 | D 4 |
| Kilsyth Dr | SC | 49 | F 4-5 |
| Kim Ct | SC | 27 | E 4 |
| Kimbark Blvd | NY | 6 | E 1 |
| Kimbark Blvd | T | 6 | E 1 |
| Kimberdale Cr | SC | 31 | B 5 |
| Kimberley Av | T | 15 | E 4-5 |
| Kimbermount Dr | SC | 31 | D 5 |
| Kimbolton Ct | SC | 49 | D 5 |
| Kimbourne Av | EY | 15 | A 2-3 |
| Kimloch Cr | NY | 9 | F 4 |
| Kimridge Av | SC | 25 | B-C 3 |
| Kimroy Gr | SC | 39 | B 1 |
| Kincort St | NY | 16 | E 2-3 |
| Kincort St | T | 16 | E 2-3 |
| King Arthurs Ct | SC | 47 | E 4 |
| King David Dr | NY | 10 | D 2 |
| King Edward Av | ET | 15 | D 2-3 |
| King George's Dr | Y | 16 | C 3 |
| King George's Rd | NY | 28 | E 5 |
| King Georges' Rd | ET | 24 | D-E 3 |
| King Henrys Blvd | SC | 31 | D 5-6 |
| King High Av | NY | 8 | B 2-3 |
| King Louis Cr | SC | 31 | D 5 |
| King Maple Pl | NY | 11 | E 5 |
| King St | Y | 3 | E 5-6 |
| King St E | T | 3 | A-D 1 |
| King St W | T | 12 | B-C 1 |
| King St W | T | 2 | A-F 1 |
| King St W | T | 3 | A 1 |
| Kingdom St | ET | 26 | E 2 |
| Kinghorn Av | Y | 26 | F 5-6 |
| Kingland Cr | NY | 21 | A 5 |
| King's College Cir | T | 4 | E 4-5 |
| Kings Lynn Rd | ET | 24 | D 2-3 |
| Kings Park Blvd | EY | 15 | A 3 |
| Kings Park Blvd | SC | 5 | E-F 3 |
| Kings Point Dr | ET | 24 | E 5 |
| Kingsborough Cr | ET | 26 | A 3 |
| Kingsbridge Cr | NY | 10 | C 4 |
| Kingsbury Cr | SC | 25 | C 4 |
| Kingscourt Dr | SC | 31 | E 4 |
| Kingscross Sq | ET | 24 | E 5 |
| Kingsdale Av | NY | 11 | A-C 5 |
| Kingsdown Dr | SC | 27 | D-E 2-3 |
| Kingsfold Ct | SC | 26 | B 4-5 |
| Kingsgarden Rd | ET | 24 | D-E 2 |
| Kingsgate Dr | ET | 24 | C-D 2 |
| Kingsgrove Blvd | ET | 28 | B 1 |
| Kingsknowe Pl | ET | 28 | B 1 |
| Kingsknowe Rd | SC | 30 | A 6 |
| Kingslake Rd | ET | 21 | B-E 4-5 |
| Kingslea Ct | ET | 24 | D 2 |
| Kingslea Gdns | ET | 24 | D-E 2 |
| Kingsley Av | T | 14 | E 2 |
| Kingsmere Cr | SC | 37 | D 4 |
| Kingsmere Rd | T | 7 | B 6 |
| Kingsmill Rd | ET | 24 | E 3 |
| Kingsmoor Cr | ET | 30 | A-B 5 |
| Kingsmount Park Rd | T | 15 | C 4-5 |
| Kingsplate Ct | ET | 40 | B 5 |
| Kingston Rd | SC | 25 | A-F 1-5 |
| Kingston Rd | SC | 27 | A-F 2-6 |
| Kingston Rd | SC | 47 | A 1-2 |
| Kingston Rd | SC | 49 | A-F 3-6 |
| Kingston Rd | T | 15 | B-F 5-6 |
| Kingsview Blvd | ET | 38 | E-F 5-6 |
| Kingsview Blvd | ET | 38 | E-F 6 |
| Kingsway, The | ET | 24 | D-E 1-2 |
| Kingsway, The | ET | 26 | A-C 4-6 |
| Kingswell Cr | SC | 27 | A 5 |
| Kingswood Rd | T | 13 | F 5 |
| Kingswood Rd | T | 15 | E 5 |
| Kinora Dr | NY | 18 | D-E 6 |
| Kinloss Rd | ET | 28 | A 1 |
| Kinnie Ct | NY | 20 | B 3 |
| Kinsdale Blvd | ET | 24 | E-F 5 |
| Kinsdale La | ET | 24 | E 5 |
| Kinsmen Gt | SC | 37 | B 3 |
| Kintail Rd | NY | 30 | C 5 |
| Kintyre Av | T | 5 | D 6 |
| Kipling Av | ET | 22 | A 1-6 |
| Kipling Av | ET | 24 | A 1-6 |
| Kipling Av | ET | 32 | F 1-4 |
| Kipling Av | ET | 34 | F 1-6 |
| Kipling Av | ET | 36 | F 1-6 |
| Kipling Av | ET | 38 | F 1-6 |
| Kipling Av | ET | 40 | F 1-6 |
| Kippendavie | T | 13 | D 6 |
| Kippendavie Av | T | 15 | D 6 |
| Kipping Dr | Y | 16 | E 6 |
| Kirah Ct | NY | 28 | F 5 |
| Kirby Rd | NY | 28 | F 4 |
| Kirk Bradden Rd E | ET | 24 | D-E 4-5 |
| Kirkdale Cr | NY | 30 | C 5 |
| Kirkdene Dr | SC | 47 | D-E 4 |
| Kirker Av | SC | 37 | E 1-2 |
| Kirkhams Rd | SC | 51 | B-E 5-6 |
| Kirkland Blvd | NY | 8 | B-C 6 |
| Kirknewton Rd | Y | 16 | F 4 |
| Kirkside Ct | ET | 40 | E 2 |
| Kirkton Rd | NY | 8 | A 3 |
| Kirkwood Rd | NY | 9 | F 3 |
| Kirtling Pl | NY | 9 | E 3 |
| Kiskadee Dr | ET | 40 | D-E 4 |
| Kiswick St | T | 5 | F 4-5 |
| Kitchener Av | Y | 16 | E-F 4 |
| Kitchener Rd | SC | 47 | A-B 1-2 |
| Kite Hawkway | NY | 10 | B 1 |
| Kitson Dr | SC | 25 | F 1 |
| Kittery Blvd | SC | 31 | E 5 |
| Kittiwake Av | ET | 40 | D-E 4 |
| Kliburn Pl | ET | 28 | B 2-3 |
| Klondike Dr | NY | 30 | D 1 |
| Knight St | EY | 15 | B 2-3 |
| Knighton Dr | NY | 17 | E-F 1-2 |
| Knightsbridge Rd | SC | 27 | A 5 |
| Knightswood Rd | NY | 9 | B 4-5 |
| Knob Hill Dr | NY | 28 | D 4-5 |
| Knockbolt Cr | SC | 31 | E-F 4 |
| Knoll Dr | ET | 26 | E 4 |
| Knollview Cr | NY | 11 | E 4 |
| Knollwood St | NY | 9 | C 2-3 |
| Knowland Dr | ET | 26 | D-E 4 |
| Knowlton Dr | SC | 37 | C 4 |
| Knox Av | NY | 30 | B 2 |
| Knox Av | T | 15 | A 6 |
| Knox Av | T | 13 | D 1 |
| Kodiak Cr | NY | 20 | F 5-6 |
| Kollar Dr | SC | 37 | D 1-2 |
| Koning Ct | SC | 47 | B 4 |
| Koos Rd | ET | 34 | C 3 |
| Kootenay Cr | SC | 37 | A 2 |
| Korol Av | ET | 26 | C 1 |
| Koven Pl | NY | 21 | C-D 5 |
| Krieger Cr | NY | 8 | A 5 |
| Kris Ct | ET | 34 | B 1 |
| Kuhl Av | ET | 36 | E 4 |
| Kylemore Cr | ET | 26 | C 3 |

## L

| Street | Muni | Map | Grid |
|---|---|---|---|
| La Dolce Dr | NY | 16 | A 2 |
| La Peer Blvd | SC | 31 | B 2-3 |
| La Plante Av | T | 4 | F 5 |
| La Rose Av | ET | 26 | B-E 2 |
| La Rush Dr | ET | 26 | D-E 2 |
| La Scala La | T | 4 | F 4 |
| Labatt Av | T | 5 | C 6 |
| Laburnham Av | ET | 32 | E-F 4 |
| Lace Fernway | NY | 21 | A 3 |
| Lacewood Ct | NY | 19 | C-D 4-5 |
| Lacey Av | NY | 16 | D 4 |
| Lachine Ct | ET | 36 | C 4 |
| Lackman St | ET | 26 | B 2 |
| Laconia Dr | NY | 10 | D 2 |
| Lactonia St | ET | 28 | B-C 2 |
| Ladbrooke Rd | ET | 36 | E-F 2 |
| Ladner Dr | NY | 21 | E 6 |
| Lady Bank Rd | ET | 24 | B 6 |
| Lady Bower Cr | SC | 41 | F 4 |
| Lady Churchill St | SC | 31 | F 3 |
| Lady Fernway | NY | 21 | B 4 |
| Lady Sarah Ct | SC | 41 | B 3 |
| Lady York Av | NY | 18 | F 3-4 |
| Ladyfield Ct | NY | 18 | C 1 |
| Ladykirk Av | T | 15 | A 6 |
| Ladysbridge Dr | SC | 39 | F 5-6 |
| Ladyshot Cr | NY | 20 | B-C 5 |
| Ladysmith Av | T | 15 | A 3-4 |
| Ladywood Dr | ET | 30 | B 5 |
| Lafferty St | ET | 36 | A 6 |
| Lagos Rd | ET | 30 | A 6 |
| Lailey Cr | NY | 11 | B-C 4 |
| Laing St | T | 15 | A 6 |
| Laird Dr | EY | 7 | E 3-5 |
| Lake Cr | ET | 22 | C-D 4 |
| Lake Pr | ET | 32 | C-F 1 |
| Lake Shore Av | T | 2 | C-F 3-6 |
| Lake Shore Av | T | 3 | A-B 4-6 |
| Lake Shore Blvd E | T | 3 | A-B 2 |

| STREET NAME | MUNICIPALITY | MAP NO | MAP AREA |
|---|---|---|---|
| Lake Shore Blvd E | T | 3 | D-F 1-2 |
| Lake Shore Blvd E | T | 13 | D-F 1 |
| Lake Shore Blvd W | ET | 22 | A-F 1-4 |
| Lake Shore Blvd W | ET | 32 | D-F 4-5 |
| Lake Shore Blvd W | T | 14 | A-D 6 |
| Lake Shore Blvd W | T | 2 | A-E 2-3 |
| Lake Shore Blvd W | T | 12 | B-C 2-3 |
| Lake Shore Dr | ET | 22 | A-C 4-5 |
| Lakehill Cr | SC | 25 | F 5 |
| Lakehurst Cr | SC | 25 | D 4 |
| Lakehurst Dr | SC | 25 | D 4 |
| Lakeland Cr | SC | 39 | E 5 |
| Lakeland Dr | ET | 30 | A 5 |
| Lakeridge Dr | SC | 47 | F 2 |
| Lakeshore Rd E | M | 32 | B 5 |
| Lakeside Av | SC | 25 | C 5 |
| Lakeview Av | T | 4 | B 5 |
| Lakewood Av | SC | 25 | E 3 |
| Lalton Pl | SC | 47 | A 3 |
| Lamay Cr | SC | 51 | A-B 4 |
| Lamb Av | T | 15 | A 3-4 |
| Lambert Av | T | 16 | E 6 |
| Lambertlodge Av | T | 4 | B 2 |
| Lamberton Blvd | NY | 20 | B-C 4-5 |
| Lambeth Ct | ET | 26 | C 6 |
| Lambeth Rd | ET | 24 | C 1 |
| Lambeth Rd | ET | 26 | C 6 |
| Lambeth Sq | SC | 31 | A 1 |
| Lambton Av | Y | 16 | A-B 4 |
| Lambton Av | Y | 26 | F 4 |
| Lamella Rd | ET | 30 | A 4 |
| Lamont Av | NY | 28 | E 5 |
| Lamont Av | SC | 29 | E 1 |
| Lamont Av | Y | 28 | E 5 |
| L'Amoreaux Cr | SC | 31 | B-C 3 |
| Lamport Av | T | 5 | B 3 |
| Lanark Av | Y | 6 | A-B 4 |
| Lanbrooke Av | NY | 10 | D 3 |
| Lancaster Av | T | 5 | A 5 |
| Lancefield Av | SC | 27 | B 4 |
| Landfair Cr | SC | 37 | C 2 |
| Landigo Dr | ET | 36 | E 1 |
| Landour Av | Y | 26 | C 1 |
| Landron Cr | ET | 26 | B 3 |
| Landry Av | SC | 25 | B 3 |
| Landseer Rd | SC | 27 | D-E 3 |
| Lanewood Cr | SC | 31 | A 4 |
| Lang St | T | 13 | D 1 |
| Langbourne Pl | NY | 19 | A 6 |
| Langdale Ct | NY | 20 | B 4 |
| Langden Av | Y | 16 | A-B 4-5 |
| Langemark Av | T | 4 | A 5 |
| Langevin Cr | SC | 49 | F 6 |
| Langfield Ct | ET | 40 | F 2-3 |
| Langford Av | EY | 5 | F 3 |
| Langford Av | T | 5 | F 3 |
| Langholm Dr | NY | 18 | C 2 |
| Langley Av | T | 5 | D-E 5 |
| Langmuir Cr | Y | 24 | E-F 2-3 |
| Langmuir Gdns | Y | 24 | F 2 |
| Langside Av | NY | 28 | E 4-5 |
| Langton Av | T | 9 | B 5 |
| Lankin Blvd | EY | 15 | B 3 |
| Lanni Ct | ET | 28 | B 5 |
| Lanor Av | ET | 32 | D-F 2 |
| Lansbury Dr | SC | 41 | B 3 |
| Lansdowne Av | NY | 16 | F 1-2 |
| Lansdowne Av | T | 14 | E-F 1-6 |
| Lansing Sq | NY | 19 | F 1 |
| Lansing Sq | NY | 29 | A 1 |
| Lantana Cr | NY | 17 | F 2 |
| Lantos Ct | NY | 18 | A-B 4 |
| Lanyard Rd | NY | 30 | C-D 4 |
| Lapp St | Y | 16 | E 6 |
| Lappin Av | T | 14 | E-F 2 |
| Lapsley Rd | SC | 39 | E 1 |
| Lapworth Cr | SC | 31 | D 2 |
| Larabee Cr | NY | 19 | C-D 4 |
| Larch St | T | 4 | E 6 |
| Larchmere Av | NY | 30 | A-B 6 |
| Larchmount Av | T | 3 | F 1 |
| Larchwood Rd | NY | 30 | B-C 4 |
| Laredo Ct | NY | 11 | B-C 3 |
| Largo La | SC | 37 | A 2 |
| Lariviere Rd | NY | 10 | F 4 |
| Lark St | T | 15 | C 6 |
| Larkfield Dr | NY | 9 | F 6 |
| Larkhall Av | SC | 37 | A 4 |
| Larkin Av | T | 14 | A 4 |
| Larkin Av | T | 24 | F 5 |
| Larksong Ct | NY | 17 | E 3 |
| Larkspur La | NY | 19 | B 6 |
| Larmere Ct | SC | 25 | D 1 |
| Larratt St | T | 6 | E 4 |
| Larstone Av | ET | 24 | B-C 5 |
| Larwood Blvd | SC | 25 | E 5-6 |
| Lascelles Blvd | T | 5 | F 3-4 |
| Lash Ct | SC | 49 | B 4-5 |
| Laskay Cr | NY | 20 | A-B 3 |
| Latham Av | T | 5 | E 2-3 |
| Latimer Av | T | 4 | A 6 |
| Latton Rd | ET | 34 | D 3-4 |
| Lauder Av | T | 4 | A 1 |
| Lauder Av | Y | 6 | A 4-6 |
| Lauderdale Dr | NY | 9 | D-E 2-3 |
| Laughton Av | M | 32 | A-B 2 |
| Laughton Av | T | 14 | E 1-2 |
| Laura Rd | NY | 30 | F 5-6 |
| Laura Secord Walk | SC | 29 | C 5 |
| Lauralynn Cr | SC | 31 | F 5-6 |
| Laurel Av | ET | 34 | E 2-3 |
| Laurel Av | SC | 27 | E 5-6 |
| Laurel Gr | ET | 34 | E 3 |
| Laurelcrest Av | NY | 8 | B-C 2 |
| Laureleaf Rd S | NY | 11 | E 1 |
| Laurelwood Cr | ET | 26 | B 2 |
| Lauren Ct | NY | 7 | C 2 |
| Laurence Av W | NY | 26 | D-E 1 |
| Laurence Av W | NY | 26 | E-F 1 |
| Laurentia Cr | NY | 8 | C 3-4 |
| Laurentide Dr | NY | 19 | C-D 3-4 |
| Laurie Shepway | NY | 21 | A 6 |
| Laurier Av | T | 5 | B 4 |
| Lausanne Cr | SC | 47 | A 3 |
| Lavender Rd | NY | 16 | D 5 |
| Laver Rd | ET | 34 | A 1 |
| Lavery Tr | SC | 49 | E 3 |
| Lavington Dr | ET | 36 | E-F 1 |
| Lavinia Av | T | 14 | A 4 |
| Lawlor Av | T | 15 | F 4-5 |
| Lawndale Rd | SC | 37 | C 4 |
| Lawnhurst Blvd | T | 6 | C 2-3 |
| Lawnmere Cr | SC | 39 | A 1 |
| Lawnside Dr | NY | 18 | A 5 |
| Lawnview Dr | NY | 11 | C 4 |
| Lawrence Av | NY | 16 | A-F 1 |
| Lawrence Av E | NY | 17 | A-F 1 |
| Lawrence Av E | NY | 19 | A-F 6 |
| Lawrence Av E | NY | 7 | B-F 1 |
| Lawrence Av E | NY | 9 | A-F 6 |
| Lawrence Av E | SC | 27 | A-F 1 |
| Lawrence Av E | SC | 29 | A-F 6 |
| Lawrence Av E | SC | 37 | A-F 1 |
| Lawrence Av E | SC | 39 | A-F 6 |
| Lawrence Av E | SC | 47 | A-F 1 |
| Lawrence Av E | ET | 27 | D-F 5-6 |
| Lawrence Av E | SC | 49 | A-F 6 |
| Lawrence Ct | T | 7 | A-B 1 |
| Lawrence Av W | NY | 18 | A-F 6 |
| Lawrence Av W | NY | 6 | A-E 1 |
| Lawrence Av W | NY | 8 | A-E 6 |
| Lawrence Av W | T | 6 | E-F 1 |
| Lawrence Av W | T | 8 | E-F 6 |
| Lawrence Av W | T | 7 | B 1 |
| Lawrence Service Rd N | NY | 18 | E 6 |
| Laws St | T | 4 | E 3 |
| Lawson Rd | SC | 47 | D 4 |
| Lawson Rd | SC | 49 | D-E 5 |
| Lawton Blvd | T | 6 | F 5-6 |
| Laxford Av | SC | 31 | F 5-6 |
| Laxis Av | NY | 26 | F 3 |
| Laxton Av | T | 12 | B 1 |
| Le Page Ct | NY | 20 | D-E 4 |
| Lea Av | T | 7 | D-E 5 |
| Leacock Cr | NY | 9 | F 5 |
| Leacrest Rd | EY | 7 | D-E 5-6 |
| Leacroft Cr | NY | 9 | E-F 6 |
| Leadale Av | EY | 7 | D 5-6 |
| Leadenhall Rd | NY | 11 | C 4 |
| Leader La | T | 3 | A 1 |
| Leading Rd | ET | 40 | D 1-2 |
| Leaf Villaway | NY | 11 | F 5 |
| Leafield Dr | SC | 31 | A 4 |
| Leafield Dr S | SC | 31 | A 4 |
| Leafy Woodway | NY | 17 | F 4 |
| Leagate Rd | ET | 34 | E 3 |
| Leagrove Cr | SC | 27 | B 5 |
| Leahann Dr | SC | 27 | D 2 |
| Leahurst Dr | SC | 27 | A-B 5 |
| Leameadow Way | SC | 49 | E 2 |
| Leamington Av | ET | 24 | C 4 |
| Leander Ct | NY | 15 | E 1 |
| Learmont Dr | ET | 36 | E-F 1 |
| Leaside Park Dr | EY | 7 | F 5 |
| Leavenworth Cr | ET | 34 | C 3 |
| Leavey Ct | NY | 11 | F 2 |
| Lebos Rd | NY | 21 | C 2-3 |
| Lebovic Av | SC | 27 | B 4-5 |
| Ledbury St | NY | 6 | E 1 |
| Ledbury St | NY | 8 | E 5-6 |
| Ledge Rd | SC | 37 | C 6 |
| Leduc Dr | ET | 28 | A-B 2-3 |
| Lee Av | T | 13 | E 5-6 |
| Lee Av | T | 15 | E 5-6 |
| Lee Centre Dr | SC | 39 | B 2 |
| Leeds St | T | 4 | B 3 |
| Leeswood Cr | SC | 31 | F 4 |
| Leeward Glenway | NY | 17 | C 5 |
| Legacy Cr | NY | 9 | C 2 |
| Legato Ct | NY | 19 | B 5 |
| Leggett Av | ET | 26 | D-E 2 |
| Legion Rd | ET | 22 | E 2 |
| Legume Rd | NY | 30 | C 4 |
| Lehar Cr | NY | 21 | A-B 3 |
| Leigh St | Y | 16 | B 5-6 |
| Leighton Ct | ET | 40 | E 2 |
| Leila La | NY | 8 | B 5 |
| Leisure La | SC | 25 | E 2 |
| Leith Ct | ET | 26 | E 4 |
| Leith Hill Rd | NY | 21 | B 5-6 |
| Leith Pl | T | 9 | A 6 |
| Lejune Rd | SC | 29 | D 1-2 |
| Leland Av | ET | 24 | B-C 4 |
| Lemay Rd | T | 7 | C 5 |
| Lemonwood Dr | ET | 26 | D-E 4 |
| Lemsford Rd | ET | 28 | B 3 |
| Lennox St | T | 4 | C-D 4 |
| Lenore Av | T | 3 | B 5 |
| Lenthall Av | SC | 41 | D 6 |
| Lenworth Dr | M | 34 | A 4-5 |
| Leo Starway | NY | 19 | D 1 |
| Leona Dr | NY | 9 | B 1 |
| Leonard Av | T | 4 | D 5 |
| Leonard Cir | T | 15 | E 5 |
| Leonard Pl | T | 4 | D 5 |
| Leopold St | T | 12 | B 1 |
| Lepus Starway | NY | 19 | D 1-2 |
| Leroy Av | EY | 15 | A 3 |
| Lescon Rd | NY | 21 | A-B 5 |
| Lesgay Cr | NY | 21 | A 4-5 |
| Leslie Garden La | T | 5 | F 6 |
| Leslie St | NY | 11 | F 1-6 |
| Leslie St | NY | 17 | A 1-3 |
| Leslie St | NY | 19 | A 1-6 |
| Leslie St | NY | 21 | A 1-6 |
| Leslie St | T | 7 | F 1-3 |
| Leslie St | T | 9 | F 1-6 |
| Leslie St | T | 15 | A 4-6 |
| Leslie St | T | 3 | F 1-2 |
| Leslie St | T | 5 | F 1-6 |
| Leslie St | T | 13 | D 1-2 |
| Lesmar Dr | ET | 36 | F 1 |
| Lesmill Rd | NY | 19 | A-B 2-3 |
| Lesmount Av | EY | 15 | A 1-2 |
| Lessard Av | ET | 24 | E 3 |
| Lesskim Ct | SC | 31 | F 4 |
| Lester Av | Y | 16 | D 3 |
| Lesterwood Cr | SC | 29 | F 5 |
| L'Estrange Pl | Y | 24 | E 2-3 |
| Leswyn Rd | NY | 18 | E 6 |
| Letchworth Cr | NY | 18 | B-C 6 |
| Lethbridge Av | ET | 26 | C 1 |
| Leuty Av | T | 13 | E 6 |
| Leuty Av | T | 15 | E 6 |
| Leverhume Cr | SC | 37 | E 3 |
| Lewes Cr | NY | 7 | C 1 |
| Lewis St | T | 3 | D 1 |
| Lewiston Rd | SC | 29 | D 4 |
| Lexfield Av | NY | 18 | A-B 2-3 |
| Lexington Av | ET | 40 | D-E 2-3 |
| Leyton Av | SC | 25 | B 2-4 |
| Lia Cr | NY | 19 | B 3 |
| Liberty St | T | 2 | A 2 |
| Lichee Dr | SC | 29 | B 5-6 |
| Lichen Pl | NY | 19 | E 4 |
| Lido Rd | NY | 30 | E 6 |
| Lightbourn Av | T | 14 | F 1-2 |
| Lighthall Cr | SC | 41 | E 4 |
| Lightwood Dr | ET | 30 | A 5 |
| Lilac Av | NY | 28 | C 3 |
| Lilian Dr | SC | 29 | B 5-6 |
| Lillian St | NY | 11 | B 1-2 |
| Lillian St | T | 7 | A 4 |
| Lillibet Rd | ET | 24 | C 4-5 |
| Lillington Av | SC | 25 | D 3 |
| Lilywood Rd | NY | 6 | A 2 |
| Lime Treeway | NY | 10 | C 2 |
| Limerick Av | NY | 28 | E 4 |
| Limestone Cr | NY | 20 | E 1 |
| Limevale Cr | SC | 47 | A 2 |
| Limewood St | NY | 19 | B 6 |
| Limoges Cr | NY | 11 | D 1 |

L

| Name | Mun. | Page | Grid | No. |
|---|---|---|---|---|
| Lincoln Av | T | 14 | A-B | 2 |
| Lincoln Woods Ct | ET | 26 | C | 5 |
| Lincolnshire Blvd | M | 32 | B | 2-3 |
| Lindal Av | SC | 27 | A | 6 |
| Linden Av | SC | 27 | E | 5-6 |
| Linden St | T | 5 | A-B | 4 |
| Linderwood Dr | SC | 49 | F | 4 |
| Lindner St | T | 14 | F | 4 |
| Lindsey Av | T | 4 | A | 4 |
| Lindsey Av | T | 4 | A | 4 |
| Lindylou Rd | NY | 30 | C-D | 4 |
| Linelle St | NY | 8 | F | 2 |
| Ling Rd | SC | 47 | B | 1 |
| Lingarde Dr | SC | 27 | B | 2 |
| Links Rd The | NY | 9 | A-B | 2-3 |
| Linkwood La | NY | 17 | C-D | 4-5 |
| Linnsmore Cr | EY | 15 | A | 1-3 |
| Linnsmore Cr | T | 15 | A | 3 |
| Linstead Ct | ET | 26 | A | 3 |
| Linthurst Av | NY | 18 | B | 2 |
| Linton Av | SC | 15 | F | 4 |
| Linton Av | SC | 25 | A | 4 |
| Linus Rd | NY | 21 | B | 3-4 |
| Linville Rd | SC | 39 | E | 5 |
| Linwood Av | SC | 31 | E | 5 |
| Lioda Dr | SC | 25 | B | 1 |
| Lionel Heights Cr | NY | 19 | E-F | 5 |
| Lionhead Tr | SC | 49 | E | 1-2 |
| Lippincott St | T | 4 | D | 4-5 |
| Lippincott St E | NY | 26 | F | 2 |
| Lippincott St W | NY | 26 | E-F | 2 |
| Lipton Av | T | 5 | E | 3 |
| Lisa Rd | SC | 39 | E-F | 6 |
| Lisburn Cr | NY | 21 | B-D | 5 |
| Lisgar Dr | T | 4 | A | 4-5 |
| Lisgar St | T | 2 | A | 1 |
| Lisgar St | T | 4 | A | 5-6 |
| Lismore Rd | T | 6 | E | 3 |
| Lissom Cr | NY | 10 | D | 2 |
| Lister Dr | NY | 10 | D | 2-3 |
| List Gr | NY | 21 | A | 3 |
| Litchfield Ct | ET | 40 | E | 3 |
| Little Av | Y | 28 | E | 4 |
| Little Blvd | Y | 16 | E | 3-4 |
| Little Norway Cr | T | 2 | C-D | 3 |
| Little Rock Dr | SC | 37 | B | 4 |
| Littleborough Ct | SC | 49 | E | 3 |
| Littledean Ct | NY | 30 | B | 2-3 |
| Littleleaf Dr | SC | 41 | D-E | 5-6 |
| Littleriver Cr | ET | 40 | E | 4 |
| Littles Rd | SC | 51 | B | 4-5 |
| Littlewood Cr | ET | 36 | C | 4 |
| Littoral Pl | ET | 26 | E | 2 |
| Liveoak Dr | M | 32 | A-B | 3 |
| Liverpool St | Y | 16 | A | 6 |
| Livingston Rd | SC | 37 | E | 2-4 |
| Livingstone Av | Y | 6 | A-B | 3 |
| Livonia Pl | SC | 39 | F | 3 |
| Lloyd Av | T | 14 | D | 1 |
| Lloyd George Av | ET | 32 | C | 4 |
| Lloyd Manor Rd | ET | 36 | E-F | 3-6 |
| Lloydminster Cr | NY | 11 | B-C | 1-2 |
| Lobb Av | T | 4 | B | 6 |
| Lochinvar Dr | NY | 19 | C-D | 3 |
| Lochleven Dr | SC | 37 | C | 4 |
| Lochway Ct | ET | 34 | F | 2 |
| Lockdare St | SC | 39 | B-C | 1 |
| Lockerbie Av | NY | 28 | F | 5 |
| Lockheed Blvd | ET | 28 | D | 6 |
| Lockie Av | SC | 31 | E | 6 |
| Lockington Ct | NY | 30 | C | 4 |
| Lockmere Terr | NY | 21 | A | 4-5 |
| Lockport Ct | ET | 34 | E | 5 |
| Locksley Av | NY | 6 | A | 2-3 |
| Locksley Av | Y | 6 | A | 3-4 |
| Lockton Ct | NY | 11 | E | 6 |
| Lockwood Rd | T | 15 | C | 6 |
| Locust St | Y | 16 | A-B | 3 |
| Lodestar Rd | NY | 20 | F | 4-5 |
| Lofthouse Sq | SC | 31 | B | 3 |
| Lofty Hillway | NY | 21 | B | 1 |
| Log Fernway | NY | 21 | B | 3-4 |
| Logan Av | EY | 5 | E | 2-5 |
| Logan Av | T | 5 | E | 3-6 |
| Logan Av | T | 5 | E | 2-6 |
| Loganberry Cr | NY | 21 | B | 1 |
| Logandale Rd | NY | 11 | A | 4 |
| Logie Pl | T | 8 | B | 6 |
| Logstone Cr | SC | 39 | E | 2-3 |
| Logwood Ct | ET | 34 | A | 2 |
| Loire Ct | ET | 34 | F | 2 |
| Lois Av | NY | 6 | A-B | 1-2 |
| Lola Rd | T | 4 | B | 6 |
| Loma Rd | ET | 24 | C | 6 |
| Lomar Dr | NY | 30 | F | 6 |
| Lombard St | T | 3 | A | 1 |
| Lombardy Cr | SC | 27 | F | 4-5 |
| Lomond Dr | ET | 24 | B | 3 |
| Lonborough Av | Y | 16 | D-E | 3 |
| London Green Ct | NY | 20 | A-B | 4-5 |
| London St | T | 4 | C | 3 |
| Londonderry Blvd | M | 32 | A | 3-4 |
| Loney Av | NY | 28 | F | 3 |
| Long Branch Av | ET | 32 | E | 4-5 |
| Long Cr | T | 15 | E | 5 |
| Long Island Cr | SC | 47 | F | 3 |
| Longboat Av | T | 3 | A-B | 2-3 |
| Longbourne Dr | ET | 36 | D-E | 2 |
| Longbow Sq | SC | 31 | B | 2 |
| Longfellow Rd | ET | 26 | A | 1 |
| Longfield Rd | ET | 36 | F | 4 |
| Longford Cr | SC | 31 | A-B | 4 |
| Longhope Pl | NY | 21 | A | 6 |
| Longhouse Pl | SC | 39 | C | 6 |
| Longmore St | NY | 11 | B | 3-6 |
| Longspur Rd | EY | 17 | C | 6 |
| Longsword Dr | SC | 41 | B | 3 |
| Longview Dr | NY | 28 | F | 5 |
| Longwood Dr | NY | 9 | F | 4 |
| Lonsdale Rd | T | 6 | C-F | 6 |
| Lonsmount Dr | T | 6 | D | 5-6 |
| Lonsmount Dr | Y | 6 | D | 6 |
| Lonson Blvd | SC | 25 | B | 4 |
| Lonsmore Dr | NY | 18 | D | 5-1 |
| Loomis Ct | NY | 20 | C | 5 |
| Loradeen Cr | SC | 41 | E | 4 |
| Lorahill Rd | ET | 24 | C | 4-5 |
| Lord Roberts Rd | NY | 9 | A-C | 1-2 |
| Lord Seaton Rd | NY | 9 | A-C | 1-2 |
| Lord Sydenham Ct | SC | 31 | B-C | 4 |
| Loreland Av | M | 34 | A | 6 |
| Lorene Dr | ET | 34 | D-E | 2 |
| Lorindale Av | T | 8 | F | 6 |
| Lormar Dr | ET | 34 | D | 2-3 |
| Lorna Rae Blvd | SC | 31 | F | 1-2 |
| Lorne Av | T | 4 | E | 6 |
| Lorne Bruce Dr | NY | 18 | B | 4 |
| Lorraine Av | SC | 27 | E-F | 4 |
| Lorraine Dr | NY | 10 | E-F | 4 |
| Lorraine Gdns | ET | 34 | E-F | 1-2 |
| Lotherton Pathway | NY | 16 | E | 1-2 |
| Lothian Av | ET | 24 | B | 3-4 |
| Lotus Ct | NY | 21 | A | 3 |
| Louisa St E | T | 22 | E | 2 |
| Louisa St | T | 4 | F | 4 |
| Louise Av | Y | 6 | C | 6 |
| Lount St | T | 15 | A | 4 |
| Louvain Av | T | 5 | E-F | 6 |
| Louvain St | Y | 16 | B | 5 |
| Love Cr | T | 15 | D-E | 5 |
| Lovekin Gr | SC | 31 | D-E | 4 |
| Lovell Av | SC | 49 | C-D | 2 |
| Lovering Rd | SC | 31 | D-E | 4 |
| Lovilla Blvd | NY | 28 | D-E | 3-4 |
| Low Meadoway | NY | 21 | C-D | 1 |
| Lowbank Cr | NY | 11 | E-F | 1 |
| Lowcrest Blvd | SC | 29 | B | 2 |
| Lowell Av | SC | 37 | B | 5 |
| Lower Jarvis St | T | 2 | F | 3 |
| Lower Jarvis St | T | 3 | A | 1-2 |
| Lower Links Rd | NY | 9 | A-B | 3 |
| Lower Portland St | T | 2 | D | 2 |
| Lower Sherbourne St | T | 3 | A-B | 1-3 |
| Lower Simcoe St | T | 2 | E | 3 |
| Lower Village Gt | T | 6 | D | 5-6 |
| Lowesmoor Av | NY | 8 | C | 2 |
| Lowry Sq | SC | 51 | A | 6 |
| Lowther Av | T | 4 | D-E | 3 |
| Loyalist Rd | ET | 24 | B | 2 |
| Lozoway Dr | SC | 27 | D | 2-3 |
| Lucania Pl | SC | 31 | B | 2 |
| Lucerne Ct | SC | 39 | D | 6 |
| Lucifer Dr | NY | 21 | E | 4 |
| Lucinda Ct | NY | 18 | B | 1 |
| Lucy Av | SC | 25 | A | 4 |
| Ludgate Dr | ET | 30 | A | 6 |
| Ludlow Av | NY | 21 | E | 4 |
| Ludstone Dr | ET | 36 | E-F | 1 |
| Luella St | SC | 37 | C-D | 3 |
| Lukow Terr | T | 14 | E | 5 |
| Lumberdale Av | T | 14 | E-F | 5 |
| Lumley Av | T | 5 | E | 4 |
| Lumsden Av | EY | 15 | C-E | 2 |
| Lund Av | NY | 30 | B | 6 |
| Lundy Av | Y | 24 | E | 1 |
| Lunness Rd | ET | 32 | D | 2-3 |
| Lunsfield Cr | SC | 41 | A | 4 |
| Lupin Dr | SC | 29 | B | 3 |
| Lurgan Dr | NY | 10 | D-E | 4 |
| Luton Gt | NY | 11 | E | 3 |
| Luttrell Av | T | 15 | F | 3-4 |
| Luverne Av | NY | 8 | B-C | 4 |
| Lyall Av | T | 15 | E-F | 5 |
| Lydia Ct | T | 15 | A | 4 |
| Lydon Av | Y | 26 | E-F | 6 |
| Lyme Regis Cr | SC | 25 | E-F | 5 |
| Lympstone Av | T | 7 | A-B | 1 |
| Lynch Rd | NY | 21 | A-B | 4 |
| Lyncroft Dr | SC | 47 | A | 3 |
| Lynd Av | T | 14 | E | 4-5 |
| Lyndale Dr | NY | 9 | B | 1 |
| Lyndhurst Av | T | 4 | D | 1-2 |
| Lyndhurst Ct | T | 4 | D | 2 |
| Lynedock Cr | NY | 19 | E-F | 3 |
| Lynmont Rd | ET | 40 | D-E | 4-5 |
| Lynn Gate Av | SC | 29 | C | 1 |
| Lynn Rd | SC | 25 | B | 4 |
| Lynnbrook Dr | SC | 39 | B | 4-5 |
| Lynndale Rd | SC | 25 | A | 5 |
| Lynnford Dr | ET | 34 | D-E | 4 |
| Lynngrove Av | ET | 24 | B-C | 2 |
| Lynnhaven Rd | NY | 8 | B | 5-6 |
| Lynnvalley Cr | SC | 19 | F | 6 |
| Lynvalley Cr | SC | 29 | A | 5 |
| Lynwood Av | T | 4 | E | 1 |
| Lyon Ct | Y | 6 | B | 3 |
| Lyon Heights Rd | SC | 29 | F | 5-6 |
| Lyonsgate Dr | NY | 8 | D | 3 |
| Lyra Starway | NY | 19 | D | 1 |
| Lyric La | NY | 9 | F | 4-5 |
| Lysander Ct | SC | 41 | B | 3-4 |
| Lytton Blvd | NY | 6 | C-D | 2 |
| Lytton Blvd | T | 6 | D-F | 2 |

## M

| Name | Mun. | Page | Grid | No. |
|---|---|---|---|---|
| Mabelle Av | ET | 24 | A-B | 2-3 |
| Maberley Cr | SC | 47 | D-E | 5 |
| Macaulay Av | T | 14 | E | 3 |
| MacDonald Av | Y | 28 | E-F | 6 |
| Macdonald St | ET | 22 | C | 3 |
| Macdonell Av | T | 14 | E | 5-6 |
| MacDuff Cr | SC | 37 | A | 5 |
| MacGregor Av | T | 14 | A-B | 2 |
| Machockie Rd | EY | 15 | B | 1-2 |
| Mack Av | SC | 25 | D | 3 |
| MacKay Av | T | 14 | F | 1 |
| MacKay St | T | 4 | A | 1 |
| Mackenzie Cr | T | 4 | A | 5-6 |
| Mackinac Cr | SC | 37 | A | 4 |
| Macklem Av | T | 4 | A | 5 |
| Macklingate Ct | SC | 41 | A | 4 |
| MacLean Av | T | 13 | E | 5-6 |
| MacLean Av | T | 15 | E | 6 |
| MacLennan Av | T | 5 | B | 2 |
| MacLeod St | NY | 18 | D | 4-5 |
| MacNaughton Rd | EY | 7 | D | 4-5 |
| MacPherson Av | T | 4 | D-E | 2 |
| Madawaska Av | NY | 11 | A-B | 1 |
| Madelaine Av | SC | 25 | A | 3 |
| Madeline Rd | NY | 10 | F | 4 |
| Madill St | ET | 28 | B-C | 6 |
| Madison Av | T | 4 | E | 2-3 |
| Madoc Dr | NY | 6 | C | 1 |
| Madonna Gdns | NY | 30 | B | 1 |
| Madras Cr | SC | 39 | F | 4-5 |
| Madrid St | SC | 39 | A | 4 |
| Madron Ct | NY | 20 | C | 4 |
| Mafeking Cr | SC | 39 | D | 4 |
| Magdalena Ct | ET | 40 | E | 1 |
| Magellan Dr | NY | 18 | B | 1-2 |
| Magnetic Dr | NY | 10 | A | 1-2 |
| Magnetic Dr | NY | 20 | F | 1 |
| Magnificent Rd | ET | 22 | B | 2-3 |
| Magnolia Av | SC | 27 | E | 5-6 |
| Magnum Way | SC | 49 | C | 2 |
| Magpie Cr | NY | 9 | F | 3 |
| Magwood Ct | Y | 24 | F | 1-2 |
| Mahoney Av | NY | 16 | A | 3 |
| Maida Vale | SC | 27 | D | 3 |
| Maidacroft Pl | ET | 26 | C | 3 |
| Maidstone St | NY | 18 | A | 4-5 |
| Main St | EY | 15 | E | 2-3 |
| Main St | T | 15 | E | 3-5 |
| Mainshep Rd | NY | 28 | D | 1 |
| Maitland Pl | T | 5 | A | 4 |
| Maitland St | T | 4 | F | 4 |
| Maitland St | T | 5 | A | 4 |
| Maitland Terr | T | 5 | A | 4-5 |
| Majestic Ct | NY | 6 | B | 1 |
| Major Oak Terr | SC | 41 | A-B | 4 |
| Major St | T | 4 | D | 4-5 |
| Malabar Pl | NY | 9 | F | 6 |
| Malamute Cr | SC | 29 | C | 1-2 |
| Malcolm Rd | EY | 7 | E | 5 |
| Mallaby Rd | NY | 11 | F | 2 |
| Mallard Rd | NY | 19 | B | 4 |
| Malley Rd | SC | 27 | B-C | 5 |

**M**

| STREET NAME | MUNICIPALITY | MAP NO | MAP AREA |
|---|---|---|---|
| Mallingham Ct | NY | 11 | C 6 |
| Mallon Av | T | 10 | B 6 |
| Mallory Cr | EY | 7 | D 6 |
| Mallory Gdns | T | 6 | D 6 |
| Mallow Rd | NY | 19 | B 6 |
| Malta St | SC | 25 | D-E 2 |
| Malvern St | SC | 41 | D 6 |
| Mammoth Hall Tr | SC | 41 | D-E 6 |
| Manadon Dr | NY | 10 | E 2 |
| Manaham Rd | SC | 20 | D 1-2 |
| Manchester Av | T | 4 | B 3 |
| Manchester St | ET | 22 | D 2 |
| Mandarin Rd | SC | 27 | F 6 |
| Mandarin Rd | SC | 37 | A 6 |
| Mandel Cr | NY | 11 | F 3 |
| Manderley Dr | SC | 25 | B 4 |
| Mandy St | NY | 20 | B 6 |
| Manfred Av | ET | 40 | E 2 |
| Mango Dr | NY | 11 | D-E 3 |
| Mangrove Rd | NY | 18 | B 6 |
| Manhattan Dr | SC | 29 | B-C 5-6 |
| Manilow St | SC | 31 | B 1 |
| Manitoba St | ET | 22 | D 1 |
| Manitou Blvd | T | 6 | C 2-3 |
| Maniza Rd | NY | 18 | F 2-3 |
| Mann Av | T | 7 | C 3 |
| Manning Av | T | 4 | C 2-6 |
| Manor Haven Rd | NY | 8 | B-C 5-6 |
| Manor Rd E | T | 7 | A-C 4-5 |
| Manor Rd W | T | 4 | F 4 |
| Manorcrest Dr | NY | 11 | C 3-4 |
| Manorglen Cr | SC | 29 | F 2 |
| Manorhampton Dr | ET | 26 | B-C 3 |
| Manorpark Ct | NY | 19 | A-B 1 |
| Manorwood Rd | SC | 39 | A 5 |
| Manresa La | NY | 18 | C 6 |
| Manse Rd | SC | 47 | B 1-3 |
| Manse Rd | SC | 49 | B 5-6 |
| Mansewood Gdns | SC | 47 | B-C 1 |
| Mansfield Av | T | 4 | E 4 |
| Mansion Av | SC | 25 | A 4 |
| Manston Rd | ET | 34 | B-C 6 |
| Manville Rd | SC | 27 | B-C 4-5 |
| Maple Av | T | 5 | B 3 |
| Maple Blvd | ET | 22 | B-C 4 |
| Maple Bush Av | NY | 28 | C 4 |
| Maple Gate Ct | ET | 34 | A 3 |
| Maple Grove Av | T | 14 | F 6 |
| Maple Leaf Dr | NY | 18 | B-D 5 |
| Maplebranch Path | ET | 28 | B 5-6 |
| Mapledawn Rd | ET | 34 | B 3 |
| Maplehurst Av | NY | 11 | A-B 6 |
| Maplelea Rd | SC | 49 | D 3 |
| Mapleview Av | T | 14 | B 2 |
| Maplewood Av | Y | 6 | B-C 6 |
| Marathon Cr | NY | 10 | D 2 |
| Marawa Ct | SC | 39 | E 4-5 |
| Marble Arch Cr | SC | 27 | B 2-3 |
| Marblehead Rd | ET | 26 | A 1 |
| Marblemount Cr | SC | 31 | B 6 |
| Marbury Cr | NY | 19 | B 2-3 |
| Marcel Rd | ET | 28 | A 3 |
| Marcella St | SC | 37 | E 1 |
| Marcelline Cr | NY | 11 | E 6 |
| Marchbank Ct | ET | 40 | B 2-3 |
| Marchington Cir | SC | 29 | A-B 4 |
| Marchmont Rd | T | 4 | E 2 |
| Marchwood Dr | NY | 8 | B 2 |
| Marcia Av | NY | 16 | E 1 |
| Marconi Ct | NY | 21 | B 1 |
| Marcos Blvd | SC | 39 | E-F 1-2 |
| Mare Cr | ET | 40 | C 5-6 |
| Marengo Av | SC | 27 | E 3 |
| Maresfield Dr | SC | 41 | B 2 |
| Maretta Av | SC | 27 | C 4 |
| Margaret Av | NY | 21 | E 5 |
| Margaret La | T | 14 | E 6 |
| Margaret Rose Ct | NY | 14 | B 2 |
| Margaret Rose Ct | Y | 26 | F 2 |
| Margate Cr | SC | 25 | B 3 |
| Margdon Rd | T | 14 | B 3 |
| Margrath Pl | ET | 36 | C 5 |
| Margueretta St | T | 4 | F 3-5 |
| Maria St | T | 14 | B 1 |
| Marianfeld Av | NY | 16 | F 1 |
| Maribeth Av | T | 5 | A-B 5 |
| Marigold Av | T | 3 | F 1 |
| Marilake Dr | SC | 29 | F 4 |
| Marilyn Av | SC | 31 | E 6 |
| Marilyn Dr | EY | 17 | D 6 |
| Marina Av | ET | 32 | D-E 4 |
| Marine Approach Dr | SC | 47 | D 6 |
| Marion St | T | 14 | D-E 6 |
| Marionville Dr | M | 32 | A 3 |
| Mariposa Av | Y | 16 | A 6 |
| Maris Shepway | NY | 21 | A 6 |
| Marisa Ct | NY | 21 | B 1 |
| Marjory Av | T | 5 | F 5-6 |
| Mark St | T | 5 | C 6 |
| Markay St | NY | 20 | B 6 |
| Markbrook La | ET | 30 | A 1 |
| Markbrook La | ET | 40 | F 1 |
| Markburn Ct | ET | 34 | A 2 |
| Markdale Av | Y | 6 | B-C 4-5 |
| Marker Ct | NY | 20 | C 6 |
| Market St | T | 3 | A 1-2 |
| Markhall Av | ET | 34 | E 4 |
| Markham Av | EY | 7 | D-E 4 |
| Markham Rd | SC | 37 | C-D 1-5 |
| Markham Rd | SC | 39 | C-D 1-6 |
| Markham Rd | SC | 41 | C-D 1-6 |
| Markham St | T | 4 | C 3-6 |
| Markland Dr | ET | 34 | A-B 2-4 |
| Markwood Cr | ET | 34 | B 3-4 |
| Marlawr Gt | SC | 39 | D 5 |
| Marlbank Rd | SC | 29 | C 2 |
| Marlborough Av | T | 4 | F 2 |
| Marlborough Pl | T | 4 | E-F 2 |
| Marlebon Rd | ET | 40 | D-E 2 |
| Marlee Av | NY | 6 | B 1-3 |
| Marlee Av | Y | 6 | B 3-4 |
| Marlena Dr | SC | 47 | A 1-2 |
| Marlington Dr | NY | 28 | F 3 |
| Marlow Av | EY | 15 | A 2-3 |
| Marlow Av | T | 15 | A 3 |
| Marmac Cr | M | 38 | C 5 |
| Marmaduke St | T | 14 | D-E 4 |
| Marmion Av | T | 10 | D 5 |
| Marmora St | NY | 28 | E 3 |
| Marmot St | T | 7 | B 4 |
| Maroon Millway | NY | 9 | D 3 |
| Marowyne Dr | NY | 21 | A 5 |
| Marquette Av | NY | 8 | C 4 |
| Marquis Av | T | 14 | F 6 |
| Marrakesh Dr | SC | 41 | B 4-5 |
| Mars Rd | ET | 40 | D 2 |
| Marsdale Cr | SC | 51 | B 4 |
| Marsh Grassway | NY | 30 | F 5 |
| Marsh Rd | SC | 25 | D 1 |
| Marsh Rd | SC | 27 | D 6 |
| Marsha Dr | SC | 29 | D 1-2 |
| Marshall Blvd | Y | 16 | A 4 |
| Marshall St | T | 14 | F 5 |
| Marshlynn Av | NY | 18 | A 6 |
| Marta Av | SC | 25 | D 1 |
| Martha Eaton Way | NY | 16 | B 2 |
| Marthclare Av | NY | 19 | E 6 |
| Martin Cr | T | 7 | B 5 |
| Martin Grove Rd | ET | 34 | E 1-3 |
| Martin Grove Rd | ET | 36 | E 1-6 |
| Martin Grove Rd | ET | 40 | E 1-6 |
| Martin Rd | T | 7 | B 5 |
| Martin Ross Av | NY | 20 | F 4 |
| Martin St | Y | 6 | A 5 |
| Martindale Rd | SC | 37 | B 5 |
| Martinview Ct | ET | 36 | E 6 |
| Martorino Dr | SC | 27 | D 4-5 |
| Marwill St | T | 4 | E 5 |
| Marwood Ct | T | 6 | B 2 |
| Marwood Rd | T | 6 | B 2-3 |
| Marydon Cr | SC | 31 | F 5-6 |
| Maryhill Dr | ET | 40 | F 2 |
| Maryland Blvd | EY | 15 | E 3 |
| Maryland Blvd | T | 15 | F 3 |
| Maryport Av | NY | 18 | C 1-2 |
| Mascot Pl | NY | 10 | C 4 |
| Mason Blvd | T | 6 | F 3-4 |
| Mason Rd | SC | 37 | C 4-5 |
| Massey Sq | EY | 15 | F 3 |
| Massey St | T | 2 | B 1 |
| Masseygrove Cr | ET | 40 | F 4 |
| Massie St | SC | 39 | C 1 |
| Massingham Rd | ET | 36 | E 4 |
| Matane Ct | SC | 29 | D 3 |
| Mathews Gt | NY | 28 | D 3-4 |
| Matilda St | T | 5 | D 6 |
| Mattari Ct | ET | 40 | C 4 |
| Mattawa Av | M | 34 | A-B 5-6 |
| Mattice Av | ET | 34 | F 2 |
| Mattson Rd | NY | 28 | F 3 |
| Maud St | T | 2 | D 1 |
| Maughan Cr | T | 15 | B-C 6 |
| Maureen Dr | NY | 11 | E 6 |
| Mavety St | T | 14 | C 2-3 |
| Maxim Cr | SC | 29 | D 4 |
| Maxine Rd | ET | 40 | F 1 |
| Maxome Av | NY | 11 | B-C 1-4 |
| Maxwell Av | T | 6 | F 3-4 |
| Maxwell St | NY | 10 | A-B 4-6 |
| May Sq | T | 5 | B 3 |
| May St | T | 5 | B 3 |
| Mayall Av | NY | 28 | F 2-3 |
| Maybank Av | T | 16 | B-C 6 |
| Mayberry Rd | NY | 30 | F 6 |
| Maybourne Av | SC | 25 | B 4 |
| Maybrook Dr | SC | 41 | C 2 |
| Maydolph Rd | ET | 34 | D-E 2 |
| Mayfair Av | T | 6 | D 3-4 |
| Mayfield Av | T | 14 | A 4 |
| Mayfield Av | T | 24 | F 4 |
| Mayflower Av | SC | 29 | B 3 |
| Mayhill Cr | SC | 37 | E 1 |
| Mayland Av | ET | 34 | B-C 3 |
| Maynard Av | T | 12 | B 1 |
| Mayo Dr | NY | 18 | B 4-5 |
| Maypole St | ET | 34 | E 4 |
| Maytree Rd | NY | 9 | B 4 |
| Maywood Pk | SC | 27 | D 5 |
| McAdam Av | NY | 18 | F 5 |
| McAllister Rd | NY | 8 | B-D 1 |
| McAlpine St | T | 4 | F 3 |
| McArthur St | ET | 28 | B 5-6 |
| McBain Av | NY | 7 | C 3 |
| McCallum Ct | ET | 24 | C 6 |
| McCaul St | T | 2 | E 1 |
| McCaul St | T | 4 | E 5-6 |
| McClear Pl | T | 5 | A 5 |
| McClinchy Av | SC | 24 | D 1-2 |
| McClure Cr | SC | 39 | E-F 1 |
| McConnell Av | T | 5 | E 4 |
| McCool Ct | SC | 31 | F 2 |
| McCord Rd | T | 7 | B 5 |
| McCormack St | NY | 16 | B-C 5-6 |
| McCormack St | T | 16 | B-C 5-6 |
| McCowan Rd | SC | 37 | B 1-6 |
| McCowan Rd | SC | 39 | B 1-6 |
| McCowan Rd | SC | 41 | A-B 1-6 |
| McCulley St | SC | 49 | F 6 |
| McCulloch Av | ET | 38 | E 4-5 |
| McDairmid Rd | SC | 29 | F 2 |
| McDonald Av | SC | 25 | B 3 |
| McDonald's Pl | NY | 17 | D 3 |
| McDougall La | T | 2 | D 1 |
| McFarland Av | T | 14 | F 1 |
| McFarrens La | T | 3 | B 1 |
| McGee St | T | 3 | B 1 |
| McGill St | T | 5 | A 5 |
| McGillivray Av | SC | 31 | D 5 |
| McGillivray Av | NY | 8 | D-E 4 |
| McGinty Pl | SC | 41 | E 4 |
| McGlashan Ct | NY | 8 | F 4 |
| McGlashan Rd | NY | 8 | F 4 |
| McGrath Ct | SC | 49 | F 6 |
| McGregor Rd | SC | 27 | D 1 |
| McGriskin Rd | SC | 41 | B-C 6 |
| McInnes Cr | SC | 51 | B 4 |
| McIntosh Av | ET | 24 | D 6 |
| McIntosh St | SC | 25 | E 2-3 |
| McKayfield Rd | EY | 15 | B 2 |
| McKee Av | NY | 11 | A-C 5 |
| McKenzie Av | T | 5 | B 3 |
| McKnight Dr | SC | 51 | A-B 5 |
| McLachlan Dr | SC | 38 | B 6 |
| McLaughlin Rd | NY | 20 | C 1 |
| McLevin Av | SC | 41 | D-F 5-6 |
| McLevin Av | SC | 51 | A-B 5-6 |
| McManus Rd | ET | 26 | C 1 |
| McMaster Av | T | 4 | E 2 |
| McMillan Av | SC | 49 | D 6 |
| McMurray Av | T | 14 | C 1-2 |
| McMurrich St | T | 4 | F 3 |
| McNab Blvd | SC | 25 | B 4 |
| McNab Blvd | SC | 37 | B 5-6 |
| McNairn Av | T | 8 | F 5 |
| McNicoll Av | NY | 21 | A-F 2 |
| McNicoll Av | SC | 31 | A-F 2 |
| McNicoll Av | SC | 41 | A-E 2 |
| McRae Dr | EY | 7 | D-E 4-5 |
| McRoberts Av | T | 16 | E 4-5 |
| McRoberts Av | Y | 16 | E 4-5 |
| Mead Ct | NY | 9 | D 3 |
| Meadow Av | SC | 15 | F 5 |
| Meadow Av | SC | 25 | A 5 |
| Meadow Lane Av | NY | 28 | F 3 |
| Meadow Larkway | NY | 11 | C 6 |

| Street | Mun. | Pg | Col | Row |
|---|---|---|---|---|
| Meadowacres Dr | SC | 29 | A | 2 |
| Meadowbank Rd | ET | 34 | D | 1-2 |
| Meadowbrook Rd | NY | 6 | B | 1 |
| Meadowcliffe Dr | SC | 37 | B-C | 5-6 |
| Meadowcrest Rd | ET | 24 | C | 4 |
| Meadowglade Cr | NY | 19 | B-C | 1 |
| Meadowglen Pl | SC | 39 | D | 4 |
| Meadowvale Dr | ET | 24 | B-D | 3 |
| Meadowvale Rd | SC | 47 | E | 1 |
| Meadowvale Rd | SC | 49 | E | 1-6 |
| Meadowvale Rd | SC | 51 | E | 3-6 |
| Meaford Av | ET | 32 | F | 5 |
| Meandering Tr | SC | 51 | C | 6 |
| Meath Rd | ET | 30 | A | 6 |
| Mechanic Av | T | 14 | F | 5 |
| Medaca St | NY | 21 | C-E | 4 |
| Medal La | NY | 20 | B | 5-6 |
| Medalist Rd | NY | 9 | B-C | 2-3 |
| Medford Av | SC | 25 | B | 3 |
| Medhurst Rd | EY | 15 | F | 2 |
| Medici Ct | SC | 27 | E | 2 |
| Medina Cr | SC | 27 | F | 1-2 |
| Medland Cr | T | 14 | C | 2-3 |
| Medland St | T | 14 | C | 2 |
| Medley Cr | SC | 37 | A | 5 |
| Medonte Av | SC | 27 | A | 3 |
| Medulla Av | ET | 34 | E | 5-6 |
| Medway Cr | SC | 29 | F | 6 |
| Meegwetch La | T | 2 | B-C | 1 |
| Megan Av | SC | 49 | C | 6 |
| Meighen Av | EY | 15 | F | 1-2 |
| Meighen Av | EY | 25 | A | 1-2 |
| Melbert Rd | ET | 34 | B | 1 |
| Melbourne Av | T | 2 | A | 1 |
| Melbourne Pl | T | 12 | C | 1 |
| Melchior Dr | SC | 47 | C | 1-2 |
| Meldazy Dr | SC | 39 | A-B | 5 |
| Melford Dr | SC | 41 | D-E | 4-5 |
| Melgund Rd | T | 4 | D | 1 |
| Melham Ct | SC | 41 | D | 5 |
| Melinda St | T | 2 | F | 1 |
| Melinda St | T | 3 | A | 1 |
| Melita Av | T | 4 | B-C | 2 |
| Melita Cr | T | 4 | B | 2 |
| Mellanby Pl | NY | 19 | A | 6 |
| Mellor Rd | ET | 24 | D | 2 |
| Mellowood Dr | NY | 9 | F | 3 |
| Melody Rd | NY | 28 | D-E | 3 |
| Melpham Ct | ET | 40 | E | 4 |
| Melrose Av | NY | 8 | D-E | 5 |
| Melrose Av | T | 8 | E-F | 5 |
| Melrose St | ET | 22 | B-E | 2 |
| Melton Grove St | NY | 10 | D | 3 |
| Melva Cr | SC | 41 | A | 3 |
| Melville Av | T | 4 | B | 2 |
| Memorial Park Av | EY | 15 | A-B | 2 |
| Memory Gardens La | NY | 21 | B-D | 2 |
| Memory La | T | 13 | D | 1 |
| Mendel Av | T | 15 | C-D | 4 |
| Mendip Cr | SC | 29 | D | 4-5 |
| Mendota Rd | ET | 22 | D-E | 1 |
| Menin Rd | Y | 6 | B | 4 |
| Mentor Blvd | NY | 21 | C-E | 2 |
| Mercedes Dr | ET | 40 | E-F | 1 |
| Mercer St | T | 2 | E | 1 |
| Mercury Rd | ET | 38 | D-E | 1 |
| Mercury Rd | ET | 40 | D-E | 6 |
| Mere Ct | NY | 17 | F | 2 |
| Meredith Cr | T | 5 | A | 3 |
| Meridian Rd | ET | 36 | C | 1-2 |
| Merkley Sq | SC | 39 | E-F | 4-5 |
| Merredin Pl | NY | 19 | A | 4 |
| Merrian Rd | SC | 27 | E | 4 |
| Merrick St | T | 14 | D | 6 |
| Merriday St | ET | 22 | B-C | 2 |
| Merrill Av | T | 28 | F | 6 |
| Merrill Av E | T | 15 | C-D | 4 |
| Merrill Bridge Rd | T | 15 | C | 4 |
| Merritt Rd | EY | 15 | E | 1 |
| Merritt Rd | EY | 17 | E-F | 6 |
| Merryfield Dr | SC | 29 | C-D | 6 |
| Merrygale Cr | ET | 36 | E | 6 |
| Merton St | T | 7 | A-C | 5 |
| Mervyn Av | ET | 34 | E-F | 3 |
| Meta St | NY | 9 | E | 2 |
| Metcalfe St | T | 5 | B | 4-5 |
| Meteor Dr | ET | 36 | B | 1 |
| Methuen Av | ET | 24 | F | 2-3 |
| Metropolitan Rd | SC | 29 | B-C | 3 |
| Mewata St | NY | 19 | E | 6 |
| Mewburn Av | SC | 25 | D-E | 2 |
| Michael Dr | NY | 21 | A-B | 2 |
| Michener Ct | T | 2 | C | 1 |
| Michigan Dr | NY | 11 | B | 1 |
| Micmac Cr | NY | 21 | E | 3-4 |
| Mid Pines Rd | SC | 39 | E | 5 |
| Midburn Av | EY | 15 | E-F | 3 |
| Midcroft Dr | SC | 29 | F | 2 |
| Midden Cr | ET | 36 | E | 2 |
| Middlefield Rd | SC | 41 | B | 1-5 |
| Middleport Cr | SC | 41 | F | 4 |
| Middleport Cr | SC | 51 | A | 4 |
| Middleton St | T | 14 | F | 5 |
| Mid-Dominion Acres | SC | 39 | C | 2 |
| Midhurst Dr | ET | 40 | D-E | 4 |
| Midholm Dr | SC | 27 | D | 3 |
| Midhurst Av | SC | 25 | E | 1-3 |
| Midland Av | SC | 27 | C | 1-6 |
| Midland Av | SC | 29 | E-F | 1-6 |
| Midland Av | SC | 31 | E | 1-6 |
| Midvale Rd | NY | 8 | C | 2 |
| Midwest Rd | SC | 29 | E | 4-6 |
| Mikado Av | NY | 8 | B | 4-5 |
| Milady Rd | NY | 30 | B | 3-4 |
| Milan St | T | 5 | B | 6 |
| Mildenhall Rd | NY | 7 | C | 1-2 |
| Mildenhall Cr | NY | 9 | B | 6 |
| Mildred Av | NY | 26 | F | 6 |
| Milepost Pl | EY | 7 | F | 6 |
| Miles Pl | T | 4 | B | 2-3 |
| Miles Rd | ET | 22 | E | 4 |
| Milford Av | NY | 16 | D | 1-2 |
| Milford Haven Dr | SC | 39 | E | 4 |
| Military Tr | SC | 39 | E-F | 2-4 |
| Military Tr | SC | 49 | A-C | 3-5 |
| Milkwood Av | ET | 40 | E | 5 |
| Milky Way | T | 12 | C | 1 |
| Mill Cove | ET | 24 | E | 2 |
| Mill Rd | ET | 34 | A-B | 1-4 |
| Mill St | NY | 9 | A | 4 |
| Mill St | NY | 8 | A | 4 |
| Mill St | T | 3 | B-D | 2 |
| Millbank Av | T | 6 | D | 5 |
| Millbridge Gt | SC | 29 | E-F | 5 |
| Millbrook Cr | T | 5 | D-E | 4 |
| Millburn Dr | ET | 36 | E | 5 |
| Millcar Ct | SC | 51 | C | 6 |
| Milldock Dr | SC | 47 | E | 4-5 |
| Millennium Dr | NY | 16 | A | 2 |
| Miller St | T | 14 | D | 1-2 |
| Millersgrove Dr | NY | 16 | F | 4 |
| Millerson Av | Y | 6 | A | 6 |
| Millgate Cr | NY | 11 | D | 5-6 |
| Millhouse Cr | SC | 49 | D | 1-2 |
| Millicent St | T | 14 | F | 3 |
| Millicent St | T | 4 | A | 3 |
| Milliken Blvd | SC | 31 | E | 3-4 |
| Millington St | T | 5 | B-C | 5 |
| Millmere Dr | SC | 39 | D | 5 |
| Millport Dr | NY | 30 | C | 3 |
| Millsborough Cr | ET | 36 | A-B | 5 |
| Millview Ct | ET | 38 | D | 1 |
| Millview Cr | ET | 40 | E | 6 |
| Millview Cr | ET | 38 | D | 1 |
| Millview Cr | ET | 40 | E | 6 |
| Millwick Dr | NY | 30 | B-C | 2-3 |
| Millwood Rd | EY | 7 | A-F | 5-6 |
| Milmink St | ET | 40 | F | 1 |
| Milmink St | ET | 40 | F | 6 |
| Milne Av | SC | 25 | B-C | 3 |
| Milner Av | SC | 39 | B-F | 1-2 |
| Milner Av | SC | 49 | A-B | 1-2 |
| Milner Business Ct | SC | 39 | D | 2 |
| Milroy Cr | SC | 49 | C | 4 |
| Milton St | EY | 15 | B | 1-2 |
| Milton St | T | 2 | F | 1 |
| Milvan Dr | NY | 30 | B-C | 2-3 |
| Milverton Blvd | EY | 15 | D | 3 |
| Milverton Blvd | T | 15 | A-C | 3 |
| Milverton Blvd | T | 5 | F | 3 |
| Mimico Av | ET | 22 | D-E | 3 |
| Min Av | NY | 18 | B | 1 |
| Mincing La | T | 2 | F | 1 |
| Minden Cr | ET | 24 | E | 5 |
| Minerva Av | SC | 27 | F | 4 |
| Minerva Av | SC | 37 | A | 6 |
| Minford Av | SC | 27 | B | 3 |
| Mingleharte Dr | ET | 40 | C | 1 |
| Minho Blvd | T | 4 | B | 2 |
| Miniot Cir | SC | 47 | D | 2 |
| Minnacote Av | SC | 49 | C | 6 |
| Minnie Av | NY | 30 | B | 2 |
| Minnowburn St | SC | 29 | C | 2 |
| Minorca Pl | NY | 19 | C-D | 3 |
| Minos Cr | SC | 39 | E | 3 |
| Minstrel Dr | ET | 24 | E | 5 |
| Minto St | T | 13 | D | 1 |
| Minton Pl | EY | 15 | D | 1 |
| Mintwood Dr | NY | 11 | F | 1-2 |
| Minuk Acres | SC | 47 | D | 2 |
| Miramar Cr | SC | 37 | A | 2 |
| Miranda Av | Y | 16 | F | 3-4 |
| Mirrow Ct | NY | 49 | B | 4 |
| Mission Dr | NY | 19 | E-F | 5 |
| Mistflower Rd | NY | 21 | B | 2 |
| Misthollow Sq | SC | 39 | F | 2 |
| Misty Cr | NY | 9 | D-E | 4 |
| Misty Hills Tr | SC | 51 | A | 4 |
| Mitcham Dr | ET | 32 | C | 2 |
| Mitchell Av | T | 2 | C | 1 |
| Mitre Pl | NY | 26 | A | 1-2 |
| Moatfield Dr | NY | 19 | B | 3 |
| Moberly Av | T | 15 | C | 3-4 |
| Mobile Dr | NY | 17 | E | 3 |
| Moccasin Tr | NY | 17 | B-C | 2 |
| Mockingbird Cr | NY | 10 | B | 2 |
| Model Av | NY | 8 | B | 3 |
| Modern Rd | SC | 27 | C | 5 |
| Moeller Ct | SC | 49 | A | 2 |
| Moffatt Ct | ET | 40 | F | 4 |
| Moford Cr | ET | 36 | F | 1 |
| Mogul Dr | NY | 21 | C-D | 2 |
| Moir Av | Y | 6 | B | 5 |
| Moira Av | SC | 25 | D | 2 |
| Moline Dr | ET | 26 | A | 2 |
| Mollard Rd | SC | 31 | F | 4-5 |
| Molson St | T | 4 | F | 2 |
| Mona Dr | T | 6 | E | 1-2 |
| Monaco Ct | NY | 30 | F | 2 |
| Monarch Park Av | EY | 15 | B | 2-3 |
| Monarch Park Av | T | 15 | B | 3-4 |
| Monarch Rd | T | 14 | D | 5-6 |
| Monarchdale Av | NY | 16 | B | 2 |
| Monarchwood Cr | NY | 19 | E | 6 |
| Monastery La | SC | 27 | B | 5-6 |
| Monclova Rd | NY | 18 | A | 2-3 |
| Moncrieff Dr | ET | 28 | A | 1-2 |
| Mondeo Dr | SC | 29 | D | 3-4 |
| Monet Av | ET | 34 | B | 1 |
| Monklands Av | ET | 24 | B | 3 |
| Monkton Av | ET | 24 | B | 3-4 |
| Monmouth Cr | SC | 39 | B | 4 |
| Monogram Pl | ET | 28 | A-B | 5 |
| Montague Pl | SC | 31 | B | 2 |
| Montana Av | NY | 18 | B | 4 |
| Montavista St | SC | 39 | E | 4 |
| Montcalm Av | SC | 16 | E | 3-4 |
| Montclair Av | T | 6 | C-E | 6 |
| Montcrest Blvd | T | 5 | D | 4 |
| Montebello Gdns | ET | 34 | D | 1 |
| Monteith St | T | 5 | A | 4 |
| Monterrey Dr | ET | 30 | A | 4 |
| Montesson St | ET | 34 | E-F | 3 |
| Montezuma Tr | SC | 31 | D | 3-4 |
| Montford Dr | NY | 11 | B | 3-4 |
| Montgomery Av | SC | 31 | E-F | 6 |
| Montgomery Av | T | 6 | F | 3 |
| Montgomery Rd | ET | 24 | B-C | 2-3 |
| Montressor Dr | NY | 9 | B-C | 1-2 |
| Montrose Av | T | 4 | B | 3-5 |
| Montvale Dr | SC | 25 | F | 1 |
| Montya Av | Y | 14 | A | 2 |
| Montye Av | Y | 24 | F | 2 |
| Moon Valley Dr | ET | 40 | E | 5-6 |
| Moonbeam Av | SC | 51 | A | 6 |
| Moonstone Byway | NY | 21 | B | 2 |
| Moore Av | EY | 7 | C-D | 5 |
| Moore Av | T | 7 | A-C | 6 |
| Moore Park Av | NY | 10 | D-F | 1 |
| Moorecroft Cr | SC | 27 | E | 3 |
| Moorefield Dr | SC | 47 | E | 3 |
| Mooregate Av | SC | 27 | E | 2-3 |
| Moorehill Dr | EY | 5 | C | 1 |
| Moorehill Dr | EY | 7 | C | 6 |
| Moorehouse Dr | SC | 31 | F | 2 |
| Moorehead Dr | ET | 34 | B-C | 2 |
| Moraine Hill Dr | SC | 29 | C | 1-2 |
| Moran Rd | SC | 31 | F | 5-6 |
| Moray Pl | SC | 27 | B | 1 |
| Morbank Dr | SC | 31 | D | 3 |
| Moreau Tr | SC | 25 | B | 1 |
| Morecambe Gt | SC | 27 | E | 2 |
| Morecambe Gt | SC | 31 | A | 3 |
| Morewood Cr | NY | 11 | D-E | 6 |
| Morgan Av | ET | 22 | D | 1 |
| Morgandale Cr | SC | 31 | B | 5 |
| Morland Rd | Y | 14 | A | 1 |
| Morley Ct | ET | 26 | D | 4 |
| Morna Av | SC | 47 | A | 3 |
| Mornelle Ct | SC | 49 | A | 3-4 |
| Morning Dew Rd | SC | 47 | C | 1-2 |
| Morning Gloryway | NY | 11 | F | 1 |
| Morningside Av | SC | 47 | B | 1-4 |
| Morningside Av | SC | 49 | A-B | 1-6 |
| Morningside Av | SC | 51 | A-B | 4-6 |
| Morningside Av | T | 14 | A-B | 4 |
| Morningside Av | T | 24 | F | 4 |

M

| STREET NAME | MUNICIPALITY | MAP NO | MAP | AREA |
|---|---|---|---|---|
| Mornington Gt | SC | 39 | D | 5 |
| Morningview Tr | SC | 51 | B | 4-5 |
| Morrish Rd | SC | 49 | C-D | 2-5 |
| Morrison Av | T | 16 | E-F | 5 |
| Morrison St | ET | 22 | A-B | 3 |
| Morrison St | T | 2 | D | 1 |
| Morrow Av | T | 14 | E | 4 |
| Morse St | T | 3 | E | 1-2 |
| Mortimer Av | EY | 15 | A-D | 5 |
| Mortimer Av | EY | 5 | D-E | 4 |
| Morton Rd | T | 15 | D | 3-4 |
| Mosedale Cr | NY | 21 | C-E | 4 |
| Moselle Dr | ET | 40 | E | 1 |
| Mosley St | T | 3 | F | 1 |
| Mosque Cr | ET | 40 | E | 5 |
| Moss St | SC | 47 | B | 3 |
| Mossbank Av | SC | 39 | E | 5-6 |
| Mossbrook Cr | SC | 31 | B | 2 |
| Mossford Ct | ET | 36 | E | 4-5 |
| Mossgrove Tr | NY | 9 | E-F | 3 |
| Mossom Pl | T | 24 | F | 4 |
| Mossom St | T | 24 | F | 4 |
| Mosswood La | ET | 40 | D-E | 1 |
| Mould Av | Y | 16 | A | 3 |
| Mount Dennis Dr | NY | 26 | F | 2-3 |
| Mount Olive Dr | ET | 40 | E-F | 1-3 |
| Mount Pleasant Rd | T | 5 | A-B | 1-3 |
| Mount Pleasant Rd | T | 7 | B | 1-6 |
| Mount Pleasant Rd | T | 9 | A | 5-6 |
| Mount Royal Av | | 4 | B | 1 |
| Mountain Ash Ct | ET | 34 | B | 4 |
| Mountalan Av | T | 15 | A | 4 |
| Mountbatten Rd | ET | 26 | D-E | 1 |
| Mountcastle Gt | SC | 31 | B | 1 |
| Mountjoy Av | T | 15 | A-B | 4 |
| Mountland Dr | SC | 39 | D | 4-5 |
| Mountnoel Av | T | 15 | A | 4 |
| Mountstephen St | T | 5 | D | 5 |
| Mountview Av | T | 14 | C | 3 |
| Moutray St | T | 14 | F | 6 |
| Moutray St | T | 14 | C | 3 |
| Mowat Av | T | 2 | A | 1-2 |
| Moyles Ct | ET | 34 | B | 1 |
| Moynes Av | ET | 24 | C | 2 |
| Mozart Av | SC | 27 | D | 2-3 |
| Muir Av | NY | 30 | A-B | 2 |
| Muir Av | T | 14 | F | 4 |
| Muir Dr | SC | 37 | D | 4 |
| Muirbank Blvd | SC | 49 | E | 3-4 |
| Muircrest Dr | NY | 19 | E-F | 6 |
| Muirdale Av | ET | 26 | A | 2-3 |
| Muirhead Rd | NY | 21 | E | 5-6 |
| Muirkirk Rd | NY | 10 | E | 2 |
| Muirlands Dr | SC | 41 | B | 2 |
| Muirpoint Rd | SC | 49 | E | 3 |
| Mulberry Ct | Y | 6 | B | 5 |
| Muldrew Av | SC | 27 | B | 2 |
| Mulgrove Dr | ET | 34 | C | 2 |
| Mulham Pl | ET | 26 | D | 3-4 |
| Mullet Rd | NY | 11 | A | 3 |
| Mulock Av | T | 14 | D | 1 |
| Muncey Av | ET | 28 | B | 2 |
| Munford Cr | EY | 15 | C | 2 |
| Munhall Rd | ET | 26 | D | 2 |
| Munham St | SC | 29 | E | 5 |
| Municipal Dr | Y | 16 | C | 3-4 |
| Munition St | T | 3 | C-D | 2 |
| Munro Blvd | NY | 9 | B-C | 3 |
| Munro Park Av | T | 13 | F | 6 |
| Munro Park Av | T | 15 | F | 6 |
| Munro St | T | 5 | D | 5-6 |
| Munson Cr | SC | 29 | F | 4 |
| Munster Av | ET | 24 | A | 4 |
| Murchison Ct | ET | 40 | E | 2 |
| Murdock Av | T | 15 | C | 4 |
| Murellen Cr | NY | 17 | F | 1-2 |
| Muriel Av | EY | 5 | E | 3 |
| Muriel Av | T | 5 | E | 3 |
| Murison Blvd | SC | 39 | A | 1 |
| Murison Blvd | SC | 49 | A | 1 |
| Murmurth Rd | SC | 29 | D | 2 |
| Murray Av | SC | 29 | F | 1-2 |
| Murray Glen Dr | SC | 29 | A-B | 5 |
| Murray Rd | NY | 18 | E | 3 |
| Murray Ross Pkwy | NY | 20 | B-D | 1-3 |
| Murray St | T | 4 | E | 1 |
| Murrie St | ET | 22 | C | 4 |
| Musgrave St | T | 25 | A | 4 |
| Muskoka Av | ET | 32 | D-E | 5 |
| Mutual St | T | 5 | A | 4-5 |
| Myers La | NY | 21 | C | 4 |
| Mylesview Pl | NY | 10 | D | 6 |
| Myrna La | SC | 31 | F | 3 |
| Myrtle Av | T | 5 | F | 5 |
| Mystic Av | SC | 25 | C | 3 |

## N

| STREET NAME | MUNICIPALITY | MAP NO | MAP | AREA |
|---|---|---|---|---|
| Nabob Cr | SC | 51 | A-B | 5-6 |
| Nagel Rd | NY | 18 | A-B | 3 |
| Nahanni Terr | SC | 41 | E | 6 |
| Nairn Av | T | 16 | F | 5-6 |
| Nairn Av | Y | 16 | F | 4-5 |
| Namco Rd | ET | 38 | F | 4 |
| Nancy Av | SC | 25 | A | 1 |
| Nancy Pocock Pl | T | 4 | B-C | 4 |
| Nanton Av | T | 5 | B | 3 |
| Napanee Ct | T | 4 | D | 6 |
| Nash Dr | NY | 18 | C | 3 |
| Nashdene Rd | SC | 41 | B-D | 3 |
| Nashland Av | SC | 36 | E | 5 |
| Nashville Av | Y | 16 | C | 5 |
| Nasmith Av | T | 5 | C | 6 |
| Nassau St | T | 4 | D-E | 5 |
| Natal Av | SC | 25 | E | 1-2 |
| Nature Pathway | SC | 49 | F | 3 |
| Navaho Dr | NY | 21 | E-F | 3 |
| Navarre Cr | SC | 37 | F | 3-4 |
| Navenby Cr | NY | 30 | B | 2-3 |
| Navy Wharf Ct | T | 2 | E | 2 |
| Nealon Av | EY | 5 | D-E | 3 |
| Neames Cr | NY | 28 | F | 2-3 |
| Neapolitan Dr | SC | 39 | A | 4-5 |
| Neartic Cr | ET | 38 | D | 2 |
| Nearwood Gt | SC | 31 | D | 4 |
| Nebula Starway | NY | 19 | C-D | 2 |
| Neddie Dr | SC | 29 | D | 1 |
| Needham Dr | ET | 38 | F | 1 |
| Needham Dr | T | 4 | F | 6 |
| Needle Firway | NY | 30 | F | 4 |
| Neepawa Av | T | 14 | E | 4 |
| Neilor Cr | ET | 34 | B | 3 |
| Neilson Av | SC | 25 | A | 4-5 |
| Neilson Av | T | 5 | A | 6 |
| Neilson Dr | ET | 34 | B-C | 3-4 |
| Neilson Dr | SC | 39 | F | 1-4 |
| Neilson Rd | SC | 41 | B-E | 1-6 |
| Neiltree Ct | SC | 34 | B-C | 4 |
| Nelles Av | T | 14 | A | 3 |
| Nelson Av | NY | 20 | C | 2 |
| Nelson Dr | SC | 39 | E | 4 |
| Nelson St | T | 2 | E | 1 |
| Nelson St | T | 4 | D | 5 |
| Neptune Dr | NY | 8 | B-C | 4-5 |
| Neris Ct | M | 32 | B | 2 |
| Nero Ct | SC | 27 | F | 3 |
| Nesbitt Dr | EY | 5 | C | 1 |
| Nesbitt Dr | T | 7 | C | 6 |
| Ness Dr | NY | 19 | F | 3 |
| Neston Av | SC | 27 | F | 4 |
| Net Dr | T | 14 | B | 4 |
| Netheravon Rd | SC | 39 | E | 3 |
| Netherby Cr | ET | 40 | F | 2 |
| Nettle Creek Cr | SC | 41 | A | 1 |
| Nevada Av | NY | 11 | C | 1 |
| Neville Park Blvd | T | 13 | F | 5-6 |
| Neville Park Blvd | T | 15 | F | 5-6 |
| New Brunswick Av | T | 2 | B | 2-3 |
| New Forest Sq | SC | 31 | D | 1 |
| New Haven Dr | T | 6 | D-E | 3 |
| New St | T | 4 | F | 3 |
| Newark St | SC | 39 | E | 4 |
| Newbold Av | T | 15 | B | 5 |
| Newbridge Rd | ET | 34 | B | 5-6 |
| Newbury La | NY | 8 | D | 2 |
| Newcastle St | T | 22 | C-D | 2 |
| Newcross Dr | ET | 36 | D | 5-6 |
| Newdawn Cr | SC | 31 | F | 3-4 |
| Newell Ct | ET | 26 | D | 4 |
| Newfoundland Rd | T | 2 | B | 2-3 |
| Newgale Gt | SC | 41 | E | 3 |
| Newgate Rd | T | 6 | B | 2-3 |
| Newholm Rd | ET | 24 | E | 5 |
| Newington Ct | ET | 36 | B | 5 |
| Newlands Av | SC | 25 | D | 1 |
| Newlin Cr | NY | 18 | B-C | 2 |
| Newlove Ct | SC | 49 | E | 4 |
| Newmains Ct | SC | 49 | E | 4 |
| Newman Av | EY | 15 | E | 3 |
| Newmarket Av | T | 15 | D-E | 3 |
| Newmill Gt | SC | 41 | B-C | 2 |
| Newport Av | SC | 25 | A | 3 |
| Newstead Rd | ET | 26 | C | 2-3 |
| Newton Dr | NY | 11 | A-C | 2 |
| Newtonbrook Blvd | NY | 10 | F | 3 |
| Niagara St | T | 2 | C-D | 1-2 |
| Niagara St | T | 4 | C-D | 3 |
| Niantic Cr | NY | 19 | F | 3 |
| Nichol La | T | 4 | E | 4 |
| Nicholas Av | T | 5 | C | 6 |
| Nickle Av | Y | 16 | A | 3 |
| Nicolan Rd | ET | 37 | A | 5-6 |
| Nida Ct | M | 32 | A | 1-2 |
| Nightingale Pl | SC | 39 | E | 6 |
| Nile St | NY | 18 | A | 5 |
| Nina St | T | 4 | D | 1 |
| Nineteenth St | ET | 32 | F | 4 |
| Ninth St | ET | 22 | B | 4-5 |
| Nipigon Av | NY | 11 | A-B | 1 |
| Nipissing Dr | ET | 34 | D | 2-3 |
| Niska Rd | NY | 20 | B | 3 |
| Niven St | ET | 38 | F | 1 |
| Nob La | NY | 17 | C | 2 |
| Nobert Rd | SC | 29 | A | 1-2 |
| Noble St | T | 14 | F | 6 |
| Noel Av | NY | 7 | C | 6 |
| Noganosh Rd | SC | 25 | B | 3 |
| Nomad Cr | NY | 9 | E | 4 |
| Nomad Rd | NY | 47 | F | 4 |
| Nootka Cr | NY | 21 | E | 3 |
| Nora Rd | ET | 24 | A | 2 |
| Noranda Dr | NY | 16 | B | 2 |
| Norbert Cr | ET | 34 | A-B | 1 |
| Norbrook Cr | ET | 40 | D | 4 |
| Norbury Cr | SC | 29 | E-F | 5-6 |
| Norby Cr | ET | 26 | B-C | 2-3 |
| Norcap Av | SC | 31 | D-E | 4 |
| Norcrest Dr | NY | 18 | C | 5 |
| Norcross Rd | NY | 8 | B | 3 |
| Nordale Cr | NY | 16 | B | 1 |
| Norden Cr | NY | 19 | A | 6 |
| Nordic Pl | NY | 19 | E | 6 |
| Nordin Av | ET | 24 | A-B | 6 |
| Noreen Dr | SC | 27 | A | 3 |
| Norelco Dr | NY | 30 | E-F | 4 |
| Norfield Cr | ET | 28 | B-C | 2-3 |
| Norfinch Dr | NY | 30 | F | 1-3 |
| Norfolk Av | ET | 32 | C | 2 |
| Norfolk St | T | 14 | F | 5 |
| Norgrove Cr | ET | 26 | C | 2-3 |
| Norham Cr | ET | 26 | B | 2 |
| Norhead Av | SC | 41 | A | 4 |
| Norlington Dr | NY | 9 | E | 2 |
| Norlong Blvd | EY | 15 | C | 1-2 |
| Norma Cr | T | 14 | B | 3 |
| Norman Av | T | 16 | E | 6 |
| Normandale Cr | NY | 9 | B | 2 |
| Normandy Blvd | T | 15 | C | 4-5 |
| Normanna Av | Y | 6 | B | 6 |
| Norris Cr | ET | 22 | D-E | 3 |
| Norris Glen Rd | ET | 34 | C | 5 |
| Norris Pl | NY | 28 | D | 2 |
| Norseman St | ET | 24 | A-C | 5 |
| North Beatrice St | T | 4 | B | 4 |
| North Bonnington Av | SC | 25 | D | 1-2 |
| North Carson St | ET | 32 | E | 2-3 |
| North Dr | ET | 26 | D | 4-5 |
| North Dr | SC | 25 | A | 4 |
| North Edgely Av | SC | 25 | D | 1-2 |
| North Heights Rd | ET | 36 | E-F | 5 |
| North Hills Terr | NY | 17 | B | 2 |
| North Kingslea Dr | ET | 24 | E | 4 |
| North Park Dr | NY | 18 | D-E | 6 |
| North Queen St | ET | 34 | C-F | 6 |
| North Service Rd | M | 32 | A | 2-3 |
| North View Terr | T | 4 | B | 3 |
| North W Gt | NY | 20 | C | 1 |
| North Wind Pl | SC | 41 | A | 5-6 |
| North Woodrow Blvd | SC | 29 | D | 2 |
| North Woodrow Blvd | SC | 27 | D | 6 |
| North York Blvd | NY | 10 | F | 5 |
| Northampton Dr | ET | 6 | E | 2 |
| Northbrook Rd | EY | 15 | A | 1-2 |
| Northcliffe Blvd | T | 4 | A | 1 |
| Northcliffe Blvd | Y | 6 | A | 4-6 |
| Northcote Av | T | 2 | A | 1 |
| Northcote Av | T | 4 | A | 6 |
| Norcrest Rd | ET | 26 | A-B | 1 |
| Northdale Rd | EY | 17 | D-E | 5-6 |
| Northdale Rd | NY | 9 | D-E | 5-6 |
| Northern Dancer Blvd | T | 13 | F | 1 |
| Northern Pl | T | 14 | F | 5 |
| Northey Dr | NY | 9 | F | 2 |
| Northfield Rd | SC | 45 | E-F | 5-6 |
| Northgate Dr | NY | 18 | E-F | 4 |
| Northglen Av | ET | 34 | E | 1 |
| Northland Av | T | 16 | C | 5 |
| Northland Av | Y | 16 | B | 5 |
| Northleigh Dr | SC | 39 | B | 4-5 |

| Street | Area | Page | Grid |
|---|---|---|---|
| Northline Rd | EY | 17 | D-F 4 |
| Northline Rd | NY | 17 | D-F 5 |
| Northmount Av | NY | 8 | D 3 |
| Northolt Ct | ET | 26 | B 6 |
| Northover St | NY | 18 | B-C 3 |
| Northridge Av | EY | 15 | B 1-2 |
| Northrop Rd | ET | 24 | B 4 |
| Northumberland St | T | 4 | A-B 3 |
| Northview Av | SC | 16 | F 3 |
| Northview Av | SC | 25 | A 5 |
| Northwestern Av | Y | 16 | D-E 3 |
| Northwood Dr | NY | 11 | B-C 2 |
| Norton Av | NY | 11 | A-B 5 |
| Norton Av | T | 16 | F 6 |
| Nortonville Dr | SC | 31 | B 6 |
| Norval St | Y | 6 | A 6 |
| Norvalley Ct | SC | 49 | B 4 |
| Norwalk St | SC | 37 | C 3 |
| Norway Av | T | 13 | D 5 |
| Norway Av | T | 15 | C-E 5-6 |
| Norwich Pl | ET | 30 | A 5 |
| Norwin St | NY | 10 | E 2 |
| Norwood Rd | T | 15 | E 4 |
| Norwood Terr | T | 15 | E 4 |
| Notley Pl | EY | 15 | E 1-2 |
| Nottawa Av | T | 3 | B 5 |
| Nottawasaga Ct | ET | 40 | F 5 |
| Nottingham Dr | ET | 24 | B 1-2 |
| Nottinghill Gt | ET | 36 | E 4 |
| Nova Rd | ET | 34 | C 6 |
| Nova Scotia Av | T | 2 | A 2 |
| Novopharm Ct | SC | 39 | D 2 |
| Nubana Av | NY | 28 | D 4 |
| Nuffield Dr | SC | 37 | F 3 |
| Nugent Rd | ET | 26 | A 1 |
| Nugget Av | SC | 41 | B-D 6 |
| Nursewood Rd | T | 13 | F 6 |
| Nursewood Rd | T | 15 | F 6 |
| Nursewood Rd | T | 25 | A 6 |
| Nymark Av | NY | 21 | A-B 5 |

## O

| Street | Area | Page | Grid |
|---|---|---|---|
| Oak Hampton Blvd | ET | 24 | B 2 |
| Oak Park Av | EY | 15 | D 4 |
| Oak Park Av | T | 15 | D 2-3 |
| Oak St | NY | 28 | D 5 |
| Oak St | T | 5 | B 5 |
| Oak St | Y | 28 | D 5 |
| Oakburn Cr | NY | 9 | A-B 1 |
| Oakburn Pl | NY | 9 | B 1 |
| Oakcrest Av | T | 15 | D-E 4 |
| Oakdale Rd | NY | 30 | F 4-6 |
| Oakdene Cr | T | 15 | A 3 |
| Oaken Gateway | NY | 9 | A-B 2 |
| Oakfield Dr | ET | 24 | E 2 |
| Oakhaven Dr | SC | 41 | A 2 |
| Oakhurst Dr | NY | 11 | D 2 |
| Oakland Av | NY | 28 | E 3-4 |
| Oaklands Av | T | 4 | E-F 2 |
| Oaklawn Gdns | T | 6 | E 4 |
| Oakley Blvd | SC | 29 | F 4-5 |
| Oakley Pl | NY | 9 | A 3 |
| Oakmeadow Blvd | SC | 39 | E-F 2-3 |
| Oakmount Rd | T | 14 | C 3 |
| Oakridge Dr | SC | 37 | A-B 5 |
| Oakvale Av | T | 15 | A 4 |
| Oakview Av | T | 14 | B 3 |
| Oakwood Av | T | 4 | A 4-6 |
| Oakwood Av | Y | 6 | A 4-6 |
| Oakworth Cr | SC | 27 | E 3 |
| Oarsman Dr | T | 12 | B 2 |
| Oban St | ET | 32 | C 2 |
| Obris Cr | SC | 41 | A 5 |
| Ockwell Manor Dr | SC | 31 | D 1 |
| O'Connor Dr | EY | 15 | A-D 1 |
| O'Connor Dr | EY | 17 | D-F 5-6 |
| O'Connor Dr | EY | 5 | E-F 1 |
| O'Connor Dr | NY | 17 | F 4 |
| O'Connor Dr | T | 5 | E-F 1 |
| Ocra Villaway | NY | 11 | F 5-6 |
| Odessa Av | T | 36 | C 5 |
| O'Donnell Av | ET | 22 | C 2 |
| Ogden Pl | ET | 22 | C 2 |
| O'Halloran Cr | SC | 31 | F 1 |
| O'Hara Av | T | 14 | F 6 |
| O'Hara Pl | T | 14 | F 6 |
| O'Henry Gr | SC | 41 | E 6 |
| Ojibway Av | T | 3 | B 5 |
| O'Keefe La | T | 5 | A 5 |
| Old Bridle Path | T | 5 | B 1 |
| Old Burnhamthorpe Rd | ET | 34 | A-B 1-2 |
| Old Colony Rd | NY | 9 | D-E 2 |
| Old Dundas St | ET | 24 | E 1 |
| Old Dundas St | Y | 24 | E 1 |
| Old Eglinton Av E | NY | 17 | E 3-4 |
| Old Finch Av | SC | 51 | A-E 4 |
| Old Forest Hill Rd | T | 6 | B-E 3-4 |
| Old George Pl | T | 5 | B 2 |
| Old Kingston Rd | SC | 49 | B-C 5-6 |
| Old Lawrence Av | NY | 17 | D 1 |
| Old Lawrence Av | NY | 19 | D 6 |
| Old Leslie St | NY | 11 | F 6 |
| Old Leslie St | NY | 19 | A 1 |
| Old Leslie St | NY | 9 | F 1 |
| Old Meadow La | NY | 8 | B 6 |
| Old Mill Dr | T | 24 | F 4 |
| Old Mill Dr | Y | 24 | F 4 |
| Old Mill Rd | ET | 24 | E-F 3 |
| Old Mill Terr | ET | 24 | E 3 |
| Old Oak Dr | ET | 24 | C 1 |
| Old Oak Rd | ET | 24 | B-C 1-2 |
| Old Orchard Gr | NY | 8 | D-E 5 |
| Old Orchard Gr | T | 8 | E-F 5 |
| Old Park Rd | T | 6 | B 2-3 |
| Old Scarlett Rd | NY | 26 | E 4 |
| Old Sheppard Av | NY | 21 | E-F 6 |
| Old Stock Yards Rd | T | 14 | C 1 |
| Old Weston Rd | T | 14 | D 1-2 |
| Old Weston Rd | T | 16 | D 5-6 |
| Old Weston Rd | Y | 16 | D 5-6 |
| Old Yonge St | NY | 9 | A-B 2-4 |
| Old York Mills Rd | NY | 9 | A 3 |
| Oldborough Cir | NY | 21 | C-E 4 |
| Oldham Rd | ET | 26 | A-B 3-4 |
| Olean Ct | NY | 11 | E 2 |
| O'Leary Av | Y | 6 | A 5 |
| Olive Av | NY | 11 | A-C 4 |
| Olive Av | T | 4 | C 3 |
| Olivewood Rd | ET | 24 | A 4 |
| Ollerton Rd | NY | 20 | B 5 |
| Olsen Dr | NY | 19 | B-D 3 |
| Olympia Pl | NY | 16 | B 1 |
| Olympus Av | T | 14 | B 4 |
| Omagh Av | NY | 28 | C 3 |
| Omaha Av | T | 3 | A-B 5 |
| O'Meara Ct | NY | 21 | A 4 |
| Omni Dr | SC | 39 | A 3 |
| Oneida Av | T | 3 | A-B 5 |
| Ongar Rd | NY | 18 | E 2 |
| Onslow Cr | T | 6 | A 4 |
| Ontario Dr | T | 2 | A 2-3 |
| Ontario Place Blvd | T | 2 | B 3 |
| Ontario St | T | 3 | B 1 |
| Ontario St | T | 5 | B 4-6 |
| Opal Ct | NY | 40 | E 4 |
| Orangewood Cr | SC | 31 | A 4 |
| Orator Gr | SC | 41 | B 4 |
| Orchard Cr | ET | 24 | C 4 |
| Orchard Crest Rd | Y | 24 | E-F 2-3 |
| Orchard Green | EY | 7 | C 6 |
| Orchard Haven Ridge | M | 32 | A-B 3 |
| Orchard Park Rd | M | 32 | B 3 |
| Orchard Park Blvd | T | 15 | B-C 6 |
| Orchard Park Dr | SC | 49 | B 5-6 |
| Orchard View Blvd | T | 6 | E-F 3 |
| Orchardcroft Cr | NY | 20 | C 6 |
| Orchid Ct | NY | 9 | F 3 |
| Orchid Pl | SC | 39 | D 1 |
| Orde St | T | 4 | E 5 |
| Ordnance St | T | 2 | B 3 |
| Ordway Rd | SC | 27 | F 4 |
| Oregon Tr | ET | 34 | D-E 3 |
| Orford Pl | T | 28 | B 2 |
| Orfus Rd | NY | 18 | E-F 5 |
| Orianna Dr | ET | 32 | C 3 |
| Oriole Cr | T | 6 | E-F 6 |
| Oriole Gdns | T | 6 | E 3-5 |
| Oriole Pkwy | T | 6 | E 3-5 |
| Oriole Rd | T | 6 | E 6 |
| Orkney Cr | ET | 26 | A 4 |
| Orland Ct | SC | 39 | F 2 |
| Orlando Blvd | SC | 29 | A-B 4 |
| Orleans Dr | SC | 49 | E 3 |
| Orley Av | EY | 15 | D-E 5 |
| Orman Av | Y | 16 | B 5 |
| Ormerod St | SC | 41 | D 6 |
| Ormont Dr | NY | 30 | C-F 2 |
| Ormsby Cr | T | 6 | D 4 |
| Ormskirk Av | T | 14 | A 5 |
| Ormskirk Ct | T | 14 | A 4 |
| Orpen La | T | 14 | F 5 |
| Orpington Cr | ET | 40 | E-F 4 |
| Orrell Av | ET | 24 | A-B 5 |
| Orton Park Rd | SC | 39 | E-F 4-6 |
| Orville Rd | SC | 37 | C 1 |
| Osborne Av | T | 15 | E 4-5 |
| Oscar Ct | NY | 11 | D-E 4 |
| Oscar Romero Pl | Y | 16 | B 6 |
| O'Shea Cr | NY | 21 | B 4 |
| Osler St | T | 14 | D-E 1-2 |
| Osmund Ct | NY | 21 | A 2 |
| Ossington Av | T | 2 | B 1 |
| Ossington Av | T | 4 | B 1-5 |
| Ossington Cr | T | 4 | B 5 |
| Osterhout Pl | SC | 41 | E-F 6 |
| Oswald Cr | T | 7 | A 4 |
| Oswego Rd | SC | 37 | A 4 |
| Otonabee Av | NY | 11 | A-C 1 |
| Ottawa Rd | NY | 9 | E 4 |
| Ottawa St | T | 5 | A 1-2 |
| Otter Cr | NY | 6 | E 1 |
| Otter Cr | T | 6 | E 1 |
| Ourland Av | ET | 22 | B 2 |
| Outlook Av | Y | 16 | A 4 |
| Outlook Garden Blvd | Y | 16 | A 4 |
| Outlook, The | ET | 36 | D 5 |
| Ovendon Sq | SC | 31 | E-F 4 |
| Overbank Cr | NY | 19 | E 4 |
| Overbrook Pl | NY | 10 | A-B 5 |
| Overdale Rd | T | 6 | B 3 |
| Overend St | T | 3 | C 1-2 |
| Overland Dr | NY | 17 | A-B 1-2 |
| Overlea Blvd | EY | 17 | A 5 |
| Overlea Blvd | NY | 17 | B 5 |
| Overlea Blvd | NY | 7 | E-F 5-6 |
| Overlord Cr | ET | 41 | F 4 |
| Overskate Ct | ET | 40 | E 1-2 |
| Overton Cr | NY | 19 | A-B 5-6 |
| Overton Pl | NY | 19 | B 5 |
| Overture Rd | SC | 37 | F 1-2 |
| Overture Rd | SC | 39 | F 6 |
| Ovida Av | ET | 34 | E 4 |
| Owen Blvd | NY | 9 | A-C 3 |
| Owen Dr | ET | 32 | C 4 |
| Oxbow Rd | NY | 9 | D 3-4 |
| Oxenden Cr | ET | 36 | B 6 |
| Oxford Dr | NY | 16 | A 3 |
| Oxford St | T | 22 | A-E 1 |
| Oxford St | T | 4 | D-E 5 |
| Oxhorn Rd | SC | 47 | E 6 |
| Oxley St | T | 2 | E 1 |
| Oxton Av | T | 6 | E 5 |
| Ozark Cr | T | 5 | D 3 |

## P

| Street | Area | Page | Grid |
|---|---|---|---|
| Pachino Blvd | SC | 29 | A 3 |
| Pacific Av | T | 14 | C 2-3 |
| Packard Blvd | SC | 39 | A 4-5 |
| Paddington Pl | ET | 26 | B 2 |
| Paddock Ct | NY | 9 | D 3 |
| Page Av | ET | 24 | F 1 |
| Page Av | NY | 11 | E 4-5 |
| Page St | T | 4 | B-C 4 |
| Pagebrook Dr | ET | 26 | D 2 |
| Paget Ct | SC | 49 | F 4 |
| Paget Rd | NY | 7 | A 4 |
| Pagoda Pl | ET | 30 | B 5 |
| Pailton Cr | T | 7 | A 5-6 |
| Painswick Cr | NY | 21 | E-F 5-6 |
| Painted Post Dr | SC | 39 | B-E 4-6 |
| Paisley Av | T | 5 | E 6 |
| Pakenham Dr | ET | 28 | B 1-2 |
| Palace Arch Dr | ET | 26 | B 4 |
| Palace Pier Ct | ET | 22 | F 1 |
| Palacky St | SC | 37 | D 2 |
| Palamar Rd | NY | 18 | B 3 |
| Pale Moon Cr | SC | 31 | B 2 |
| Palisades The | T | 14 | B 4 |
| Palm Dr | NY | 8 | B-C 2 |
| Palmdale Dr | SC | 29 | B 1-2 |
| Palmer St | EY | 15 | E 3 |
| Palmerston Av | T | 2 | C 1 |
| Palmerston Av | T | 4 | C 2-6 |
| Palmerston Blvd | T | 4 | C 3-4 |
| Palmerston Gdns | T | 4 | C 3 |
| Palmerston Sq | T | 4 | C 3 |
| Paloma Pl | SC | 37 | A 2 |
| Palomino Cr | NY | 11 | D 5 |
| Pamcrest Dr | NY | 11 | B 2 |
| Pamela Ct | ET | 40 | E 3 |
| Pamille Pl | NY | 16 | A 1 |
| Pamure Cr | SC | 27 | F 2 |
| Panama Ct | SC | 39 | C 5 |
| Pandora Cir | SC | 39 | B-D 5 |
| Pannahill Rd | NY | 10 | A-B 5 |
| Panorama Ct | ET | 30 | A 3 |
| Panorama Ct | ET | 40 | F 3 |
| Pape Av | EY | 5 | E 1-3 |
| Pape Av | T | 3 | E 1 |
| Pape Av | T | 5 | E 3-6 |
| Paperbirch Dr | NY | 17 | A-B 1 |
| Par Av | SC | 39 | E 6 |
| Parade Sq | SC | 49 | E 3 |
| Paradelle Cr | NY | 21 | F 5-6 |
| Paragon Rd | ET | 26 | A-B 2 |
| Paramount Ct | NY | 16 | C 2 |

N
O
P

| STREET NAME | MUNICIPALITY | MAP NO | MAP AREA |
|---|---|---|---|
| Pardee Av | T | 2 A | 2 |
| Parent Av | NY | 18 B-C | 3 |
| Parfield Dr | NY | 19 B-C | 1 |
| Paris Ct | NY | 19 C-D | 3 |
| Park Blvd | ET | 32 D-E | 5 |
| Park Dr Reservation | T | 5 A-B | 2-3 |
| Park Glen Dr | NY | 19 B | 5 |
| Park Hill Rd | T | 6 B | 3-4 |
| Park Home Av | NY | 10 D-F | 5 |
| Park La | ET | 24 E | 6 |
| Park Lane Cir | T | 7 E-F | 1 |
| Park Lane Cir | NY | 9 D | 5-6 |
| Park Lawn Rd | ET | 22 E-F | 1-2 |
| Park Lawn Rd | ET | 24 E | 4-6 |
| Park Manor Dr | ET | 34 E | 1 |
| Park Rd | T | 5 A | 3 |
| Park Royal Blvd | M | 32 A-B | 3 |
| Park Vista | ET | 5 E-F | 2 |
| Parkborough Blvd | SC | 39 D | 1 |
| Parkchester Rd | NY | 16 B | 3-4 |
| Parkcrest Dr | SC | 37 C | 5 |
| Parkdale Rd | T | 14 D | 6 |
| Parkdene Ct | SC | 31 A | 4 |
| Parke St | Y | 28 D | 5 |
| Parker Av | ET | 24 B | 6 |
| Parker Av | SC | 25 B | 3 |
| Parkette Pl | SC | 25 D | 3 |
| Parkfield Av | T | 15 A | 5 |
| Parkhurst Blvd | EY | 7 D-E | 4 |
| Parkington Cr | SC | 39 B | 4 |
| Parkland Av | SC | 25 A | 4-5 |
| Parklea Dr | EY | 7 D-E | 4 |
| Parkman Av | T | 14 B | 4 |
| Parkmount Rd | T | 15 B | 3-4 |
| Parkridge RD | M | 32 B | 3 |
| Parkview Av | NY | 11 A-C | 5 |
| Parkview Av | T | 5 C | 4 |
| Parkview Gdns | T | 14 B | 3 |
| Parkview Hill Cr | EY | 15 B-D | 1 |
| Parkview Hill Cr | EY | 17 B-D | 6 |
| Parkview Hts | SC | 25 A | 4-5 |
| Parkway Av | T | 14 E | 6 |
| Parkway Forest Dr | NY | 19 C-D | 1-2 |
| Parkway Forest Dr | NY | 21 B | 5-6 |
| Parkwood Av | T | 4 E | 1 |
| Parkwood Av | T | 6 D | 6 |
| Parkwoods Village Dr | NY | 19 E-F | 4 |
| Parlette Av | SC | 47 D | 5 |
| Parliament St | T | 3 B | 1-3 |
| Parliament St | T | 5 B | 6 |
| Parma Ct | NY | 17 F | 5 |
| Parmalea Ct | ET | 26 A | 2 |
| Parmbelle Cr | NY | 19 B-D | 1 |
| Parndon Pl | SC | 39 B | 5 |
| Parnell Av | SC | 25 D | 2 |
| Parr St | T | 4 A | 5 |
| Parravano Ct | NY | 10 D | 5 |
| Parsborough Ct | SC | 49 E-F | 2-3 |
| Parsell Sq | SC | 39 F | 1 |
| Parson Ct | NY | 16 F | 6 |
| Parsonage Dr | SC | 41 F | 5 |
| Parsonage St | SC | 51 A | 5 |
| Partridge La | SC | 31 B | 5 |
| Pasadena Gdns | Y | 24 E-F | 2 |
| Pashler Av | T | 5 E | 4 |
| Passmore Av | SC | 31 D-E | 1 |
| Passmore Av | SC | 41 B-F | 1 |
| Passy Cr | NY | 20 C | 2 |
| Pastrano Ct | SC | 37 A | 6 |
| Path Hill Pl | SC | 41 B | 4 |
| Patika Av | Y | 28 F | 4 |
| Patina Dr | NY | 21 A | 1-2 |
| Paton Rd | T | 14 E-F | 3 |
| Patricia Av | SC | 31 D-E | 1 |
| Patricia Dr | NY | 10 D-F | 2 |
| Patricia Dr | T | 15 D | 3-4 |
| Patrick Blvd | NY | 21 E-F | 6 |
| Patrick Blvd | NY | 31 A | 6 |
| Patsfield Gt | SC | 31 F | 4 |
| Patterson Av | SC | 25 B | 2-3 |
| Paul David St | NY | 18 F | 5 |
| Paul Markway | NY | 21 A | 4 |
| Paula Blvd | ET | 32 E | 1-2 |
| Paulander Av | SC | 47 E | 1 |
| Paulart Dr | ET | 34 E | 1 |
| Pauline Av | T | 14 F | 2 |
| Paulson Rd | Y | 16 B-C | 3 |
| Paultiel Dr | NY | 11 C | 1-2 |
| Paulvale Cr | NY | 20 C | 4 |
| Pavane Linkway | NY | 17 C-D | 5 |
| Pawnee Rd | NY | 21 E-F | 3 |
| Paxman Rd | ET | 34 C | 5 |
| Paxtonia Blvd | NY | 18 D | 3 |
| Paynter Dr | NY | 21 B | 1 |
| Payzac Av | SC | 37 F | 2 |
| Peace Dr | SC | 39 D | 4 |
| Peach Tree Path | ET | 28 B | 5-6 |
| Peach Villaway | NY | 11 F | 5 |
| Peacham Cr | NY | 18 A-B | 2 |
| Peacock Av | ET | 32 D-E | 5 |
| Pear Tree Mews | T | 14 E | 3 |
| Peard Rd | EY | 17 F | 6 |
| Peardale Av | NY | 8 B | 3-4 |
| Pearen St | Y | 16 A | 3-4 |
| Pearl St | T | 2 E-F | 1 |
| Pears Av | T | 4 E-F | 2 |
| Pearson Av | T | 14 D-E | 6 |
| Pearwood Cr | NY | 9 A | 4-5 |
| Pebble Byway | NY | 21 B-D | 2 |
| Pebble Valley La | ET | 34 A | 1 |
| Pebblehill Sq | SC | 31 F | 4 |
| Pebblewood Av | SC | 41 B | 2 |
| Pecan Ct | NY | 18 B-C | 1 |
| Peckford Rd | NY | 10 D | 2-3 |
| Peckham Av | NY | 10 E | 1-2 |
| Peebles Av | NY | 7 F | 1-2 |
| Peel Av | T | 14 F | 6 |
| Peel Rd | T | 4 A | 6 |
| Pegasus Tr | SC | 39 D-E | 3 |
| Peking Rd | SC | 37 C | 2-3 |
| Pelham Av | T | 14 D-E | 6 |
| Pelham Park Gdns | T | 14 D-E | 6 |
| Pelican Gt | NY | 30 F | 4 |
| Pell St | SC | 25 E | 2-3 |
| Pellatt Av | NY | 28 D-E | 4 |
| Pelmar Pl | SC | 37 D | 2 |
| Pelmo Cr | NY | 28 F | 5 |
| Pember Dr | NY | 18 C | 5 |
| Pemberton Av | NY | 11 A-B | 3 |
| Pemberton St | T | 3 B | 2 |
| Pembroke St | T | 5 A | 5-6 |
| Pembury Av | NY | 7 C-D | 1 |
| Pemican Ct | NY | 30 E | 4 |
| Penaire St | SC | 25 A | 4 |
| Pendeen Av | Y | 26 F | 4-5 |
| Pender Cr | SC | 29 D | 2 |
| Pendermere Pkwy | SC | 47 D | 4 |
| Pendle Hill Ct | SC | 39 C | 4 |
| Pendrith La | T | 4 B | 3 |
| Pendrith St | T | 4 B | 3 |
| Penetang Cr | SC | 27 F | 2 |
| Pengarth Gt | NY | 8 A | 5 |
| Pengelly Ct | SC | 25 C | 1 |
| Pengelly Ct | SC | 27 C | 6 |
| Penhale Dr | ET | 26 D | 2 |
| Penhurst Av | T | 22 D | 1 |
| Penlea Av | ET | 40 F | 4 |
| Penmarric St | SC | 41 A | 1 |
| Penn Dr | NY | 30 C | 3-4 |
| Pennard Ct | NY | 10 D-E | 3 |
| Penny La | NY | 15 B | 6 |
| Pennybrook La | SC | 39 C | 1 |
| Pennyhill Dr | SC | 41 A | 4-5 |
| Pennyhill St | SC | 41 A | 4-5 |
| Penrose Rd | T | 7 B | 4 |
| Pentland Pl | T | 36 E | 5 |
| Pently Cr | SC | 29 D-E | 2 |
| Penwood Cr | NY | 9 E | 4-5 |
| Penworth Rd | SC | 29 A-B | 3 |
| Penzance Dr | SC | 27 F | 2 |
| Pepler Av | EY | 5 E | 1 |
| Pepper Tree Dr | SC | 47 E-F | 2 |
| Pepper Vineway | NY | 11 F | 4 |
| Peppermill Pl | SC | 41 B | 1 |
| Percy St | T | 3 C | 1 |
| Peregrine Way | T | 6 D | 5 |
| Pergola Rd | ET | 38 E | 1 |
| Pergola St | T | 4 E | 6 |
| Perivale Cr | SC | 37 D-E | 4 |
| Permfield Path | SC | 34 C | 1 |
| Perry Av | T | 24 A-B | 3 |
| Perry Cr | T | 26 B | 6 |
| Persimmon Ct | SC | 37 B | 5 |
| Perth Av | T | 14 E | 5-6 |
| Perthshire St | SC | 31 D | 3 |
| Petal Ct | NY | 17 F | 4 |
| Peter Kaiser St | NY | 20 A | 1 |
| Peter Kaiser Gt | NY | 30 F | 1 |
| Peter St | T | 2 E | 1 |
| Peterborough Av | T | 14 F | 1 |
| Peterborough St | T | 4 A | 3 |
| Peterdale Rd | NY | 18 B | 6 |
| Peterlee Av | ET | 34 D-E | 3 |
| Peterson Dr | NY | 30 F | 4 |
| Petiole Rd | NY | 30 F | 4 |
| Petman Av | T | 7 B | 4 |
| Petrolia Rd | NY | 20 E | 1-2 |
| Pettibone Sq | SC | 31 A | 3 |
| Pettit Dr | ET | 26 A | 2-3 |
| Petworth Cr | SC | 31 E | 4 |
| Peveril Hill N | Y | 6 C | 4 |
| Peverill Hill S | Y | 6 C | 4 |
| Pewter Rd | NY | 8 F | 1 |
| Phalen Ct | SC | 41 A | 2 |
| Pharmacy Av | SC | 25 A | 1-3 |
| Pharmacy Av | SC | 27 A | 1-6 |
| Pharmacy Av | SC | 29 A | 1-6 |
| Pharmacy Av | SC | 31 A | 2-6 |
| Pheasant La | ET | 26 A-B | 6 |
| Pheasant Rd | NY | 11 B | 2 |
| Phenix Dr | SC | 25 C | 3-4 |
| Phillip Av | SC | 25 E | 2-3 |
| Phin Av | T | 15 A | 4 |
| Phipps St | T | 4 F | 4 |
| Phlox Av | ET | 32 E | 4 |
| Phoebe St | T | 2 D | 1 |
| Photography Dr | Y | 16 B | 4 |
| Phyllis Av | SC | 37 A-B | 5 |
| Picaro Dr | NY | 30 F | 4 |
| Picasso Rd | SC | 49 C | 2 |
| Pickering St | T | 15 F | 4-5 |
| Pickford Rd | SC | 49 A | 5 |
| Pickwick Rd | SC | 29 A | 5 |
| Picola Cr | NY | 21 C | 2 |
| Picton Cr | NY | 18 D | 3 |
| Pictorial Ct | SC | 49 C | 2-3 |
| Pilgrim Ct | NY | 16 B-C | 2 |
| Pilkey Cr | SC | 39 F | 1 |
| Pilot St | SC | 37 F | 2 |
| Pimlico Rd | NY | 18 C | 6 |
| Pindar Cr | NY | 21 E-F | 6 |
| Pine Av | T | 15 E-F | 6 |
| Pine Cr | T | 13 E | 6 |
| Pine Cr | T | 15 E | 5-6 |
| Pine Crest Rd | T | 14 B | 3 |
| Pine Forest Rd | NY | 7 B | 2 |
| Pine Glen Rd | T | 15 E | 6 |
| Pine Hill Rd | T | 5 A | 3 |
| Pine Ridge Dr | SC | 37 B-C | 5-6 |
| Pine St | T | 26 F | 1 |
| Pine St | Y | 28 F | 5-6 |
| Pine Terr | T | 15 F | 6 |
| Pinebrook Av | NY | 17 F | 4 |
| Pinecone Dr | ET | 40 A-B | 4 |
| Pinedale Dr | T | 7 B | 4 |
| Pinegrove Av | SC | 25 D | 3 |
| Pinehill Cr | Y | 26 F | 3 |
| Pinehurst Cr | ET | 26 B-C | 6 |
| Pinemeadow Blvd | SC | 31 A-B | 4 |
| Pinemore Cr | NY | 19 F | 4 |
| Pineslope Cr | SC | 39 E-F | 2 |
| Pineway Blvd | NY | 11 F | 2-3 |
| Pinewood Av | Y | 6 B | 5-6 |
| Pinewoods Dr | ET | 28 C | 1-2 |
| Pinnacle Rd | NY | 9 E-F | 3 |
| Pintail Cr | NY | 19 F | 3-4 |
| Pinto Dr | NY | 21 E | 4 |
| Pioneer Av | NY | 26 F | 2 |
| Pioneer Pathway | SC | 41 F | 5-6 |
| Pioneer Pathway | SC | 51 A | 6 |
| Piper St | T | 2 F | 2 |
| Piperbrook Cr | SC | 47 B | 3 |
| Pipers Green Av | SC | 41 A | 4 |
| Pipestone Pl | ET | 28 C | 2 |
| Pippin Pl | ET | 24 A | 1 |
| Pippin Pl | ET | 26 A | 6 |
| Pitcairn Cr | NY | 17 E | 3 |
| Pitfield Rd | SC | 29 F | 2 |
| Pitfield Rd | SC | 39 A-B | 1 |
| Pitkin Ct | NY | 16 B | 2 |
| Pitt Av | SC | 25 A | 1-2 |
| Pittsboro Dr | ET | 40 E | 4 |
| Pixley Cr | SC | 47 B | 2-3 |
| Placentia Blvd | SC | 41 B | 4-5 |
| Placer Ct | NY | 21 E | 2 |
| Placid Rd | ET | 24 C | 4-5 |
| Plainfield Rd | NY | 26 F | 1-2 |
| Plainfield Rd | ET | 26 F | 1-2 |
| Plains Rd | EY | 15 A-C | 2 |
| Plant Blvd | SC | 49 C | 4 |
| Plastics Av | ET | 22 B | 1 |
| Plateau Cr | NY | 17 C | 1-2 |
| Platinum Dr | NY | 16 A | 2 |
| Plaxton Cr | EY | 15 E | 1 |
| Plaxton Dr | EY | 15 E | 1 |
| Playdell Ct | ET | 30 A | 6 |
| Playfair St | NY | 16 E-F | 1 |
| Playter Blvd | T | 5 D | 3 |
| Playter Cr | T | 5 D-E | 3 |

| STREET NAME | MUNICI-PALITY | MAP NO | MAP AREA |
|---|---|---|---|
| Ranstone Gdns | SC | 27 | D-E 2 |
| Ranwood Dr | NY | 28 | E 5 |
| Raoul Wallenberg Rd | NY | 8 | D-E 1 |
| Rappert Av | NY | 7 | C 3 |
| Raquel Ct | Y | 26 | F 6 |
| Rathburn Rd | ET | 26 | A-B 6 |
| Rathburn Rd | ET | 36 | A-F 6 |
| Rathgar Av | ET | 34 | B-C 2 |
| Rathlyn Ct | ET | 40 | E 4 |
| Rathmore Av | SC | 25 | B 4 |
| Rathnelly Av | T | 4 | E 2 |
| Ravel Rd | NY | 21 | A 3 |
| Raven Rd | NY | 18 | A 5 |
| Ravenal St | Y | 16 | B 6 |
| Ravenbury Rd | NY | 21 | A 5 |
| Ravencliff Cr | SC | 31 | A-B 5 |
| Ravenhill Rd | NY | 8 | E 3 |
| Ravenrock Ct | NY | 18 | A 5 |
| Ravensbourne Cr | ET | 26 | A-B 4 |
| Ravenscrest Dr | ET | 36 | E-F 5-6 |
| Ravenscroft Cir | NY | 11 | D 5 |
| Ravenview Dr | SC | 47 | C-D 1-2 |
| Ravenwood Pl | EY | 15 | E 2 |
| Ravina Cr | T | 5 | F 4 |
| Ravine Dr | SC | 37 | B-C 6 |
| Ravine Park Cr | SC | 47 | D 5 |
| Rawlings Av | T | 5 | C 4-5 |
| Rawlinson Av | T | 7 | A 3 |
| Ray Av | Y | 16 | A-B 3 |
| Ray La | T | 3 | B 1 |
| Raybould St | Y | 14 | A-B 1 |
| Raymead St | SC | 47 | C 2 |
| Raymond Av | Y | 24 | F 2 |
| Raymore Dr | ET | 26 | E 1-2 |
| Rayoak Dr | NY | 19 | F 3-4 |
| Rayside Dr | SC | 34 | C 3-4 |
| Rayward Ct | SC | 41 | D-E 6 |
| Reading Ct | ET | 38 | B-C 6 |
| Rean Dr | NY | 9 | E 1 |
| Rebecca St | T | 4 | B 6 |
| Rectory Rd | NY | 28 | D 5 |
| Red Cedarway | NY | 20 | A 1-2 |
| Red Deer Av | SC | 25 | D 4 |
| Red Maple Ct | NY | 11 | D 6 |
| Red Oaks Cr | EY | 5 | C 1 |
| Red Oaks Cr | EY | 7 | C 6 |
| Red River Cr | SC | 49 | C 2 |
| Red Robinway | NY | 10 | C 4 |
| Redbank Rd | NY | 16 | C 1 |
| Redberry Pkwy | NY | 18 | D 6 |
| Redbird Gt | SC | 31 | A 4 |
| Redbud Cr | SC | 39 | A 2 |
| Redcar Av | ET | 34 | D 3 |
| Redcastle Cr | SC | 31 | B 6 |
| Redcliff Blvd | ET | 28 | A 2 |
| Reddins Rd | SC | 29 | A 3 |
| Redfern Av | NY | 18 | B 3 |
| Redgrave Dr | ET | 36 | D-E 2-3 |
| Redhead Cr | SC | 41 | B 3 |
| Redheugh Cr | SC | 31 | B-C 6 |
| Redhill Av | Y | 16 | E-F 4 |
| Redland Cr E | SC | 25 | C 4 |
| Redland Cr W | SC | 25 | E 6 |
| Redlea Av | SC | 31 | E 1 |
| Redmount Rd | NY | 8 | B 2-3 |
| Rednor Rd | EY | 15 | D 2 |
| Redpath Av | T | 7 | A 3-4 |
| Redstone Path | ET | 34 | A 1-2 |
| Redthorn Ct | NY | 34 | B 1 |
| Redwater Dr | ET | 28 | A-B 2-3 |
| Redwater Dr | ET | 38 | F 3 |
| Redway Rd | EY | 7 | E 5-6 |
| Rediwillow Dr | NY | 19 | B 5 |
| Redwing Pl | NY | 17 | B 2 |
| Redwood Av | NY | 15 | A 5 |
| Reed Grassway | NY | 30 | F 4-5 |
| Rees St | T | 2 | E 2 |
| Reesor Rd | SC | 51 | C-D 1-4 |
| Reeve Av | SC | 25 | C 1 |
| Regatta Cr | NY | 10 | D 5 |
| Regency Sq | SC | 37 | D 2 |
| Regent Rd | NY | 18 | E-F 3 |
| Regent St | T | 5 | B 6 |
| Regina Av | NY | 8 | B-C 3 |
| Regis Dr | NY | 11 | B 4 |
| Reiber Cr | NY | 11 | F 2-3 |
| Reid Manor | ET | 24 | D 4 |
| Reidmount Av | SC | 31 | E 6 |
| Reigate Rd | ET | 36 | B 1 |
| Reiner Rd | NY | 8 | A-C 1 |
| Relmar Gdns | T | 6 | D 6 |
| Relmar Rd | T | 6 | D 5-6 |
| Relroy Ct | SC | 31 | A 2 |
| Remembrance Dr | T | 2 | B-C 2-3 |
| Remington Dr | ET | 24 | A 1 |
| Remington Dr | ET | 26 | A 6 |
| Remora Royalway | NY | 21 | B 3 |
| Renata Royalway | NY | 21 | B 2-3 |
| Renault Cr | ET | 26 | D 2-3 |
| Renfield St | NY | 16 | A 1 |
| Renforth Dr | ET | 34 | B 1-3 |
| Renforth Dr | ET | 36 | A-B 2-6 |
| Renfrew Pl | T | 4 | E 6 |
| Rennie Terr | T | 14 | B 4 |
| Reno Dr | SC | 27 | D 3 |
| Renoak Dr | NY | 10 | C 1-2 |
| Renova Dr | ET | 34 | B 1 |
| Renown Rd | ET | 24 | A 3 |
| Rensburg Dr | SC | 27 | D 3 |
| Renshaw St | NY | 18 | C 2-3 |
| Renwick Cr | T | 3 | E 1 |
| Replin Rd | NY | 8 | C 4 |
| Research Rd | EY | 7 | E-F 4 |
| Resolution Cr | NY | 21 | B 2 |
| Resever Gt | ET | 28 | A 1 |
| Resources Rd | ET | 28 | B-C 4 |
| Restwell Cr | NY | 11 | E 5 |
| Reuben Av | NY | 28 | C 3 |
| Revcoe Dr | NY | 11 | B 3 |
| Revere Pl | ET | 24 | B 4 |
| Revlis Cr | SC | 31 | D 3 |
| Rex Gt | ET | 38 | F 4 |
| Rexdale Blvd | ET | 28 | A-B 3 |
| Rexdale Blvd | ET | 38 | A-F 1-3 |
| Rexdale Blvd | ET | 40 | A-C 6 |
| Rexford Rd | Y | 14 | A 1 |
| Rexleigh Dr | EY | 15 | E 1-2 |
| Rexton Rd | ET | 34 | B-C 2 |
| Reynolds St | T | 5 | A 3 |
| Rhinestone Dr | ET | 36 | B-C 5 |
| Rhodes Av | T | 15 | B 3-6 |
| Rhydwen Av | SC | 25 | D 3 |
| Rhyl Av | T | 15 | D 5 |
| Rialto Dr | NY | 19 | E 6 |
| Riant St | SC | 37 | C 4 |
| Ricardo Rd | NY | 18 | B 5 |
| Richard Av | T | 15 | A-B 5 |
| Richard Clark Dr | NY | 18 | A-B 3 |
| Richardson Av | Y | 16 | D 3-4 |
| Richardson St | T | 3 | A 2 |
| Richbourne Ct | SC | 31 | B 6 |
| Richdale Ct | ET | 36 | F 4 |
| Richelieu Rd | NY | 2 | C 3-4 |
| Richgrove Dr | ET | 36 | D-E 3 |
| Richland Cr | ET | 36 | B 5 |
| Richlea Cir | EY | 7 | E 3 |
| Richmond Park Blvd | SC | 41 | B 3 |
| Richmond St E | T | 2 | F 1 |
| Richmond St E | T | 3 | A-C 1 |
| Richmond St W | T | 2 | B-F 1 |
| Richmond St W | T | 3 | A 1 |
| Richome Ct | SC | 27 | D 3 |
| Richview Av | T | 6 | D 4-5 |
| Richview Rd | ET | 26 | D-E 3 |
| Richwood St | Y | 16 | C 1 |
| Ricklan Dr | NY | 30 | F 6 |
| Rickshaw Av | ET | 34 | C 4 |
| Rideau Av | T | 14 | E 5 |
| Rideau Rd | NY | 20 | D 1 |
| Ridelle Av | T | 6 | B-E 3 |
| Ridelle Av | Y | 16 | F 3 |
| Ridelle Av | Y | 6 | A-B 3 |
| Riderwood Dr | NY | 9 | F 3 |
| Ridge Dr | T | 5 | A-B 1 |
| Ridge Drive Pk | T | 5 | A 1 |
| Ridge Hill Dr | T | 6 | B-D 3 |
| Ridge Point Cr | NY | 16 | B 1 |
| Ridge Rd | NY | 18 | B 5 |
| Ridgecross Rd | ET | 26 | B 4-5 |
| Ridgefield Rd | NY | 7 | C 2 |
| Ridgegate Cr | ET | 24 | D 5 |
| Ridgehampton Ct | ET | 24 | B 4-5 |
| Ridgemoor Av | SC | 25 | E 2-3 |
| Ridgemount Rd | ET | 26 | D 2-3 |
| Ridgetop Rd | SC | 29 | C-D 3 |
| Ridgevale Dr | NY | 8 | B-C 5 |
| Ridgevalley Cr | ET | 26 | B 5 |
| Ridgewood Rd | SC | 47 | D-E 4-5 |
| Ridgewood Rd | T | 6 | C-D 5 |
| Ridley Blvd | NY | 8 | E-F 2-4 |
| Ridley Blvd | NY | 8 | F 5 |
| Ridley Gdns | T | 14 | D 5-6 |
| Ridout St | T | 14 | D 4 |
| Ridvale Cr | SC | 49 | E 3-4 |
| Rifle Ct | ET | 36 | B 1 |
| Rima Ct | ET | 36 | B 5 |
| Rimilton Av | ET | 32 | C-F 2-3 |
| Rimrock Rd | NY | 20 | F 5 |
| Rinfret Av | ET | 24 | E-F 6 |
| Ringley Av | ET | 24 | E-F 6 |
| Ringway Cr | NY | 28 | B 3 |
| Ringwood Cr | NY | 19 | B 1 |
| Rintella Ct | SC | 29 | F 5 |
| Ripley Av | Y | 14 | A 5-6 |
| Ripon Rd | EY | 15 | F 1 |
| Ripon Rd | EY | 25 | A 1 |
| Rippleford Rd | NY | 9 | F 5 |
| Ripplewood Rd | ET | 26 | C 5 |
| Risa Blvd | NY | 16 | F 2 |
| Risa Blvd | NY | 6 | E 2 |
| Risdon Ct | ET | 36 | B 4 |
| Risebrough Av | NY | 11 | B-C 3 |
| Rita Dr | NY | 20 | A 6 |
| Ritchie Av | T | 14 | E 4 |
| Ritz Garden Ct | SC | 49 | C-D 4 |
| Rivalda Rd | NY | 30 | D-E 5-6 |
| River St | T | 5 | C 6 |
| River Valley Cr | ET | 24 | F 5 |
| Riverband Dr | ET | 24 | B 2 |
| Rivercourt Blvd | EY | 5 | F 1 |
| Rivercrest Rd | Y | 24 | F 3 |
| Riverdale Av | T | 5 | D-F 5 |
| Riverdale Dr | ET | 28 | B 1 |
| Riverdale Dr | ET | 28 | A 1 |
| Riverdale Park Rd | T | 5 | C 5 |
| Rivergrove Dr | SC | 31 | B 1 |
| Riverhead Dr | ET | 28 | A-B 1 |
| Riverhead Dr | ET | 30 | A 5-6 |
| Riverlea Dr | ET | 28 | D 6 |
| Riverlea Dr | ET | 28 | D 6 |
| Riverlea Rd | ET | 28 | D-E 6 |
| Riverside Cr | T | 24 | F 4 |
| Riverside Dr | NY | 30 | A 2 |
| Riverside Dr | T | 14 | A 5-6 |
| Riverside Dr | T | 24 | F 4-5 |
| Riverside Dr | T | 24 | F 4 |
| Riverside Tr | T | 24 | F 4 |
| Riverstone Dr | ET | 26 | E 1 |
| Riverton Dr | NY | 30 | A 2 |
| Riverview Dr | NY | 9 | B 5-6 |
| Riverview Dr | T | 9 | B 5 |
| Riverview Gdns | T | 24 | F 4 |
| Riverview Gdns | T | 24 | F 3 |
| Riverview Hts | ET | 28 | D 5-6 |
| Riverwood Pkwy | ET | 24 | E-F 4-5 |
| Riviera Dr | SC | 25 | E 3 |
| Roanoke Rd | NY | 19 | D-E 6 |
| Robalon Rd | ET | 26 | B-C 4 |
| Robbie Av | NY | 8 | B-C 3 |
| Robbins Av | T | 15 | B 5-6 |
| Robbinstone Dr | SC | 41 | D 6 |
| Robert Hicks Dr | NY | 10 | B 3 |
| Robert St | NY | 28 | E 5 |
| Robert St | T | 4 | D 4-5 |
| Robert Woodhead Cr | NY | 20 | D 6 |
| Roberta Dr | NY | 8 | B-C 5-6 |
| Robertsfield Cr | SC | 29 | A 4-5 |
| Robertson Cir | T | 2 | E 3 |
| Robin Hood Rd | ET | 24 | B 1 |
| Robina Av | Y | 6 | A 5-6 |
| Robina Av | Y | 16 | A 3 |
| Robindale Av | ET | 32 | E 3 |
| Robinglade Dr | ET | 36 | D 5-6 |
| Robingrove Rd | NY | 10 | C 2 |
| Robinson Av | SC | 25 | B 3 |
| Robinson St | T | 4 | B-D 6 |
| Rointer Dr | NY | 11 | C 1-2 |
| Robin Ct | ET | 36 | D 4 |
| Robinwood Av | T | 6 | D 6 |
| Roblin Av | EY | 15 | C 1-2 |
| Roblocke Av | T | 4 | B 3 |
| Robron Pl | NY | 10 | B 3 |
| Rochdale Av | Y | 16 | E-F 5 |
| Rochefort Dr | NY | 17 | A-B 4 |
| Rochelle Cr | NY | 21 | B 5-6 |
| Rochester Av | NY | 7 | B-C 1 |
| Rochester Av | T | 7 | B-C 5 |
| Rochmon Blvd | SC | 39 | B-D 5-6 |
| Rock Fernway | NY | 21 | A-B 4 |
| Rock Mossway | NY | 21 | B 1 |
| Rockaway Cr | SC | 25 | A 6 |
| Rockaway Cr | T | 13 | F 5 |
| Rockbank Cr | NY | 28 | E 2 |
| Rockcastle Dr | ET | 26 | A 2-3 |
| Rockcliffe Blvd | Y | 16 | A 4-6 |
| Rockcliffe Dr | Y | 16 | A-B 5-6 |
| Rockelm Rd | SC | 27 | B 6 |
| Rockfield Dr | ET | 34 | E 2 |
| Rockford Rd | NY | 10 | B-C 1-2 |

R

| Street | Area | Pg | Col | Row |
|---|---|---|---|---|
| Rockingham Dr | ET | 26 | A-B | 6 |
| Rockland Dr | NY | 11 | E | 1 |
| Rockport Dr | SC | 47 | F | 2 |
| Rockvale Av | Y | 6 | A | 5 |
| Rockwell Av | T | 16 | D-E | 6 |
| Rockwood Dr | SC | 37 | B | 4-5 |
| Rodarick Dr | SC | 47 | E | 1 |
| Rodd Av | SC | 47 | F | 4 |
| Rodda Blvd | SC | 49 | A | 5-6 |
| Roden Pl | T | 4 | F | 3 |
| Rodeo Ct | NY | 10 | F | 2-3 |
| Rodeo Pathway | SC | 25 | B | 4-5 |
| Roding St | NY | 18 | C | 2-3 |
| Rodney Blvd | NY | 11 | B-C | 5 |
| Roe Av | NY | 8 | E | 5 |
| Roe Av | T | 8 | E | 5 |
| Roebuck Dr | T | 27 | D | 4-5 |
| Roehampton Av | T | 7 | A-D | 3 |
| Rogate Pl | SC | 37 | E | 5 |
| Rogers Rd | T | 16 | B-F | 5 |
| Rogers Rd | Y | 6 | A | 5 |
| Roker Ct | SC | 31 | E | 5-6 |
| Rolark Dr | SC | 29 | C | 3-4 |
| Rolland Rd | EY | 7 | D | 5 |
| Rollet Dr | NY | 18 | D-E | 6 |
| Rolling Meadows | SC | 47 | E-F | 1 |
| Rollingwood Dr | NY | 21 | B-D | 2 |
| Rollins Pl | ET | 34 | D | 3 |
| Rollscourt Dr | NY | 9 | D | 2-3 |
| Rolph Rd | EY | 7 | | 5-6 |
| Rolyat St | T | 4 | B | 5 |
| Romac Dr | SC | 49 | D | 4 |
| Romana Dr | SC | 25 | E-F | 3 |
| Romanway Cr | NY | 26 | F | 1 |
| Romar Cr | NY | 18 | D | 5 |
| Romeo St | NY | 18 | D | 5 |
| Rometown Dr | M | 32 | A-B | 2-3 |
| Romfield Dr | NY | 20 | D | 4 |
| Romfield La | NY | 20 | D | 4 |
| Romey Rd | ET | 26 | D | 5 |
| Romney Rd | NY | 8 | D | 2 |
| Romulus Dr | SC | 27 | E | 2 |
| Ronald Av | Y | 16 | E | 2-3 |
| Ronan Av | T | 9 | A | 5-6 |
| Roncesvalles Av | T | 14 | E | 4-6 |
| Rondale Blvd | NY | 8 | B | 6 |
| Rondeau Dr | NY | 21 | A | 1 |
| Ronson Dr | ET | 38 | E-F | 4-6 |
| Ronway Cr | SC | 37 | C | 3 |
| Rooksgrove Pl | NY | 16 | C | 2 |
| Rooksnest Tr | SC | 41 | B | 5 |
| Roosevelt Rd | EY | 15 | B | 2-3 |
| Rory Rd | NY | 18 | C | 4 |
| Rosalie Av | NY | 28 | F | 3 |
| Rosalind Cr | SC | 27 | A | 6 |
| Roscoe Rd | SC | 49 | E | 1 |
| Rose Av | T | 5 | B | 4-5 |
| Rose Park Cr | T | 7 | A | 6 |
| Rose Park Dr | T | 7 | A-B | 6 |
| Rose Valley Cr | Y | 16 | E-F | 5 |
| Rosebank Dr | SC | 39 | D | 1 |
| Rosebank Rd | SC | 47 | F | 1 |
| Rosecliffe Av | Y | 6 | A | 5 |
| Rosedale Heights Dr | T | 5 | B-C | 1 |
| Rosedale Valley Rd | T | 5 | A-C | 3-4 |
| Rosefair Cr | ET | 38 | D-E | 2 |
| Roseglen Cr | NY | 30 | F | 5 |
| Roseglor Cr | SC | 29 | F | 6 |
| Rosegrove Pl | SC | 29 | F | 2 |
| Roseheath Av | T | 5 | C | 3-4 |
| Rosehill Av | T | 5 | A | 1 |
| Roseland Dr | ET | 32 | C | 3 |
| Roselawn Av | T | 16 | F | 3 |
| Roselawn Av | Y | 6 | B-F | 3 |
| Roselawn Av | Y | 16 | F | 3 |
| Roselawn Av | T | 6 | A-B | 3 |
| Roselm Av | SC | 27 | C | 1 |
| Roselm Rd | SC | 29 | B-C | 6 |
| Rosemarie Dr | SC | 29 | B | 6 |
| Rosemary La | T | 6 | C-D | 4 |
| Rosemary Rd | T | 6 | D | 4-5 |
| Rosemeade Av | ET | 24 | B | 6 |
| Rosemount Av | T | 14 | F | 1 |
| Rosemount Av | T | 4 | A-B | 1 |
| Rosemount Av | T | 4 | A-B | 1 |
| Rosemount Dr | SC | 27 | D | 2-3 |
| Roseneath Gdns | Y | 6 | B | 5-6 |
| Rosethorn Av | T | 16 | D | 5-6 |
| Rosethorn Av | T | 16 | D | 5-6 |
| Rosette Ct | NY | 30 | C | 4 |
| Rosevear Av | EY | 15 | E-F | 3 |
| Rosewell Av | T | 6 | D | 4-5 |
| Rosewell Av | T | 8 | E | 6 |
| Rosewood Av | ET | 24 | B-C | 6 |
| Rosita Cr | SC | 27 | A | 6 |
| Roskell Cr | NY | 20 | C | 4-5 |
| Roslin Av | T | 8 | F | 5 |
| Roslin Av | T | 9 | A-B | 5-6 |
| Ross Av | SC | 31 | E | 6 |
| Ross St | T | 4 | E | 5 |
| Rossander Ct | SC | 37 | B | 2 |
| Rossburn Dr | ET | 34 | B-C | 2-3 |
| Rosscowan Cr | SC | 31 | A | 5 |
| Rosscowan Ct | SC | 31 | A | 5 |
| Rossdean Dr | NY | 30 | E | 1 |
| Rosseau Rd | NY | 8 | C | 2-3 |
| Rossford Rd | SC | 29 | B | 5 |
| Rossini Pl | SC | 47 | A | 3 |
| Rossmore Rd | T | 4 | C | 2-3 |
| Rosswood Cr | SC | 29 | F | 5 |
| Rostrevor Rd | Y | 6 | C | 4 |
| Rotary Dr | SC | 49 | E | 1-2 |
| Rotherham Av | Y | 16 | B-C | 4 |
| Rothmere Dr | NY | 9 | B | 5 |
| Rothsay Av | ET | 24 | B | 6 |
| Rothwell Rd | SC | 29 | A | 3 |
| Rotunda Pl | SC | 29 | B | 2 |
| Rouge Highland Dr | SC | 47 | D | 2 |
| Rouge Hills Dr | SC | 47 | E-F | 4-5 |
| Rouge River Dr | SC | 51 | C | 6 |
| Rougedate Ct | SC | 51 | C | 6 |
| Roughfield Cr | SC | 41 | B | 4 |
| Roughwood Ct | NY | 20 | B | 5 |
| Roundwood Ct | SC | 31 | B | 5 |
| Rovinelli Rd | SC | 41 | F | 4 |
| Rovinelli Rd | SC | 51 | A | 4 |
| Rowallan Dr | SC | 47 | A | 2 |
| Rowan Av | T | 16 | F | 4 |
| Rowanwood Av | T | 5 | A | 2 |
| Rowatson Rd | SC | 37 | E | 3-4 |
| Rowena Dr | NY | 19 | F | 5 |
| Rowland St | T | 14 | B | 2 |
| Rowley Av | NY | 7 | C | 3 |
| Rowley Av | T | 7 | C | 3 |
| Rowntree Av | T | 16 | D-E | 5 |
| Rowntree Mill Rd | NY | 30 | A-B | 2-3 |
| Rowse Cr | ET | 26 | B | 1-2 |
| Roxaline St | ET | 26 | D | 1 |
| Roxaline St | ET | 28 | D | 6 |
| Roxanne Cr | SC | 41 | A | 1 |
| Roxborough Dr | T | 5 | A-C | 2 |
| Roxborough St E | T | 5 | A | 2 |
| Roxborough St W | T | 4 | E-F | 2 |
| Roxton Rd | T | 4 | B | 3-5 |
| Roxville Av | EY | 7 | D | 3 |
| Royal Albert Cr | SC | 31 | D | 3 |
| Royal Doulton Dr | NY | 19 | E | 5 |
| Royal Oak Dr | NY | 7 | E-F | 2 |
| Royal Palm Ct | NY | 30 | C | 6 |
| Royal Rouge Tr | SC | 49 | F | 2-3 |
| Royal St | Y | 16 | A | 6 |
| Royal York Ct | ET | 22 | D | 1 |
| Royal York Rd | ET | 22 | C-D | 1-6 |
| Royal York Rd | ET | 24 | C-D | 1-6 |
| Royal York Rd | ET | 26 | C | 1-6 |
| Royalavon Cr | ET | 24 | A | 2-3 |
| Royalcrest Rd | ET | 40 | D-E | 2 |
| Royaleigh Av | ET | 28 | D | 6 |
| Royalwood Ct | ET | 26 | A | 3 |
| Roycroft Cr | NY | 10 | D-E | 6 |
| Roydawn Ct | SC | 49 | E | 5 |
| Roy's Sq | T | 5 | A | 3-4 |
| Roy's Sq | T | 5 | A | 3-4 |
| Roywood Dr | NY | 19 | E-F | 2-3 |
| Rozell Rd | SC | 47 | D | 4 |
| Rozell Rd | SC | 49 | F | 4 |
| Rubic Cr | SC | 29 | F | 2 |
| Rubicon Dr | SC | 41 | C | 3 |
| Ruby Cr | NY | 6 | D | 2 |
| Rudydale Gdns | NY | 30 | B | 3 |
| Ruddell Pl | SC | 49 | D | 5 |
| Ruddington Dr | NY | 11 | D | 2-3 |
| Ruden Cr | NY | 19 | B-D | 3 |
| Rufford Rd | ET | 32 | C | 2 |
| Rumi Cr | NY | 17 | E-F | 4 |
| Rumike Rd | NY | 30 | C | 4 |
| Rumney Rd | EY | 15 | D | 1 |
| Rumsey Rd | EY | 7 | D | 3-5 |
| Runnymede Rd | T | 14 | B | 1-4 |
| Runnymede Rd | T | 16 | A | 5 |
| Runnymede Rd | T | 16 | A | 6 |
| Rupert Av | SC | 25 | D | 2 |
| Rural Av | SC | 31 | E-F | 5 |
| Ruscica Dr | NY | 17 | E-F | 2-3 |
| Ruscoe Cr | ET | 26 | C | 1-2 |
| Rush La | T | 2 | D | 1 |
| Rushbrooke Av | T | 3 | F | 1 |
| Rushley Dr | SC | 27 | F | 1 |
| Rushley Dr | SC | 29 | F | 6 |
| Rusholme Dr | T | 4 | A | 5 |
| Rusholme Park Cr | T | 4 | A | 5 |
| Rusholme Rd | T | 4 | A | 3-5 |
| Rushton Rd | Y | 6 | B | 5-6 |
| Rushton Rd T | T | 4 | A | 5 |
| Ruskin Av | T | 14 | E | 3 |
| Russell Hill Dr | T | 4 | D-E | 1 |
| Russell Hill Rd | T | 4 | E | 1-2 |
| Russell Hill Rd | T | 6 | E | 4-6 |
| Russell Rd | ET | 26 | C | 3 |
| Russell St | T | 4 | D-E | 5 |
| Russett Av | T | 4 | C-F | 3 |
| Russfax Dr | NY | 10 | C | 1 |
| Rustic Rd | NY | 18 | A-E | 5 |
| Rusty Crestway | NY | 21 | B | 4 |
| Rustywood Dr | NY | 19 | E-F | 5 |
| Ruth Av | NY | 11 | C | 2 |
| Rutherford Av | Y | 16 | A | 3 |
| Rutherglen Rd | EY | 7 | D-E | 5 |
| Ruthmar Cr | NY | 30 | F | 2-3 |
| Ruthven Pl | Y | 16 | A | 4 |
| Rutland St | T | 14 | E | 1 |
| Rutledge Av | SC | 27 | E | 3 |
| Rutter St | SC | 37 | C | 3 |
| Ryding Av | T | 14 | B | 1 |
| Rye Meadoway | NY | 21 | C-D | 1 |
| Ryecliffe Ct | SC | 49 | F | 3 |
| Ryerson Av | T | 4 | D | 6 |
| Ryewood Dr | NY | 30 | F | 6 |
| Rykert Cr | EY | 7 | E-F | 3 |
| Rylander Blvd | SC | 49 | E-F | 3 |
| Rymer Rd | ET | 36 | B | 6 |

## S

| Street | Area | Pg | Col | Row |
|---|---|---|---|---|
| Saber Ct | NY | 10 | E | 3 |
| Sabine La | ET | 36 | E | 4-5 |
| Sable St | NY | 16 | E | 1-2 |
| Sabrina Dr | ET | 36 | E-F | 1 |
| Sachems Pl | SC | 41 | E | 6 |
| Sackville Green | T | 5 | B | 6 |
| Sackville Pl | T | 5 | B | 6 |
| Sackville Pl | T | 5 | B | 6 |
| Sackville St | T | 5 | B | 4-6 |
| Saddle Ridge Dr | NY | 17 | F | 4 |
| Saddleback Ct | SC | 49 | D | 2 |
| Saddletree Dr | NY | 11 | F | 1 |
| Saddle Cove Cr | SC | 41 | A | 2 |
| Sadler Dr | SC | 25 | D | 1 |
| Safari St | SC | 27 | E | 4 |
| Safeway Cr | M | 32 | A | 2 |
| Saffron Cr | ET | 36 | B-C | 6 |
| Sagamore Cr | ET | 36 | B | 4 |
| Sage Av | NY | 16 | F | 1 |
| Sagebrush La | NY | 19 | E | 4 |
| Sagewood Dr | NY | 9 | E | 4 |
| Saguenay Av | NY | 6 | E | 1 |
| Saint Albans Rd | ET | 34 | F | 3-4 |
| Saint Andrews St | T | 4 | D-E | 5 |
| Saint Andrews Blvd | ET | 28 | A-B | 5 |
| Saint Andrews Blvd | ET | 38 | F | 5 |
| Saint Andrews Gdns | T | 5 | B | 2 |
| Saint Andrews Rd | SC | 39 | A-B | 5 |
| Saint Anne's Rd | T | 4 | A | 5 |
| Saint Aubyns Cr | NY | 7 | C | 1 |
| Saint Clair Av E | Y | 24 | E | 1 |
| Saint Clair Av E | EY | 15 | C-F | 1 |
| Saint Clair Av E | EY | 17 | C-F | 6 |
| Saint Clair Av E | SC | 25 | A-F | 1 |
| Saint Clair Av E | EY | 7 | A-F | 1 |
| Saint Clair Av E | SC | 37 | A | 6 |
| Saint Clair Av W | T | 7 | A-B | 6 |
| Saint Clair Av W | T | 6 | A-F | 1 |
| Saint Clair Pl | Y | 24 | E | 1 |
| Saint Clare Av E | T | 5 | A-B | 1 |
| Saint Clair Av W | T | 16 | B-F | 1 |
| Saint Clare Av W | Y | 16 | A | 6 |
| Saint Clarens Av | T | 14 | F | 1-6 |
| Saint Clements Av | T | 6 | C-F | 3 |
| Saint Columba Pl | EY | 15 | E | 1 |
| Saint Crispins Dr | SC | 31 | D | 5 |
| Saint Cuthberts Rd | EY | 7 | D | 5 |
| Saint David Walk | T | 5 | B | 6 |
| Saint Dennis Dr | NY | 17 | C | 3-4 |
| Saint Dunstan Dr | SC | 25 | A | 3 |
| Saint Edmund's Dr | T | 7 | A | 1 |
| Saint Enoch's Sq | T | 5 | A | 6 |
| Saint George St | ET | 22 | C | 2 |
| Saint George St | T | 4 | C | 4-6 |
| Saint Georges Blvd | ET | 28 | A-B | 5 |
| Saint George's Rd | ET | 24 | C | 1 |
| Saint Germain Av | NY | 8 | C-E | 5 |
| Saint Germain Av | T | 8 | C-E | 5 |
| Saint Helens Av | T | 14 | E | 4-5 |
| Saint Hilda's Av | T | 7 | A | 2 |
| Saint Hubert Av | EY | 15 | A | 1-2 |

| STREET NAME | MUNICIPALITY | MAP NO | MAP AREA |
|---|---|---|---|
| Saint Ives Av | .T | 7 | B | 1 |
| Saint Ives Cr | .NY | 7 | B | 1 |
| Saint Ives Ct | .T | 7 | B | 1 |
| Saint James Av | .M | 32 | B | 5 |
| Saint James Av | .T | 5 | B | 4 |
| Saint James Ct | .T | 5 | C | 4 |
| Saint Johns Pl | .T | 14 | B | 1 |
| Saint John's Rd | .T | 14 | B | 2 |
| Saint John's Rd | .Y | 14 | A | 2 |
| Saint John's Rd | .Y | 24 | F | 2 |
| Saint Joseph St | .T | 4 | F | 4 |
| Saint Lawrence Av | .ET | 22 | B | 6 |
| Saint Lawrence St | .T | 3 | C | 1 |
| Saint Leonard's Av | .NY | 7 | A-B | 1 |
| Saint Leonard's Av | .T | 7 | A-B | 1 |
| Saint Leonard's Cr | .NY | 7 | B | 1-2 |
| Saint Leonard's Cr | .T | 7 | B | 1-2 |
| Saint Lucie Dr | .NY | 30 | C-D | 5-6 |
| Saint Magnus Dr | .SC | 49 | F | 4 |
| Saint Margarets Dr | .Y | 9 | B | 4 |
| Saint Marks Rd | .Y | 24 | E-F | 2 |
| Saint Mary St | .T | 4 | F | 4 |
| Saint Mary's Av | .M | 32 | A-B | 5 |
| Saint Mathias Pl | .T | 4 | C | 5-6 |
| Saint Matthews Rd | .T | 5 | D | 5 |
| Saint Maurice Cr | .ET | 28 | A | 5-6 |
| Saint Nicholas St | .T | 4 | F | 4 |
| Saint Paschal Ct | .NY | 10 | E | 1 |
| Saint Patrick St | .T | 4 | E | 5-6 |
| Saint Patricks Market | .T | 4 | E | 4 |
| Saint Patricks Sq | .T | 4 | E | 4 |
| Saint Paul St | .T | 3 | B | 1 |
| Saint Pauls Sq | .T | 4 | E | 4 |
| Saint Phillips Rd | .ET | 28 | C | 5-6 |
| Saint Regis Cr | .NY | 20 | D-E | 5 |
| Saint Regis Cr N | .NY | 20 | D-E | 5 |
| Saint Stevens Ct | .ET | 26 | C | 4 |
| Saint Thomas St | .T | 4 | F | 3-4 |
| Saintfield Av | .NY | 7 | E-F | 1-2 |
| Saintsbury Sq | .SC | 41 | A-B | 2 |
| Salem Av | .T | 4 | A | 2-3 |
| Salem Av N | .T | 4 | A | 1-2 |
| Salinger Ct | .NY | 21 | E | 2 |
| Salisbury Av | .T | 5 | B-C | 5 |
| Salome Dr | .SC | 29 | F | 1-2 |
| Salonica Rd | .NY | 7 | F | 2 |
| Salvation Sq | .T | 4 | F | 1 |
| Salvi Ct | .NY | 17 | E | 2 |
| Sam Frustaglio Dr | .NY | 26 | F | 1-2 |
| Samba Dr | .NY | 30 | F | 2 |
| Sammon Av | .EY | 15 | A-D | 3 |
| Sammon Av | .EY | 15 | E-F | 3 |
| Samor Rd | .NY | 18 | F | 5-6 |
| Samson Cr | .SC | 37 | E | 1-2 |
| Samuel Teitel Ct | .SC | 51 | A-B | 3 |
| Samya Ct | .SC | 27 | B | 1-2 |
| San Antonioway | .NY | 30 | F | 2 |
| San Carmeloway | .NY | 30 | F | 2 |
| San Lucaway | .NY | 30 | F | 2 |
| San Robertoway | .NY | 20 | A | 4 |
| San Roccoway | .NY | 20 | A | 3-4 |
| San Romanoway | .NY | 20 | A | 3-4 |
| San Varoway | .NY | 20 | A-B | 4 |
| San Vitoway | .NY | 20 | A | 4 |
| Sancrest Dr | .SC | 39 | A | 4-5 |
| Sanctbury Pl | .ET | 36 | B | 4-5 |
| Sand Beach Rd | .ET | 22 | C | 4 |
| Sand Fernway | .NY | 21 | B | 3 |
| Sandale Gdns | .NY | 10 | A | 6 |
| Sandalwood Pl | .NY | 19 | A | 5 |
| Sandbar Villaway | .NY | 17 | E | 5 |
| Sandbourne Cr | .NY | 21 | C-E | 3 |
| Sandcliff Rd | .T | 26 | F | 5 |
| Sanderling Pl | .NY | 17 | B | 1 |
| Sanderson Rd | .ET | 28 | B | 1 |
| Sanderson Rd | .ET | 40 | F | 1 |
| Sanderstead Av | .Y | 16 | E | 3-4 |
| Sandfield Rd | .NY | 8 | E | 3-4 |
| Sandford Av | .T | 15 | A | 3 |
| Sandhill Dr | .ET | 30 | A-B | 4 |
| Sandhurst Cir | .SC | 51 | A-B | 3-4 |
| Sandhurst Cir | .SC | 39 | D | 6 |
| Sandover Dr | .NY | 19 | B | 3 |
| Sandown Av | .SC | 25 | E | 1-2 |
| Sandown Rd | .NY | 8 | E | 3 |
| Sandpiper Ct | .NY | 19 | C-D | 1 |
| Sandra Rd | .EY | 15 | D | 5 |
| Sandra Rd | .EY | 17 | D | 4 |
| Sandrift Sq | .SC | 39 | F | 2 |
| Sandringham Dr | .NY | 8 | D-F | 2-3 |
| Sandstone La | .T | 15 | A | 4 |
| Sandusky Cr | .SC | 27 | B | 2 |
| Sandwell Dr | .ET | 36 | E | 1-2 |
| Sandy Haven Dr | .SC | 31 | B | 2 |
| Sandyhook Sq | .SC | 31 | B | 1 |
| Santa Barbara Rd | .NY | 10 | E-F | 4 |
| Santamonica Blvd | .SC | 25 | B-C | 1 |
| Santamonica Blvd | .SC | 27 | C | 6 |
| Sanwin Ct | .NY | 21 | E | 5 |
| Sanwood Blvd | .SC | 31 | D | 2 |
| Sapling Ct | .ET | 34 | B | 3 |
| Saraband St | .ET | 40 | D | 4 |
| Sarah Ashbridge Av | .T | 13 | F | 1 |
| Sarah St | .T | 4 | C | 6 |
| Saratoga Dr | .SC | 39 | A | 4 |
| Sari Cr | .SC | 37 | F | 3 |
| Sarnia Av | .T | 14 | E | 3 |
| Saskatchewan Rd | .T | 2 | A | 2 |
| Saskatoon Dr | .ET | 26 | B-C | 1 |
| Satchell Blvd | .SC | 49 | E | 4-5 |
| Satok Terr | .SC | 47 | D-E | 1-2 |
| Satterly Rd | .NY | 30 | B | 2 |
| Saturn Rd | .ET | 34 | B | 2 |
| Saugeen Cr | .SC | 27 | E | 4 |
| Saulter St | .T | 5 | D | 1 |
| Saulter St S | .T | 3 | D-E | 2 |
| Saunders Av | .T | 14 | E | 6 |
| Saunders Ct | .ET | 24 | C | 6 |
| Saunders Rd | .SC | 37 | E | 3 |
| Saunders St | .NY | 8 | E | 3-4 |
| Savalon Ct | .ET | 36 | E | 6 |
| Savarin St | .SC | 37 | A | 3 |
| Savona Dr | .ET | 32 | B-C | 2 |
| Savory Av | .EY | 15 | C-D | 2 |
| Sawden Av | .T | 15 | A | 5 |
| Sawley Dr | .NY | 19 | D | 2 |
| Sawmill Rd | .NY | 20 | B | 5-6 |
| Saxony Cr | .T | 26 | E | 2 |
| Saybrook Av | .ET | 24 | A | 5 |
| Scadding Av | .T | 3 | A-B | 2-3 |
| Scarbell Dr | .SC | 49 | D | 3 |
| Scarboro Av | .SC | 49 | D | 3-4 |
| Scarboro Beach Blvd | .T | 13 | E | 6 |
| Scarboro Beach Blvd | .T | 15 | E | 6 |
| Scarboro Cr | .SC | 25 | F | 2-3 |
| Scarboro Hts Blvd | .SC | 25 | F | 4-5 |
| Scarborough Golf Club Rd | .SC | 37 | D-E | 1-4 |
| Scarborough Golf Club Rd | .SC | 39 | E | 4-6 |
| Scarborough Heights Blvd | .SC | 37 | B | 6 |
| Scarborough Rd | .T | 13 | F | 5 |
| Scarborough Rd | .T | 15 | F | 4-6 |
| Scarborough-Pickering Townline | .SC | 51 | F | 1-4 |
| Scarcliff Gdns | .SC | 47 | A | 3-4 |
| Scarfair Pathway | .SC | 51 | A | 5-6 |
| Scarden Av | .SC | 29 | B-C | 2 |
| Scarlett Rd | .ET | 26 | D-E | 1-4 |
| Scarlett Rd | .ET | 28 | D | 6 |
| Scarlett Rd | .Y | 26 | E | 4-6 |
| Scarlett Rd | .Y | 28 | D | 6 |
| Scarlettwood Ct | .ET | 26 | E | 2 |
| Scarsdale Rd | .NY | 19 | A | 3-4 |
| Scarth Rd | .T | 5 | A-B | 3 |
| Scenic Hill Ct | .SC | 49 | C | 5 |
| Scenic Millway | .NY | 9 | C-D | 3 |
| Schell Av | .Y | 16 | E-F | 3 |
| Schick Ct | .SC | 29 | F | 1 |
| Scholfield Av | .T | 5 | B | 2 |
| Schooner L | .SC | 47 | D | 6 |
| Schubert Dr | .SC | 47 | A | 3-4 |
| Scollard St | .T | 4 | F | 3 |
| Scotchdale Av | .SC | 37 | B | 3 |
| Scotia Av | .SC | 25 | B | 3 |
| Scotland Rd | .SC | 31 | E | 5 |
| Scotney Gr | .SC | 51 | A | 4 |
| Scotswood Rd | .SC | 29 | A-B | 4 |
| Scott La | .T | 3 | A | 2 |
| Scott Rd | .Y | 16 | D | 4-5 |
| Scott St | .T | 3 | A | 1-2 |
| Scottfield Dr | .SC | 41 | B-C | 4 |
| Scoville Sq | .SC | 31 | F | 1 |
| Scranton Rd | .SC | 39 | D | 5 |
| Scunthorpe Rd | .SC | 39 | C | 1-2 |
| Sea Grassway | .NY | 30 | F | 1 |
| Sea Hawkway | .NY | 10 | C | 1 |
| Sea Robinway | .NY | 10 | C | 1 |
| Seabrook Av | .NY | 18 | A | 5 |
| Seaburn Pl | .SC | 31 | E | 5 |
| Seabury Gt | .SC | 29 | A | 2 |
| Seacliffe Blvd | .NY | 30 | B | 2-3 |
| Seaforth Av | .T | 14 | E-F | 6 |
| Seagrave Cr | .SC | 31 | B | 2 |
| Sealcove Dr | .ET | 34 | B-C | 2 |
| Sealstone Terr | .SC | 39 | E-F | 2 |
| Seamist Cr | .SC | 41 | B | 1 |
| Searle Av | .NY | 10 | A-C | 6 |
| Sears St | .T | 13 | D | 1 |
| Seaton St | .T | 5 | C | 1 |
| Second Av | .ET | 22 | B-C | 4-5 |
| Second St | .T | 3 | B | 4 |
| Secord Av | .EY | 15 | E | 3 |
| Secord Ct | .EY | 40 | B | 5 |
| Secretariat Dr | .ET | 40 | F | 2 |
| Secroft Cr | .NY | 30 | F | 1 |
| Secroft Ct | .NY | 20 | A | 2-3 |
| Sedan Av | .Y | 16 | A | 2-3 |
| Sedgebrook Cr | .ET | 36 | D | 5 |
| Sedgeley Dr | .ET | 36 | E | 2 |
| Sedgemount Dr | .SC | 39 | C | 5-6 |
| Sedgewick Cr | .SC | 27 | E | 3 |
| Seeley Dr | .SC | 49 | E | 4 |
| Sego Royalway | .NY | 21 | B | 2-3 |
| Seguin Ct | .ET | 40 | E | 3 |
| Selby St | .T | 5 | A-B | 4 |
| Select Av | .SC | 41 | B-C | 1 |
| Selkirk St | .T | 5 | E-F | 3 |
| Sellers Av | .T | 16 | F | 5-6 |
| Sellers Av | .Y | 16 | F | 5-6 |
| Sellmar Rd | .ET | 26 | C | 2 |
| Selwood Av | .T | 13 | E | 6 |
| Selwyn Av | .EY | 15 | E | 4 |
| Selwyn Av | .EY | 17 | E | 6 |
| Seminole Av | .SC | 37 | A-B | 2 |
| Senator Blvd | .SC | 37 | E | 3 |
| Seneca Av | .T | 3 | A-B | 5 |
| Seneca Av | .SC | 16 | B-C | 5 |
| Seneca Hill Dr | .NY | 21 | A-B | 3-4 |
| Seneca St | .NY | 9 | B | 3 |
| Seneca St | .NY | 10 | E | 4-6 |
| Senlac Rd | .NY | 9 | B | 1 |
| Senlac Rd | .NY | 8 | E | 1 |
| Sentinel Rd | .NY | 20 | C | 2-6 |
| Sepia Dr | .NY | 21 | E | 4 |
| Service Rd | .SC | 37 | C-D | 4 |
| Servington Cr | .T | 7 | A | 4 |
| Sesame St | .SC | 31 | A | 5-6 |
| Seton Park Rd | .NY | 19 | B | 3-4 |
| Settlers Rd | .NY | 19 | E-F | 1-2 |
| Sevenoaks Av | .ET | 24 | A | 5 |
| Seventeenth St | .ET | 22 | A | 3-4 |
| Seventh St | .ET | 22 | B | 4-5 |
| Severn Rd | .NY | 20 | D | 1 |
| Severn St | .T | 5 | A | 3 |
| Seville Av | .ET | 34 | C | 4 |
| Sewells Rd | .SC | 41 | F | 6 |
| Sewells Rd | .SC | 51 | A-B | 1-5 |
| Sexton Cr | .NY | 21 | C-E | 2-3 |
| Seymour Av | .T | 15 | A | 4 |
| Shadberry Dr | .NY | 21 | C-D | 2 |
| Shaddock Cr | .SC | 37 | A | 3 |
| Shademaster Ct | .SC | 41 | E | 6 |
| Shadetree Rd | .ET | 34 | B | 3-4 |
| Shadowbrook Dr | .ET | 36 | E | 4 |
| Shadowood Ct | .SC | 49 | A | 1 |
| Shadwell Pl | .NY | 19 | A | 5 |
| Shady Glen Rd | .ET | 40 | C | 4 |
| Shady Golfway | .NY | 17 | D | 4 |
| Shady Hollow Dr | .SC | 41 | B | 2 |
| Shady Oaks Cr | .NY | 7 | E-F | 2 |
| Shaft Rd | .ET | 38 | F | 4-5 |
| Shaftesbury Av | .T | 5 | A | 2 |
| Shaftesbury Pl | .T | 5 | A | 2 |
| Shaftesbury St | .NY | 10 | A | 4-5 |
| Shale Gt | .NY | 20 | E | 1 |
| Shallice Ct | .SC | 49 | F | 3 |
| Shallmar Blvd | .T | 6 | B | 6 |
| Shalom Cr | .ET | 40 | B | 5 |
| Shamokin Dr | .NY | 19 | C-D | 3 |
| Shamrock Av | .ET | 32 | E | 5 |
| Shand Av | .ET | 24 | D | 2 |
| Shandara Cr | .SC | 27 | A | 2 |
| Shandon Dr | .SC | 29 | A | 2-3 |
| Shangarry Dr | .SC | 27 | A | 2-3 |
| Shank St | .T | 2 | B | 3 |
| Shanly St | .T | 4 | A-B | 3 |
| Shannon St | .T | 4 | B | 3 |
| Sharbot Av | .SC | 39 | C | 5-6 |
| Sharlyn Rd | .M | 34 | A | 4 |
| Sharpe St | .SC | 25 | E | 1-2 |
| Sharpecroft Blvd | .NY | 20 | D | 5-6 |
| Sharron Dr | .T | 7 | D | 6 |
| Sharrowbay Ct | .SC | 31 | B | 2 |
| Shaughnessy Blvd | .NY | 19 | B | 1 |
| Shaughnessy Blvd | .NY | 21 | B | 4-6 |
| Shaunavon Heights Cr | .NY | 19 | F | 5-6 |
| Shaver Av N | .ET | 34 | E | 1-3 |

| Street | Mun. | Map | Col | Row |
|---|---|---|---|---|
| Shaver Av S | ET | 34 | E | 3-4 |
| Shaver Ct | ET | 34 | E | 1 |
| Shaw St | T | 2 | B | 1 |
| Shaw St | T | 4 | B | 2-6 |
| Shawbridge Av | ET | 24 | A | 4 |
| Shawfield Cr | NY | 19 | E | 5 |
| Shawford Cr | SC | 39 | D | 6 |
| Shawnee Cir | NY | 21 | E | 3 |
| Shea Ct | SC | 49 | F | 6 |
| Sheard St | T | 5 | A | 5 |
| Sheath Rd | ET | 36 | B | 6 |
| Shediac Rd | SC | 27 | F | 2 |
| Sheffield St | NY | 16 | E | 1-2 |
| Sheffley Cr | ET | 26 | A | 2 |
| Sheila Ct | ET | 40 | F | 2 |
| Shelborne Av | NY | 6 | C-E | 1 |
| Sheldon Av | ET | 32 | D | 2-3 |
| Sheldonbury Cr | SC | 31 | A-B | 5 |
| Sheldrake Blvd | T | 7 | A-B | 2 |
| Shellamwood Tr | SC | 37 | F | 4 |
| Shendale Dr | ET | 28 | B-C | 2 |
| Shenley Rd | SC | 27 | E | 2 |
| Shenstone Rd | NY | 10 | B-C | 1 |
| Shepmore Terr | SC | 41 | E | 5-6 |
| Sheppard Av E | NY | 19 | A-F | 6 |
| Sheppard Av E | NY | 21 | A-F | 6 |
| Sheppard Av E | NY | 9 | A-F | 1 |
| Sheppard Av E | NY | 11 | A-F | 6 |
| Sheppard Av E | SC | 29 | A-F | 1 |
| Sheppard Av E | SC | 31 | A-F | 6 |
| Sheppard Av E | SC | 39 | A-F | 1 |
| Sheppard Av E | SC | 41 | A-F | 6 |
| Sheppard Av E | SC | 49 | A-F | 1-3 |
| Sheppard Av E | SC | 51 | A-E | 6 |
| Sheppard Av W | NY | 10 | A-F | 6 |
| Sheppard Av W | NY | 18 | A-F | 1 |
| Sheppard Av W | NY | 20 | A-F | 5-6 |
| Sheppard Av W | NY | 30 | D-F | 6 |
| Sheppard Av W | NY | 8 | A-F | 1 |
| Sheppard Av W | NY | 40 | D-F | 1 |
| Sheppard Sq | NY | 9 | D-E | 1 |
| Shepton Way | SC | 31 | D | 2 |
| Sherbourne St | T | 3 | B | 1 |
| Sherbourne St | T | 5 | B | 4-6 |
| Sherbourne St N | T | 5 | B | 3 |
| Sheridan Av | T | 14 | F | 5-6 |
| Sherin Ct | ET | 26 | C | 1 |
| Sherman Ct | NY | 18 | B | 2 |
| Shermount Av | NY | 6 | B | 1-2 |
| Sherry Rd | SC | 27 | B-C | 4 |
| Sherway Dr | ET | 32 | A-B | 2 |
| Sherway Gt | ET | 32 | B | 1-2 |
| Sherwood Av | SC | 27 | A-B | 1 |
| Sherwood Av | T | 7 | A-B | 2 |
| Sherwood La | T | 7 | A | 2-3 |
| Shetland St | NY | 10 | E | 1-2 |
| Sheva Ct | SC | 27 | F | 1 |
| Shields Av | T | 6 | E | 3 |
| Shilton Rd | SC | 31 | F | 5-6 |
| Shipley Rd | ET | 36 | F | 2 |
| Shipman St | T | 14 | B | 1 |
| Shippigan Cr | NY | 21 | A-B | 5 |
| Shirley Cr | SC | 37 | C-D | 4-5 |
| Shirley St | T | 14 | F | 5 |
| Shoalhaven Dr | SC | 47 | D | 6 |
| Shockley Dr | ET | 40 | E | 1 |
| Shootfield Cr | SC | 41 | B | 4-5 |
| Shoredale Dr | SC | 37 | E | 1 |
| Shoreham Cr | NY | 20 | A-B | 2 |
| Shoreham Dr | NY | 20 | A-B | 2 |
| Shoreham Dr | NY | 30 | F | 2 |
| Shoreland Cr | SC | 37 | E | 2 |
| Shoreview Dr | SC | 47 | B | 2 |
| Shorncliffe Av | T | 6 | D | 6 |
| Shorncliffe Av | ET | 34 | F | 4-5 |
| Shorting Rd | SC | 41 | B | 6 |
| Shortland Cr | ET | 26 | B | 2-3 |
| Shortridge Ct | NY | 30 | F | 2 |
| Shortt St | Y | 16 | F | 3-4 |
| Shouldice Ct | NY | 9 | F | 2 |
| Shrewsbury Sq | SC | 29 | B | 2 |
| Shropshire Dr | SC | 29 | D-E | 4-5 |
| Shudell Av | T | 15 | A | 4 |
| Shudell Av | T | 5 | A | 4 |
| Shuter St | T | 5 | A-C | 6 |
| Sibley Av | EY | 15 | F | 4 |
| Sidford Ct | Y | 24 | E-F | 2 |
| Sidney Belsey Cr | Y | 26 | F | 2 |
| Sidney St | T | 3 | B | 1 |
| Sierra Dr | SC | 29 | D | 3-4 |
| Sifton Ct | NY | 11 | E | 6 |
| Sighthill Av | T | 5 | B | 1 |
| Sigmont Rd | ET | 36 | C | 5 |
| Signal Hill Av | ET | 40 | B | 1 |
| Signet Dr | NY | 30 | E | 1-4 |
| Silas Hill Dr | NY | 21 | A | 4 |
| Silbury Dr | SC | 41 | B | 3-4 |
| Silkwood Ct | NY | 19 | B | 1 |
| Silurian Rd | SC | 39 | C | 5 |
| Silvan Carseway | NY | 10 | C | 4 |
| Silver Av | T | 14 | E | 4 |
| Silver Birch | T | 13 | F | 5-6 |
| Silver Birch Av | T | 15 | F | 5-6 |
| Silver Dart Dr | ET | 36 | A-B | 1-3 |
| Silver Shadow Path | ET | 34 | A-B | 2 |
| Silver Springs Blvd | SC | 31 | C-D | 2-4 |
| Silver Spruce Dr | SC | 31 | A-B | 3 |
| Silver Star Blvd | SC | 31 | E | 3 |
| Silverbell Gr | SC | 41 | F | 6 |
| Silvercrest Av | ET | 32 | D | 3 |
| Silverdale Cr | NY | 19 | C-D | 3-4 |
| Silvergrove Rd | NY | 9 | E | 1-2 |
| Silverhill Dr | ET | 34 | D-E | 3-4 |
| Silversand Pl | SC | 39 | E | 2 |
| Silversted Dr | SC | 41 | A-B | 5 |
| Silverstone Dr | ET | 40 | D-F | 2-4 |
| Silverthorn Av | T | 16 | D-E | 4-6 |
| Silverthorn Av | Y | 16 | D-E | 4-5 |
| Silverthorne Bush Dr | ET | 34 | A | 3 |
| Silvertip Cr | SC | 49 | A | 5-6 |
| Silverton Av | NY | 8 | C | 2-3 |
| Silverview Dr | NY | 11 | A-B | 2-3 |
| Silverwood Av | T | 6 | D | 5 |
| Silvio Av | SC | 25 | D | 1 |
| Simcoe St | T | 2 | E | 1-2 |
| Simcoe St | T | 4 | E | 5-6 |
| Simeon Ct | NY | 11 | C | 2 |
| Simpson Av | ET | 22 | B-C | 2 |
| Simpson Av | T | 5 | D-E | 5 |
| Sims Cr | ET | 28 | B | 1 |
| Sinclair St | T | 22 | C | 1 |
| Singleton Rd | SC | 27 | A | 2-3 |
| Sinnott Rd | SC | 27 | C | 4-5 |
| Sinton Ct | NY | 18 | B | 2 |
| Sir Raymond Dr | SC | 37 | E | 4 |
| Sir Williams La | ET | 26 | A | 5 |
| Sirocco Dr | NY | 21 | A | 1-2 |
| Six Nations Av | SC | 39 | C | 6 |
| Six Point Rd | ET | 24 | A-B | 4 |
| Sixteenth St | ET | 22 | A | 3-4 |
| Sixth St | ET | 22 | B | 4-5 |
| Sixth St | T | 3 | B | 4 |
| Skagway Av | SC | 37 | A | 5 |
| Skelmore Cr | NY | 19 | E | 3 |
| Skelton St | ET | 22 | E | 2 |
| Skey La | T | 4 | A | 5-6 |
| Skipton Ct | NY | 18 | C | 2 |
| Skopie Ct | NY | 17 | F | 5 |
| Skye Ct | NY | 30 | F | 2 |
| Skyes Av | NY | 26 | F | 2 |
| Skylark Rd | M | 24 | F | 1 |
| Skyline Dr | M | 32 | A-B | 3 |
| Skymark Dr | NY | 21 | B | 3 |
| Skyridge Rd | SC | 39 | F | 2 |
| Skyview Cr | NY | 19 | B-C | 1-2 |
| Skyway Av | ET | 36 | C | 1-2 |
| Slade Av | T | 4 | C | 1 |
| Slan Av | SC | 39 | E | 4 |
| Slane Ct | ET | 40 | E | 4-5 |
| Slater Ct | NY | 18 | B | 1 |
| Slender Fernway | NY | 21 | B | 3-4 |
| Slidell Cr | NY | 19 | E | 3 |
| Sloane Av | NY | 17 | F | 2-3 |
| Sloley Rd | SC | 25 | E-F | 5 |
| Small St | T | 3 | B | 2 |
| Smallwood Dr | NY | 18 | A-B | 3 |
| Smith Cr | ET | 24 | C | 6 |
| Smithfield Dr | ET | 24 | E | 4 |
| Smithwood Dr | ET | 34 | E | 2-3 |
| Snapdragon Dr | NY | 21 | E | 6 |
| Snaresbrook Ct | ET | 28 | A | 2 |
| Snaresbrook Dr | ET | 38 | F | 2 |
| Sneath Av | SC | 25 | A | 3-4 |
| Snider Av | NY | 16 | E | 3-4 |
| Snowball Cr | SC | 41 | A | 6 |
| Snowberry Av | NY | 11 | E | 4-5 |
| Snowcrest Av | NY | 11 | E | 2-3 |
| Snowden St | NY | 28 | F | 3-4 |
| Snowdon Dr | T | 9 | A-B | 5 |
| Snowellen Av | ET | 34 | C | 4 |
| Snowhill Cr | SC | 39 | A | 2 |
| Snowood Ct | NY | 30 | F | 5-6 |
| Snowshoe Millway | NY | 9 | D | 3 |
| Soho Sq | T | 4 | E | 6 |
| Soho St | T | 4 | E | 6 |
| Solway Ct | SC | 31 | B | 5 |
| Sombrero Ct | NY | 30 | B | 1 |
| Somerdale Sq | SC | 37 | F | 3 |
| Somers Av | EY | 15 | A | 3 |
| Somers Av | EY | 5 | F | 3 |
| Somerset Av | T | 4 | B | 1-2 |
| Somerville Av | Y | 16 | A | 3 |
| Sommerset Way | NY | 11 | A | 4 |
| Sonata Ct | NY | 9 | E | 4 |
| Song Meadoway | NY | 21 | C-D | 1 |
| Songwood Dr | NY | 30 | B-C | 4 |
| Sonmore Dr | SC | 29 | F | 1-2 |
| Sonneck Sq | SC | 37 | E | 4-5 |
| Sonnet Ct | NY | 18 | A | 5 |
| Sonoma Way | ET | 40 | E | 1 |
| Sonora Terr | SC | 25 | E | 3 |
| Sophia Dr | SC | 39 | C | 5-6 |
| Sophia Loren Ct | ET | 40 | F | 1 |
| Sorauren Av | T | 14 | E | 4-6 |
| Sorlyn Av | NY | 18 | B | 6 |
| Sorrel Ct | NY | 11 | E | 5 |
| Sorrento Ct | NY | 20 | A | 6 |
| Soudan Av | T | 7 | A-C | 4 |
| South Bonnington Av | SC | 39 | D | 2-3 |
| South Dr | T | 5 | A-B | 2-3 |
| South Edgely Av | SC | 25 | D | 2-3 |
| South Kingslea Dr | ET | 24 | E | 4 |
| South Kingsway | T | 14 | A | 4-6 |
| South Kingsway | T | 24 | F | 4-5 |
| South Marine Dr | SC | 37 | E | 5 |
| South Service Rd | M | 32 | A | 3 |
| South Shields Av | SC | 31 | E-F | 3 |
| South Station St | Y | 28 | E | 6 |
| South Woodrow Blvd | SC | 25 | D | 2-3 |
| Southampton Dr | SC | 27 | F | 3 |
| Southbourne Av | NY | 8 | D | 3 |
| Southcreek Rd | M | 34 | B | 4-5 |
| Southdown Av | NY | 8 | D | 3 |
| Southgate Av | NY | 8 | D | 3 |
| Southill Dr | NY | 17 | B | 1-2 |
| Southlawn Dr | SC | 31 | E | 5 |
| Southlea Av | EY | 7 | D | 5-6 |
| Southmead Rd | SC | 27 | A | 4 |
| Southport St | T | 14 | A-B | 6 |
| Southridge Av | EY | 15 | B | 2 |
| Southvale Dr | EY | 7 | D-E | 5-6 |
| Southview Av | T | 14 | A | 3 |
| Southway Rd | ET | 26 | C | 5-6 |
| Southwell Dr | NY | 19 | A | 4 |
| Southwood Dr | T | 15 | E | 5-6 |
| Sovereign Av | NY | 18 | B | 4 |
| Spadina Av | T | 2 | E | 1-2 |
| Spadina Av | T | 4 | E | 4-6 |
| Spadina Cr | T | 4 | D-E | 4-5 |
| Spadina Rd | T | 4 | E | 1-3 |
| Spadina Rd | T | 6 | D | 3-6 |
| Spain Rd | SC | 29 | D | 5 |
| Spalding Rd | NY | 18 | E-F | 3 |
| Spanbridge Rd | NY | 17 | C | 5 |
| Spanish Mossway | NY | 21 | A-B | 1 |
| Sparkhall Av | T | 5 | D-E | 4 |
| Sparks Av | NY | 21 | E-F | 2 |
| Sparrow Av | NY | 8 | A | 5 |
| Sparta Rd | NY | 18 | D | 6 |
| Sparwood Ct | NY | 11 | E-F | 1 |
| Spears St | NY | 16 | B | 5-6 |
| Speers Av | NY | 26 | F | 1 |
| Spencer Av | ET | 26 | C | 1-2 |
| Spencer Av | T | 12 | C | 1-2 |
| Spenvalley Dr | NY | 20 | A-B | 6 |
| Spindlewood Dr | NY | 21 | A | 4 |
| Spinney Ct | NY | 19 | C-D | 3-4 |
| Spire Hillway | NY | 21 | B | 1 |
| Split Maple Ct | SC | 49 | A | 1 |
| Springarod Gt | SC | 39 | E | 4 |
| Spring Forest St | SC | 39 | C | 1 |
| Spring Forest Gt | SC | 39 | C | 1 |
| Spring Garden Av | NY | 11 | A-C | 6 |
| Spring Garden Rd | ET | 24 | B-C | 3-4 |
| Spring Grove Av | T | 14 | E | 1 |
| Spring Rd | T | 14 | C | 4-6 |
| Springbank Av | SC | 26 | A-D | 3 |
| Springbrook Gdns | ET | 24 | B-C | 4 |
| Springdale Blvd | EY | 15 | A-D | 3 |
| Springhouse Sq | SC | 31 | A | 2 |
| Springhurst Av | T | 12 | B-C | 1-2 |
| Springmount Av | T | 4 | A | 1 |
| Springmount Av | T | 28 | E | 6 |
| Springside Rd | NY | 21 | A | 4 |
| Springvale Av | NY | 18 | A | 4 |
| Springwood Dr | NY | 28 | A | 5 |
| Sproat Av | T | 15 | A | 5 |
| Sproat Av | T | 5 | F | 5 |
| Spruce Ct | T | 5 | C | 5 |
| Spruce Hill Rd | T | 13 | E | 5 |
| Spruce Hill Rd | T | 15 | E | 5-6 |
| Sprucedale Pl | EY | 15 | D-E | 1 |
| Sprucewood Ct | SC | 31 | A | 4 |
| Spy Appleway | NY | 19 | F | 6 |
| Squires Av | EY | 15 | F | 6 |

**S**

| STREET NAME | MUNICIPALITY | MAP NO | MAP AREA |
|---|---|---|---|
| Squires Av | EY | 17 | F | 6 |
| St Gentin Av | SC | 25 | E | 4 |
| St. Olaves Rd | T | 14 | A-B | 5 |
| Stable Rd | ET | 38 | A-C | 2-3 |
| Stacy St | T | 15 | B-C | 4 |
| Stadacona Dr | NY | 8 | C | 3-4 |
| Stadium Rd | T | 2 | C | 2-3 |
| Stafford Rd | NY | 10 | D | 4-5 |
| Stafford St | T | 2 | B | 1 |
| Staffordshire Pl | ET | 32 | E | 1 |
| Stag Hill Dr | EY | 15 | E | 1 |
| Staines Rd | SC | 41 | A | 1-4 |
| Stainforth Dr | SC | 31 | E | 5 |
| Staley Terr | SC | 31 | C-D | 3 |
| Stamford Sq N | SC | 27 | A | 4 |
| Stamford Sq S | SC | 27 | A | 4 |
| Stanbridge Av | SC | 51 | A | 1-4 |
| Standish Av | T | 5 | C | 1 |
| Stanhope Av | EY | 5 | E | 1 |
| Stanland Dr | SC | 37 | B-C | 4 |
| Stanley Av | ET | 22 | D-E | 2-3 |
| Stanley Av | T | 2 | C | 1 |
| Stanley Greene Pk | NY | 18 | D-E | 2 |
| Stanley Rd | NY | 30 | F | 6 |
| Stanley Terr | T | 2 | B | 1 |
| Stanmills Rd | T | 24 | B | 1 |
| Stansbury Cr | SC | 27 | F | 3 |
| Stanthorpe Ct | ET | 36 | F | 1 |
| Stanton Av | T | 15 | A | 5 |
| Stanwell Dr | SC | 39 | A | 4 |
| Stanwood Cr | NY | 30 | C | 4 |
| Stapleton Dr | ET | 26 | B | 1-2 |
| Starcross Ct | NY | 30 | A | 2 |
| Stardew Pl | NY | 8 | A | 4 |
| Starfire Dr | SC | 49 | D | 3 |
| Stark Appleway | NY | 19 | F | 6 |
| Starlite Cr | SC | 39 | E | 4 |
| Starspray Blvd | SC | 47 | E | 4-5 |
| Starview Dr | NY | 28 | E | 2 |
| Starview La | NY | 28 | D-E | 2 |
| State Crown Blvd | SC | 41 | C | 1 |
| Statesman Sq | SC | 41 | B | 4 |
| Station Rd | ET | 22 | D | 2-3 |
| Station St | T | 2 | E-F | 2 |
| Statler Av | ET | 34 | E | 3 |
| Stavely Av | SC | 27 | F | 4 |
| Stavely Cr | ET | 28 | A-B | 2-3 |
| Staverton Cr | SC | 31 | E | 1 |
| Staverton Rd | SC | 49 | B | 3 |
| Stayner Av | NY | 6 | A-B | 2 |
| Steeles Av E | SC | 41 | A-F | 1 |
| Steeles Av E | NY | 11 | A-F | 1 |
| Steeles Av E | NY | 41 | A-F | 1 |
| Steeles Av E | SC | 51 | A-F | 1 |
| Steeles Av W | ET | 30 | A | 1 |
| Steeles Av W | ET | 40 | A-F | 1 |
| Steeles Av W | NY | 10 | A-F | 1 |
| Steeles Av W | NY | 20 | A-F | 1 |
| Steeles Av W | NY | 30 | A-F | 1 |
| Steepmaple Gr | SC | 39 | F | 2 |
| Steeprock Dr | NY | 20 | E-F | 5 |
| Steeton Rd | ET | 40 | B-C | 2 |
| Stella St | NY | 18 | A | 5 |
| Stellarton Rd | SC | 27 | A | 5-6 |
| Stephanie St | T | 4 | E | 6 |
| Stephen Dr | ET | 24 | F | 5-6 |
| Stephen Mews | ET | 24 | E-F | 6 |
| Stephenfrank Rd | SC | 29 | F | 3 |
| Stephenson Av | T | 14 | D | 4 |
| Stephney Dr | ET | 32 | C | 2 |
| Sterling Rd | T | 14 | E | 4-5 |
| Steven Av | NY | 6 | A | 2 |
| Stevenharris Dr | ET | 34 | C | 3-4 |
| Stevenson Rd | ET | 40 | E-F | 3 |
| Stevenvale Dr | SC | 37 | D | 1-2 |
| Stevenwood Rd | SC | 37 | D | 1 |
| Stewart Av | ET | 30 | B | 6 |
| Stewart Smith Dr | NY | 16 | A-B | 2 |
| Stewart St | T | 2 | C-D | 1 |
| Stibbard Av | T | 7 | A-B | 2 |
| Stilecroft Dr | NY | 20 | C | 5-6 |
| Stillbrook Ct | SC | 47 | C | 1 |
| Stillwater Cr | NY | 10 | B | 1 |
| Stinson Cir | EY | 17 | B | 1 |
| Stock Av | ET | 24 | A | 6 |
| Stockbridge Av | ET | 24 | A | 4-5 |
| Stockton Rd | NY | 8 | A | 4 |
| Stoffel Dr | ET | 36 | D-E | 1 |
| Stokewell Pl | SC | 29 | F | 4-5 |

| STREET NAME | MUNICIPALITY | MAP NO | MAP AREA |
|---|---|---|---|
| Stone Ct | ET | 30 | D | 6 |
| Stonebridge Av | SC | 37 | B | 4 |
| Stonecraft Pl | T | 39 | F | 2 |
| Stonecrop La | ET | 40 | E | 5 |
| Stonecutters La | T | 3 | B | 1 |
| Stonedale Placeway | NY | 19 | A | 4 |
| Stonedale Placeway | NY | 9 | F | 4 |
| Stonedene Blvd | NY | 10 | C | 1-2 |
| Stonefield Cr | SC | 39 | F | 2 |
| Stonegate Rd | ET | 24 | F | 5 |
| Stoneglen Dr | ET | 34 | B | 2 |
| Stoneham Rd | ET | 34 | A | 2 |
| Stonehenge Cr | SC | 39 | D | 4-5 |
| Stonehill Ct | SC | 31 | B | 4 |
| Stonehouse Cr | T | 14 | E | 4 |
| Stoneleigh Rd | Y | 26 | F | 5 |
| Stonemanse Ct | SC | 37 | E | 2 |
| Stoneton Dr | SC | 39 | A | 1 |
| Stoneybrook Dr | NY | 26 | F | 5 |
| Stong Ct | NY | 20 | A-B | 3 |
| Stonewall Rd | SC | 39 | A | 1 |
| Stoney Creek Dr | SC | 47 | C | 1 |
| Storer Dr | SC | 30 | C | 5 |
| Storey Cr | ET | 30 | C | 5 |
| Stormont Av | NY | 6 | C-E | 1 |
| Stornoway Ct | SC | 49 | B-C | 1 |
| Strachan Av | T | 2 | B | 1-2 |
| Strachan Av | T | 4 | B | 6 |
| Strader Av | Y | 6 | A-B | 4 |
| Strandhill Rd | SC | 37 | C | 2 |
| Stratford Cr | NY | 7 | B-C | 2 |
| Strath Av | ET | 24 | D-E | 2 |
| Strath Humber Ct | ET | 24 | D | 1 |
| Strathavon Dr | ET | 6 | D-E | 2 |
| Strathallan Blvd | NY | 6 | C-D | 2 |
| Strathallan Wood | NY | 6 | C-D | 2 |
| Strathcona Av | T | 15 | E-F | 4 |
| Strathdee Dr | ET | 26 | A-B | 3 |
| Strathearn Blvd | NY | 6 | D | 5 |
| Stratheden Rd | NY | 7 | B-C | 2 |
| Strathgowan Av | T | 7 | B | 2 |
| Strathgowan Cr | T | 7 | B | 2 |
| Strathgowan Rd | T | 7 | B-C | 2 |
| Strathmore Blvd | EY | 15 | D | 3 |
| Strathmore Blvd | T | 5 | F | 3 |
| Strathmore Blvd | T | 15 | A-D | 3 |
| Strathmore Blvd | T | 16 | D-E | 3 |
| Stratton Av | SC | 27 | E | 3 |
| Stratton Cr | T | 14 | D | 6 |
| Strawberry Hills Dr | SC | 41 | A | 1 |
| Streatham Pl | ET | 36 | E | 4 |
| Strickland Av | T | 14 | F | 6 |
| Strode Dr | SC | 37 | A | 3 |
| Struthers St | ET | 22 | C | 2 |
| Stuart Av | NY | 8 | E-F | 2 |
| Stuart Cr | NY | 8 | E-F | 2 |
| Stubbs Dr | NY | 9 | F | 2 |
| Stubbswood Sq | SC | 31 | E-F | 5 |
| Sturton Rd | ET | 26 | B | 1 |
| Subway Cr | ET | 34 | F | 4 |
| Sudbury Hall Dr | SC | 49 | C-D | 2 |
| Sudbury St | T | 2 | A-B | 1 |
| Sufferance Rd | SC | 49 | E | 4 |
| Sufi Cr | NY | 17 | E-F | 4 |
| Sugar Millway | NY | 9 | E | 4 |
| Sugarbush Sq | SC | 49 | D | 4 |
| Sulgrave Cr | NY | 9 | D-E | 3 |
| Sulkara Ct | NY | 17 | E | 2 |
| Sullivan St | T | 4 | E | 6 |
| Sully Cr | T | 4 | B | 5 |
| Sultan Pool Dr | ET | 40 | E | 4 |
| Sultan St | T | 4 | F | 4 |
| Sultana Av | NY | 8 | B-C | 5 |
| Sumach St | T | 3 | C | 1 |
| Sumach St | T | 5 | C | 4-6 |
| Summer Dr | SC | 27 | E | 5 |
| Summerbridge Rd | SC | 37 | E | 1-2 |
| Summerfield Cr | ET | 36 | C | 5 |
| Summerglade Dr | SC | 29 | F | 2 |
| Summerhill Av | T | 5 | A-C | 1-2 |
| Summerhill Gdns | T | 5 | A | 1-2 |
| Summerhill Rd | ET | 22 | D-E | 3 |
| Summerside Cr | NY | 21 | A | 2-3 |
| Summerton Pl | SC | 31 | B | 5-6 |
| Summerville Cr | M | 34 | B | 5 |
| Summit Av | NY | 16 | E | 5 |
| Summitcrest Dr | ET | 26 | B-C | 3 |
| Sumner Heights Dr | NY | 11 | D | 4-5 |
| Sun Av | SC | 29 | D | 5 |
| Sun Valley Dr | Y | 24 | E-F | 2 |
| Sunbeam Av | NY | 8 | B | 3 |
| Sunbury Ct | SC | 37 | E | 2 |
| Sunbird Cr | SC | 31 | D | 1 |
| Sunburst Sq | SC | 41 | D | 6 |

| STREET NAME | MUNICIPALITY | MAP NO | MAP AREA |
|---|---|---|---|
| Suncrest Dr | NY | 7 | E-F | 2 |
| Sundance Cr | SC | 39 | E | 5 |
| Sundel Av | Y | 16 | E | 4 |
| Sunderland Cr | SC | 39 | B | 4 |
| Sundial Cr | NY | 17 | E | 2 |
| Sundridge Dr | SC | 27 | A | 4 |
| Sunfield Rd | NY | 18 | C | 1 |
| Sunforest Ct | NY | 10 | E | 2-3 |
| Sunlight Park Rd | T | 3 | D | 1 |
| Sunmount Rd | SC | 29 | C | 1-2 |
| Sunny Glenway | NY | 17 | B | 5 |
| Sunnybrae Av | Y | 16 | A | 3 |
| Sunnybrook Rd | T | 14 | A | 4 |
| Sunnybrook Rd | T | 24 | F | 4 |
| Sunnycove Dr | M | 32 | B | 2 |
| Sunnycrest Rd | NY | 10 | B-C | 1-2 |
| Sunnydale Dr | ET | 24 | F | 4 |
| Sunnydene Cr | NY | 7 | C | 2 |
| Sunnylea Av E | ET | 24 | D-E | 4 |
| Sunnylea Av W | ET | 24 | D | 4 |
| Sunnypoint Cr | SC | 25 | E | 5-6 |
| Sunnyside Av | T | 14 | D | 4-6 |
| Sunplains Cr | ET | 34 | A | 3-4 |
| Sunray Cr | NY | 18 | C | 3-4 |
| Sunrise Av | NY | 17 | E-F | 5 |
| Sunrise Cr | ET | 26 | B | 1-3 |
| Sunset Av | ET | 32 | C | 3-4 |
| Sunset Tr | NY | 28 | D-E | 3 |
| Sunshine St | NY | 8 | D | 4 |
| Suntract Rd | ET | 28 | F | 4-5 |
| Sunvale Dr | ET | 36 | E-F | 2 |
| Superior Av | ET | 22 | D-E | 2-3 |
| Supertest Rd | NY | 10 | A | 2-3 |
| Supertest Rd | NY | 20 | F | 2 |
| Suraty Av | SC | 39 | A | 5 |
| Surrey Av | SC | 27 | A-B | 2 |
| Surrey Pl | T | 4 | D | 4 |
| Susan St | SC | 37 | E | 1 |
| Sussex Av | T | 4 | D-E | 4 |
| Sussex Dr | ET | 22 | D | 4 |
| Sussex Mews | T | 4 | D | 4 |
| Sutton Av | T | 3 | B | 6 |
| Sutherland Av | EY | 15 | F | 3 |
| Sutherland Av | ET | 25 | A | 3 |
| Sutherland Dr | T | 7 | D-E | 3-5 |
| Suzy St | ET | 40 | B | 6 |
| Swallow Ct | NY | 19 | B | 5 |
| Swan Av | ET | 34 | E | 2 |
| Swansdown Dr | NY | 9 | E-F | 2 |
| Swansea Av | T | 14 | A | 5 |
| Swansea Mews | T | 14 | B | 5-6 |
| Swanwick Av | SC | 15 | F | 4 |
| Swanwick Av | T | 15 | E-F | 4 |
| Sweeney Dr | NY | 17 | E-F | 4 |
| Sweet Grassway | NY | 30 | F | 4-5 |
| Sweet Pea Path | ET | 28 | F | 5 |
| Sweetbriar Ct | NY | 17 | F | 2 |
| Sweetland Rd | ET | 26 | B | 2 |
| Sweetwood Gt | NY | 21 | C | 1 |
| Swift Dr | NY | 17 | B | 3 |
| Swiftdale Pl | NY | 19 | B | 5 |
| Swindon Rd | ET | 26 | B | 5 |
| Swiss Ct | NY | 10 | C | 2-3 |
| Sword St | T | 5 | C | 5 |
| Swordbill Dr | ET | 26 | D | 3-4 |
| Sycamore Pl | T | 15 | E-F | 6 |
| Sydenham St | T | 5 | B | 6 |
| Sydnor Rd | NY | 11 | B | 1 |
| Sylla Av | SC | 29 | B | 3 |
| Sylvan Av | SC | 37 | C-E | 4-6 |
| Sylvan Av | T | 4 | A | 6 |
| Sylvestre Dr | SC | 31 | C | 1 |
| Symes Rd | NY | 16 | B | 5-6 |
| Symes Rd | Y | 16 | B | 5-6 |
| Symington Av | T | 14 | A | 1-3 |
| Symons St | ET | 22 | C-D | 4 |
| Syndicate Av | Y | 16 | A-B | 4 |
| Syracuse Cr | SC | 47 | A | 4 |

**T**

| STREET NAME | MUNICIPALITY | MAP NO | MAP AREA |
|---|---|---|---|
| Tabard Gt | ET | 36 | B | 5 |
| Taber Rd | ET | 38 | E-F | 2 |
| Tacoma Av | T | 5 | A | 2 |
| Tadcaster Pl | NY | 19 | A | 5 |
| Taddle Creek Rd | T | 4 | E | 5 |
| Tahoe Ct | NY | 9 | E | 4 |
| Talara Dr | NY | 9 | E | 4 |
| Talbot Rd | NY | 10 | E-F | 3-4 |
| Talbot St | T | 14 | E | 1 |
| Talent Cr | NY | 30 | D | 6 |
| Talgarth Rd | ET | 36 | D | 5 |
| Tallforest Cr | ET | 34 | A | 3 |
| Tallon Rd | ET | 26 | B-C | 2 |
| Tallpines Ct | NY | 49 | E | 2 |

        *Trellanock*

| Street | Area | Pg | Grid | Ref |
|---|---|---|---|---|
| Tally La | NY | 11 | E | 5 |
| Talwood Dr | NY | 19 | A | 5-6 |
| Tamarisk Dr | ET | 40 | D-E | 4 |
| Tamblyn La | T | 5 | A | 1 |
| Tamblyn La | T | 7 | A | 5 |
| Tambrook Dr | SC | 31 | C | 3-4 |
| Tamerlane Ct | ET | 34 | E | 3-4 |
| Tammy La | ET | 40 | E | 5 |
| Tamora Ct | SC | 31 | E | 2 |
| Tampa Terr | NY | 30 | D | 5 |
| Tamworth Rd | NY | 10 | E-F | 5 |
| Tanager Av | EY | 7 | D | 3 |
| Tanbark Cr | NY | 9 | E-F | 5 |
| Tanburn Pl | NY | 19 | E | 4 |
| Tandridge Cr | ET | 28 | C | 1 |
| Tangamo Rd | ET | 36 | F | 1 |
| Tangiers Rd | NY | 20 | E | 3-4 |
| Tangle Briarway | NY | 11 | F | 4-5 |
| Tanglewood Terr | ET | 24 | F | 1 |
| Tangmere Rd | NY | 19 | A | 6 |
| Tangreen Ct | NY | 10 | F | 1 |
| Tanis Ct | SC | 49 | D | 4 |
| Tanjoe Cr | NY | 10 | E | 1 |
| Tanner Ct | NY | 11 | C | 3 |
| Tansley Av | SC | 30 | A | 4 |
| Tanvalley Ct | NY | 9 | E | 3 |
| Tanya Pl | SC | 31 | E | 5 |
| Tapestry La | NY | 8 | B | 6 |
| Tapley Dr | ET | 36 | E | 1-2 |
| Tapscott Rd | SC | 41 | E | 1-5 |
| Tara Av | SC | 27 | E | 2 |
| Tarbert Rd | NY | 11 | E | 1 |
| Tardree Pl | SC | 29 | B | 4-5 |
| Tarlton Rd | T | 6 | E | 4 |
| Tarn Rd | M | 32 | B | 2 |
| Tarsus Cr | SC | 49 | C | 3 |
| Tartan Av | SC | 25 | B-C | 1 |
| Taunton Rd | T | 7 | B | 4 |
| Taverly Rd | NY | 21 | E-F | 4 |
| Tavistock Rd | NY | 18 | B-C | 2 |
| Taylor Ct | EY | 15 | B-C | 1 |
| Taylor Rd | SC | 47 | E | 4 |
| Taylorwood Dr | ET | 26 | D-E | 4 |
| Taymall Av | ET | 22 | C | 1 |
| Tayrow Rd | ET | 28 | A | 1 |
| Taysham Cr | ET | 30 | A | 4-5 |
| Teagarden Ct | NY | 11 | C | 6 |
| Teak Av | NY | 17 | E | 2 |
| Teakwood Gr | NY | 9 | F | 5 |
| Teal Ct | NY | 19 | C-D | 4 |
| Tealham Dr | ET | 40 | E | 3 |
| Tecumseth Pl | T | 2 | C | 1 |
| Tecumseth St | T | 2 | C | 1-2 |
| Tecumseth St | T | 4 | C | 6 |
| Tedder St | NY | 2 | F | 1 |
| Teddington Park Av | T | 9 | A-B | 3 |
| Tedford Dr | SC | 27 | B | 2 |
| Teesdale Pl | SC | 25 | A | 3 |
| Tefft Rd | SC | 49 | B | 6 |
| Tefley Rd | NY | 10 | E | 3 |
| Teignmouth Av | Y | 16 | E-F | 5 |
| Telco Cr | NY | 28 | E | 4 |
| Temagami Ct | NY | 11 | B | 1 |
| Temperance St | T | 2 | F | 1 |
| Templar Dr | ET | 26 | A | 2 |
| Temple Av | T | 12 | C | 2 |
| Temple Av | T | 2 | A | 2 |
| Temple Bar Cr | SC | 31 | C | 5 |
| Templeton Ct | SC | 37 | F | 1-2 |
| Tempo Av | NY | 21 | E-F | 2 |
| Tenby St | NY | 24 | D | 6 |
| Tennis Cr | T | 11 | B | 4 |
| Tenth St | ET | 22 | B | 4-5 |
| Tepee Ct | NY | 21 | C-D | 6 |
| Teresa Ct | ET | 40 | E | 4 |
| Terlean Rd | NY | 9 | A | 1 |
| Ternhill Cr | NY | 17 | A | 1 |
| Terrace Av | NY | 10 | C-D | 4 |
| Terrington Ct | NY | 9 | F | 5 |
| Terry Dr | NY | 16 | A-B | 6 |
| Terrydale Dr | NY | 10 | A | 4 |
| Terryellen Cr | ET | 34 | C | 4 |
| Terryhill Cr | NY | 39 | A | 1-2 |
| Tesson Pl | SC | 49 | E | 6 |
| Teston Blvd | Y | 16 | A | 4-5 |
| Tetbury Cr | NY | 19 | C-D | 4 |
| Tettenhall Rd | ET | 26 | A | 4 |
| Tewsley Pl | ET | 26 | C | 2 |
| Texas Roseway | NY | 9 | C | 1 |
| Thackeray St | T | 5 | E | 5-6 |
| Thames Av | ET | 32 | B-C | 2 |
| Thamesford Ct | NY | 8 | B | 2 |
| Thane Ct | NY | 21 | E | 5 |
| Thatcher Av | SC | 25 | E | 5 |
| Thelma Av | T | 6 | D-E | 6 |
| Thelmere Pl | ET | 36 | F | 2 |
| Theresa Av | NY | 10 | E | 2-3 |
| Thermos Rd | SC | 27 | C | 3-4 |
| Thicket Rd | ET | 34 | B | 2 |
| Thicketwood Dr | SC | 37 | A | 3 |
| Thimble Berryway | NY | 21 | B | 1 |
| Third St | ET | 22 | B | 4-5 |
| Third St | T | 3 | B | 4 |
| Thirteenth St | ET | 22 | A | 4-5 |
| Thirtieth St | ET | 32 | E | 2-3 |
| Thirty-Eighth St | ET | 32 | E | 4 |
| Thirty-Fifth St | ET | 32 | D | 4-5 |
| Thirty-Ninth St | ET | 32 | E | 4-5 |
| Thirty-Second St | ET | 32 | E | 4 |
| Thirty-Seventh St | ET | 32 | D | 4-5 |
| Thirty-Sixth St | ET | 32 | D | 4-5 |
| Thirty-Third St | ET | 32 | E | 4-5 |
| Thistle Down Blvd | ET | 30 | B-C | 5 |
| Thistlewaite Cr | SC | 39 | C | 1 |
| Thome Cr | T | 4 | B | 1 |
| Thompson Av | ET | 24 | C | 3-4 |
| Thompson Rd | NY | 20 | C | 1 |
| Thompson St | T | 5 | D | 6 |
| Thora Av | SC | 25 | A | 3-4 |
| Thorburn Av | NY | 12 | C | 2 |
| Thorn La | NY | 19 | B | 5-6 |
| Thornbeck Dr | SC | 39 | E-F | 4 |
| Thornbush Cr | ET | 34 | B | 2 |
| Thorncliffe Av | T | 5 | D | 3 |
| Thorncliffe Park Dr | EY | 17 | A | 5-6 |
| Thorncliffe Park Dr | EY | 7 | F | 5-6 |
| Thorncrest Rd | ET | 26 | A-B | 4-5 |
| Thorndale Av | ET | 24 | E | 1 |
| Thornhill Av | Y | 24 | F | 2 |
| Thornly Cr | ET | 36 | F | 6 |
| Thornmount Dr | SC | 51 | B | 6 |
| Thornton Av | Y | 16 | E-F | 4 |
| Thornwood Rd | T | 5 | A | 2 |
| Thorny Vineway | NY | 11 | F | 4 |
| Thorold Gt | NY | 30 | B | 1 |
| Thoroughbred Cr | ET | 40 | B | 5 |
| Thorpe Rd | ET | 36 | E | 2 |
| Threadneedle Cr | NY | 21 | A-B | 2 |
| Three Valleys Dr | NY | 19 | B-D | 4-5 |
| Thrush Rd | SC | 27 | E | 4 |
| Thunder Gr | SC | 41 | B | 4 |
| Thurloe Av | T | 7 | A-B | 4 |
| Thurodale Av | NY | 16 | A-B | 1 |
| Thurrock Rd | NY | 18 | B | 1 |
| Thurstfield Cr | EY | 7 | E-F | 3 |
| Thurston Rd | T | 7 | B | 8 |
| Thwaite Av | NY | 20 | B | 6 |
| Thyme Ct | ET | 40 | E | 4 |
| Thyra Av | EY | 15 | F | 3 |
| Tiago Av | EY | 17 | E-F | 6 |
| Tichester Rd | Y | 6 | C-D | 6 |
| Tidefall Dr | SC | 31 | A | 5-6 |
| Tidemore Av | ET | 38 | D | 2-3 |
| Tideswell Blvd | SC | 49 | E | 2-3 |
| Tidworth Sq | SC | 39 | A | 1 |
| Tiffany Ct | NY | 17 | F | 2 |
| Tilfield Rd | SC | 41 | B-C | 2-3 |
| Tigerlily Ct | NY | 10 | E | 3 |
| Tilburn Pl | SC | 25 | A | 4 |
| Tilbury Dr | NY | 18 | D-E | 3 |
| Tilden Cr | ET | 26 | E | 1-2 |
| Tillbrook Ct | SC | 51 | A | 6 |
| Tilley Dr | SC | 47 | D | 4 |
| Tilley Dr | SC | 49 | F | 5 |
| Tillingham Keep | NY | 8 | A | 2 |
| Tillplain Rd | NY | 10 | A | 5-6 |
| Tilson Rd | T | 7 | B | 4 |
| Timberbank Blvd | SC | 31 | B-D | 4-5 |
| Timberglade Ct | NY | 9 | D-E | 5 |
| Timberlane | NY | 8 | D-E | 2 |
| Times Rd | Y | 6 | A | 2-3 |
| Times Rd | Y | 6 | A | 3-4 |
| Timgren Dr | SC | 29 | B | 4-5 |
| Timothy Ct | ET | 26 | D | 3 |
| Tina Ct | NY | 20 | B | 6 |
| Tinbury Pl | SC | 39 | F | 1 |
| Tinder Cr | NY | 17 | E-F | 3 |
| Tineham Ct | NY | 40 | E | 2 |
| Tineta Cr | SC | 39 | B | 1 |
| Tingle Cr | SC | 37 | E | 2 |
| Tintagel Rd | NY | 9 | E | 1 |
| Tinton Cr | ET | 40 | D-E | 2-3 |
| Tippett Rd | NY | 8 | B | 3-4 |
| Tisdale Av | NY | 17 | F | 4 |
| Titan Rd | ET | 24 | A-B | 5 |
| Tiverton Av | T | 5 | E | 6 |
| Tivoli Ct | SC | 47 | A | 3 |
| Tizzard Av | ET | 24 | D | 5 |
| Toba Dr | NY | 9 | C | 3 |
| Tobermory Dr | NY | 20 | B | 3-4 |
| Tobruk Cr | NY | 11 | A | 2 |
| Todd Baylis Blvd | Y | 16 | B | 2-3 |
| Todd Brook Dr | ET | 30 | A | 5 |
| Todd Rd | SC | 31 | F | 5 |
| Todmorden La | EY | 5 | F | 2 |
| Toffee Ct | ET | 22 | B | 3-4 |
| Toffoli Pl | NY | 11 | C | 2 |
| Tofield Cr | ET | 28 | A | 2 |
| Tofino Cr | NY | 9 | F | 4 |
| Tokay Ct | NY | 10 | B | 6 |
| Toledo Rd | ET | 34 | B | 2-3 |
| Tollerton Av | NY | 11 | D | 3-4 |
| Tollington Rd | ET | 36 | E | 1 |
| Tomar Villaway | NY | 11 | F | 6 |
| Tonon Dr | NY | 30 | F | 6 |
| Tonwell Ct | ET | 34 | F | 2 |
| Tooklea Cr | SC | 41 | B | 4 |
| Topaz Gt | NY | 11 | F | 1 |
| Topbank Cr | ET | 40 | A-B | 4 |
| Topcliff Av | NY | 20 | B | 4 |
| Topeka Rd | NY | 30 | B | 3 |
| Topham Rd | EY | 17 | E-F | 6 |
| Topview Ct | NY | 6 | A | 2 |
| Torbarrie Rd | NY | 28 | E-F | 1-3 |
| Torbolton Dr | ET | 28 | B | 3-4 |
| Torbrick Rd | T | 15 | A | 4-5 |
| Tordale Cr | SC | 29 | F | 4-5 |
| Torham Pl | SC | 41 | E | 3 |
| Torlake Cr | ET | 32 | F | 2 |
| Toro Rd | NY | 20 | D-E | 4 |
| Torrance Rd | SC | 37 | B | 2-3 |
| Torrens Av | EY | 15 | A | 2 |
| Torrens Av | EY | 5 | E-F | 2 |
| Torresdale Av | NY | 10 | B-C | 1-4 |
| Torrington Dr | ET | 36 | B | 6 |
| Torryburn Pl | NY | 19 | A | 4 |
| Toryork Dr | NY | 30 | B-D | 2-3 |
| Toshill Rd | NY | 30 | A | 2 |
| Tottenham Rd | NY | 17 | A | 1-2 |
| Totteridge Rd | ET | 26 | A | 4-5 |
| Touchstone Dr | NY | 16 | A | 2 |
| Toulon Rd | SC | 39 | D | 6 |
| Touraine Av | NY | 8 | B-C | 4 |
| Tourmaline Gr | SC | 29 | C | 2 |
| Tournament Dr | NY | 9 | B | 3 |
| Tower Dr | SC | 27 | B | 1 |
| Tower Dr | SC | 29 | B-C | 5-6 |
| Tower Rd | T | 4 | E | 4 |
| Towercrest Dr | NY | 19 | A | 4 |
| Towercrest Dr | NY | 9 | F | 4 |
| Town Centre Ct | SC | 39 | A-B | 4 |
| Town Haven Pl | ET | 27 | E | 4 |
| Townley Av | SC | 27 | A | 1 |
| Townley Av | SC | 29 | A | 6 |
| Towns Rd | ET | 32 | F | 3 |
| Townsend Rd | NY | 21 | B-D | 1 |
| Townsley St | T | 16 | D | 6 |
| Toynbee Tr | SC | 37 | E-F | 4 |
| Toyota Pl | SC | 39 | B-C | 2 |
| Tracy St | T | 3 | B | 1 |
| Tracy St | T | 5 | B | 6 |
| Tradewind Av | NY | 9 | A | 1 |
| Trafford La | NY | 8 | B | 5 |
| Trail View Ct | SC | 51 | C | 6 |
| Trailridge Cr | SC | 39 | F | 3 |
| Trailside Dr | NY | 21 | A-B | 5 |
| Trailsmoke Cr | ET | 34 | A-B | 4 |
| Tralee Av | SC | 39 | E | 4 |
| Tranby Av | T | 4 | E | 3 |
| Tranmer Av | T | 6 | E-F | 4 |
| Tranquil Ct | ET | 34 | B | 2 |
| Transfer Pl | SC | 41 | C | 6 |
| Transit Rd | NY | 8 | A-B | 2-3 |
| Transway Cr | SC | 27 | E | 4 |
| Transwell Av | NY | 10 | D | 3 |
| Traymore Ct | NY | 24 | F | 4 |
| Traymore Cr | Y | 24 | F | 3 |
| Treadgold Cr | NY | 19 | E-F | 4 |
| Treadway Blvd | EY | 15 | B | 1-2 |
| Treasure Gr | SC | 31 | E | 5 |
| Tredvalley Gr | SC | 47 | E | 1 |
| Tree Sparroway | NY | 11 | F | 3 |
| Treeland Way | NY | 18 | C | 1 |
| Treelawn Pkwy | NY | 18 | E | 5-6 |
| Treeline Ct | ET | 34 | B | 3 |
| Treerun Av | SC | 37 | E | 2 |
| Treetops Ct | SC | 41 | B | 2 |
| Treeview Dr | ET | 32 | E | 2-3 |
| Treewood St | SC | 29 | E-F | 6 |
| Trefann St | T | 5 | B | 6 |
| Treford Pl | T | 4 | B-C | 5 |
| Tregellis Rd | NY | 8 | E | 2-3 |
| Trehorne Dr | ET | 26 | C | 2 |
| Trelevan Pl | SC | 27 | B | 1 |
| Trellanock Av | SC | 47 | D | 6 |

T

| STREET NAME | MUNICIPALITY | MAP NO | MAP AREA |
|---|---|---|---|
| Tremayne Av | ET | 24 | D 2 |
| Tremely Cr | SC | 27 | E 3 |
| Tremont Av | NY | 19 | A 6 |
| Tremont Rd | ET | 34 | E 3-4 |
| Trent Av | T | 15 | B 1 |
| Trenton Av | EY | 15 | C-D 1 |
| Trenton Terr | T | 12 | C 2 |
| Tresillian Rd | NY | 8 | D 2-3 |
| Trestleside Cr | SC | 29 | A 5 |
| Trethewey Dr | NY | 16 | A-B 1-2 |
| Trethewey Dr | Y | 16 | A-B 2-3 |
| Treverton Dr | SC | 27 | E 2-3 |
| Triangle Villas Dr | SC | 31 | B-C 2 |
| Triburnham Pl | ET | 34 | B 2 |
| Triller Av | T | 12 | B 1 |
| Triller Av | T | 14 | E 6 |
| Trillium Terr | ET | 24 | F 5 |
| Trimontium Cr | EY | 15 | C 1 |
| Trinity Dr | T | 4 | B 6 |
| Trinity Dr | T | 4 | B 6 |
| Trinity St | T | 3 | B 1-2 |
| Trinnel Blvd | SC | 25 | C 1 |
| Trio Av | T | 26 | C 1-2 |
| Triple Crown Rd | ET | 40 | C 5-6 |
| Tripp Cr | SC | 27 | D 2 |
| Tristan Cr | NY | 21 | B 2-3 |
| Triton Rd | NY | 39 | A 4 |
| Trojan St | SC | 31 | D 6 |
| Tromley Dr | ET | 36 | E-F 4 |
| Troon Ct | NY | 9 | C 2 |
| Trophy Dr | NY | 17 | E-F 3 |
| Trott Sq | SC | 41 | E 4 |
| Troutbeck Av | SC | 41 | F 4 |
| Troutbeck Cr | SC | 41 | F 4 |
| Troutbeck Dr | SC | 51 | A 4 |
| Troutbrooke Dr | NY | 18 | A-B 2 |
| Trowell Av | T | 16 | D 3 |
| Trudelle St | SC | 37 | A-B 3 |
| Trudy Rd | NY | 21 | A 3-4 |
| Trueman Av | ET | 24 | A 6 |
| Truman Rd | NY | 9 | D-E 2 |
| Truro Cr | SC | 31 | F 1 |
| Truxford Rd | NY | 19 | F 6 |
| Tucker St:NY | | 17 | E-F 5 |
| Tudor Dr | NY | 9 | D 4 |
| Tudro Glen Cr | SC | 47 | D 4 |
| Tufton Cr | NY | 17 | F 3 |
| Tulane Cr | NY | 19 | E-F 3 |
| Tulip Dr | SC | 29 | B 4 |
| Tullamore Dr | NY | 9 | F 4 |
| Tullis Dr | T | 7 | A 4 |
| Tumbleweed Rd | NY | 21 | B 4 |
| Tumpane St | NY | 18 | B 3 |
| Tuna Ct | NY | 19 | C-D 3 |
| Tunbridge Cr | ET | 34 | B 1-2 |
| Tundra La | NY | 19 | A 4 |
| Tunmead Sq | SC | 41 | E 4-5 |
| Tupper Av | ET | 32 | F 3 |
| Turbina Av | SC | 41 | D 2 |
| Turbine Dr | NY | 30 | C 1 |
| Turf Grassway | NY | 30 | F 1 |
| Turks Rd | NY | 18 | A 1-2 |
| Turnberry Av | T | 16 | D-E 6 |
| Turner Rd | T | 4 | B 1-2 |
| Turnvale Rd | ET | 40 | D-E 5 |
| Turpin Av | ET | 28 | B 2 |
| Turret Hillway | NY | 21 | B 1 |
| Turpan Gt | NY | 20 | E 5 |
| Tuscarora Dr | NY | 21 | E-F 3 |
| Tuxedo Ct | SC | 39 | C-D 3 |
| Tweed Cr | SC | 29 | B 4 |
| Tweedrock Cr | SC | 49 | A 4 |
| Tweedsmuir Av | Y | 6 | D 6 |
| Twelfth St | ET | 32 | A 4-5 |
| Twentieth St | ET | 32 | F 4 |
| Twenty-Eighth St | ET | 32 | E 4-5 |
| Twenty-Fifth St | ET | 32 | F 4 |
| Twenty-First St | ET | 32 | F 4 |
| Twenty-Fourth St | ET | 32 | F 4 |
| Twenty-Ninth St | ET | 32 | E 4 |
| Twenty-Second St | ET | 32 | F 4 |
| Twenty-Seventh St | ET | 32 | E 4-5 |
| Twenty-Sixth St | ET | 32 | F 4 |
| Twenty-Third St | ET | 32 | F 4-5 |
| Twin Circle Ct | NY | 10 | C 1 |
| Twin Pauls Cr | SC | 29 | B 4 |
| Twyford Ct | ET | 26 | A 3 |
| Twyford Rd | ET | 26 | A-B 3 |
| Twyn Rivers Dr | NY | 21 | E 1 |
| Twyn Rivers Dr | SC | 51 | E-F 4 |
| Tycos Dr | NY | 16 | E-F 2 |
| Tyler Pl | ET | 26 | A 1 |
| Tyndall Av | T | 12 | C 1-2 |
| Tyndall Av. | T | 2 | A 1-2 |
| Tyne Ct | SC | 27 | F 4 |
| Tynevale Dr | ET | 36 | E-F 2 |
| Tyre Av | ET | 24 | A 2-3 |
| Tyre Av | ET | 34 | F 2-3 |
| Tyrone Av | NY | 26 | F 3 |
| Tyrrel Av | T | 4 | B-C 1 |
| Tyson Shepway | NY | 21 | A 6 |
| **U** | | | |
| Ullswater Ct | ET | 40 | E 2 |
| Ulster St | T | 4 | C-D 4 |
| Ulverston Rd | ET | 34 | B-C 1 |
| Ulysses Pl | SC | 31 | F 4 |
| Undercliff Dr | SC | 25 | F 3 |
| Underhill Dr | NY | 19 | E 4-5 |
| Underpass Gt | NY | 19 | C-E 3 |
| Underwood Av | ET | 24 | F 1-2 |
| Underwriters Rd | SC | 27 | C 1-2 |
| Unicorn Av | NY | 11 | E 3 |
| Union St | T | 16 | D 5-6 |
| Unita Gr | SC | 41 | E 6 |
| United Sq | SC | 39 | F 1 |
| United Sq | SC | 49 | F 1 |
| Unity Dr | T | 15 | A 4 |
| Universal Dr | M | 34 | A-B 4-5 |
| University Av | T | 2 | F 1-2 |
| University Av | T | 4 | E-F 5-6 |
| Uno Ct | SC | 24 | C 6 |
| Uno Dr | SC | 24 | C 5-6 |
| Unser Gt | NY | 30 | C 4-5 |
| Unsworth Av | T | 8 | F 6 |
| Unwin Av | T | 3 | C-F 2-4 |
| Uphill Av | NY | 28 | F 5 |
| Upjohn Rd | NY | 19 | B 3-4 |
| Upland Rd | ET | 24 | C 2-3 |
| Upminster Cr | ET | 36 | E 4-5 |
| Upper Canada Dr | NY | 9 | A-C 1-3 |
| Upper Highland Cr | NY | 9 | B 2-3 |
| Upper Humber Dr | ET | 40 | A 3-4 |
| Upper Rouge Ct | SC | 51 | C 6 |
| Upton Rd | SC | 27 | B-C 5 |
| Upwood Av | NY | 18 | A 6 |
| Urban Ct | NY | 28 | B 3 |
| Urbandale Av | NY | 11 | C 2 |
| Ursa Starway | NY | 19 | D 1 |
| Usher Av | NY | 24 | D 2 |
| Usherwood Ct | SC | 49 | A 1 |
| Uxbridge Ct | T | 14 | E 1-2 |
| **V** | | | |
| Val Fior Pl | T | 15 | B 4 |
| Valdane Dr | SC | 27 | A 5 |
| Valdor Dr | SC | 31 | E-F 3 |
| Vale Carseway | NY | 10 | C 4 |
| Valecrest Dr | ET | 26 | D 4-5 |
| Valencia Ct | NY | 18 | B-C 6 |
| Valentine Dr | NY | 19 | C-D 3 |
| Valerie Rd | SC | 27 | D 2 |
| Valermo Dr | ET | 32 | D-F 2 |
| Valetta Ct | ET | 40 | F 2-3 |
| Valewood Av | Y | 6 | B-C 5 |
| Valhalla Blvd | SC | 25 | C 5 |
| Valhalla Inn Rd | ET | 34 | D 2 |
| Valia Rd | ET | 47 | F 1 |
| Valiant Rd | ET | 24 | C 2 |
| Valley Centre Dr | SC | 51 | B 4 |
| Valley Dr | T | 16 | B-C 5 |
| Valley Rd | NY | 9 | B-C 4 |
| Valley Ridge Pl | NY | 9 | C 4 |
| Valley Stream Dr | SC | 41 | B 2 |
| Valley View | T | 5 | B-C 1 |
| Valley Woods Rd | NY | 19 | D-E 3-4 |
| Valleyanna Dr | NY | 7 | D 1-2 |
| Valleybrook Dr | NY | 19 | B 2-3 |
| Valleymede Rd | T | 14 | B 4 |
| Valleyview Gdns | Y | 24 | F 4 |
| Valmount Av | SC | 49 | E 4 |
| Valois Ct | ET | 30 | A 4 |
| Valor Blvd | ET | 17 | E-F 6 |
| Valparaiso Av | SC | 37 | A 1 |
| Valparaiso Av | SC | 39 | A 1 |
| Valport Cr | T | 26 | F 6 |
| Van Allan Rd | SC | 37 | D 1 |
| Van Camp Pl | ET | 36 | D-E 2 |
| Van De Water Cr | T | 2 | E 2 |
| Van Dusen Blvd | ET | 24 | A-C 3 |
| Van Horne Av | NY | 21 | A-F 4 |
| Van Horne Av | NY | 31 | A 4 |
| Van Stassen Blvd | Y | 24 | F 1-2 |
| Vanauley Ct | T | 4 | D 5 |
| Vanauley St | T | 4 | D 5 |
| Vanbrugh Av | SC | 25 | E 1-2 |
| Vancho Cr | ET | 26 | B 4 |
| Vancouver Av | T | 15 | A 6 |
| Vanderbrent Cr | ET | 36 | E 1 |
| Vanderhoof Av | EY | 7 | D-F 4 |
| Vandorf St | SC | 49 | E-F 2 |
| Vanellan Ct | ET | 24 | C 3 |
| Vanevery St | ET | 22 | C 3 |
| Vange Cr | ET | 40 | E 2-3 |
| Vanhill Av | NY | 30 | B 2 |
| Vanier La | NY | 20 | C 2 |
| Vanier La | NY | 19 | F 4 |
| Vankirk Rd | SC | 29 | D 5 |
| Vankoughnet St | T | 4 | D 5 |
| Vanley Cr | NY | 20 | E-F 4-5 |
| Vansco Rd | ET | 34 | E-F 6 |
| Vantage La | NY | 8 | A 6 |
| Vanwart Dr | SC | 37 | D 1-2 |
| Varley La | ET | 24 | D 3 |
| Varna Dr | NY | 8 | B 5-6 |
| Varsity Rd | Y | 24 | E-F 1-2 |
| Vassar Dr | ET | 36 | F 6 |
| Vaughan Rd | T | 5 | C 1 |
| Vaughan Rd | Y | 6 | A-C 4-6 |
| Vaughan St | EY | 7 | E 4 |
| Vauxhall Dr | SC | 26 | C-D 6 |
| Veerland Dr | NY | 18 | B 5 |
| Veery Pl | NY | 17 | A 1 |
| Vega Starway | NY | 19 | D 1 |
| Velma Dr | ET | 24 | B 3 |
| Vendome Pl | NY | 17 | C 4 |
| Venetian Cr | NY | 20 | A 4 |
| Venice Dr | NY | 18 | B 5-6 |
| Venn Cr | Y | 16 | D-E 4 |
| Venta Av | M | 32 | A 2 |
| Ventnor Av | EY | 15 | C-D 1 |
| Venture Dr | SC | 51 | B 6 |
| Verbena Av | T | 14 | A 4 |
| Verbena Av | T | 24 | F 4 |
| Verdun Av | SC | 27 | E-F 4 |
| Verlaine Pl | SC | 29 | F 4 |
| Vermont Av | T | 4 | C 2 |
| Vernadale Cr | SC | 25 | A 1 |
| Vernadale Cr | SC | 27 | A 6 |
| Verne Cr | SC | 41 | D 6 |
| Vernham Av | NY | 9 | E 3 |
| Vernham Cr | NY | 9 | E 3 |
| Vernon Av | T | 14 | B 2 |
| Vernon Rd | SC | 27 | A 2-3 |
| Verobeach Blvd | NY | 30 | C-D 6 |
| Verona Av | NY | 26 | F 3 |
| Verral Av | T | 5 | E 6 |
| Versailles Ct | NY | 9 | E 3-4 |
| Versend Dr | NY | 19 | E 3 |
| Verwood Av | NY | 8 | C 1 |
| Vesper Ct | SC | 37 | B 1 |
| Vesta Dr | T | 6 | C-D 3-4 |
| Via Aurelia Dr | NY | 16 | A 3 |
| Via Cassia Dr | NY | 16 | A-B 2 |
| Via Italia | T | 14 | F 1 |
| Via Torre Dr | NY | 16 | A 2 |
| Viamede Cr | NY | 18 | E 4-5 |
| Vianney Dr | SC | 25 | B 1 |
| Vibe Rd | ET | 22 | A 1 |
| Vicarage Ct | ET | 36 | E 1 |
| Vicdave St | NY | 26 | E 5 |
| Vice Regent Blvd | ET | 38 | D 2 |
| Vickers Rd | ET | 34 | D 4-5 |
| Vickson Cr | ET | 34 | D-E 3 |
| Vicora Linkway | NY | 17 | C-D 5 |
| Vicross Rd | EY | 17 | F 1 |
| Vicross Rd | EY | 17 | F 6 |
| Victor Av | T | 5 | D-E 5 |
| Victor Av | ET | 22 | D 2-3 |
| Victoria Av | Y | 26 | F 2 |
| Victoria Av W | Y | 26 | F 2 |
| Victoria Blvd | Y | 16 | A 3 |
| Victoria Park Av | EY | 15 | F 1-4 |
| Victoria Park Av | EY | 17 | F 5-6 |
| Victoria Park Av | T | 15 | F 1-4 |
| Victoria Park Av | NY | 19 | F 1-6 |
| Victoria Park Av | NY | 21 | F 1-6 |
| Victoria Park Av | SC | 25 | A 1-6 |
| Victoria Park Av | SC | 27 | A 1-6 |
| Victoria Park Av | SC | 29 | A 1-6 |
| Victoria Park Av | SC | 31 | A 1-6 |
| Victoria St | T | 13 | F 5 |
| Victoria St | T | 15 | F 4-6 |
| Victoria St | ET | 22 | E 2 |
| Victoria St | T | 3 | A 1 |
| Victoria St | T | 5 | A 5-6 |
| Victoria Street La | T | 5 | A 6 |
| Victoria Woods Gt | NY | 21 | F 5 |
| Victory Dr | NY | 18 | C-D 3 |
| View Green Cr | ET | 40 | A 5 |
| Viewbank Rd | SC | 25 | C 5 |
| Viewmount Av | NY | 6 | B-D 3 |
| Viking Rd | ET | 34 | F 3 |

| Street | Area | Map | Grid | No. |
|---|---|---|---|---|
| Villa Rd | ET | 32 | C | 5 |
| Village Greenway | NY | 19 | C-D | 2 |
| Village Gt | T | 10 | D | 1 |
| Village Station Rd | EY | 7 | E | 5 |
| Villata Gdns | NY | 20 | D | 4 |
| Villiers St | T | 3 | C-E | 2 |
| Vimy Av | Y | 28 | F | 6 |
| Vinci Cr | NY | 8 | B | 3 |
| Vine Av | T | 14 | C | 1-2 |
| Violet Av | T | 13 | E | 6 |
| Virgilwood Dr | NY | 10 | C | 3-4 |
| Virgin Pl | T | 3 | B-C | 1 |
| Virginia Av | EY | 15 | B-C | 2 |
| Virgo Starway | NY | 19 | D | 1 |
| Virtue St | T | 14 | E | 6 |
| Vista Humber Dr | ET | 26 | E | 1 |
| Vita Dr | NY | 16 | A | 2 |
| Vonda Av | NY | 9 | C | 1 |
| Voyager Ct N | ET | 36 | B | 2 |
| Voyager Ct S | ET | 36 | B | 2 |
| Vradenberg Dr | SC | 29 | B | 4 |
| Vulcan St | ET | 38 | D-E | 4 |
| Vyner Rd | NY | 9 | C | 2 |

**W**

| Street | Area | Map | Grid | No. |
|---|---|---|---|---|
| Wabash Av | T | 14 | E | 5 |
| Waddington Cr | NY | 21 | C-E | 4-5 |
| Wade Av | NY | 14 | E-F | 3 |
| Wagner Av | SC | 47 | A | 2 |
| Wagon Trailway | NY | 21 | E | 6 |
| Wagstaff Dr | T | 15 | A | 5 |
| Wainfleet Rd | SC | 27 | E | 3 |
| Wainwright Dr | ET | 26 | B | 6 |
| Wakefield Cr | SC | 31 | C | 4-5 |
| Wakehood St | SC | 15 | F | 4 |
| Wakunda Pl | NY | 17 | E | 5 |
| Walbon Rd | SC | 27 | B | 2 |
| Walby Dr | NY | 30 | B | 2-3 |
| Walder Av | NY | 7 | C | 2 |
| Walder Av | T | 7 | C | 3 |
| Walding Gt | SC | 49 | C | 4 |
| Waldock St | SC | 47 | A | 4 |
| Wales Av | T | 4 | D | 5 |
| Walford Rd | ET | 24 | E | 1-2 |
| Walgreen Ct | SC | 29 | B | 2 |
| Walker Av | T | 4 | F | 2 |
| Walker Rd | NY | 28 | B | 6 |
| Wall Av | NY | 28 | B | 6 |
| Wallace Av | T | 14 | E-F | 3 |
| Wallasey Av | NY | 28 | D-E | 3 |
| Wallbridge Ct | NY | 10 | D | 4 |
| Wallenberg Rd | NY | 8 | D | 1 |
| Waller Av | T | 14 | A-B | 4 |
| Wallingford Rd | NY | 19 | E-F | 4 |
| Wallington Av | EY | 15 | D-E | 2 |
| Wallis Cr | ET | 40 | F | 4 |
| Wallsend Dr | SC | 47 | A | 2 |
| Walmer Av | T | 4 | D | 5 |
| Walmer Rd | Y | 6 | D | 6 |
| Walmsley Blvd | T | 6 | E-F | 6 |
| Walnut Av | T | 2 | B-C | 1 |
| Walnut Av | T | 4 | B | 6 |
| Walnut Cr | ET | 32 | E | 4-5 |
| Walpole Av | T | 15 | A-B | 5 |
| Walsh Av | NY | 28 | D | 4 |
| Walter St | T | 15 | E | 5 |
| Waltham Dr | ET | 30 | A | 4 |
| Walton St | T | 4 | F | 5 |
| Waltonice Rd | SC | 25 | F | 1 |
| Waltonice Rd | SC | 27 | F | 1 |
| Walwyn Av | NY | 28 | E | 4-5 |
| Wanda Rd | T | 14 | D | 3 |
| Wandering Tr | SC | 51 | B | 3-4 |
| Wandle Av | NY | 18 | B | 3 |
| Waniska Av | ET | 24 | E-F | 6 |
| Wanita Rd | SC | 49 | E | 6 |
| Wanless Av | T | 9 | A-B | 5 |
| Wanless Cr | NY | 7 | B | 1 |
| Wanless Cr | NY | 9 | B | 6 |
| Wanless Cr | T | 7 | B | 1 |
| Wanless Cr | T | 9 | B | 6 |
| Wansey Rd | ET | 28 | A | 1 |
| Wanstead Av | SC | 25 | A | 3 |
| Wantanopa Cr | SC | 39 | C | 5 |
| Warbeck Pl | ET | 26 | A | 1 |
| Ward St | T | 14 | E | 2-3 |
| Wardell St | T | 5 | E | 6 |
| Warden Av | SC | 25 | B | 1-5 |
| Warden Av | SC | 27 | B | 1-6 |
| Warden Av | SC | 29 | B | 1-6 |
| Warden Av | SC | 31 | B | 1-6 |
| Wardencourt Dr | SC | 31 | A | 4 |
| Wardlaw Cr | ET | 30 | B | 1 |
| Wareside Rd | ET | 34 | B | 1 |
| Warfield Dr | NY | 21 | E | 4 |
| Waring Ct | NY | 11 | B | 4 |
| Waringstown Dr | SC | 29 | A | 3-4 |
| Warland Av | EY | 5 | F | 1 |
| Warlingham Ct | ET | 34 | B | 1 |
| Warlock Cr | NY | 11 | E | 3 |
| Warner Av | T | 17 | F | 4 |
| Warner Gt | NY | 17 | F | 4 |
| Warnica Av | ET | 24 | A-B | 6 |
| Warnsworth St | SC | 49 | A-B | 5 |
| Warren Av | Y | 24 | E | 1 |
| Warren Rd | T | 4 | C | 4-6 |
| Warren Rd | T | 6 | E | 4-6 |
| Warrendale Ct | ET | 40 | F | 4 |
| Warrender Av | ET | 36 | F | 4 |
| Warvet Cr | EY | 15 | E | 1 |
| Warvet Cr | EY | 17 | F | 6 |
| Warwick Av | Y | 6 | B-D | 4 |
| Warwick Castle Gt | SC | 51 | A | 6 |
| Warwood Rd | ET | 34 | E | 1-2 |
| Wascana Av | T | 5 | C | 6 |
| Wasdale Cr | NY | 8 | C | 4 |
| Washburn Way | SC | 41 | E | 5-6 |
| Washington Av | T | 4 | E | 4 |
| Water St | T | 3 | C | 1-2 |
| Water Tower Gt | SC | 51 | B | 6 |
| Water Wheelway | NY | 21 | B | 1 |
| Waterbeach Cr | ET | 38 | E | 1 |
| Waterbridge Way | NY | 21 | F | 1-2 |
| Waterbury Dr | ET | 36 | E | 1-2 |
| Watercliffe Rd | ET | 30 | A | 3-6 |
| Waterfield Dr | SC | 29 | F | 4 |
| Waterford Dr | ET | 26 | A-B | 2-3 |
| Waterfront Dr | ET | 22 | F | 2 |
| Watergarden Way | NY | 11 | D | 4 |
| Waterloo Av | NY | 10 | A-C | 6 |
| Waterloo Av | T | 4 | A | 6 |
| Waterloo Terr | T | 2 | D | 1 |
| Waterman Av | ET | 17 | D-E | 5 |
| Waterton Rd | ET | 26 | E | 1-2 |
| Watford Av | Y | 6 | B | 6 |
| Watkinson Av | T | 14 | D | 2 |
| Watling St | ET | 26 | C | 3 |
| Watney Cr | NY | 20 | B | 6 |
| Watson Av | T | 24 | F | 1-2 |
| Watson St | SC | 49 | C | 4-5 |
| Watt Av | Y | 16 | D | 5 |
| Waulron St | ET | 34 | B | 5 |
| Waverley Av | T | 13 | D | 5 |
| Waverley Rd | T | 13 | D | 5 |
| Waverley Rd | T | 15 | D | 5-6 |
| Wax Myrtleway | NY | 19 | B | 5 |
| Waxham Rd | ET | 38 | E-F | 1 |
| Waxham Rd | ET | 40 | E-F | 6 |
| Waxwing Pl | ET | 17 | C | 1 |
| Wayford Cr | SC | 51 | A | 6 |
| Wayland Av | T | 15 | E | 4-5 |
| Wayne Av | SC | 27 | B | 1-2 |
| Ways La | T | 4 | C | 6 |
| Wayside Av | SC | 31 | D | 5 |
| Weatherell St | T | 14 | A | 3 |
| Weatherell St | T | 24 | F | 3 |
| Weatherstone Cr | NY | 11 | F | 3 |
| Webb Av | T | 14 | B | 2 |
| Webster Av | T | 4 | E-F | 3 |
| Wedge Ct | NY | 20 | A | 5 |
| Wedgeport Pl | NY | 11 | B | 5 |
| Wedgewood Dr | ET | 34 | E | 2 |
| Wedgewood Dr | T | 11 | A-C | 2 |
| Wedmore Av | NY | 17 | F | 4 |
| Weetwood Av | NY | 8 | E | 5 |
| Weir Cr | SC | 49 | A | 5-6 |
| Welby Cir | T | 15 | B | 3-4 |
| Weldon Ct | NY | 18 | B | 5 |
| Welkin Gt | T | 34 | B | 1 |
| Welland Av | T | 5 | B | 1 |
| Welland Av | T | 7 | B | 6 |
| Welland Rd | T | 8 | D | 6 |
| Wellesbourne Cr | NY | 21 | B | 2 |
| Wellesley Av | T | 5 | C | 4 |
| Wellesley Cottages | T | 5 | B | 4 |
| Wellesley La | T | 5 | A-B | 4 |
| Wellesley Pl | T | 5 | A | 4 |
| Wellesley St E | T | 5 | A-C | 4 |
| Wellesley St W | T | 4 | E-F | 4 |
| Wellesworth Dr | ET | 36 | B-C | 4-6 |
| Wellington St | T | 2 | B-F | 1 |
| Wellpark Blvd | SC | 41 | A | 3 |
| Wells Hill Av | T | 4 | D | 1-2 |
| Wells St | T | 4 | D | 3 |
| Wellwood Av | Y | 6 | B | 6 |
| Welsford Gdns | NY | 19 | F | 5 |
| Welwyn Av | SC | 39 | E | 5 |
| Wembley Av | ET | 24 | A | 2 |
| Wembley Rd | T | 6 | B-D | 3 |
| Wendell Av | NY | 28 | E | 4-5 |
| Wenderly Dr | NY | 6 | A-B | 1 |
| Wendigo Way | T | 14 | B | 4 |
| Wendover Rd | ET | 24 | D | 3 |
| Wendy Cr | NY | 8 | D | 3 |
| Wenlock Gt | SC | 31 | F | 2 |
| Wenlock Gt | SC | 41 | A | 2 |
| Wentworth Av | NY | 10 | D-E | 6 |
| Wesley St | ET | 22 | D | 1-2 |
| Wessex Pl | SC | 41 | B | 4 |
| West Av | T | 5 | E | 5-6 |
| West Burton Ct | SC | 39 | C | 1 |
| West Deane Park Dr | ET | 36 | D-E | 5-6 |
| West Deane Valley Rd | ET | 36 | D | 4 |
| West Grove Cr | NY | 6 | D | 1-2 |
| West Hill Dr | SC | 49 | B | 5-6 |
| West Lodge Av | T | 14 | F | 5-6 |
| West Lynn Av | T | 15 | C | 3-4 |
| West Mall | ET | 34 | C | 4 |
| West Mall, The | ET | 32 | B | 1-2 |
| West Mall, The | ET | 34 | B-C | 1-6 |
| West Mall, The | T | 34 | C | 6 |
| West Palm Ct | NY | 30 | C | 6 |
| West Point Av | SC | 47 | E | 4 |
| West Rd | T | 14 | B-C | 4-5 |
| West Wareside Rd | ET | 34 | B | 1 |
| Westacres Dr | Y | 16 | C | 3 |
| Westbank Cr | ET | 26 | E | 2 |
| Westbourne Av | SC | 25 | A | 1-2 |
| Westbourne Av | SC | 27 | A | 6 |
| Westbrook Av | EY | 15 | D-E | 3 |
| Westbury Cr | Y | 16 | C | 4 |
| Westchester Rd | NY | 16 | B | 2 |
| Westcliffe Rd | NY | 18 | A | 3 |
| Westcroft Dr | SC | 49 | A | 5-6 |
| Westdale Dr | NY | 18 | F | 4 |
| Westgate Blvd | NY | 8 | D-E | 2-3 |
| Westgate Cr | NY | 8 | D | 3 |
| Westglen Cr | ET | 34 | F | 4 |
| Westhampton Dr | ET | 28 | A-B | 5 |
| Westhead Rd | ET | 32 | B | 2-3 |
| Westholme Av | T | 14 | B | 2 |
| Westhumber Blvd | ET | 38 | E-F | 1 |
| Westhumber Blvd | ET | 40 | E-F | 6 |
| Westlake Av | EY | 15 | D-E | 2-3 |
| Westlake Cr | T | 15 | E | 3-4 |
| Westlake Cr | EY | 15 | D-E | 2 |
| Westlake Rd | SC | 37 | E-F | 3 |
| Westlake Rd | SC | 47 | A | 3 |
| Westlawn Pl | ET | 40 | A | 5 |
| Westleigh Cr | ET | 32 | B-C | 3 |
| Westminster Av | T | 14 | D-E | 5 |
| Westmore Dr | ET | 40 | D | 3-4 |
| Westmoreland Av | T | 4 | A | 2-3 |
| Westmoreland Av N | T | 4 | A | 1-2 |
| Westmount Av | T | 4 | A | 1 |
| Westmount Av | Y | 6 | A | 4-6 |
| Westmount Park Rd | ET | 26 | D | 2 |
| Weston Rd | NY | 28 | D-E | 1-5 |
| Weston Rd | NY | 30 | D-E | 1-6 |
| Weston Rd | T | 16 | C | 5-6 |
| Weston Rd | Y | 16 | A-C | 2-5 |
| Weston Rd | Y | 28 | D-E | 5-6 |
| Weston Wood Rd | ET | 26 | D | 2 |
| Westona St | T | 26 | D | 1 |
| Westona St | ET | 28 | D | 6 |
| Westover Hill Rd | Y | 6 | B | 4 |
| Westport Av | T | 14 | D | 1 |
| Westridge Rd | ET | 26 | D | 5 |
| Westrose Av | ET | 24 | C | 2 |
| Westroyal Rd | ET | 26 | C | 1-2 |
| Westrum Rd | ET | 36 | B | 5-6 |
| Westside Dr | ET | 34 | B | 5-6 |
| Westview Blvd | EY | 17 | E-F | 5-6 |
| Westwater Dr | SC | 31 | B-C | 3 |
| Westway, The | ET | 26 | A-C | 1-2 |
| Westway, The | ET | 36 | E-F | 2 |
| Westwood Av | EY | 5 | E-F | 2 |
| Westwynd Ct | ET | 36 | E | 2 |
| Wetherby Dr | SC | 31 | A | 3 |
| Wetherfield Pl | NY | 9 | E | 5 |
| Wexford Blvd | SC | 27 | B | 1-2 |
| Weybourne Cr | T | 7 | A | 1 |
| Weybourne Pl | ET | 26 | B | 4-5 |
| Weybridge Ct | ET | 36 | F | 5 |
| Weybright Ct | SC | 29 | E-F | 5 |
| Weymouth Av | EY | 15 | F | 3 |
| Whaley Dr | ET | 32 | C | 2 |
| Wharton Glen Av | M | 34 | A-B | 5 |
| Wharton Sq | SC | 41 | A | 2 |
| Wharton Way | M | 34 | A | 4-5 |
| Wheatfield Rd | ET | 22 | D | 3 |
| Wheaton Gr | SC | 37 | B | 3 |
| Wheatsheaf Cr | NY | 30 | F | 1 |
| Wheel Wright Cr | NY | 30 | F | 1 |

| STREET NAME | MUNICIPALITY | MAP NO | | MAP AREA |
|---|---|---|---|---|
| Wheeler Av | T | 13 | D | 5 |
| Wheeler Av | T | 15 | D | 5-6 |
| Wheeling Dr | SC | 47 | D-E | 6 |
| Whispering Willow Ptwy | SC | 51 | A | 4 |
| Whistling Hills Dr | SC | 41 | B | 2 |
| Whitaker Av | T | 4 | C | 1 |
| Whitbread Cr | NY | 20 | A | 6 |
| Whitburn Cr | NY | 18 | C | 2 |
| White Abbey Pk | SC | 29 | B | 3-4 |
| White Av | NY | 26 | F | 6 |
| White Av | SC | 49 | E | 4 |
| White Court Pl | T | 4 | D | 6 |
| White Heather Blvd | SC | 41 | B | 2-3 |
| White Oak Blvd | T | 24 | C | 3 |
| White Pine Ct | EY | 17 | C | 6 |
| Whiteacres Av | SC | 49 | D-E | 5 |
| Whitebirch Rd | SC | 25 | B | 6 |
| Whitecap Blvd | SC | 37 | C | 5 |
| Whitecroft Pl | ET | 26 | D | 4 |
| Whitefriars Dr | NY | 19 | D | 5 |
| Whitehall Rd | T | 5 | A-B | 2 |
| Whitehorn Av | NY | 21 | B-E | 3-4 |
| Whitehorse Rd | NY | 20 | F | 5 |
| Whiteleaf Cr | SC | 41 | B | 2 |
| Whiteleas Av | SC | 41 | B | 5 |
| Whitelock Cr | T | 11 | D | 5 |
| Whiterock Dr | SC | 40 | D | 5 |
| Whiteside Pl | T | 5 | C | 6 |
| Whiteway Ct | SC | 51 | B | 4 |
| Whitewood Rd | T | 7 | C | 5 |
| Whitfield Av | NY | 30 | A-B | 2 |
| Whitlam Av | ET | 32 | F | 4 |
| Whitley Av | NY | 18 | E-F | 4 |
| Whitley Castle Cr | SC | 41 | B | 3-4 |
| Whitman St | NY | 11 | B | 1 |
| Whitmore Rd | T | 16 | F | 3 |
| Whitmore Av | T | 16 | B | 3 |
| Whitmore Av | Y | 16 | B | 3 |
| Whitmore Av | Y | 6 | A-B | 3 |
| Whitney Av | T | 5 | B-C | 2 |
| Whittaker Av | NY | 11 | E | 6 |
| Whitworth Av | T | 24 | F | 6 |
| Whytock Av | T | 14 | E-F | 4 |
| Wichey Rd | SC | 47 | D | 4-5 |
| Wichey Rd | SC | 49 | F | 5 |
| Wickford Dr | NY | 18 | C | 6 |
| Wickham Ct | ET | 40 | F | 2 |
| Wickham Rd | T | 24 | F | 6 |
| Wicklow Dr | SC | 31 | B | 6 |
| Wickman Rd | ET | 32 | F | 1 |
| Wickman Rd | ET | 34 | F | 6 |
| Wickson Tr | SC | 41 | F | 6 |
| Wickson Tr | SC | 51 | A | 6 |
| Wicksteed Av | EY | 17 | A | 4 |
| Wicksteed Av | EY | 7 | A | 4 |
| Wickware Gt | SC | 29 | E | 6 |
| Widdicombe Hill | ET | 36 | E-F | 3 |
| Widdicombe Hill Blvd | ET | 36 | E | 3 |
| Wideford Pl | NY | 11 | C | 3 |
| Widmer St | T | 2 | E | 1 |
| Wigan Cr | T | 8 | B | 3 |
| Wiggens Ct | SC | 41 | E | 6 |
| Wigmore Dr | NY | 17 | E-F | 5 |
| Wilberton Rd | T | 6 | E-F | 5 |
| Wilby | NY | 26 | E | 1 |
| Wilcox Creek Pathway | SC | 51 | A | 4 |
| Wild Briarway | NY | 11 | A | 4 |
| Wild Gingerway | NY | 10 | C | 6 |
| Wildcat Rd | NY | 20 | E | 2 |
| Wilderness Dr | SC | 41 | A | 1 |
| Wildlark Dr | SC | 47 | C | 1 |
| Wildwood Cr | T | 15 | C | 4 |
| Wiley Av | EY | 15 | A | 2-3 |
| Wiley Av | T | 15 | A | 3 |
| Wilfred Av | NY | 11 | B | 4-6 |
| Wilfred Av | NY | 9 | C | 1 |
| Wilfrid Av | T | 7 | A | 4 |
| Wilgar Rd | ET | 24 | C | 3 |
| Wilket Creek Rd | NY | 17 | B | 4 |
| Wilket Rd | NY | 9 | D | 4 |
| Wilkie Av | SC | 25 | E | 1 |
| Wilkins Av | T | 3 | B | 1 |
| Wilkinson Dr | NY | 21 | A | 6 |
| Willamere Dr | SC | 37 | A | 6 |
| Willard Av | T | 14 | A | 2-4 |
| Willard Av | Y | 14 | A | 1-2 |
| Willard Gdns | T | 14 | A | 4 |
| Willcocks St | T | 4 | D-E | 1 |
| Willesden Rd | NY | 21 | A | 3 |
| William Carson Cr | NY | 9 | A | 3 |
| William Cragg Dr | NY | 18 | A-B | 4 |
| William Kitchen Rd | SC | 29 | E | 3 |
| William St | Y | 28 | F | 6 |
| Williamson Rd | T | 13 | E | 5 |
| Williamson Rd | T | 15 | E | 6 |
| Willie Ct | ET | 40 | F | 1 |
| Willimart Ct | NY | 10 | E-F | 2 |
| Willingdon Av | SC | 25 | D | 2 |
| Willingdon Blvd | ET | 24 | D | 2-3 |
| Willis St | T | 4 | C | 6 |
| Willison Pl | T | 4 | D | 6 |
| Willison Sq | T | 4 | D-E | 6 |
| Willow Av | T | 13 | F | 5-6 |
| Willow Av | T | 15 | F | 5-6 |
| Willow Av | T | 3 | B | A-5 |
| Willow Heights Ct | NY | 11 | B | 2-3 |
| Willowbank Blvd | T | 6 | E | 3 |
| Willowbrook Rd | ET | 22 | C | 2 |
| Willowdale Av | NY | 11 | B | 1-6 |
| Willowdale Av | NY | 9 | B | 1 |
| Willowhurst Cr | SC | 29 | B | 5 |
| Willowlea Dr | SC | 49 | C-D | 5 |
| Willowmount Dr | SC | 27 | C-D | 6 |
| Willowood Ct | NY | 21 | A | 5 |
| Willowridge Rd | ET | 36 | D-E | 2-3 |
| Willowvale Ct | T | 8 | B | 2-5 |
| Willrod Rd | ET | 24 | B | 3-4 |
| Willsteven Dr | SC | 37 | D | 1-2 |
| Wilmar Rd | ET | 34 | E | 3-4 |
| Wilmington Av | NY | 10 | A-B | 4-6 |
| Wilmont Dr | NY | 20 | A-B | 4 |
| Wilson Av | NY | 18 | A-F | 3-4 |
| Wilson Av | NY | 28 | D-F | 4 |
| Wilson Av | SC | 8 | A-F | 3-4 |
| Wilson Heights Blvd | NY | 10 | A | 5-6 |
| Wilson Heights Blvd | NY | 8 | B | 1-3 |
| Wilson Park | T | 12 | B | 1 |
| Wilton St | T | 3 | A-B | 2-3 |
| Wiltshire Av | T | 14 | E | 1-2 |
| Wimbleton Cr | ET | 24 | B | 6 |
| Wimbleton Cr | ET | 26 | B | 6 |
| Wimbleton Rd | ET | 24 | B-C | 1 |
| Wimbleton Rd | ET | 26 | B-C | 6 |
| Wimpole Dr | NY | 9 | D-E | 2 |
| Winchester St | T | 5 | B-C | 5 |
| Winchfield Pl | NY | 9 | E-F | 5 |
| Wincott Dr | ET | 26 | A | 1-2 |
| Wincrest Dr | SC | 39 | A | 4 |
| Windal Av | NY | 28 | D | 5 |
| Windermere Av | T | 14 | A | 2-5 |
| Windermere Av | Y | 14 | A | 1-2 |
| Windermere Pl | Y | 14 | B | 5-6 |
| Windham Dr | NY | 11 | D | 5 |
| Windhill Cr | NY | 30 | C-D | 4-5 |
| Winding Ct | SC | 49 | D | 4 |
| Windley Av | Y | 6 | B | 1 |
| Windmill Rd | EY | 7 | C | 6 |
| Windover Dr | SC | 37 | E | 1 |
| Windrush Tr | SC | 49 | C | 6 |
| Windsor Av | SC | 15 | F | 6 |
| Windsor Av | SC | 25 | A | 6 |
| Windsor Av | T | 13 | F | 5 |
| Windsor Rd | ET | 28 | A | 5-6 |
| Windsor St | T | 22 | D | 2 |
| Windsor St | T | 2 | E | 1-2 |
| Windust Gt | ET | 34 | B | 2 |
| Windwood Dr | ET | 40 | C | 4-5 |
| Windy Golfway La | NY | 17 | D | 4 |
| Windy Ridge Dr | SC | 37 | B-C | 5 |
| Winesap Pl | ET | 24 | A | 1 |
| Winesap Pl | ET | 26 | A | 6 |
| Wineva Av | T | 13 | E | 5 |
| Wineva Av | T | 13 | E | 6 |
| Wineva Av | T | 15 | E | 6 |
| Winfield Av | Y | 14 | A | 4 |
| Wingarden Ct | SC | 41 | E | 4-6 |
| Wingate Pl | T | 6 | D | 3 |
| Wingold Av | NY | 16 | E-F | 2 |
| Wingreen Ct | NY | 19 | B | 6 |
| Wingrove Hill | ET | 34 | F | 1 |
| Winlock Pk | NY | 11 | B-C | 4 |
| Winners Cir | T | 13 | F | 1 |
| Winnett Av | T | 6 | B | 4-5 |
| Winnifred Av | T | 3 | F | 1 |
| Winnipeg Rd | ET | 26 | B-C | 1 |
| Winoka Av | NY | 18 | D | 4 |
| Winona Dr | T | 4 | B | 1 |
| Winona Dr | T | 6 | B | 4-6 |
| Winsdale Rd | ET | 34 | A-B | 2-3 |
| Winsland Dr | ET | 36 | E | 3-4 |
| Winslow Av | EY | 7 | D | 3 |
| Winslow St | ET | 22 | D | 1 |
| Winsome Av | NY | 18 | D | 4 |
| Winson Rd | NY | 17 | B | 3 |
| Winstanly Cr | SC | 51 | A | 6 |
| Winston Av | T | 15 | F | 5 |
| Winston Av | SC | 25 | A | 5 |
| Winston Churchill Dr | SC | 25 | A | 4-5 |
| Winston Park Blvd | NY | 18 | E-F | 3-4 |
| Winter Av | SC | 27 | F | 4-5 |
| Winter Gardens Tr | SC | 47 | D | 5 |
| Winterbourne Ct | ET | 26 | A | 3 |
| Wintergreen Rd | T | 18 | C | 3 |
| Winterhaven Rd | M | 32 | B | 2 |
| Wintermute Blvd | SC | 31 | B-C | 1 |
| Winters Rd | NY | 20 | C | 1-2 |
| Winterset Ct | ET | 36 | D | 2-3 |
| Winterton Dr | ET | 36 | E-F | 4 |
| Winthorpe Rd | T | 15 | C | 6 |
| Winton Rd | NY | 9 | A-B | 4-5 |
| Wirral Ct | SC | 25 | F | 1 |
| Wishart Pl | NY | 18 | B | 1 |
| Wishaw Rd | SC | 49 | C-D | 4 |
| Wishbone, The | NY | 16 | A | 2 |
| Wishford Dr | SC | 51 | B | 6 |
| Wishing Well Dr | SC | 29 | A-B | 1-2 |
| Wisteria Rd | SC | 29 | B | 3 |
| Witherow St | T | 5 | D-F | 5 |
| Withrow Av | T | 3 | B | 4-5 |
| Withrow St | T | 3 | B | 4-5 |
| Withycombe Cr | SC | 31 | E-F | 1 |
| Wm. R. Allen Rd | NY | 8 | B | 1-3 |
| Wm. R. Allen Rd | NY | 6 | A-B | 1-6 |
| Wm. R. Allen Rd | T | 6 | B | 3-4 |
| Wm.Morgan Dr | EY | 17 | A | 5 |
| Woburn Av | NY | 10 | A-B | 4-6 |
| Woburn Av | NY | 9 | B | 6 |
| Woburn Av | T | 8 | E-F | 6 |
| Wolcott Av | SC | 25 | C | 3 |
| Wolfe Av | SC | 27 | E-F | 5 |
| Wolfrey Av | T | 5 | D-E | 4 |
| Wolseley St | T | 4 | C | 6 |
| Wolverleigh Blvd | T | 15 | A-D | 3 |
| Wolverton Av | EY | 5 | F | 1 |
| Wonderland Dr | SC | 39 | E | 1 |
| Wood Av | NY | 7 | C | 1 |
| Wood Fernway | NY | 21 | B | 3 |
| Wood Glen Rd | SC | 25 | B | 5 |
| Wood St | T | 4 | F | 5 |
| Wood St | T | 5 | A | 5 |
| Woodale Av | T | 15 | F | 5 |
| Woodale Av | T | 25 | A | 5 |
| Woodbank Rd | ET | 34 | E | 1 |
| Woodbine Av | T | 15 | C-D | 1-3 |
| Woodbine Av | T | 15 | C-D | 3-6 |
| Woodbine Ave | T | 13 | D | 5-6 |
| Woodbine Downs Blvd | ET | 40 | C | 3-4 |
| Woodbine Entrance | M | 38 | A | 2 |
| Woodbine Heights Blvd | EY | 17 | C-D | 5-6 |
| Woodbine Mews | T | 13 | D | 6 |
| Woodborough Av | Y | 16 | E | 3 |
| Woodbury Pl | ET | 32 | C | 2 |
| Woodbury Rd | ET | 32 | C | 3 |
| Woodcliff Pl | NY | 19 | B | 6 |
| Woodcrest Dr | ET | 26 | D-E | 4 |
| Woodcroft Cr | Y | 16 | F | 5 |
| Wooded Carseway | NY | 10 | C | 4 |
| Woodenhill Ct | Y | 16 | E | 4 |
| Woodfern Dr | SC | 27 | D | 4 |
| Woodfield Rd | T | 15 | B | 4-6 |
| Woodfield Rd | T | 13 | E | 6 |
| Woodford Park Rd | ET | 24 | E | 6 |
| Woodgarden Cr | SC | 47 | C | 2 |
| Woodgate Rd | NY | 26 | E | 5 |
| Woodgreen Pl | T | 3 | D-E | 1 |
| Woodgrove Dr | SC | 47 | C | 2 |
| Woodhaven Hts | ET | 25 | B | 3 |
| Woodington Av | EY | 15 | B | 3 |
| Woodington Av | T | 15 | B | 3 |
| Woodland Hts | T | 14 | B | 5 |
| Woodland Park Rd | SC | 25 | B | 4-5 |
| Woodlawn Av E | T | 5 | A | 1 |
| Woodlawn Av W | T | 4 | F | 1 |
| Woodlee Rd | T | 15 | D | 4 |
| Woodlot Cr | ET | 40 | B | 4 |
| Woodmere Ct | ET | 26 | C | 4-5 |
| Woodmount Av | EY | 15 | C | 1-3 |
| Woodmount Av | T | 15 | C | 2 |
| Woodpark Rd | ET | 26 | B-C | 2 |
| Woodridge Ct | NY | 16 | C | 1 |
| Woodrow Av | SC | 25 | D | 2 |
| Woodrow Av | T | 15 | B | 4 |
| Woodrow St | T | 15 | B | 4 |
| Woodsdale Ct | NY | 11 | E | 4 |
| Woodstock Pl | T | 4 | D | 6 |
| Woodsview Av | ET | 40 | C | 4 |
| Woodsworth Rd | NY | 9 | E-F | 1-2 |
| Woodthorpe Rd | T | 15 | B | 5 |
| Woodthrush Ct | NY | 11 | E | 4 |
| Woodvale Cr | EY | 15 | C | 1 |

W

Y

Z

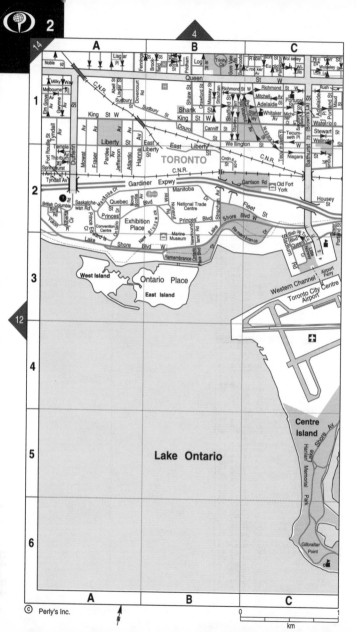

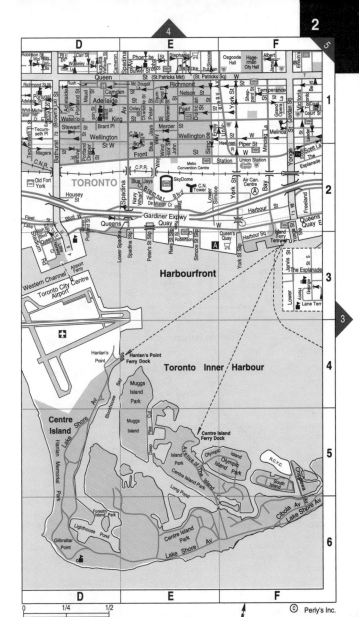

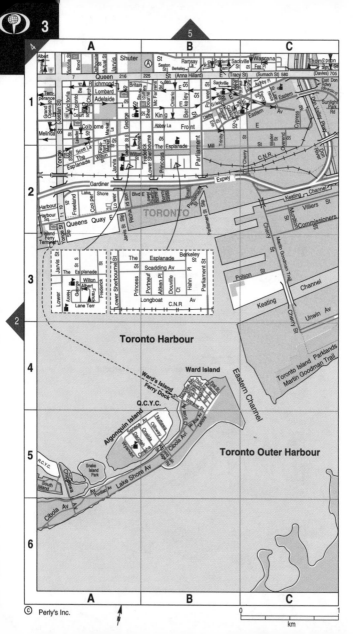

5

4

A B C

**Shuter**

Queen 216 225

Richmond Britania
Lombard
Adelaide
King
Colborne
Front
The Esplanade

**TORONTO**

Gardiner Expwy

Blvd E

Queens Quay E

Villiers St

Commissioners St

The Esplanade Berkeley
Scadding Av
Princess Porthguil Aitken Pl Douville Hahn Pl Parliament St
Longboat C.N.R Av

Polson St

Channel

Keating

Unwin Av

**Toronto Harbour**

Toronto Island Parklands
Martin Goodman Trail

**Ward Island**

Ward's Island
Ferry Dock

Q.C.Y.C.

**Algonquin Island**

Eastern Channel

**Toronto Outer Harbour**

A.C.Y.C.

Snake Island Park

South Island

Lake Shore Av

Cibola Av

A B C

© Perly's Inc.

0 1
km

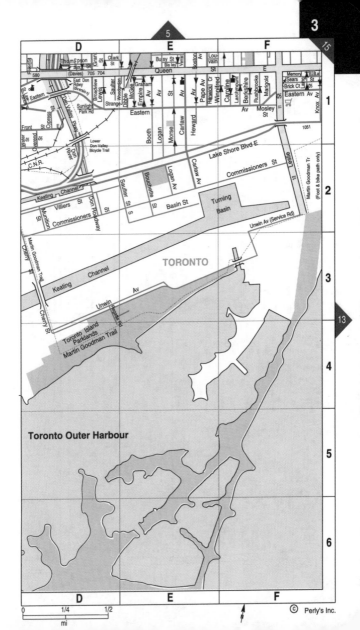

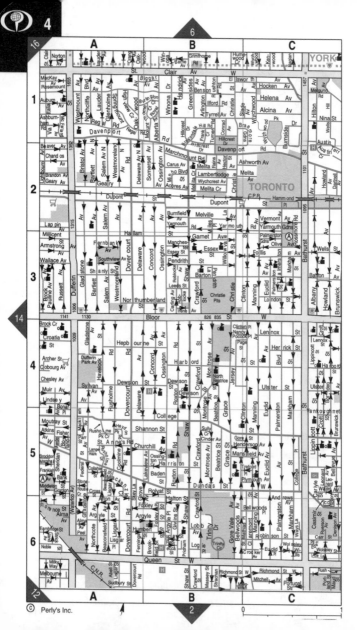

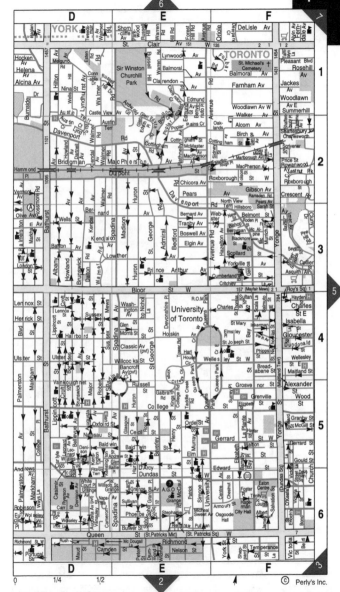

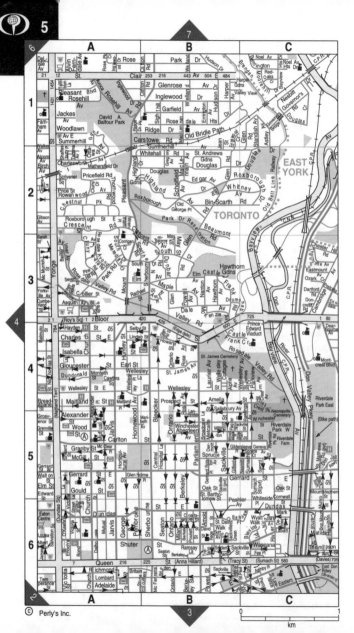

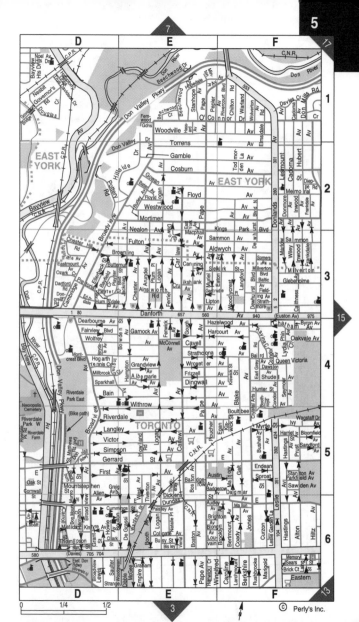

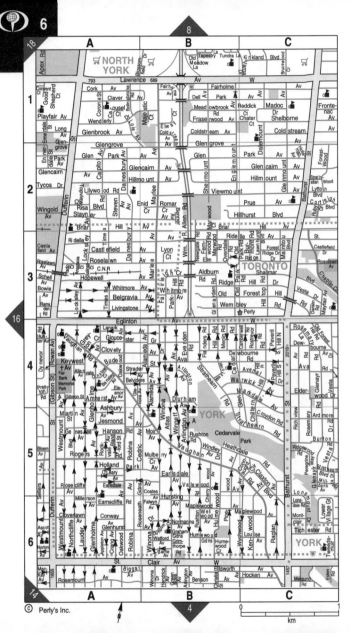

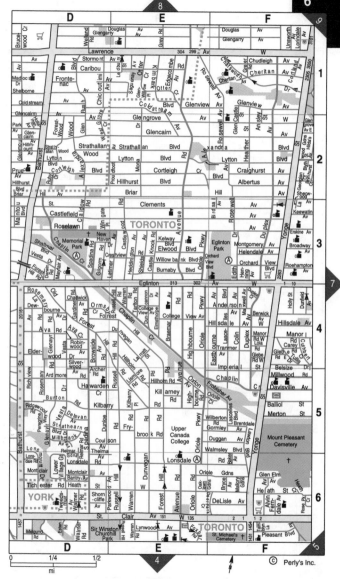

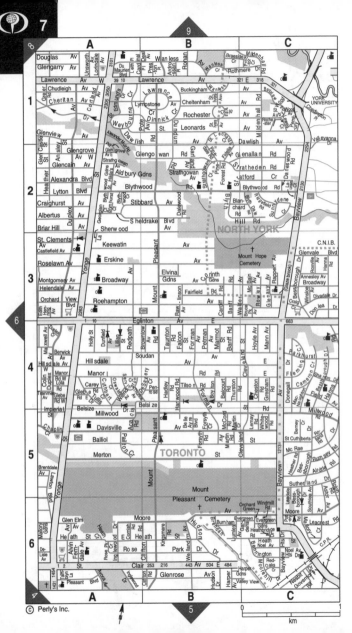

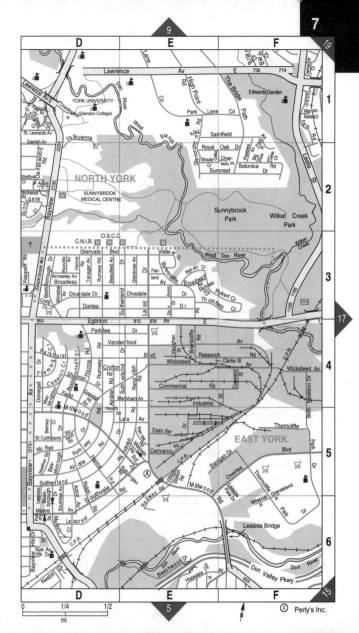

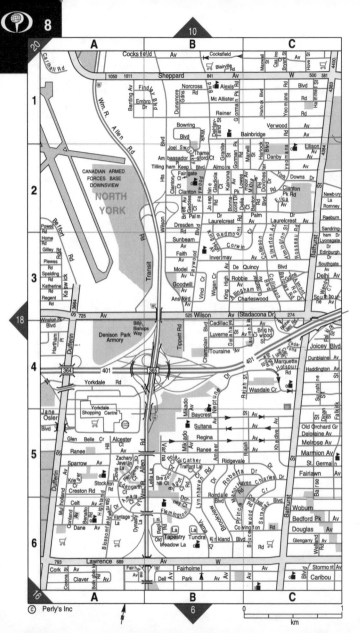

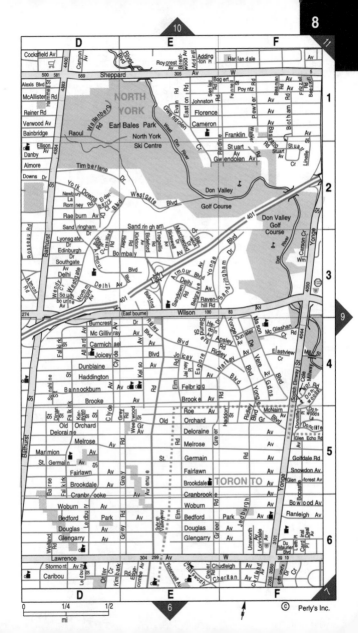

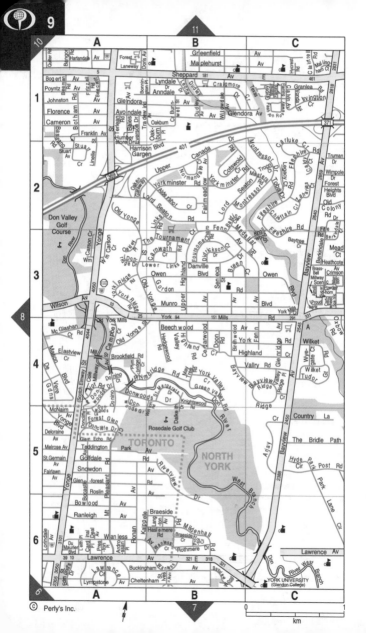

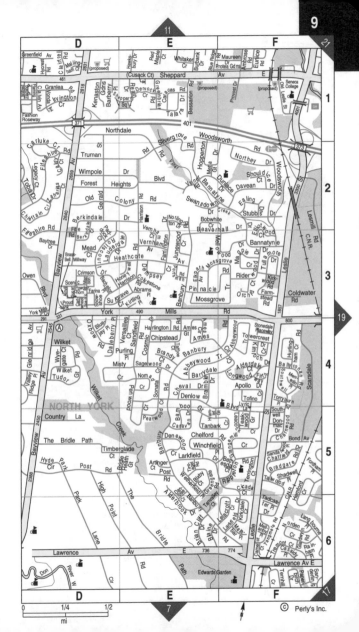

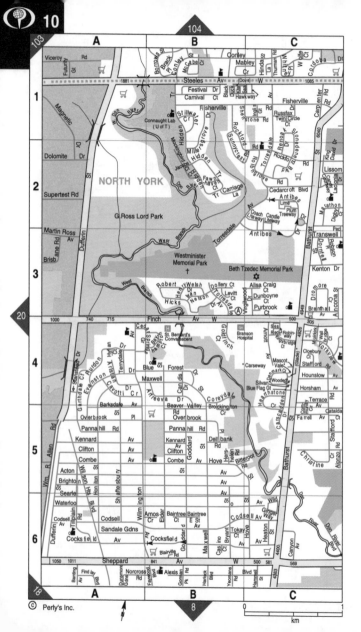

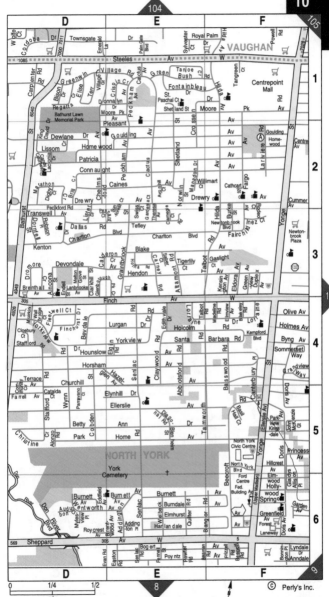

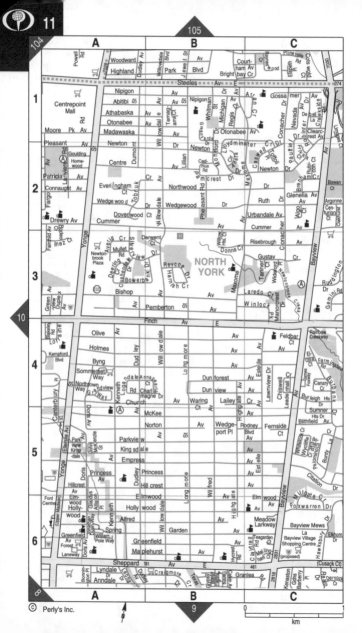

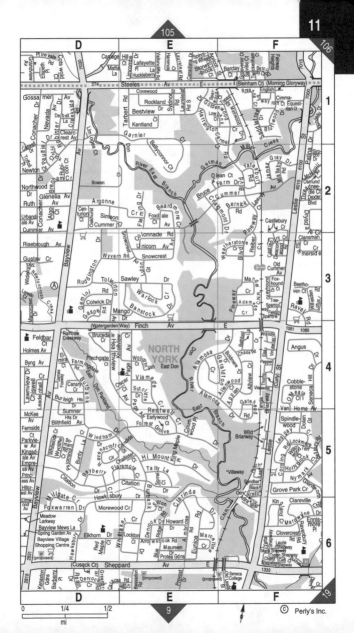

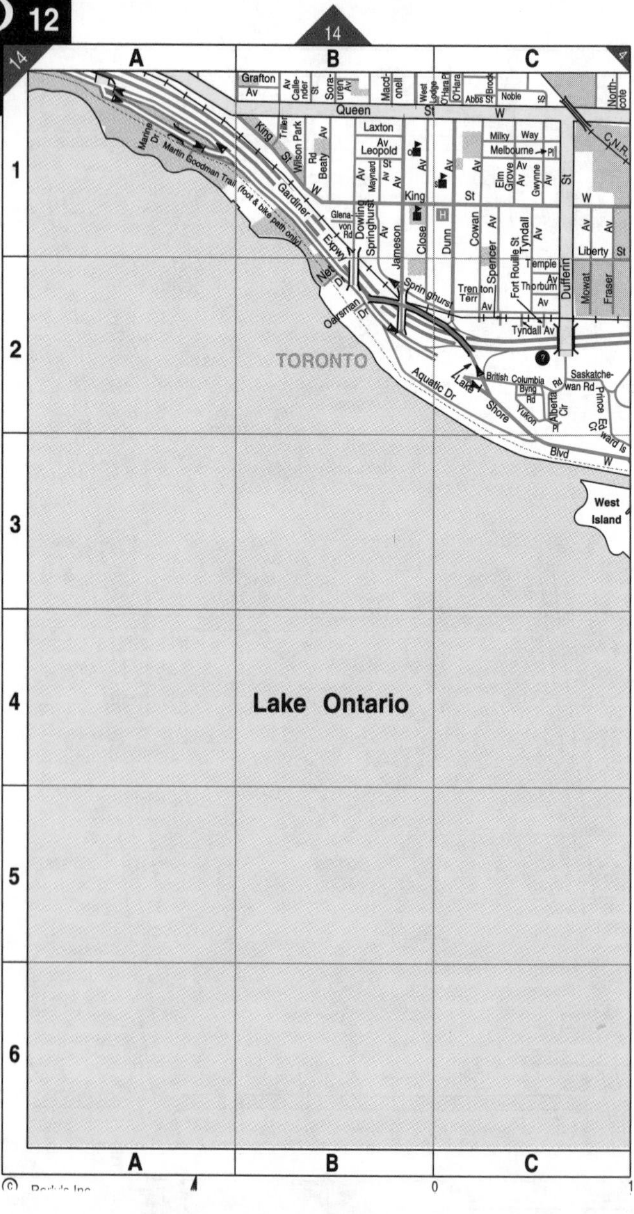

| | A | B | C |
|---|---|---|---|

Martin Goodman Trail (foot & bike path only)

Marine Dr

Grafton Av
Callander Av
Scra... ... St
Macdonell

Queen St

Laxton Av
West Lodge
O'Hara ... Av
Abbs St
Noble ... St
Northcote

C.N.R.

King St
Telfar St
Wilson Park Rd
Beaty Av

Leopold

Milky Way
Melbourne Av ... Pl
Elm Grove Av
Gwynne Av

Gardiner Expwy

Maynard Av

King St W

St

St

W

Glena... von Rd
Dowling Av
Springhurst Av
Jameson Av
Close

Dunn Av
Cowan Av
Spencer Av

Fort Rouille St
Tyndall Av
Temple Av
Dufferin St
Mowat Av
Fraser Av

Liberty St

Nr Dr

Oleraman Dr

Springhurst

Trenton Terr
Thorburn Av

Tyndall Av

**TORONTO**

Aquatic Dr

Lake Shore

British Columbia Rd

Saskatchewan Rd

ward Is

Blvd

Alberta Cr
Yukon

Prince Edward Is

Blvd W

**West Island**

# Lake Ontario

© Perly's Inc.

0                    1

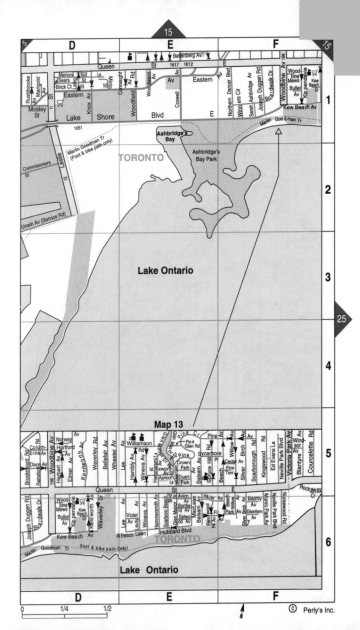

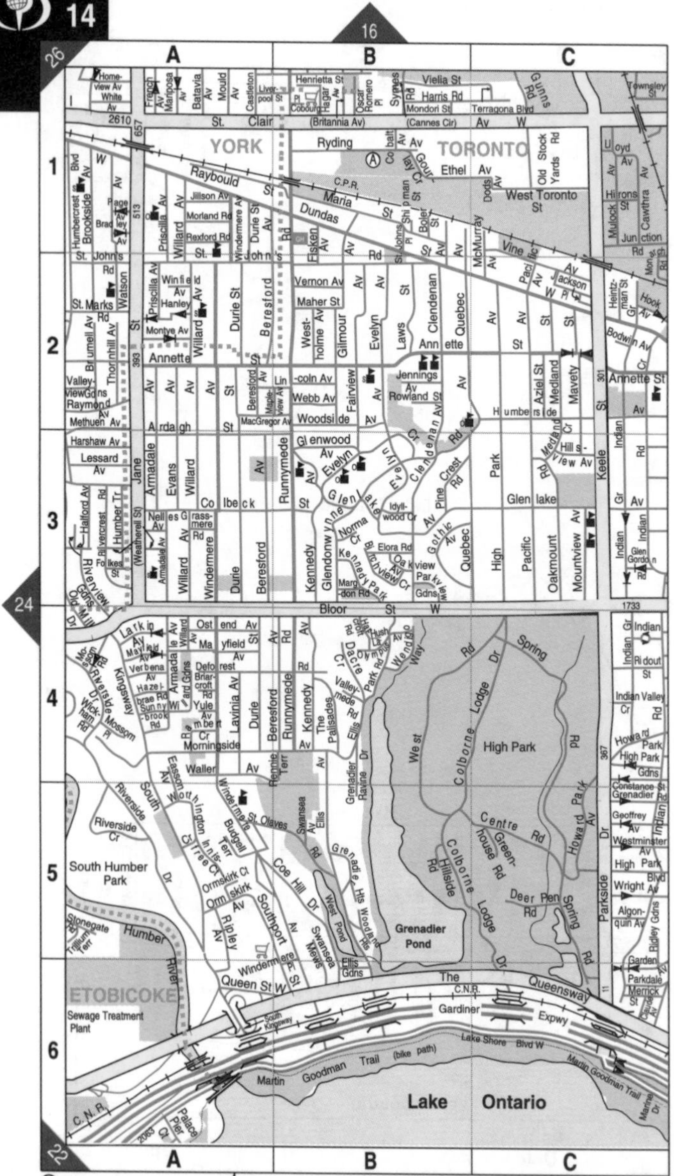

26

| | A | B | C |
|---|---|---|---|

**YORK** **TORONTO**

1

Home-view Av White Av
Fraser Av Mould St Batavia Av Castleton
Uxbridge pool St
Henrietta St Coburg Av Oscar Romeo Av Sypes
Vielia St Harris Rd Terragona Av
Gunns Rd Townsley
Lloyd Av
Hilrons
Cawtra

Humbercrest Blvd Brookside W
Brad Av
2610
657
513
St. Clair Av
Britannia Av (Cannes Cir) W
Old Stock Yards
West Toronto
Mulock Av

Raybould
Ryding Av
Cobalt Av
Ethel Av Dods Av
Junction

C.P.R.
Maria St
Gouin St
Heintzman Av Hook Av

St. John's Rd Watson Priscilla Av
Dundas St
Vine St Pacific
Jackson Av
Monti St

2

St. Marks Rd Burnell Av Winfield Av Hanley Priscilla Av Willard
Durie St Beresford
Vernon Av Maher St West-holme Av Gilmour
Clendenan St Quebec Av Pacl Av
Bodwin Av

Thorhill Av Montye Av
Annette St
Evelyn Laws St Annette St
Medland Mavety St
**Annette St**

Valley-view Gdns Raymond Methuen Av
Airdaigh St
Lin-coln Av Beresford Maple Av Webb Av Woodside Av MacGregor St Fairview Av Rowland Av
Humberside Av
Indian Av

3

Harshaw Av Lessard Av
Jane St Armadale Evans Willard
Colbeck St
Glenwood Av Evelyn St
Clendenan Av Pine Crest Rd
Park
Hills view Medland Keele St
Indian Gr Glen Gordon Indian Gr Av

Halford Rd Riverview Humber Tr Rivercrest Rd Fol kes St
Nelles Av Grassmere Rd Weatherell St Armadale Av Willard Windermere Durie St Beresford St
Glendonwynne Rd Norma Cr Kennedy Av Ellis Av Gothic Av
Idyl-wood Cr Elora Rd Parkview Gdns
Oakmount Mountview Av
Quebec Av High Pacific

24

**Bloor St W**
1733

4

Larkin Av Mayfield St Kingsway Mossom Rd Riverside Kingsway Hazel Av
Ostend Av Brian Defo rest Av
Amanda Willard Yule Av Lambert Rd
Mayfield St Runnymede Rd Durie Bereford Kennedy
Colborne Lodge Dr Spring Rd
Indian Gr Rd Ridout Indian Valley Cr
Howard Park Av High Park Gdns

Morningside Waller Av
Renne Terr
Valley Cr Park The Palisades Rd Grenadier Heights Ellis
West
High Park
Constance Av Grenadier Geoffrey Westminster Av
High Park Blvd Wright Av Algon-quin Av

5

South Humber Park
Riverside Cr
Worthington Budget Terr St Olaves Av Brule Gdns Ormsdirk Ct Ormskirk Av Southport
Woodside Av Swansea Coe Hill Dr
Centre Green Rd
Colborne House Rd Deer Pen Rd Hilliside
Parkside Garden Parkdale Merrick St

Stonegate Humber River
Ripley Windermere Av
Queen St W
Grenadier Pond
Colborne Lodge Dr Spring Rd

**ETOBICOKE**
Sewage Treatment Plant

The Queensway
C.N.R.
Gardiner Expwy
Lake Shore Blvd W

6

C.N.R.
Martin Goodman Trail (bike path)
**Lake Ontario**
Martin Goodman Trail

22

© Perly's Inc.
0 km 1

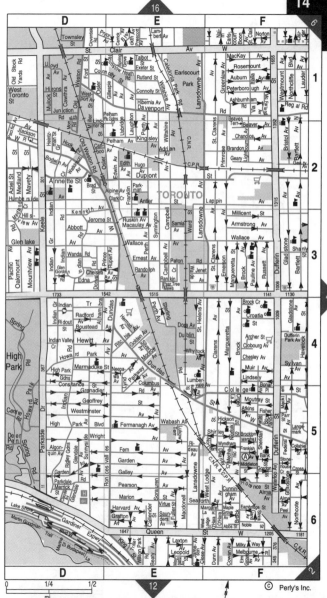

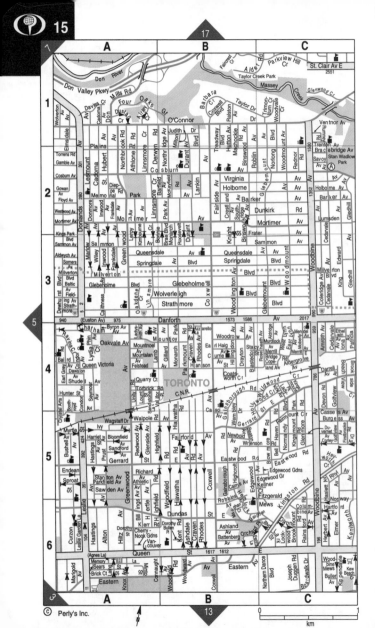

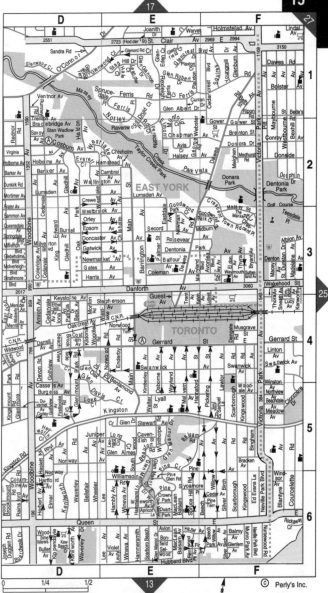

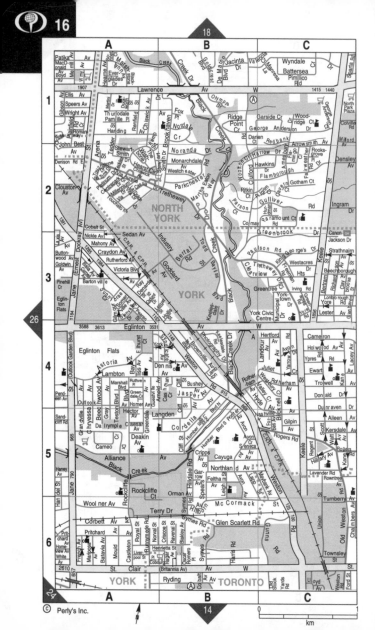

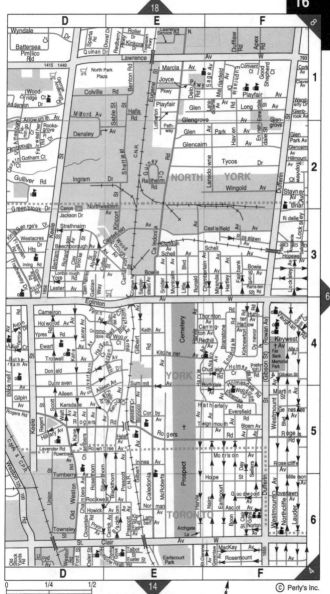

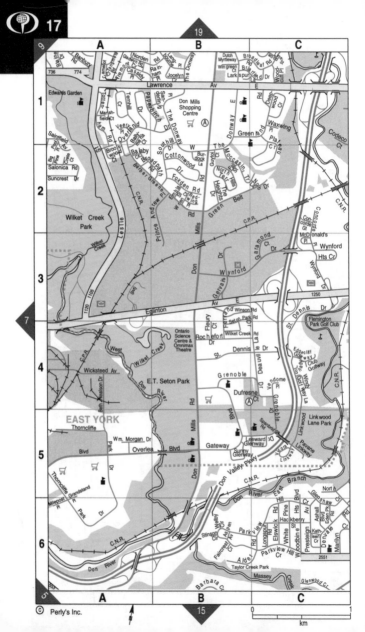

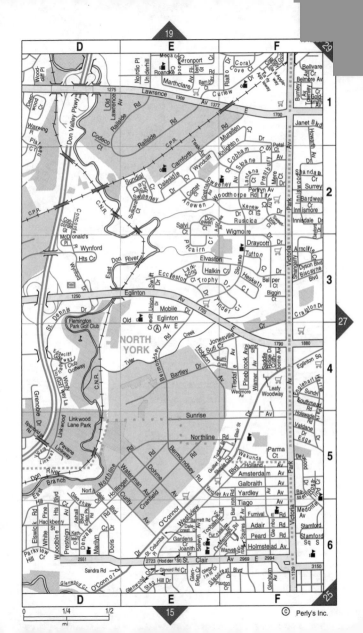

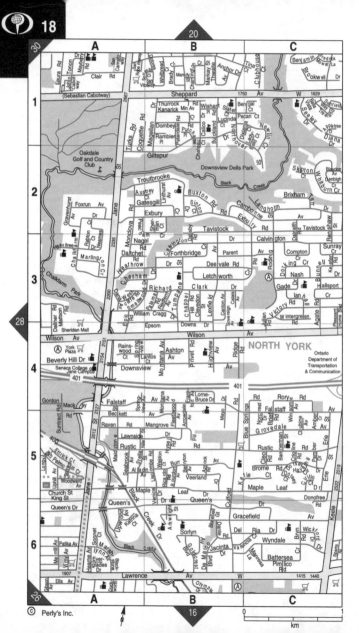

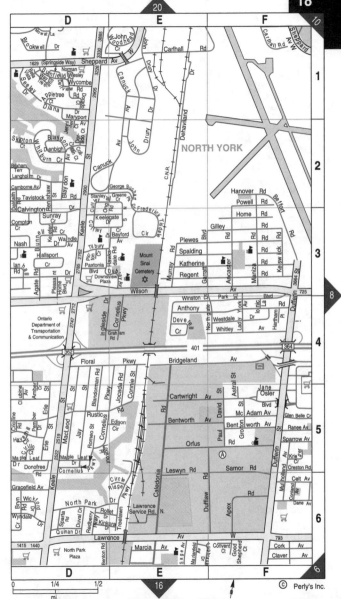

**NORTH YORK**

© Perly's Inc.

0    1/4    1/2
mi

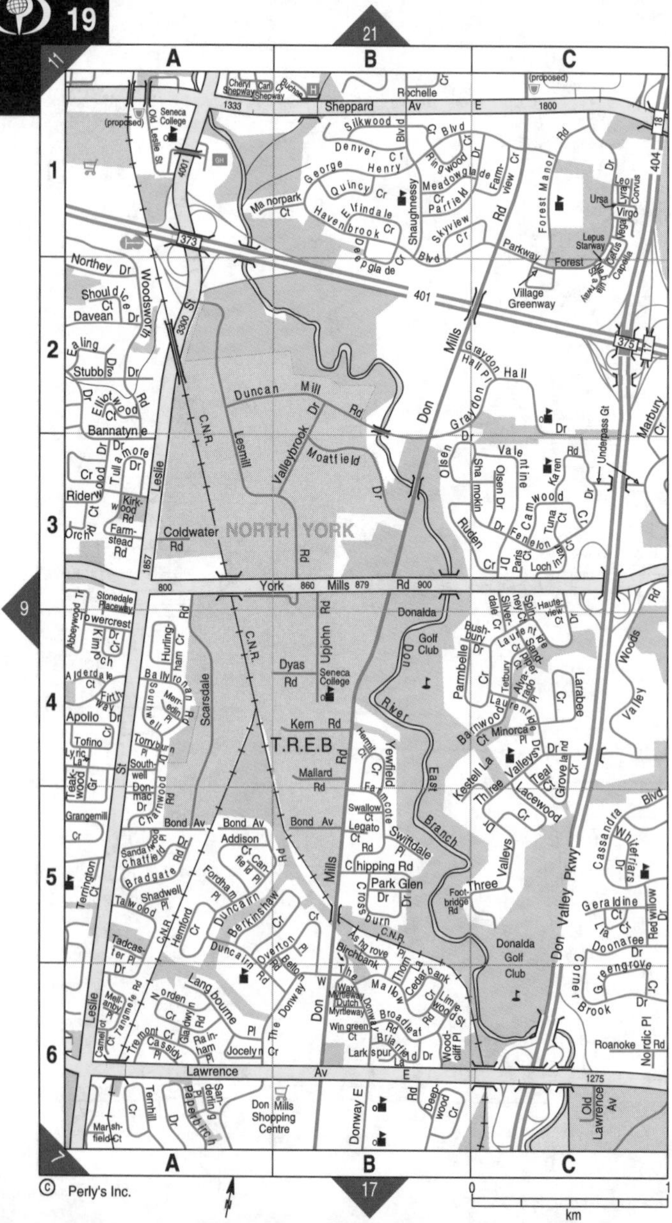

11 21 C

A B C

Rochelle Ct

Cheryl Shepway Carl Shepway

**Sheppard** Av E
1333 (proposed) 1800

Silkwood Blvd

Denver Cr Blvd
George Henry Ringwood Blvd Fern-View Rd Forest Manor Rd

Manorpark Quincy Cr Parfield Meadowland Dr Ursa

**1** Ct Shaughnessy SkyView Rd Virga Corvus

Vindale Cr Rd Lepus Starway

Havenbrook Blvd Parkway Forest 373

la de Village

Northey Dr Greenway

Should Ct Graydon

Davean Dr Hall Pl Hall Marbury

**2** Ealing Dr 401 Mills Graydon Dr Ct

Stubbs Dr Don Olsen Dr Vale Underpass Gt

Elliott Duncan Mill Rd Valentine

Cl'dood Rd Sha mokin Ka ren

Bannatyne Dr Lesmill Dr Olsen Dr Camwood

Dinmore Valleybrook Moatfield Dr Tuna Ct

Tulla Cr Fenelon

Rider Kirk Daris Ruden Loch

**3** Orch wood Rd **NORTH YORK** Cr

Farmstead Rd

Coldwater Rd

800 **York** 860 **Mills** 879 **Rd** 900

9 Stonedale Raceway Donalda Bushbury

Abberwood Tr Auburn Golf Club Haute

Wecrest Kimcoch Ballyronan Dyas Rd Parmbelle Laurel Larabee

**4** Alderda Southway Seneca Donald Cr Tetbury Woods

Apollo Dr Mern College River Barnwood Minorca

Tofino Kern Rd Minorca Ct

Lyric Tonynlyn **T.R.E.B** Kestell La Three Valleys

Teakwood Gr Southwell Yewfield Lacewood

Donmac Mallard Rd Swallow Ct Teal

Grangemill Bond Av Bond Av Legato Three Valleys

**5** Addison Swinfdale Valleys Cassandra

Sandal Chatfield Cart Chipping Rd Foot Willow

Bradgate Fordham Duncairn Park Glen bridge Rd Geraldine

Shadwell Berkinshaw Woodcliff Donaree

Talwood Overton Donwy W Three Doonavee

Tadcas Hembord Duncairn Donalda Greengrove

Far Pl Birchbank Golf Club Roanoke Brook

**6** Lang Bourne Highrove Mallow Lime Nordic Pl

Norden Dutch Broadleaf St

Rainham Myrleway Wingreen

Jocelyn Larkspur Dr Wood cliff

**Lawrence** Av E 1275

7 Temhill Don Mills Donway E Deep Old Lawrence Av

Marsh Sam denthy wood

field Shopping Centre

© Perly's Inc. 17

0 1
km

A B C

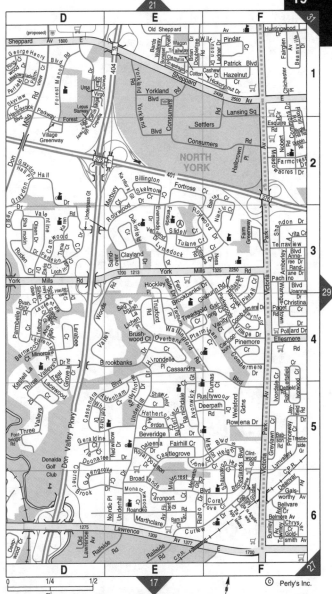

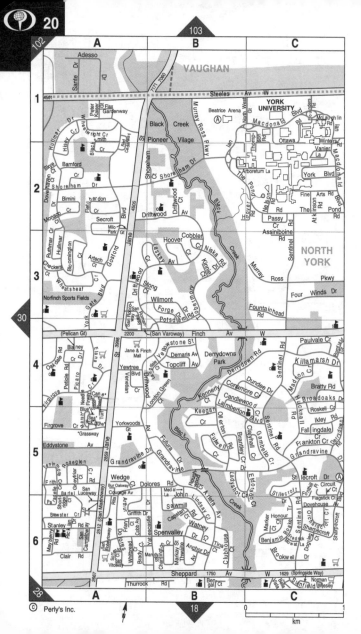

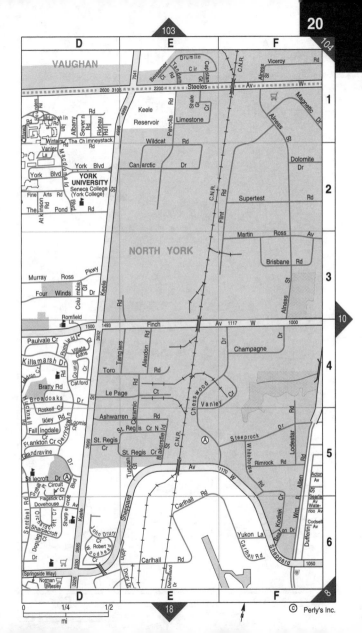

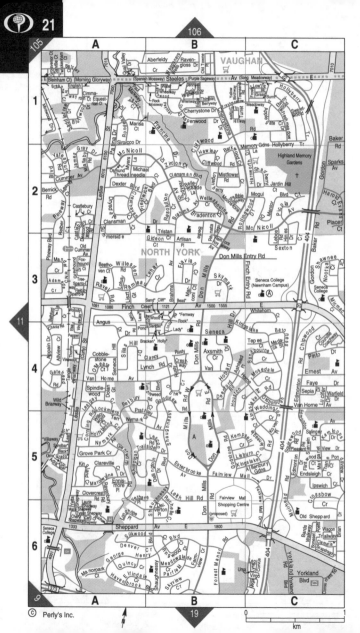

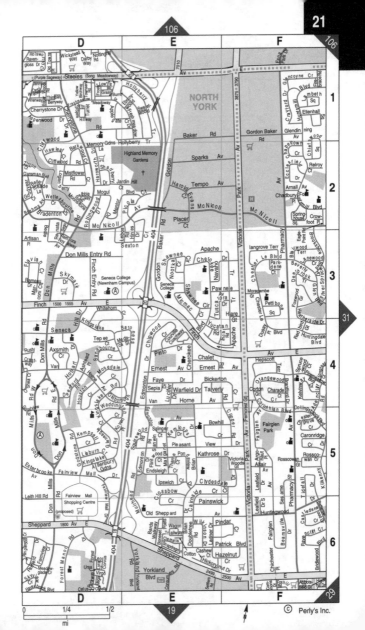

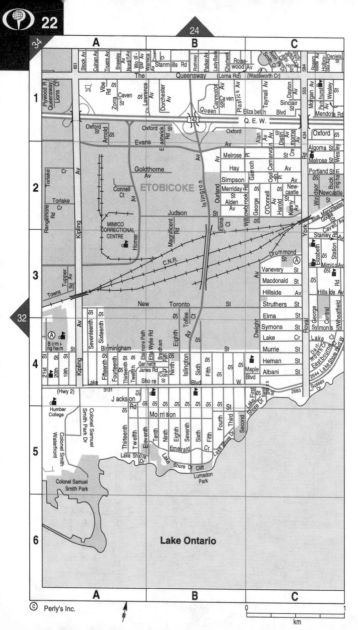

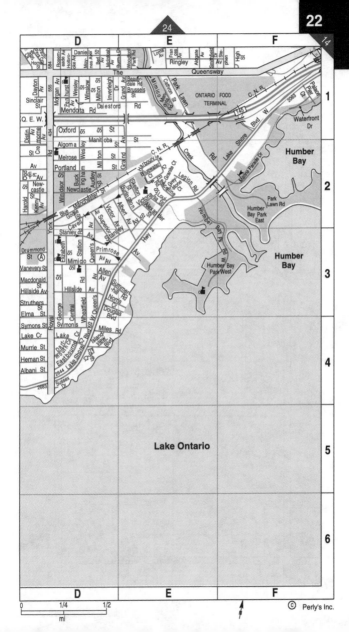

**Humber Bay**

**Humber Bay**

**Lake Ontario**

0    1/4    1/2
mi

© Perly's Inc.

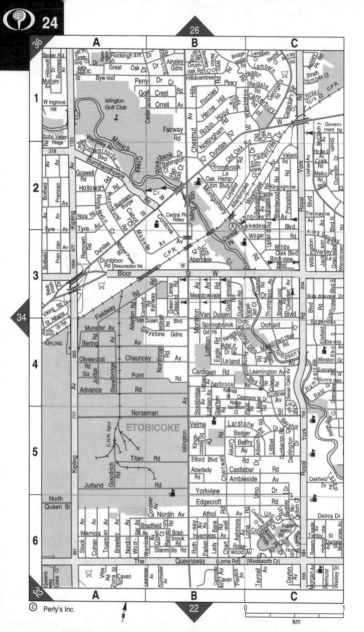

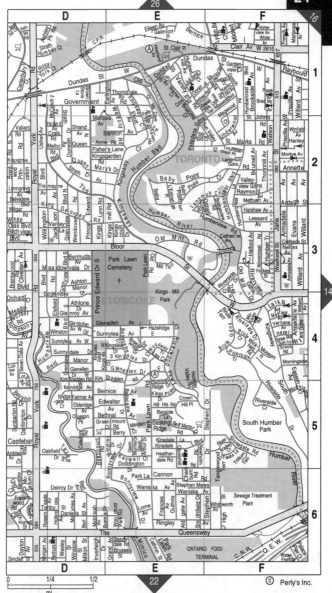

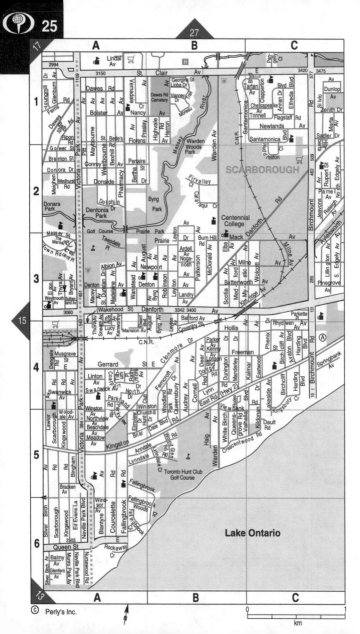

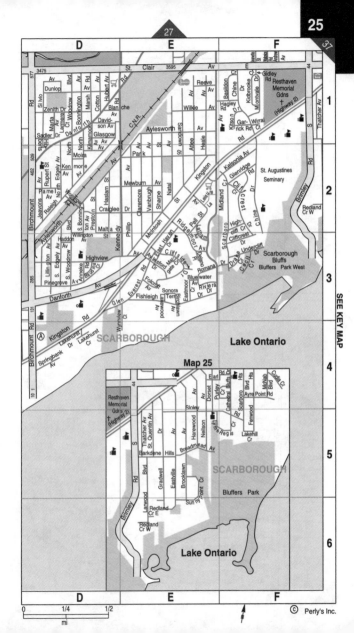

27

37

SEE KEY MAP

**D**   **E**   **F**

St. Clair   Av

Lake Ontario

**Map 25**

SCARBOROUGH

Resthaven
Memorial
Gdns
† (Highway 2)

Scarborough
Bluffs
Bluffers Park West

St. Augustines
Seminary

SCARBOROUGH

Bluffers Park

Lake Ontario

0   1/4   1/2

mi

© Perly's Inc.

**D**   **E**   **F**

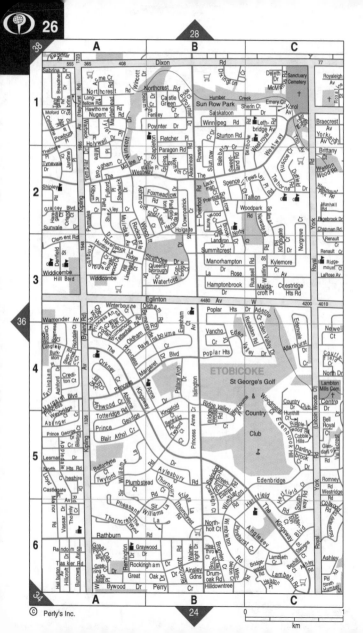

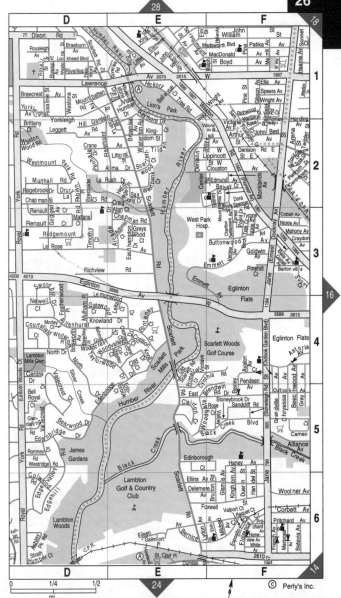

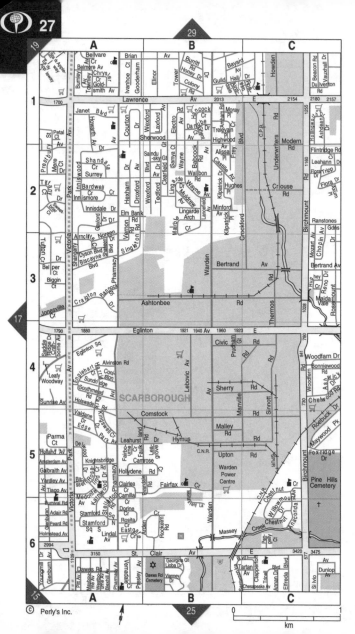

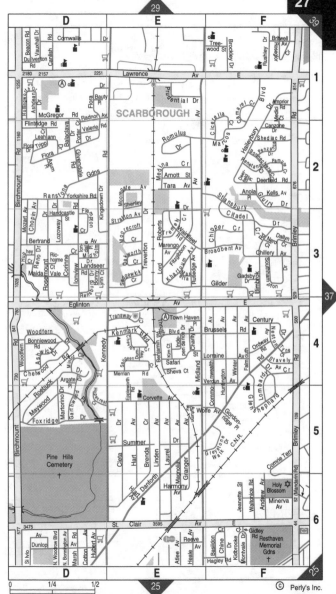

SCARBOROUGH

Perly's Inc.

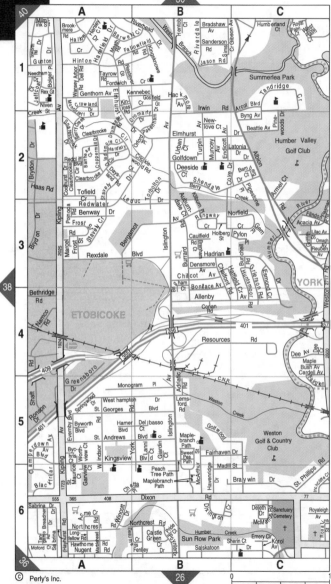

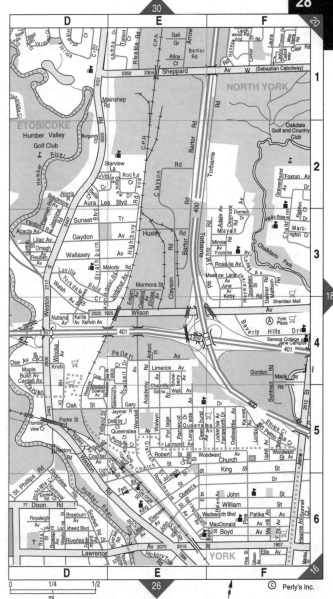

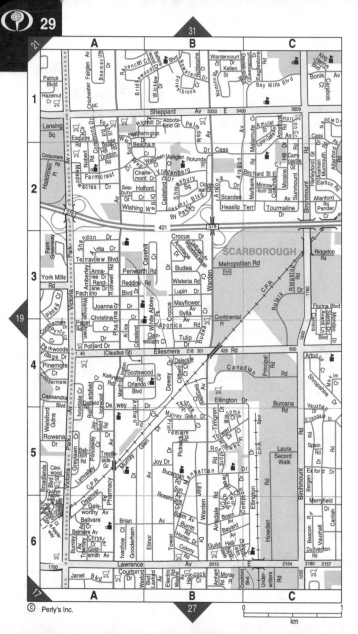

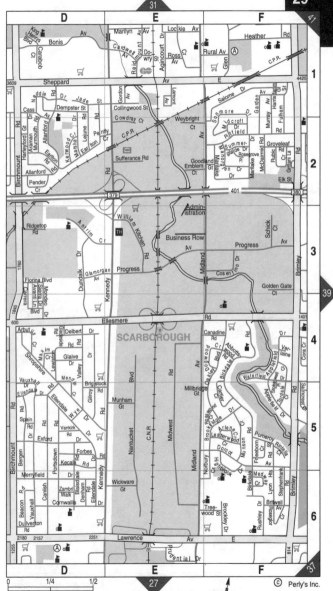

SCARBOROUGH

© Perly's Inc.

0   1/4   1/2
mi

VAUGHAN

Riverside Golf Course

101

ETOBICOKE

NORTH YORK

Finch

Steeles

Rowntree Mills Park

Rowntree Mills Park

Millwick

Emery Yard

Panorama

© Perly's Inc.

| A | B | C |

0        km        1

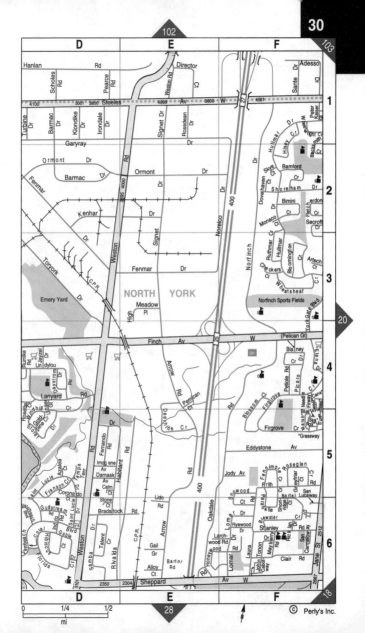

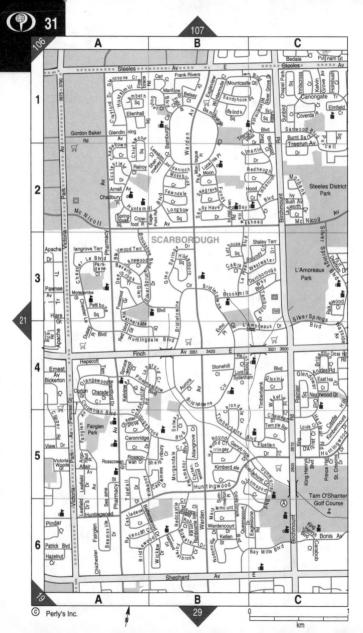

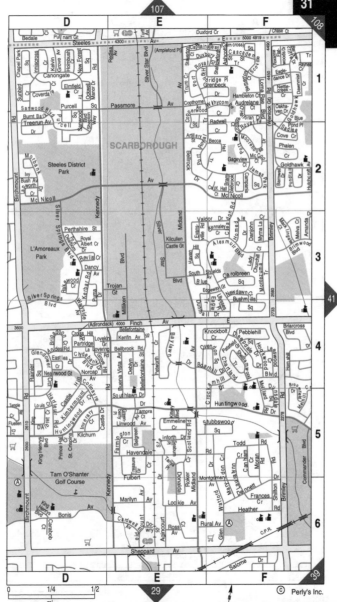

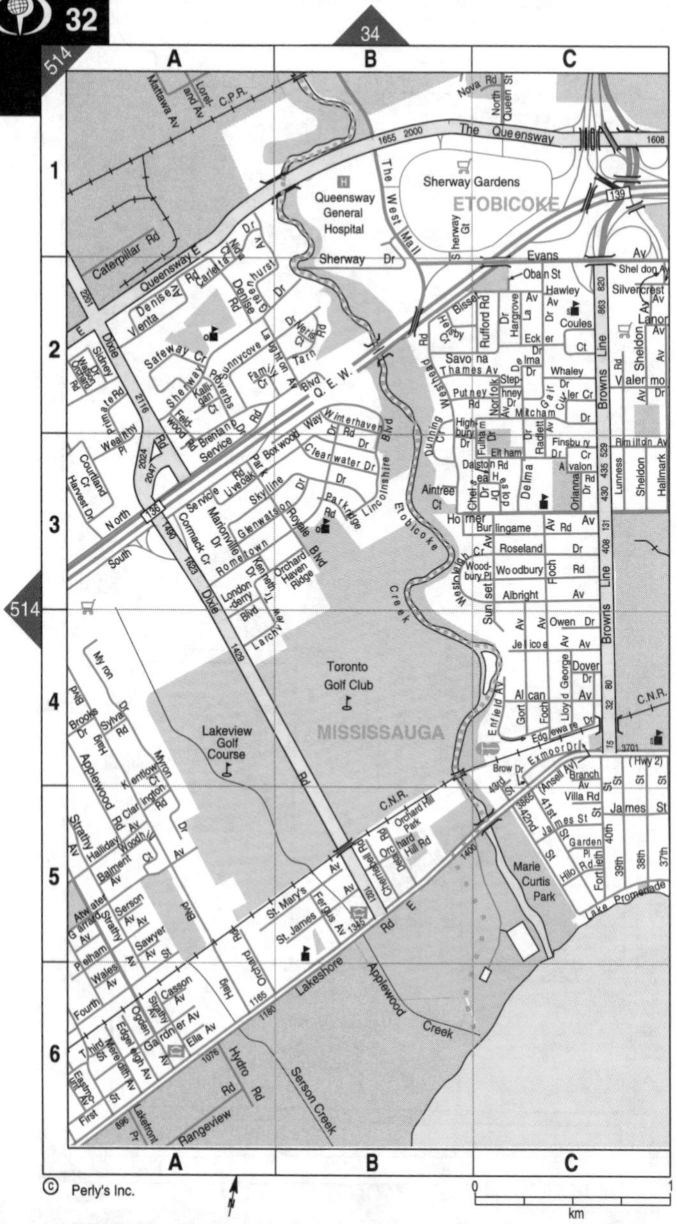

| | A | B | C |
|---|---|---|---|

The Queensway

ETOBICOKE

Sherway Gardens

Queensway General Hospital

Sherway Dr

Evans Av

Caterpillar Rd

Queensway E

Dixie Vienta

Gateway Ct

Q.E.W.

Winterhaven

Cleanwater Dr

Lincolnshire Blvd

Skyline Dr

Glenwatson Dr

Rometown

Londonderry Blvd

Orchard Haven Ridge

Toronto Golf Club

MISSISSAUGA

Etobicoke Creek

Lakeview Golf Course

Browns Line

C.N.R.

(Hwy 2)

Marie Curtis Park

James St

Lakeshore Rd E

St. Mary's Av

St. James Av

Applewood Creek

Serson Creek

Rangeview Rd

Hydro Rd

Dixie Rd

© Perly's Inc.

0 ____ 1 km

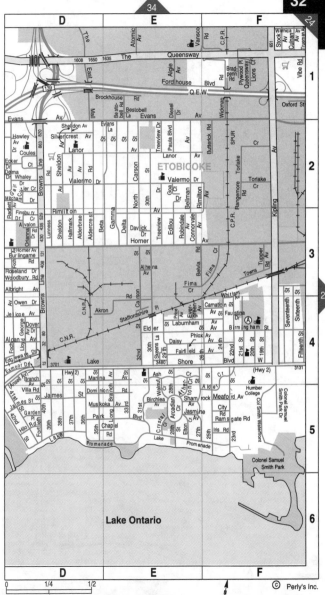

535

36

| A | B | C |

**1**

Rathburn Rd
Pebble Valley La
Esposito
Laver Rd
Elmcrest Rd
Burnham Rd
Stonecham Rd
Wading Ham
Mather Rd
Wareside
Myles
Clendon
Redthorn Ct
Emberwood Dr
Alfonsius Dr
Burnhamthorpe Rd
Windust Gt
Carsbrooke
Monet Av
Gunsey
Kris
Hensolt
Glos
Elderfield
Cheltenham
Beckenham Rd
Unwerston Av
Holiday
Path
Capri Rd
East Mall
427
Four Seasons

Burnhamthorpe Rd   551   582   425   430

**2**

Garrow hill Tr
Gametwood Park
Burnhamthorpe Rd
Silver Shadow
Thornbury
Stoneglen
Thornton
Markland
Mossdale
Rathgar Av
Saturn
Tranquil Dr
Boreal Rd
Rexton
Rd
Mooreshe
Ross Rd
Surberry Ct
Sealcove
Renforth
Mulgrove
Rd
West Eva Rd
Civic Centre Ct
Valhalla Inn Rd
Formula Ct
Gibbs Rd

Fleetwood Park
Etobicoke Creek
The Green Pines
Maple Gate
Fourpines
Markland
Westfield
Giles
Toledo
Beanbury
Clearfield
Bridge
Maryland Av
Eriksdale
West Mall
4206
4039

**3**

Golf Valley
Burnt Log
Cherry Post Ct
Silverthorne
Trailcrest
Bush
Bloor St   4258   W   4319
Broadfils
Subplains
Trailside
Markwood
Markland Dr
Mountain Ash
Cosway Ct
Greencroft
Nelor Dr
Avery
Radway Av
Neiltree Ct
Jeff Dr
Rickshaw
Seville Dr
Rayside
Stevenharris Dr
Snowelle Dr
Terryellen
Cr
Neilson Dr
West Mall
427
Collins Rd
Gordon
Park Dr
Falby Ct
Cloverdale Mall

**4**

Markland Wood Golf & Country Club
Markland Wood Country Club
Etobicoke Creek
Sharlyn
Lenworth Dr
Universal
Southcreek
Hwy 5
West Mall
ETOBICOKE
Vickers Rd
Eastside Dr
East Mall

**5**

Kirkwall
Knob
Oberon Cr
Seafield Rd
Blackbird Dr
Fairfax Ct
Treadwells Dr
Nardook Rd
Berkel Rd
Goldenridge
Wharton
Slumper ville
Creek
Waulron
Norris Glen Rd
Paxman Rd
Index Rd

**6**

Coram Cr
Mattawa Av
C.P.R.
MISSISSAUGA
Westside
Manstor Rd
Bansel Rd
Nova Rd
North Queen St
The West C.P.R.
The Queensway   1655   2000   1608
Sherway Gardens

524

| A | B | C |   139   32

© Perly's Inc.

0   1   km

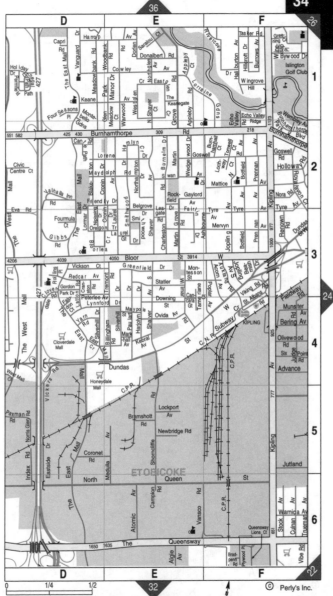

0   1/4   1/2
mi

© Perly's Inc.

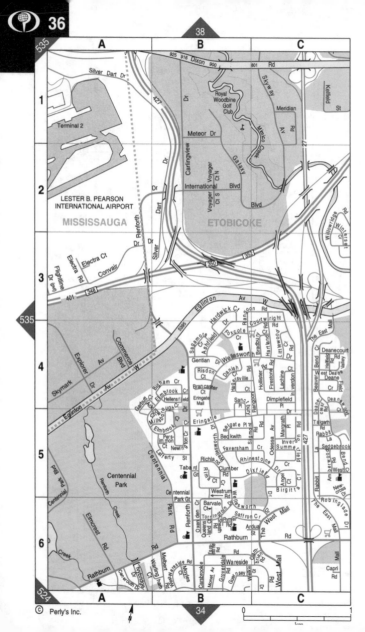

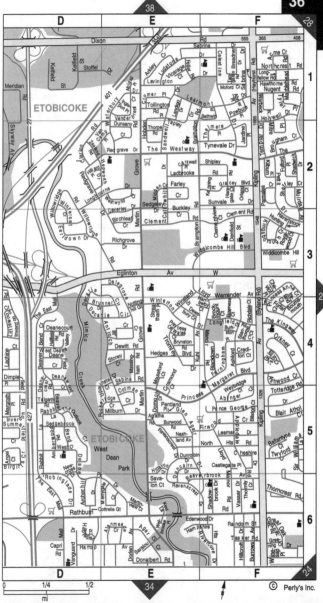

ETOBICOKE

ETOBICOKE

West Dean Park

Perly's Inc.

0    1/4    1/2
mi

29

**A**  **B**  **C**

Britwell Av

Thomson Memorial Park

Scarborough General Hospital

Ben Dorah Blvd
Benhur
Bancroft
Benhar
Ben Alder
Bentleigh
Banjolea
Ben Stanton
Ben Bella
Cr
Ben Lisa
Cr

Rockman
Six Nations
Norkville
Sharbot
Cir
Indian Mound
Cr
Greenbrae
Av

### 1

Lawrence  Av

Shelve
Melrose
Barrymore
Biltmore
Holly
hedge
Valdamar
Diagem
Perivale
Gaiety
Vesper
Ct
Bullfever Ct
Crusader  St
Greencedar Crct
Eastpark
Cedarbrae Mall
Cedarbrae Blvd
Felicity

Lanhall Av
Triicosta
Dr

Gage
Fleeton
K ingleggan Cr
Thorn
Cr
Rosande
Ct

### 2

Largo
Koolenay
La
Miramat
Mackinac
Elmdon
Bardsea
Perivale
Blvd
Fairway
Dr
Bellamy
Cheyenne
Strandhill
Landfair
Blvd
Pacal
Ridge
Blvd
Alpaca

Tansley
Seminole
Gios
Av
Paloma
Catsen
Cr
Totrance
Rd
Braleburn
Blvd
Brae
Amerilla
Chalcedor
Blvd
Alanbury
Blvd

Providence
Scotchdale
Radisson
Av
Nelson
Blakely
Barkdene
Ruth
Peking
Dr
Norwalk

### 3

Brimley
Graylee  Av
Elgar
Cr
Chillery Av
Strode  Dr
Wetherby
Dr
Danforth
Savarin St
Ticketts
St
Cunard
Adler
St
Dan-
mary
Cedar
St
Greenwich
Gr
Wheaton
Gr
Romney
Farmbrook
Porchester
Dr
Shier
Chelsea
St
Norwalk
Barketon
C.N.R.
Luella
Central
Markham

Fred Blue
Blue
Lagoon
Rd
Grace
Tollmaton
St
Bellamy
Rd N

Shaddock
Trudelle
No Frills La

27

### 4

Eglinton  Av  E

Horton
Blvd
Boyce Av
Barbados
Blvd
Oswego
Bridlewood
Castlethorpe
Dr
Granard Blvd
Adanac
Brimorton
Stanjan
Dr
Glenda Rd
Argo Rd
Markanna
Dr

C.N.R.

Tyne
Ct

Colonial
Little
Rock
Glen Muir Dr
Av
Barn
Rock
Bellamy
Chatterton Blvd
Knowlton Dr
ndowns
Riant
St
Mason

SCARBOROUGH
McCowan

Martindale
Rd
Oakridge
Dr
Parkcrest

### 5

Skagway
Av
Oakridge
Dr
Cree
Phyllis
Lowell
Rockwood
Av
Kingston
Cree
Av
Windy Ridge
Dr
Bellehaven Ct
Whitecap
Rd
Annis
Cr
Hill

MacDuff
Cr
Horfield
Av
Allister
Dorset Rd
Halbert
Pine
Ridge
Ravine
Dr

### 6

Brimley
Anson Av
Randall
Harlewood
Av
Randall
Cr
(Hwy 2)
Balcarra
Av
Faircroft Blvd
Pine
Ridge
Ledge
Rd
Dr
Meadowcliffe
Dr

Meadervcliffe Dr

William
Av
Fenmore

Eglinton  Av

Earl
Scarboro
Hts
McNab
Cudia Ct
Ayre Point Rd

Gradwell Dr
Eastville
Av
Brooklawn
Av
Sloley
Neilson
Dorset
Dudley
Av
Cathedral
Bluffs
Dr
Scarboro
Hts
Rd
Fenwood

Lake Ontario

25

23

**A**  **B**  **C**

© Perly's Inc.

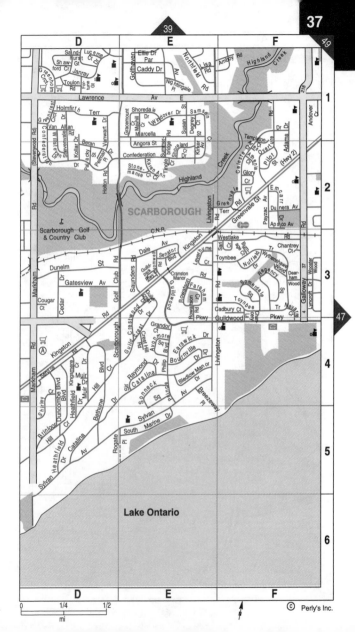

39

49

## D · E · F

SCARBOROUGH

Scarborough Golf & Country Club

C.N.R.

Lake Ontario

47

Lawrence Av E

Highland

Livingston Rd

Kingston Rd

Kingston Rd

Markham Rd

Stevenwood Rd

Golf Club Rd

Saunders Rd

Scarborough Golf Club Rd

Guildwood Pkwy

Galloway Rd

1

2

3

4

5

6

0   1/4   1/2
mi

© Perly's Inc.

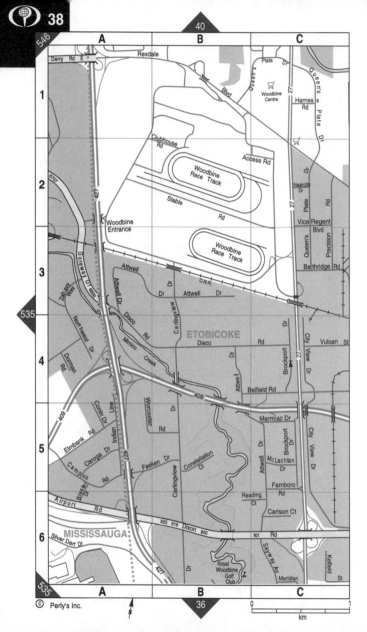

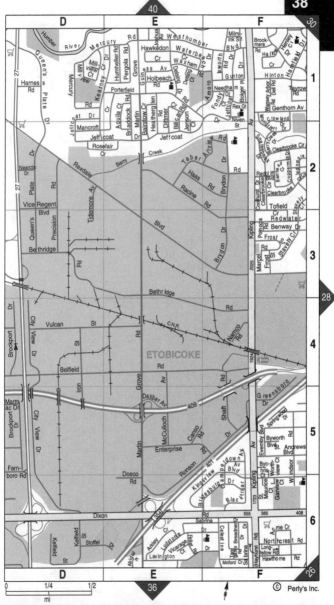

ETOBICOKE

© Perly's Inc.

0    1/4    1/2
mi

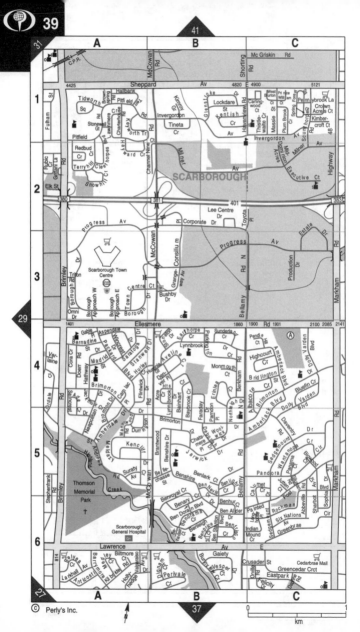

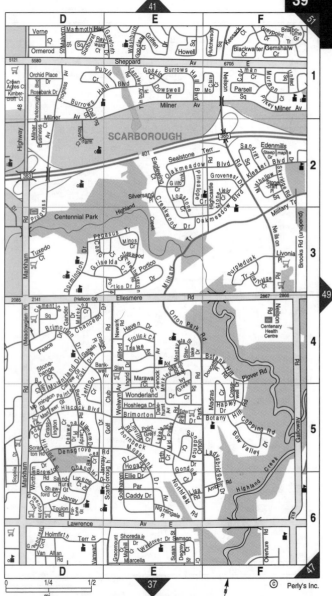

556

VAUGHAN

Steeles Av W 6838

**A**  **B**  **C**

Codlin
Abcde
Cr
St

1

Albion Rd
Cr

Signal Hill
Av
Steinway
Blvd
Goodmark Pl

Claireport

C.N.R.

ETOBICOKE

Dr

Albion

Dr

†

Glendale
Memorial
Gardens

2

427

Huddersfield Rd

Dr

Dansk Ct

Carrier

Rd

Mars
Rd

BRAMPTON

Claireville
Reservoir

Claireville

Humberline

Blvd

Carrier

27

3

Longo
Cir

Downs

Dr

Humber

Woodbine

Carrier
Dr

546

Finch

Av 6699

Sigsbee

Dr

Humber

Banky

Key

Dr

Viewcrest
Cir

Woodlot

Holyoake

Carlet

W 6590

Leesburg

Topbank

Cr

Hullen

Humberline

Woodcrest

College

6620

4

Brandon

Ford

Teeswater Rd

Gate

Custer Cr

Belmonte

Upper
Humber
Dr

Pinecone

Arbor
Cr

Holyoake
Dr

Halsall

Meyer Dr

Morning Star Dr

Humberwood

Humber

Humber
College
Blvd

Hydrock Cr
Wickstead Cr

Madiera
Rd

Av

River

Humber
Arboretum
Park

1. Corylus Ct
2. Auld Croft Rd
3. Shady Glen Rd

Etobicoke
General
Hospital

5

Magic
Rd

Netherbury
Rd

Dalcol

Chipwi

View
Green
Cr

Humberwood

West

(West Branch)

Rexwood
Rd

Hullick
West

Arwood
Dr

Secretariat

Thoroughbred
Vale

Clerkbar
Bridbury

Branch

Down Av
Mare Cr
Triple

Quinela

Stallion

Cinderstand

Hullick
Dr

Plate
Dr

Derry Rd E

Rexdale

MISSISSAUGA

ETOBICOKE

Blvd

Queens

Harness
Rd

6

Woodbine
Race Track

Woodbine
Centre

535

**A**  **B**  **C**

© Perly's Inc.

38

0          km          1

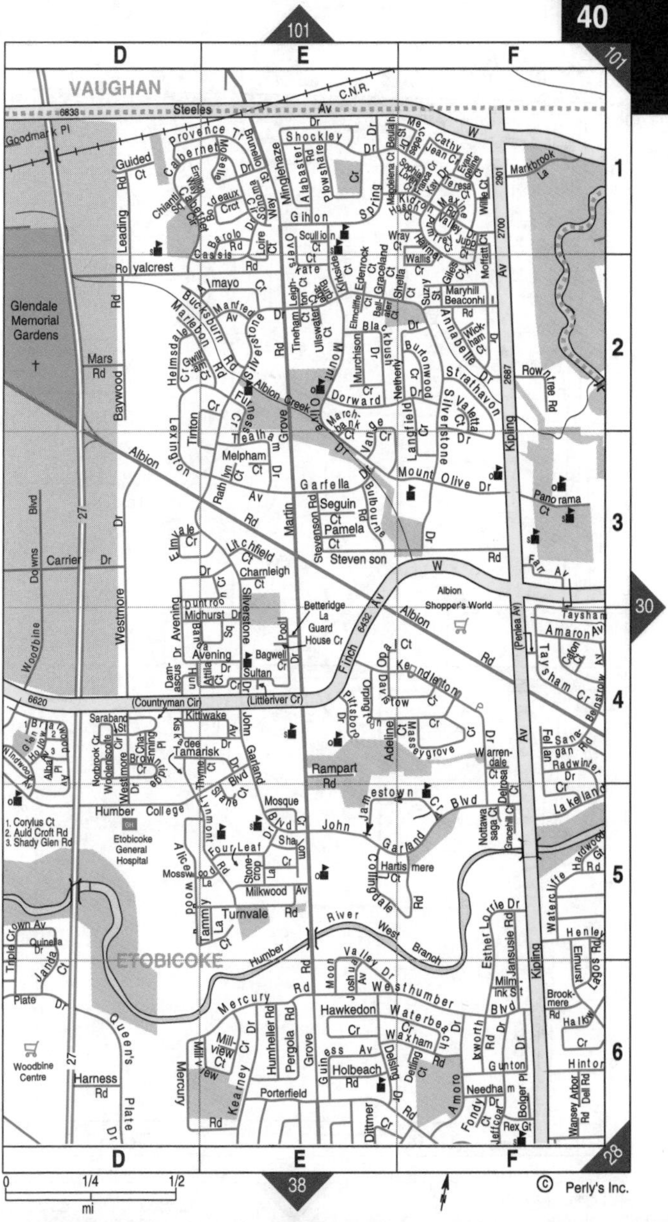

101

VAUGHAN

Steeles Av.

C.N.R.

Goodmark Pl

Glendale Memorial Gardens

Mars Rd

Barwood

Blvd

27

Downs Dr

Carrier Dr

Westmore Dr

Albion Rd

Leading Rd

Royalcrest Rd

Helmsdale

Tinton

Melpham

Albion

Rd

ETOBICOKE

Woodbine Centre

Harness Rd

Queen's Plate Dr

Humber College

Etobicoke General Hospital

Albion Shopper's World

Mount Olive Dr

Panorama Ct

Kipling Av

Rampart Rd

Mosque

Four Leaf

Milkwood

Turnvale Rd

Humber River West Branch

Westhumber Blvd

Hawkedon Cr

Waterbeach Cr

Martin Grove Rd

Finch Av

(Countryman Cir)

Steven son

Seguin Ct

Pamela Ct

Garfella

Dorward

Strathavon Dr

Silverstone Dr

Mount Olive Dr

30

Taysham Cr

Amaron

Lakeland

Kipling Av

1. Corylus Ct
2. Auld Croft Rd
3. Shady Glen Rd

0    1/4    1/2
mi

38

© Perly's Inc.

D          E          F

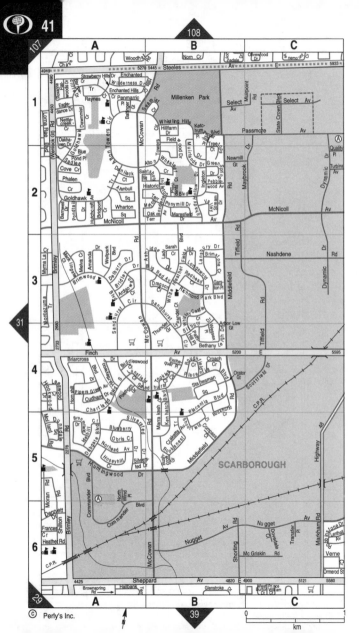

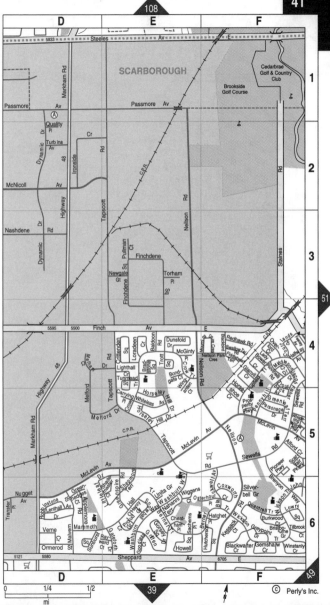

**SCARBOROUGH**

Cedarbrae
Golf & Country
Club

Brookside
Golf Course

**1**

Passmore Av

Quality
Pl
Turbina
Cr

McNicoll Av

Nashdene Rd

**2**

Passmore Av

Finchdene

Pullman
Ct

Newgale
Gt

Torham
Pl

Finchdene Sq

**3**

51

Finch Av

Dunsfold
Dr
Loradeen
Cr
Baldoon
Sq
McGinty

Crittenden

Lighthall
Cr
Tunmead
Sq

Redhawk Rd

Nelson Park

Bond-
gale Ct

Wrencliffe
arden Ct

**4**

Horseley
Hill Dr
Whiteleas
Av

Carrying
Cr

Prosperity
Pwy

Horseley Hill Dr

C.P.R.

McLevin Av

McLevin Av

Sewells Rd

**5**

Nugget
Av

Transfer
Pl

Robinstone
Lenthall Av
Dr

Greenhedges
Cres

Verne

Mammoth

Ormerod St

Malvern

Sunburst

Sheppard Av

Unita Gr

Wiggens
Ct

Osterhout
Pl

Washburn

Nanomi
Ct

Cheatham
Pl

Howell

Sachems
Pl

Hutchens
Dr

Silver-
bell Gr

Coxworth
Av

Hatchet
Pl

Quantrell Tr

Kessack
Ct

Blackwater
Cr

Weldon

Burkwood

Greypoint

Tillbrook
Sq

Lowry
Sq

Gemshaw
Cr

Winstanly
Cr

**6**

0   1/4   1/2
mi

© Perly's Inc.

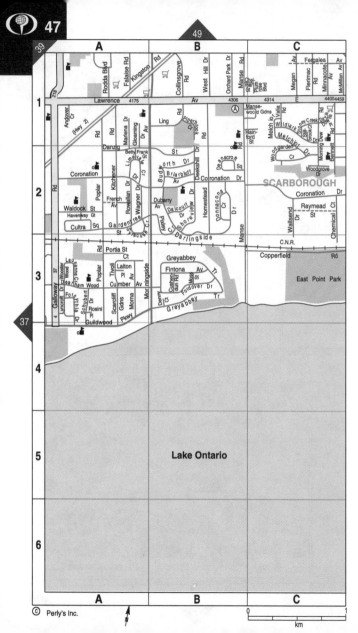

39 49 37

| | A | B | C |
|---|---|---|---|

**1**

Rodda Blvd
Falaise Rd
Kingston Rd
Collinsgrove Rd
West Hill Dr
Orchard Park Dr
Manse Rd
Chelmeri Gt
Plum rose Blvd
Megan
 Fierimac Rd
Minnacote Av
McMillan Av
Fergalea Av

Lawrence 4175 Av 4306 4314 E 44004459

Andover Cr
(Hwy 2)
Rd
Rd
Mariena Dr
Gloaming Dr
Ling Rd
piperb ook
Rd
Rd
A
Mansewood Gdns
Melch Rd
Viella
Sidney Creek Rd
Wildiard Dr
Stillbrook Rd
Morning Dew Rd
Bennett
Hainford St
Wood garden Dr
Melchior Dr

Danzig Betty Frank Gt
St
Coronation
Woodgrove Dr
Cr

Limelw w orth Dr
Deekshill Dr
beanscroft Sq
SCARBOROUGH

Coronation
Kitchener
Budw Briarbluff Av
Coronation Dr
Coronation Dr

**2**
Poplar
French Av
Rowallan Dr
Wagner Dr
Dubarry Av
Dalcourt Dr
Homestead
ponnacone Cr
Dr
Raymead St
Wallsend Dr
Chemical Ct

Waldock St
Havenway Gt
Gardenyres St
Syracuse Cr
Kaykd Cr
Shoreview Dr
Darlingside
Manse

Cultra Sq

C.N.R.

**3**
Rd
Portia St
Ct
Greyabbey
Copperfield Rd

Lau Wood
Lyncott Dr Wooster Dr
Dearham Wood
Tivoli
Lalton Pl
Cumber Av
Morningside
Fintona
Custen dun Rd
Moss Tr
Foxover Dr
Tr
East Point Park

Galloway 37
Fote Schubert Dr
Scarcliff Gdns
Morna Pkwy
Denny
Greyabbey
Rosini Pl

4
Guildwood

**4**

**5**
Lake Ontario

**6**

| | A | B | C |
|---|---|---|---|

© Perly's Inc.

0 1
km

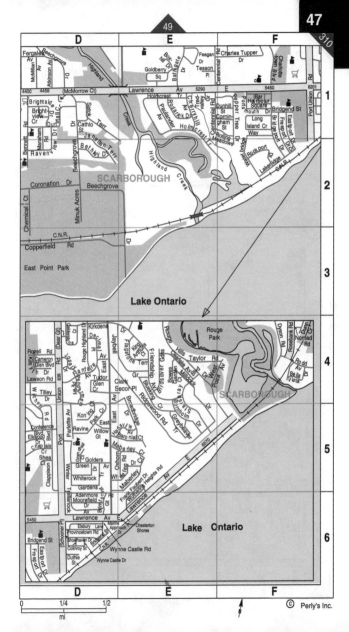

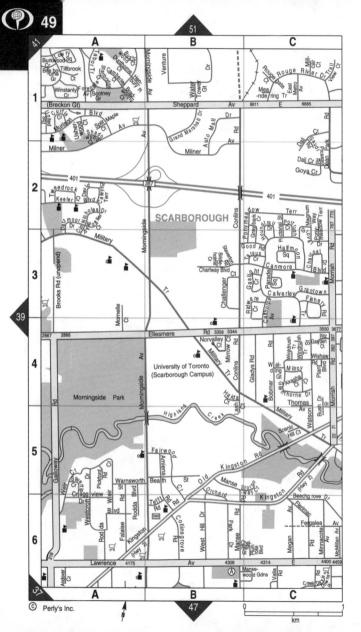

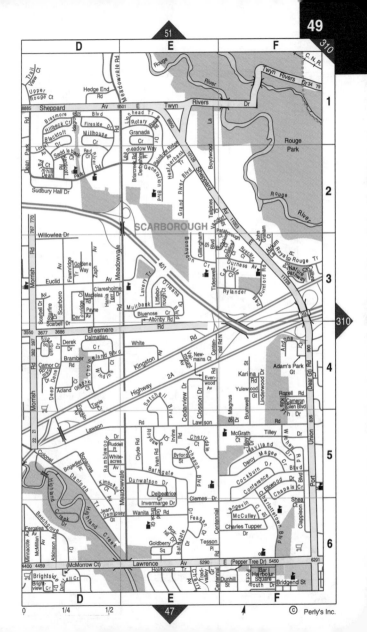

SCARBOROUGH

Steeles Av E

Cedarbrae Golf & Country Club

Woodlands Park (Private)

C.N.R

C.P.R

Old Finch Av

Finch Av

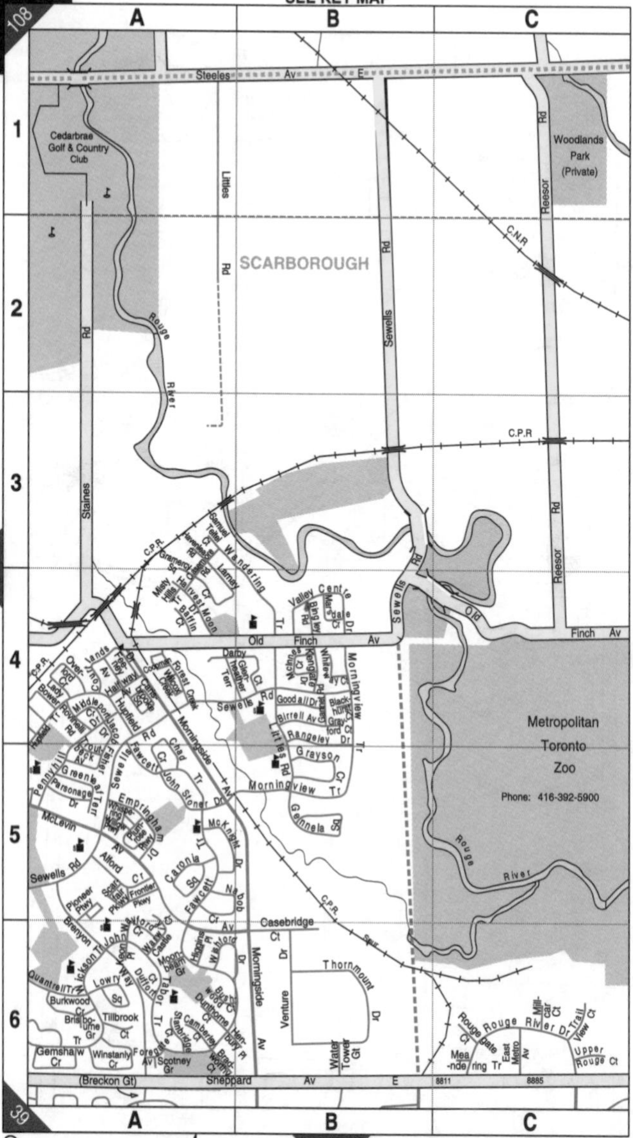

Metropolitan Toronto Zoo

Phone: 416-392-5900

Rouge River

Casebridge

Thornmount

Water Tower

Venture

Sheppard Av E

Rouge Rmer D Trail

East Metro

Upper Rouge Ct

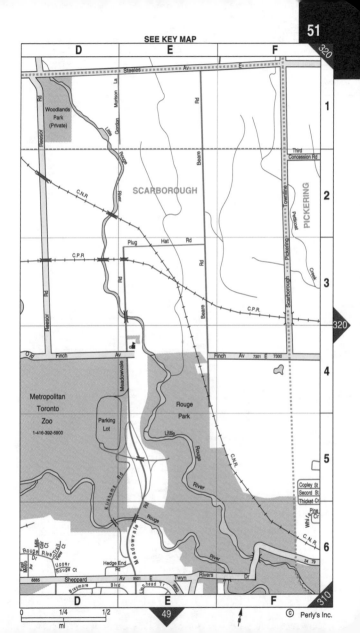

D     E     F

320

Steeles   Av   E

Heesor Rd

Woodlands Park (Private)

Munson La

Gordon La

Little Rouge River

Beare Rd

SCARBOROUGH

1

Third Concession Rd

PICKERING

C.N.R.

2

Towline

Pickering

Plug   Hat   Rd

Rd

C.P.R

Rd

Beare Rd

Scarborough

C.P.R.

Creek

320

3

Heesor Rd

Old Rd

Finch   Av

CPR

Finch   Av   7301 E   7300

4

Meadowvale

Metropolitan Toronto Zoo
1-416-392-5900

Parking Lot

Rouge Park

Little

Rouge

C.N.R.

Copley St

Secord St

Thicket Cr

5

Kirkhams Rd

River

White Pine Cr

Rouge

Meadowvale Rd

River

C.N.R.

6

East Metro

Rouge River Dr

Mill Cr Ct

Glen Ct

Yew Ct

Trail Ct

Upper Rouge Ct

Hedge End Rd

Rouge

Rivers Dr

34   79

310

8885

Sheppard   Av   9501 E

Baxmore

Blvd

Leenhead Tr   9699

Twyn

D     E     F

0    1/4    1/2

mi

49

© Perly's Inc.

| AIRLINES/CONVENTION CENTRES/GO BUS | MAP NO | MAP AREA |
|---|---|---|

## AIRLINES

| Airline | Terminal |
|---|---|
| Aeroflot | .3 |
| Air Alliance (CND) | .1 |
| Air Alliance (USA) | .2 |
| Air Canada (CND) | .2 |
| Air Canada (Int'l) | .1 |
| (except Thunder Bay & Ottawa) | |
| Air Canada (Ottawa) | .2 |
| Air Canada (Thunder Bay) | .1 |
| Air Canada (USA) | .2 |
| Air France | .3 |
| Air New Zealand | .2 |
| Air Ontario (USA) | .2 |
| Air Pacific | .3 |
| Air Transat | .3 |
| Air Ukraine | .3 |
| Alitalia | .3 |
| America West | .3 |
| American | .3 |
| American Transair | .3 |
| British Airways | .3 |
| BWIA | .3 |
| Canada 3000 | .3 |
| Canadian (Canada) | .2 |
| Canadian (Int'l) | .1 |
| Canadian (Ontario) | .1 |
| (except Thunder Bay & Ontario) | |
| Canadian (Ottawa) | .2 |
| Canadian (Thunder Bay) | .2 |
| Canadian Airlines (USA) | .2 |
| Canadian Regional | .2 |
| Cathay Pacific | .3 |
| Continental | .3 |
| ComAir | .3 |
| Cubana | .3 |
| Czech Airlines | .1 |
| Delta | .3 |
| EL AL | .3 |
| Finnair | .3 |
| Guyana | .3 |
| Henson | .3 |
| KLM | .3 |
| Korean Air | .3 |
| LACSA | .3 |
| LanChile | .3 |
| LOT | .1 |
| LTU | .3 |
| Lufthansa | .1 |
| Malev | .3 |
| Martinair | .3 |
| Mexicana | .1 |
| Midwest Express | .3 |
| Northwest | .3 |
| Olympic Airways | .3 |
| Pakistan Int'l | .3 |
| Pemair | .3 |
| Qantas-July 3, 2000 | .3 |
| Royal Airlines | .3 |
| SATA | .3 |
| Scandinavian | .1 |
| Skyservice | .3 |
| Skyway | .3 |
| Trans World | .3 |
| TWA | .3 |
| United Airlines | .2 |
| US Airways | .3 |
| Varg Brazilian | .1 |

## CONVENTION CENTRES

| | MAP NO | MAP AREA |
|---|---|---|
| International Plaza Hotel and Conference Centre . . . . .655 Dixon Rd | | |
| Metropolitan Convention Centres . . . . . . . . . . . . . . .255 Front St. W | | |
| National Trade Centre . .Exhibition Place | | |

## GO BUS TERMINALS

| | MAP NO | MAP AREA |
|---|---|---|
| Elizabeth St. . . . . . . . . . . . .4 | E | 6 |
| Scarborough . . . . . . . . . .39 | A | 3 |
| York Mills . . . . . . . . . . . . .9 | A | 3 |
| York Region . . . . . . . . . . .11 | A | 3 |
| Yorkdale . . . . . . . . . . . . . .8 | A | 5 |

| GO TRAIN/HOTELS | MAP NO | MAP AREA |
|---|---|---|

## GO TRAIN STATIONS

| | MAP NO | MAP AREA |
|---|---|---|
| Agincourt . . . . . . . . . . . . .31 | E | 6 |
| Bloor . . . . . . . . . . . . . . . .14 | E | 3 |
| Danforth . . . . . . . . . . . . . .15 | E | 4 |
| Eglinton . . . . . . . . . . . . . .37 | B | 3 |
| Etobicoke North . . . . . . . .28 | A | 4 |
| Exhibition . . . . . . . . . . . . .2 | A-B | 2 |
| Guildwood . . . . . . . . . . . .37 | F | 2 |
| Kipling . . . . . . . . . . . . . . .34 | F | 1 |
| Long Branch . . . . . . . . . .32 | C | 4 |
| Mimico . . . . . . . . . . . . . . .22 | D | 2 |
| Old Cummer . . . . . . . . . .11 | F | 3 |
| Oriole . . . . . . . . . . . . . . . .9 | F | 2 |
| Rouge Hill . . . . . . . . . . . .47 | E | 2 |
| Scarborough . . . . . . . . . .25 | E | 1 |
| Union . . . . . . . . . . . . . . . .2 | E | 2 |
| Weston . . . . . . . . . . . . . .28 | E | 6 |

## HOTELS

| | MAP NO | MAP AREA |
|---|---|---|
| 7 & 7 Motel . . . . . . . . .3458 Queen St E | | |
| A Lido Motel . . . . . . . .4674 Kingston Rd | | |
| Alexandra Apt Hotel . . . .77 Ryerson Av | | |
| Alpine Hotel . . . . . . . .1102 Kingston Rd | | |
| Andrews Motel . . . . . .2245 Kingston Rd | | |
| Andrews Motel Large . . . . . . . . . . . . . . .4434 Kingston Rd | | |
| Annex Guest House,The . . . . . . . . . . . . . . . . . .83 Spadina Rd | | |
| Avenue Motel . . . . . .1060 Dundas St E | | |
| Avenue Park Hotel . . . .138 Pears Ave | | |
| Avon Motel . . . . . . . . .2800 Kingston Rd | | |
| Beach Motel . .2183 Lakeshore Blvd W | | |
| Bell Motel . . . . . . . . . . .318 Plains Rd E | | |
| Best Western | | |
| Carlton Place Hotel . . . .33 Carlson Ct | | |
| Chestnut Park Hotel . . .108Chestnut St | | |
| Metro Inn . . . . . . . .2121 Kingston Rd | | |
| Primrose Hotel . . . . . . .111 Carlton St | | |
| Roehampton Hotel . .808 Mt Pleasant | | |
| Black Bull Hotel & Tavern298 Queen St W | | |
| Bond Place Hotel . . . . .65 Dundas St E | | |
| Bradgate Arms . . . . . . . .54 Foxbar Rd | | |
| Camberly Club Hotel . . .40 King St W | | |
| Cambridge Suites Hotel . . . . . . . . . . . . . . . . .15 Richmond St | | |
| Cameron House . . . . .408 Queen St W | | |
| Canadian Pacific Toronto East Hotel . . . . . . . . . . . . . . . .2035 Kennedy Rd | | |
| Carlingview Airport Inn . . . . . . . . . . . . . .221 Carlingview Dr | | |
| Casa Loma Inn, The . . .21 Walmer Rd | | |
| Cedar Croft Motor Court . . . . . . . . . . . . . . . . .494 Lakeshore Rd | | |
| Cityview Hotel . . . .1400 Plains Rd W | | |
| Clarion Essex Park Hotel . .300 Jarvis St | | |
| Clarkson Village Motel . . . . . . . . . . . . . . .1815 Lakeshore Rd W | | |
| Clover Leaf Motel . . . .214 Toronto Av | | |
| Colony Hotel . . . . . . . .89 Chestnut St | | |
| Comfort Hotel Downtown . . . . . . . . . . . . . . . . .15 Charles St E | | |
| Comfort Inn | | |
| Airport . . . . . . . . . . .240 Belfield Rd | | |
| Mississauga . . .1500 Matheson Blvd E | | |
| Markham . . . . . .8330 Woodbine Av | | |
| North York . . . . . . .66 Norfinch Dr | | |
| Oshawa . . . . . . . .605 Bloor St W | | |
| Pickering . . . . . . .533 Kingston Rd | | |
| Scarborough . . . .3306 Kingston Rd | | |
| Concordian Motel . . . . .7818 Dufferin | | |
| Crowne Plaza . . . . . .225 Front St W | | |
| Cruise Motel . .2083 Lakeshore Blvd W | | |
| Days Inn | | |
| Carlton . . . . . . . . . . .30 Carlton St | | |
| Mississauga . . .4635 Tomken Rd | | |
| Toronto Airport . . . .6257 Airport Rd | | |
| Toronto Downtown . .1684 Queen St E | | |
| Delta Chelsea Inn . . . .33 Gerrard St W | | |
| Delta Meadowvale Inn, The . . . . . . . . . . . . . . .6750 Mississauga Rd | | |
| Delta Toronto Airport Hotel . . . . . . . . . . . . . . . . . . .801 Dixon Rd | | |

| HOTELS | MAP NO | MAP AREA |
|---|---|---|
| Deluxe Motel . . . . .1554 The Queensway | | |
| Disera Motel . . . . . .7890 Bathurst St | | |
| Dodge Suites Hotel . . .5050 Orbitor Dr | | |
| Embassy Suites . . . . . . . . . . . . . . . . . .8500 Warden at Hwy 7 | | |
| Emerald Isle Motel . . .8700 Yonge St | | |
| Esquire Motel . . . . . .1110 Plains Rd W | | |
| Executive Motor Hotel . . .621 King St W | | |
| Executive Suites . . . .33 City Centre Dr | | |
| Isabella Hotel . . . . .556 Sherbourne St | | |
| Fort York Motel . . . . .1920 Dundas St E | | |
| Four Points Hotel . . . . . .5444 Dixie Rd | | |
| Four Seasons Hotel . . . .21 Avenue Rd | | |
| Gladstone Hotel . . . .1214 Queen St W | | |
| Glenerin Inn . . . . .1695 The Collegeway | | |
| Glengrove Suites . . . . .2837 Yonge St | | |
| Grand Motel . . . . . .4626 Kingston Rd | | |
| Grange Apt. Hotel, The . .165 Grange Av | | |
| Green Acres Motel . . . . . . . . . . . . . . . .1303 Lakeshore Rd E | | |
| Guild Inn, The . .201 Guildwood Pkwy | | |
| Hav-A-Nap Motel . . .2733 Kingston Rd | | |
| Henry's Motel . . . . . .2785 Kingston Rd | | |
| Hilton | | |
| Airport . . . . . . . . . . .5875 Airport Rd | | |
| Scarborough . . . . . . . . . .50 Estate Dr | | |
| Toronto . . . . . . . . .145 Richmond St | | |
| Hillcrest Motel .2143 Lakeshore Blvd W | | |
| Holiday Inn . . . .3063 South Service Rd | | |
| . . . . . . . . . .2125 North Sheridan Way | | |
| . . . . . . . . . . . . . . . . . .1011 Bloor St E | | |
| . . . . . . . . . . . . . . . . .7095 Woodbine Av | | |
| Brampton . . . .30 Peel Centre Dr | | |
| Express . . . . . . . . . . .30 Norfinch Dr | | |
| Etobicoke . . . . . . . . . . .2 Holiday Dr | | |
| Mississauga . . . .4635 Tomken Rd | | |
| Oakville Plaza . . . . . .590 Argus Rd | | |
| Scarborough . . . .22 Metropolitan Rd | | |
| Holiday Inn & King . . .370 King St W | | |
| Toronto West . . . .100 Britannia Rd E | | |
| Yorkdale . . . . . . . . . . .3450 Dufferin St | | |
| Crowne Plaza . . . . . .225 Front St W | | |
| Toronto Select . . . . . . .970 Dixon Rd | | |
| Toronto Airport S . . . . .Hwy 427 and Burnhamthorpe | | |
| Hostelling International Toronto . . . . . . . . . . . . . . . . . . .223 Church St | | |
| Hotel Ibis Toronto Centre . .240 Jarvis St | | |
| Hotel Intercontinental Toronto . . . . . . . . . . . . . . . . .220 Bloor St W | | |
| Howard Johnson | | |
| Clarington . . . . . . . . . . . .143 Duke St | | |
| Plaza Hotel . . . . . . . .475 Yonge St | | |
| Markham . . . . . .555 Cochrane St | | |
| Mississauga . . .2420 Surveyor Rd | | |
| North York . . . . . .2737 Keele St | | |
| Toronto East . . . . . .940 Progress Av | | |
| Airport Hotel . . . . . . .600 Dixon Rd | | |
| Idlewood Inn . . . . .4212 Kingston Rd | | |
| Inn on the Creek . .1625 Military Trail | | |
| Inn on the Lake . . . . . . . . . . . . . . . .1926 Lakeshore Blvd W | | |
| Inn on the Park, The Four Seasons . . . . . . . . . . . . . . . .1100 Eglinton Av E | | |
| International Plaza Hotel . .655 Dixon Rd | | |
| Ivy Motel . . . . . . .1417 Lakeshore Rd E | | |
| Journey's End | | |
| Comfort Inn . . . . . .5 Rutherford Rd S | | |
| Comfort Inn . .1230 Journey's End Cir | | |
| Quality Suites . . . .262 Carlingview Dr | | |
| Quality Hotel . . . . . . .280 Bloor St W | | |
| King Edward Hotel . . . . . .37 King St W | | |
| L'Hotel . . . . . . . . . . . . .225 Front St W | | |
| Lido Motel . . . . . . . . .4674 Kingston Rd | | |
| Lucien Motel . . . . . . . . .134 Byron St N | | |
| Manor Motel . . . . . . .2740 Kingston Rd | | |
| Maples Ballentrae . . . . .14248 Hwy 48 | | |
| Maple Leaf Motel . . .4540 Kingston Rd | | |
| Marriott Hotel | | |
| Toronto Airport . . . . . . .901 Dixon Rd | | |
| Toronto Marriott Eaton Centre . . . . . . . . . . . . . . . . . . .525 Bay St | | |

## HOTELS | MAP NO | MAP AREA

Maxin Inn Motel . . 2477 Lakeshore Rd W
Metropolitan Hotel . . . . . . . 108 Chestnut
Mississauga Gate Motel
. . . . . . . . . . . . . . . . . 1938 Dundas St E
Mohawk Inn . . . . . . . 9230 Guelph Line
Monte Carlo Hotel . . 1886 Dundas St E
Monte Carlo Inn . . . . . . . . 5 Derry Rd E
Motel 27 . . . . . . . . . . . . . 650 Evans Av
Neil-Wycik College Hotel
. . . . . . . . . . . . . . . . . . . 96 Gerrard St
New Edwin Hotel . . . . 650 Queen St E
Newmarket Inn . . . . . . 18667 Yonge St
New Heritage Inn . . . 385 Rexdale Blvd
New Plaza Hotel . . 4584 Kingston Rd
North American Motel
. . . . . . . . . . . . . . 2147 Lakeshore Blvd W
Novotel
  North York . . . . . . . 3 Park Home Av
  Toronto Airport . . . 135 Calingview Dr
  Toronto Centre . . . . 45 The Esplanade
  Mississauga . . . . 3670 Hurontario St
Orangeville Motel . . 633-195 Hwy 10/24
Panorama Inn . . . . 25 Broadway Av E
Park Motel . . . . . . . . 3126 Kingston Rd
Park Plaza Hotel . . . . . . . 4 Avenue Rd
Pig & Whistle Inn .5527 Lakeshore Rd E
Pinecrest Motel . . . . . . . . 2641 Hwy 7
Pine Ridge Motel . . . . . 1607 King St E
Port Darlington Marina Hotel
. . . . . . . . . . . . 70 Port Darlington Rd
Prince Hotel, The Westin
. . . . . . . . . . . . . . . 900 York Mills Rd
Midtown Quality Hotel . . 280 Bloor St W
. . . . . . . . . . . . . . . . . . 111 Lombard St
. . . . . . . . . . . . . . . . . . . . . 754 Bronte
Quality Hotel Suites . . 2180 Islington Av
Quality Inn & Suites . . 22 Metropolitan Rd
Quality Inn - Airport West
. . . . . . . . . . . . . . . . 50 Britannia Rd W
Quality Motel - Airport . . . 6090 Dixie Rd
Queensway Motel .638 The Queensway
Radisson
  Don Valley . . . . . . . 1250 Eglinton Av E
  Markham . . . . . . . . 50 East Valhalla Dr
  Plaza Hotel Admiral
. . . . . . . . . . . . . 249 Queens Quay W
  Toronto . . . . . . . . . . . . 90 Bloor St W
  Mississauga . . . . . . . 2501 Argentia Rd
Radisson Suites Toronto Airport
. . . . . . . . . . . . . . . . . . . 640 Dixon Rd
Ramada Hotel 400 - 401 1657 Wilson Av
Ramada Inn . . . . . . . . 185 Yorkland Blvd
Ramada Inn . . . . . . . . . . . 360 Argus Rd
Ramada Inn Airport . . . . . . 2 Holiday Dr
Regal Constellation Hotel .900 Dixon Rd
Rex Hotel, The . . . . . 194 Queen St W
Riviera On The Lake
. . . . . . . . . . . . . . . . . 2048 Lakeshore Rd
Roehampton Hotel .808 Mt.Pleasant Rd
Rosetown Inn . . . . . . 226 Queen St E
Royal Motel . . . . . . 2746 Kingston Rd
Royal Motel . . . . . . . . . 99 Plains Rd E
Royal York Hotel . . . . 100 Front St W
Roycroft Motel . . . . . 3137 Kingston Rd
Scarborough Inn . . . . . . . 8 Dowry St
Seahorse Inn .2095 Lake Shore Blvd W
Selby Hotel . . . . . . 592 Sherbourne St
Sheraton Centre Toronto Hotel
  Tower Toronto . . . 123 Queen St W
  Parkway Toronto North . . . 600 Hwy 7
  Sheraton GatewayToronto Airport
. . . . . . . . . . . . . . . . . . . . . Terminal 3
Sherway Inn . . . . . . . . 619 Evans Rd
Shield and Sword . . . 260 Queen E.
Shore Breeze Motel
. . . . . . . . . . . . 2175 Lakeshore Blvd W
Silver Moon Motel
. . . . . . . . . . . . 2157 Lakeshore Blvd W
SkyDome Hotel . . . . . 1 Blue Jays Way
St. Leonard Hotel . . . 418 Sherbourne St
Stage West All Suites Hotel
. . . . . . . . . . . . . . . . . . . 5400 Dixie Rd
Strathcona Hotel . . . . . . . . . 60 York St

## HOTELS/HOSPITALS | MAP NO | MAP AREA

Sunset Inn . . . . . . . . . . . 5825 Dixie Rd
Summit Motel, The . . . . 11610 Yonge St
Super 8 Motel . . . . . . . . . . . 600 Dixon
. . . . . . . . . . . . . . . . . . 5585 Ambler Rd
. . . . . . . . . . . . . . . . . . . . . 30 Clark Blvd
. . . . . . . . . . . . . . . . . . 3280 Kingston Rd
Sutton Place Hotel, The . . . . 955 Bay St
Toronto Colony Hotel . . .89 Chestnut St
Toronto Airport Hilton Int'l
. . . . . . . . . . . . . . . . . . 5875 Airport Rd
Toronto Gateway Inn .4694 Kingston Rd
Toronto Hilton . . . . . 145 Richmond St E
Toronto International Hostel
. . . . . . . . . . . . . . . . . . . . 223 Church St
Toronto Marriot Eaton Centre
. . . . . . . . . . . . . . . . . . . . . 525 Bay St
Toronto Marriot Airport . .901 Dixon Rd
Town & Country Hotel . .517 Plains Rd E
Town Inn Suites . . . . . . . 620 Church St
Travellodge ,The
  Etobicoke . . . . . . . 445 Rexdale Blvd
  Burlington . . . . . . . . 950 Walkers Line
  North York . . . . . . . . 50 Norfinch Dr
  North York . . . . 55 Hallcrown Place
  Mississauga . . . . . 5599 Ambler St
  Scarborough . . 20 Milner Business Ct
Valhalla Inn
  Etobicoke . . . . . . . 1 Valhalla Inn Rd
Venture Inn
  Toronto Airport . . . . . . 925 Dixon Rd
  Yorkville . . . . . . . . . . . 89 Avenue Rd
Victoria Hotel . . . . . . . . 56 Yonge St
Voyageur Place Hotel . .17 Yonge St N
Waverly Hotel . . . . . . 484 Spadina Av
Westin Harbour Castle . .1 Harbour Sq
White Knight Motel . . . 6965 Dixie Rd
Whitehouse Hotel . . . . . 76 Church St
Windham Bristol Place Hotel
. . . . . . . . . . . . . . . . . . . . . 950 Dixon Rd
Woodbine Motel . . . . . . 7242 Hwy 27
Woodhill Motel . . . . 3160 Queen St S
Yorkdale Inn . . . . . . . 3080 Dufferin St

### GENERAL HOSPITALS

Ajax & Pickering General Hospital
. . . . . . . . . . . . . . 580 Harwood Av S
Baycrest Hospital . . . .3560 Bathurst St
Bowmanville Memorial Hospital
. . . . . . . . . . . . . . . . 47 Liberty St S
Centenary Hospital . 2867 Ellesmere Rd
Credit Valley Hospital,The
. . . . . . . . . . . . . . . 2200 Eglinton Av W
Doctors Hospital, The . .45 Brunswick Av
Dufferin Area Hospital . . . . .32 First St
Etobicoke General Hospital,The
. . . . . . . . . . 101 Humber College Blvd
Georgetown & Dist. Memorial Hosp
. . . . . . . . . . . . . . . 1 Princess Anne Dr
Hospital for Sick Children,The
. . . . . . . . . . . . . . . . 555 University Av
Humber River Regional Hospital
. . . . . . . . . . . . . . . . . . . . 2175 Keele St
Humber River Regional Hospital
. . . . . . . . . . . . . . . . . . . 200 Church St
Joseph Brant Memorial Hospital
. . . . . . . . . . . . . 1230 North Shore Blvd
Lakeridge Health,Oshawa .1 Hospital Ct
Markham Stouffville Hospital
. . . . . . . . . . . . . . . . . . . 381 Church St
Milton District Hospital
. . . . . . . . . . . . . . . . . . . 30 Derry Rd E
Mississauga Hospital, The
. . . . . . . . . . . . . . . . 100 Queensway W
Mount Sinai Hospital . 600 University Av
North York Branson Hospital
. . . . . . . . . . . . . . . . . 555 Finch Av.W.
North York General Hospital
. . . . . . . . . . . . . . . . . . 4001 Leslie St.
Oakville-Trafalgar Memorial Hosp
. . . . . . . . . . . . . . . . . 327 Reynolds St
Peel Memorial Hospital . .20 Lynch St
Port Perry Community Memorial
. . . . . . . . . . . . . . . . . . 451 Paxton St.

## HOSPITALS | MAP NO | MAP AREA

Princess Margaret Hospital
. . . . . . . . . . . . . . . 500 Sherbourne St
Queen Elizabeth Hospital
. . . . . . . . . . . . . . . . 550 University Av
Queensway General Hospital
. . . . . . . . . . . . . . . . . . 150 Sherway Dr
Royal Victoria Hospital .201 Georgian Dr
Scarborough General Hospital
. . . . . . . . . . . . . . 3050 Lawrence Av E
Scarborough Grace General Hospital
. . . . . . . . . . . . . . . 3030 Birchmount Rd
Shouldice Genral Hosp.7750 Bayview Av
St. Michael's Hospital . . .30 Bond St
Sunnybrook Health Science Centre
. . . . . . . . . . . . . . . . 2075 Bayview Av
Toronto East General & Ortho. Hosp
. . . . . . . . . . . . . . . . . . 825 Coxwell Av
Toronto General Division
. . . . . . . . . . . . . . . . 200 Elizabeth St
Toronto Western Division
. . . . . . . . . . . . . . . . . 399 Bathurst St
Uxbridge Cottage Hospital
. . . . . . . . . . . . . . . . . . . . Campbell Dr
Wellesley Central Hospital
. . . . . . . . . . . . . . . . 160 Wellesley St E
West Park Hospital . .82 Buttonwood Av
Whitby General Hospital
. . . . . . . . . . . . . . . . . . . 300 Gordon St
Women's College Hospital
. . . . . . . . . . . . . . . . . . 76 Grenville St
York Central Hospital . . . . 10 Trench St
York County Hospital . . . 596 Davis Dr
York-Finch General Hospital
. . . . . . . . . . . . . . . . . . 2111 Finch Av W

### OTHER HOSPITALS

Addict.Research Detoxinution Unit
. . . . . . . . . . . . . . . . 501 Queen St W
Addiction Research Foundation
. . . . . . . . . . . . . . . . . . . 33 Russell St
Aisling Centre for Children/Family
. . . . . . . . . 2202 Eglinton Av E. Ste.105
Bellwood Health Services
. . . . . . . . . . . . . . . . 1020 McNicoll Av
Bloorview Children's Hospital
. . . . . . . . . . . . . . . . . . . 25 Buchan Ct
C.M Hincks Treatment Centre
. . . . . . . . . . . . . . . . . . . 440 Jarvis St
Clarke Institute of Psychiatry
. . . . . . . . . . . . . . . . . . 250 College St
Dewson Private Hospital . .47 Dewson St
Don Mills Surgical Unit Limited
. . . . . . . . . . . . . . . . . . . 20 Wynford Dr
Donwood Institute . . .175 Brentcliffe Rd
Downsview Rehabilitation Centre
. . . . . . . . . . . . . . . . . 115 Torbarrie Rd
Erinoak Treatment Centre
. . . . . . . . . . . . . . . 2277 South Millway
Grandview Rehab.& Treatment Centre
. . . . . . . . . . . . . . . 600 Townline Rd S
Hillcrest Hospital . . . . 47 Austin Terrace
Hugh MacMillan Medical Centre
. . . . . . . . . . . . . . . . . 350 Rumsey Rd
Institute of Restorative Surgery
. . . . . . . . . . . . . . . . . 215 Victoria St
Lyndhurst Hospital . . 520 Sutherland Dr
Oaklands Regional Centre . .53 Bond St
Ontario Cancer Treatment Centre
. . . . . . . . . . . . . . . 620 University Av
Orthopaedic and Arthritic Hospital
. . . . . . . . . . . . . . . . 43 Wellesley St E
Our Lady of Mercy . .100 Sunnyside Av.
Providence Centre . .3276 St.Clair Av E
Queen St. Mental Health Centre
. . . . . . . . . . . . . . . 1001 Queen St W
Riverdale Hospital . .14 St.Mathews Rd
Runnymede Chronic Care Hospital
. . . . . . . . . . . . . . . . 274 St. John's Rd
Sacred Heart Child & Family Centre
. . . . . . . . . . . . . . . 3275 St.Clair Av E
Salvation Army Toronto Grace Hosp
. . . . . . . . . . . . . . . . . 650 Church St
Southdown Treatment Centre . . . .R.R.2

## HOSPITALS/PUBLIC SCHOOLS

St. Bernard's Convalescent Hospital ......685 Finch Av W
St. John's Rehabilitation Centre ......285 Cummer Av
St. Joseph Detoxification Centre ......2769 Dundas St W
St. Joseph's Health Centre ......30 Queensway The
St. Joseph's Infirmary .3377 Bayview Av
St. Michael's Detoxification Centre ......314 Adelaide St E
Surrey Place Centre ..2 Surrey Pl
Thistletown Regional Centre ......51 Panorama Ct
Toronto East General & Detox. Unit ......109 Knox Av
Toronto Rehabilitation Centre ......345 Rumsey Rd
Toronto Western Detoxification Centre ......16 Ossington Av
Whitby Psychiatric Hospital ......700 Gordon St
Woodbridge Cosmetic Surgery Hospital ......4650 Highway 7

## PUBLIC SCHOOLS

| PUBLIC SCHOOLS | MAP NO | MAP AREA |
|---|---|---|
| Adam Beck Jr. P.S. | 15 | F 5 |
| Agincourt Jr. P.S. | 31 | E 6 |
| Agnes Macphail P.S. | 41 | A 2 |
| Albion Heights P.S. | 40 | D-E 4-5 |
| Alexander Muir/ Gladstone P.S. | 4 | A 6 |
| Alexander Stirling P.S. | 51 | A 5 |
| Alexmuir Jr. P.S. | 31 | F 3 |
| Allenby Jr. P.S. | 6 | E 3 |
| ALPHA Jr.& Sr.P.S. | 2 | D 1 |
| Alternative Primary Jr. | 6 | D 3 |
| Ancaster P.S. | 18 | B 2 |
| Annette Street Jr.& Sr.P.S. | 14 | B 3 |
| Anson Park P.S. | 37 | A 5 |
| Anson Taylor Jr. P.S. | 41 | B 4 |
| Arbor Glen P.S. | 21 | C 1 |
| Armour Heights P.S. | 8 | E 3-4 |
| Balmy Beach Jr. P.S. | 15 | E 6 |
| Banting & Best P.S. | 41 | A 1 |
| Baycrest P.S. | 8 | B 5 |
| Bayview Elem. & Mid. | 11 | D 5 |
| Beaches Alternative P.S. | 15 | E 4 |
| Beaumonde Heights Jr. & Mid. | 30 | A 4 |
| Bedford Park Jr. P.S. | 9 | A 6 |
| Bellmere Jr. P.S. | 39 | C 4 |
| Bendale Jr. P.S. | 39 | B 5 |
| Bennington Heights Jr. P.S. | 7 | D 6 |
| Berner Trail Jr. P.S. | 41 | E 4 |
| Bessborough Drive P.S. | 7 | D 4 |
| Beverly Glen Jr. P.S. | 31 | B 3 |
| Birch Cliff Heights Sch. | 25 | D 5 |
| Birch Cliff P.S. | 25 | C 4 |
| Birchmount Centre Sch. | 29 | D 5 |
| Blacksmith P.S. | 20 | A 2 |
| Blake Street Jr. P.S. | 5 | D 6 |
| Blantyre P.S. | 25 | A 4-5 |
| Blaydon P.S. | 18 | C 2 |
| Bloorview/ McMillan Centre Sch. | 21 | A 6 |
| Blythwood Jr. P.S. | 7 | B 6 |
| Bowmore Road Jr. & Sr. | 15 | E 5 |
| Braeburn Jr. P.S. | 28 | C 1 |
| Brian P.S.(Eng.& Fl.) | 21 | F 5 |
| Briar Hill Jr. | 6 | A 3 |
| Briarcrest P.S. | 36 | C 4 |
| Bridlewood Jr. P.S. | 31 | B 6 |
| Brimwood Boulevard Jr. P.S. | 41 | A 3 |
| Broadacres Jr. P.S. | 34 | B-C 1 |
| Broadlands P.S.(Sr.) | 19 | E-F 5-6 |
| Brock Jr. P.S. | 14 | F 4 |
| Brookbanks P.S.(Eng.& Fr.) | 19 | E 3-4 |
| Brookhaven P.S. | 16 | B 1 |
| Brookmill Boulevard Jr. P.S. | 31 | C 3 |
| Brooks Road P.S. | 49 | A 4 |
| Brown Jr. P.S. | 4 | E 1 |
| Bruce Jr. P.S. | 3 | F 1 |

| PUBLIC SCHOOLS | MAP NO | MAP AREA |
|---|---|---|
| Buchanan P.S. | 29 | B 5 |
| Burrows Hall Jr. P.S. | 39 | D 1 |
| C.D. Farquharson Jr. P.S. | 39 | A 1 |
| Calico P.S. | 18 | B 1 |
| Cameron P.S. | 8 | E 2 |
| Carleton Village Jr.&Sr.P.S. | 14 | D 1 |
| Cassandra P.S. | 19 | D-E 5 |
| Cedar Drive Jr. P.S. | 31 | D 3 |
| Cedarbrook Jr. P.S. | 37 | C 2-3 |
| Centennial Road Jr. P.S. | 49 | E 5 |
| Chalkfarm P.S. | 28 | F 3 |
| Charles E. Webster P.S. | 16 | C 3 |
| Charles G. Fraser Jr. P.S. | 4 | C 6 |
| Charles H Best P.S. ( West ) | 10 | A 4 |
| Charlottetown P.S. | 49 | F 6 |
| Chartland Jr. P.S. | 31 | F 2 |
| Cherokee P.S. | 21 | F 3 |
| Chester Le Jr. P.S. | 31 | A 3 |
| Chester P.S. | 5 | E 2 |
| Chief Dan George P.S. | 49 | E 2 |
| Chine Drive P.S. | 25 | F 3 |
| Church Street Jr. P.S. | 5 | A 5 |
| Churchill Heights Jr. P.S. | 39 | B 2 |
| Churchill P.S. | 10 | E 4 |
| Claireville Jr. P.S. | 40 | E 2 |
| Clairlea Jr. P.S. | 27 | A 5 |
| Cliffside P.S. | 25 | E 3 |
| Cliffwood P.S.(Eng.& Fl.) | 21 | B 1 |
| Clinton Street Jr. P.S. | 4 | C 4 |
| Cordella Jr. P.S. | 16 | B 5 |
| Cornell Jr. P.S. | 37 | D 1 |
| Corvette Jr. P.S. | 27 | E 4 |
| Cottingham Jr. P.S. | 4 | F 2 |
| Courcelette P.S. | 25 | A 5-6 |
| Crescent Town P.S. | 15 | F 5 |
| Cresthaven P.S. | 21 | B 2 |
| Crestview P.S. | 21 | B 4 |
| Dallington P.S. (Eng.& Fr.) | 21 | A 1 |
| Danforth Gardens P.S. | 25 | C 2 |
| David Hornell Jr. P.S. | 22 | E 2 |
| David Lewis P.S. | 31 | C 2 |
| Davisville Jr. P.S. | 7 | A 4 |
| Daystrom P.S. | 30 | D 4 |
| Deer Park Jr. & Sr. P.S. | 7 | A 6 |
| Denlow P.S. | 9 | F 4 |
| Dennis Avenue Community Sch. | 16 | B 4 |
| Derrydown P.S.(Eng.& Fr.) | 20 | C 4 |
| Dewson Street Jr. P.S. | 4 | B 4 |
| Diefenbaker P.S. | 15 | B 2 |
| Dixon Grove Jr. & Mid. | 36 | F 4 |
| Donwood Park Jr. P.S. | 29 | F 5 |
| Dorset Park Jr. P.S. | 29 | D 6 |
| Dovercourt Jr. P.S. | 4 | A 3 |
| Downsview P.S. | 18 | D 3 |
| Downtown Alternative Primary Sch. | 3 | A 2 |
| Dr.Marion Hilliard Sr. P.S. | 41 | C 3 |
| Driftwood P.S. | 20 | A 3 |
| Dublin Heights Elem.& Mid. | 8 | D 2 |
| Dundas Jr. P.S. | 5 | D 6 |
| Dunlace P.S.(Eng.& Fr.) | 9 | F 2 |
| Earl Beatty Jr. & Sr. P.S. | 15 | B 3 |
| Earl Haig Jr. P.S. | 15 | B 4 |
| Earlscourt Jr. P.S. | 16 | F 6 |
| Eastview Jr. P.S. | 47 | A 2 |
| Eatonville Jr. P.S. | 34 | C 3 |
| Edgewood Jr. P.S. | 29 | F 4 |
| Eglinton Jr. P.S. | 7 | B 3 |
| Elizabeth Simcoe Jr. P.S. | 37 | E 4 |
| Elkhorn P. S. | 11 | D 6 |
| Ellesmere-Statton P.S. | 29 | D 4 |
| Elmlea Jr. P.S. | 28 | C 3 |
| Emily Carr Jr. P.S. | 51 | A 6 |
| Ernest P.S. | 21 | A 4 |
| Essex Jr. & Sr. P.S. | 4 | B 3 |
| Etienne Brule Jr. P.S. | 24 | E 5 |
| F.H. Miller Jr. P.S. | 16 | E 5 |
| Fairglen Jr. P.S. | 31 | A 5 |
| Fairmount Jr. P.S. | 25 | F 5 |
| Fenside P.S. | 19 | E 2-3 |
| Fern Avenue Jr.& Sr. P.S. | 14 | E 5 |

| PUBLIC SCHOOLS | MAP NO | MAP AREA |
|---|---|---|
| Finch P.S. | 11 | C 4 |
| Firgrove P.S. | 30 | F 4 |
| First Nations Jr. & Sr. P.S. | 5 | D 6 |
| Fleming P.S. | 51 | B 5 |
| Flemingdon P.S. | 8 | B 6 |
| Forest Hill Jr. & Sr. P.S. | 6 | D 5 |
| Forest Manor P.S. | 19 | C 1 |
| Frankland Community Jr. P.S. | 5 | E 4 |
| Galloway Road P.S. | 37 | F 1 |
| Garden Avenue Jr. P.S. | 14 | D 5 |
| Gateway P.S. | 17 | D 5 |
| General Brock P.S. | 27 | C 5 |
| General Crerar P.S. | 27 | D 1 |
| General Mercer Jr. P.S. | 16 | D 5 |
| George Anderson P.S. | 16 | C 1 |
| George B. Little Jr. P.S. | 39 | E 5 |
| George P. Mackie Jr. P.S. | 37 | D 4 |
| George Peck P.S. | 27 | B 2 |
| George R. Gauld Jr. P.S. | 22 | D 2 |
| George Webster P.S. | 15 | E 2 |
| Givins Shaw Jr. & Sr. P.S. | 4 | B 6 |
| Glamorgan Jr. P.S. | 29 | D 3 |
| Gledhill Jr. P.S. | 15 | D 3 |
| Glen Park P.S.(Eng.& Fr.) | 6 | C 2 |
| Glen Ravine Jr. P.S. | 27 | F 3 |
| Golf Road Jr. P.S. | 39 | D-E 6 |
| Gosford P.S. | 20 | A 4 |
| Grace Street Jr. P.S. | 4 | B 5 |
| Gracedale P.S. | 30 | C 3 |
| Gracefield P.S. | 18 | B 6 |
| Greenholme Jr. P.S. | 40 | F 4 |
| Greenland P.S. | 17 | C 1 |
| Grenoble P.S. | 17 | B 4 |
| Grey Owl Jr. P.S. | 41 | F 6 |
| Guildwood Jr. P.S. | 37 | E 3 |
| Gulfstream P.S. | 30 | D 5 |
| H.A. Halbert Jr. P.S. | 37 | B 5 |
| H.J. Alexander Community Sch. | 28 | E 6 |
| Harrison P.S. | 9 | E 2 |
| Harwood Jr. P.S. | 16 | B 5 |
| Hawthorne II Bilingual Alt. P.S. | 4 | B 3 |
| Heather Heights Jr. P.S. | 39 | E 4 |
| Heritage Park P.S. | 51 | A 4 |
| Heron Park Jr. P.S. | 47 | B 2 |
| High Park Alternative P.S. | 14 | B 2 |
| Highcastle P.S. | 39 | F 3 |
| Highfield Jr. P.S. | 40 | F 3 |
| Highland Creek P.S. | 49 | C 4 |
| Highland Heights Jr. P.S. | 31 | D 5 |
| Highview P.S. | 18 | B 4 |
| Hillcrest Jr. P.S. | 4 | D 1 |
| Hillmount P.S. | 21 | C 2 |
| Hollywood P.S. | 11 | C 6 |
| Howard Jr. P.S. | 14 | D 4 |
| Hughes Jr. P.S. | 16 | E 5 |
| Hudson Valley Village Jr & Mid. | 26 | C 6 |
| Humbercrest Jr. P.S. | 24 | F 2 |
| Humberwood Downs Jr. & Mid. | 40 | A 4 |
| Hunter's Glen Jr. P.S. | 27 | E 2 |
| Huron Street Jr. P.S. | 4 | E 3 |
| Indian Road Crescent Jr. P.S. | 14 | D 2 |
| Inglewood Heights Jr. P.S. | 29 | D 1-2 |
| Ionview P.S. | 27 | D 3 |
| Iroquois Jr. P.S. | 41 | A 4 |
| Islington Jr. & Mid. | 24 | B 3 |
| J.G. Workman P.S. | 25 | D 2 |
| Jackman Avenue Jr. P.S. | 5 | E 3 |
| James S. Bell Jr. & Mid. | 32 | E 4 |
| Jesse Ketchum Jr. & Sr. P.S. | 4 | F 3 |
| John A. Leslie P.S. | 25 | E-F 2 |
| John D. Parker Jr. P.S. | 40 | E 1 |
| John English Jr.& Mid. | 22 | D 3 |
| John Fisher Jr. P.S. | 7 | A 3 |
| John G. Althouse Jr. & Mid. | 36 | F 5 |
| John G. Diefenbaker P.S. | 49 | D 2 |

| OTHER/SECONDARY SCHOOLS | MAP NO | MAP AREA |
|---|---|---|
| Hillside Outdoor Education Center | 51 | E 3 |
| Hilltop Mid. | 26 | C 2 |
| Hodgson Sr. P.S. | 7 | B 5 |
| Hollycrest Mid. | 36 | B 5 |
| Horizon Alternative Sr. P.S. | 4 | D 5 |
| Humber Summit Mid. | 30 | C 3 |
| Humewood Comm. Sch. | 6 | B 5 |
| Island Natural Science Sch. | 2 | D 6 |
| J.B.Tyrell Sr. P.S. | 31 | A 1 |
| J.R.Wilcox Comm. Sch. | 6 | B 4 |
| J.S. Woodsworth Sr.P.S. | 39 | C 5 |
| Jack Miner Sr. P.S. | 47 | A 4 |
| Jean-Lajoie Elm (Fr.) | 17 | E 1 |
| John Buchan Sr. P.S. | 31 | C 6 |
| John McCrae Sr. P.S. | 37 | B 3 |
| Jones Av. Adult New Canadians | 5 | F 4 |
| Joseph Brant Sr. P.S. | 47 | B 2 |
| Joseph Howe Sr. P.S. | 47 | C 5 |
| Kane Middle S. | 16 | E 3 |
| Kennedy Language Center | 31 | E 4 |
| Kent Sr. P.S. | 14 | F 4 |
| Lambton Park Community Sch. | 26 | E 6 |
| Lawrence Heights Mid. | 8 | A 5 |
| LINC (For Newcomers) | 29 | F 2 |
| Lucy McCormick Sr. P.S. | 14 | D 2 |
| Metro Toronto Sch. for the Deaf | 7 | A 4 |
| Milne Valley Mid. | 19 | E 5 |
| Oakdale Park Mid. | 20 | A 5 |
| Ontario College of Art | 4 | E 6 |
| Park Lane Circle Sch. | 7 | D 6 |
| Pierre Laporte J.H.S. | 18 | B 3 |
| Pleasant View J.H.S. | 21 | F 4 |
| Portage Middle S. | 26 | F 2 |
| Queen Alexandra Sr. P.S. | 5 | D 6 |
| Quest Alternative Sr. P.S. | 5 | E 5 |
| Rawlinson Comm. Sch. | 6 | A 5 |
| Robert Service Sr. P.S. | 27 | F 4 |
| Rockcliffe Sr.P.S. | 16 | A 5 |
| Rosthorn P.S. | 24 | A 1 |
| Royal Conservatory of Music | 4 | E 6 |
| Samuel Hearne Sr. P.S. | 25 | B 3 |
| School of Life Experience | 15 | A 4 |
| Seneca Sch. | 36 | B 6 |
| Sir Alexander MacKenzie Sr. P.S. | 31 | F 6 |
| Sir Ernest MacMillian Sr. P.S. | 31 | E 4 |
| Sir Robert L Borden Bus./Tech.Inst. | 47 | A 2 |
| Smithfield Mid. | 40 | E 2 |
| Spectrum Sr. P.S. | 7 | B 4 |
| St Andrews J.H.S. | 9 | C 3 |
| Sunny View P.S. | 7 | C 4 |
| Tecumseh Sr. P.S. | 39 | D-E 4 |
| Timothy Eaton Bus. & Tech.Inst. | 31 | C 4 |
| Valley Park Mid. | 17 | E 5 |
| Westwood J.H.S. | 5 | E 2 |
| William J McCordic Sch. | 15 | E 3 |
| Willowdale Mid.(Eng. & Fr.) | 10 | E 5 |
| Windfield J.H.S.(Eng.& Fr.) | 9 | E 3 |
| Winona Drive Sr. P.S. | 4 | B 5 |
| Woodbine J.H.S. | 21 | B 5 |
| Zion Heights J.H.S. | 11 | F 4 |

## SECONDARY SCHOOLS

| SECONDARY SCHOOLS | MAP NO | MAP AREA |
|---|---|---|
| A Y Jackson S.S. | 21 | B 1 |
| Agincourt C.I. | 31 | E-F 6 |
| Albert Campbell C.I. | 41 | A 3 |
| Alternative School Educ. (ASE) 1 | 39 | A 4 |
| Alternative Scarb. Educ. (ASE) 2 | 31 | F 4 |
| Bathurst Heights S.S. | 8 | B 4 |
| Bickford Centre | 4 | B 4 |
| Birchmount Park C.I. | 25 | D 4 |
| Bloor C.I. | 14 | F 4 |
| Brockton H.S. | 4 | F 4 |
| Burnhamthorpe C.I. | 34 | B 2 |
| C W Jefferys S.S. | 20 | B 4 |
| Cedarbrae C.I. | 37 | C 1 |
| Central Commerce C.I. | 4 | B 4 |
| Central Etobicoke H.S. | 36 | F 3 |
| Central Tech. Sch. | 4 | D 4 |
| City School (Alternative) | 14 | D 1 |
| College Street S.S. | 4 | E 6 |
| CONTACT | 4 | E 6 |
| Danforth C.T.I. | 15 | A 3 |
| David & Mary Thompson C.I. | 29 | F 6 |
| Don Mills C.I. | 17 | C 1 |
| Downsview S.S. | 18 | D 3 |
| Dr. Norman Bethune C.I. | 31 | B 2 |
| Drewry / Avon Glen S.S. | 10 | F 2 |
| Earl Haig S.S. | 11 | A 5 |
| East York Alternative Sch. | 15 | B 2 |
| East York C.I. | 15 | B 2 |
| Eastdale C.I. | 5 | E 5 |
| Eastern H.S. of Commerce | 5 | F 4 |
| Emery C.I. | 30 | D 4 |
| Emery C.I. | 30 | E 3 |
| Etobicoke C.I. | 24 | B 2 |
| Forest Hill C.I. | 6 | D 3 |
| Frank Oke S.S. | 16 | A 5 |
| George Harvey C.I. | 16 | C 4 |
| George S Henry Academy | 19 | C 2 |
| George Vanier S.S. | 21 | B 5 |
| Greenwood S.S. | 15 | A 4 |
| Harbord C.I. | 4 | C 4 |
| Heydon Park S.S. | 4 | A 5 |
| Humberside C.I. | 14 | B 2-3 |
| Inglenook S.S. | 3 | C 1 |
| Jarvis C.I. (Fr. & Eng.) | 5 | A 4 |
| Kipling C.I. | 36 | E 2 |
| L'Amoreaux C.I. | 31 | B 3 |
| Lakeshore C.I. | 32 | F 4 |
| Lawrence Park C.I. | 6 | F 1 |
| Leaside H.S. (Eng. & Fl.) | 7 | D 3-4 |
| Lester B Pearson C.I. | 41 | B 1 |
| Malvern C.I. | 15 | A 5 |
| Maplewood H.S. | 37 | F 2 |
| Marc Garneau C.I. | 17 | B 5 |
| Martingrove C.I. | 36 | E 2 |
| Massey Centre S.S. | 5 | E 4 |
| Midland Avenue C.I. | 27 | E 4 |
| Monarch Park C.I. | 15 | B 4 |
| Nelson A Boylen S.S. | 18 | B 4 |
| Newtonbrook S.S. (Eng. & Fr.) | 10 | F 1 |
| North Albion C.I. | 40 | F 3 |
| North Toronto C.I. | 7 | A 3 |
| Northern S.S. | 7 | B 3 |
| Northview Heights C.I. | 10 | C 3 |
| Oakwood C.I. | 4 | A 1 |
| Oasis Alternative S.S. | 2 | D 1 |
| Parkdale C.I. | 12 | B 1 |
| R H King Academy | 37 | A 6 |
| Richview C.I. | 26 | B 3 |
| Riverdale C.I. | 5 | F 5 |
| Rosedale Heights S.S. | 5 | C 4 |
| Runnymede C.I. | 14 | A 1 |
| S.E.E. | 28 | B 5 |
| S.E.E.D. | 4 | F 5 |
| S.O.L.E. Alternative Sch. | 15 | A 4 |
| Sa Tec @ W.A.Porter C.I. | 27 | B 5 |
| Scarborough Centre for Alter. Study | 39 | D 2 |
| Scarlett Heights C.I. | 26 | C 2 |
| Silverthorn C.I. | 34 | A 2 |
| Sir John A Macdonald C.I. | 31 | A 4 |
| Sir Oliver Mowat C.I. | 49 | F 6 |
| Sir Sandford Fleming S.S. | 8 | B 5 |
| Sir Wilfrid Laurier C.I. | 37 | E 3 |
| Sir William Osler H.S. | 31 | E 3 |
| St.Rita's Secondary School | 14 | D 2 |
| Stephen Leacock C.I. | 31 | C 4 |
| Subway Academy 1 | 5 | F 4 |
| Subway Academy 2 | 4 | D 4 |
| The City School | 14 | E 5 |
| The Student School | 5 | E 5 |
| Thistletown C.I. | 30 | B 6 |
| Ursula Franklin Academy | 14 | F 4 |
| Vaughan Road C.I. | 6 | B 5 |

| SECONDARY/SEPARATE SCHOOLS | MAP NO | MAP AREA |
|---|---|---|
| Victoria Park S.S. | 19 | E 4 |
| W L Mackenzie C.I. | 10 | A 6 |
| West End Alternative Sch. | 4 | A 5 |
| West Hill C.I. | 49 | A 5 |
| West Humber C.I. | 40 | E 5 |
| West Toronto C.I. | 14 | E 4-5 |
| Western Tech./ Commercial Sch. | 14 | B 3 |
| Weston C.I. | 28 | B 3 |
| Westview Centennial S.S. | 30 | F 4 |
| Wexford C.I. | 29 | A 6 |
| Winston Churchill C.I. | 27 | D 1 |
| Woburn C.I. | 39 | D 3 |
| York Humber H.S. | 26 | F 3 |
| York Memorial C.I. | 16 | C 3 |
| York Mills C.I. | 9 | E 3 |
| Yorkdale S.S. (Adult) | 18 | E 5 |

## SEPARATE SCHOOLS

| SEPARATE SCHOOLS | MAP NO | MAP AREA |
|---|---|---|
| All Saints Sep.S. | 26 | E 5 |
| Annunciation Sep.S. | 19 | E 4 |
| Archbishop Romero Sep.S. | 16 | B 5 |
| Bishop Allen Academy | 24 | B 5 |
| Bishop Marrocco Sep.S. | 14 | E 4 |
| Bl. Margherita of Citta di Castello | 20 | A 6 |
| Blessed Kateri Tekakwitha Sep.S. | 21 | E 5 |
| Blessed Sacrement Sep.S. | 8 | F 6 |
| Blessed Trinity Sep.S. | 11 | D 3 |
| Br Edmund Rice Sep.S. | 14 | D 2 |
| Brebeuf College | 11 | C 1 |
| Canadian Martyrs Sep.S. | 15 | C 2 |
| Cardinal Carter Academy for Arts | 11 | A 6 |
| Cardinal Leger Sep.S. | 49 | A 5 |
| Cardinal Newman Sep.S. | 25 | F 2 |
| Chaminade College | 18 | A 5 |
| Christ the King Sep.S. | 32 | C 4 |
| Corpus Christi Sep.S. | 15 | B 6 |
| D'Arcy McGee Sep.S. | 6 | A 4 |
| Dante Alighieri Academy | 16 | F 1 |
| Don Bosco Sep.S. | 28 | B 5 |
| Father Henry Carr Sep.S. ( Sec.) | 30 | A 3 |
| Father John Redmond | 32 | E 2 |
| Father Serra Sep.S. | 26 | C 2 |
| Francis Libermann Sep.S. | 41 | A 4 |
| Georges-Etienne-Carter Sep.S. (Fr.) | 15 | D 2 |
| Holy Angels Sep.S. | 24 | B 6 |
| Holy Child Sep.S. | 40 | A 4 |
| Holy Cross Sep.S. | 15 | A 2 |
| Holy Family Sep.S. | 12 | B 1 |
| Holy Name Sep.S. | 5 | E 4 |
| Holy Redeemer Sep.S. | 21 | B 4 |
| Holy Rosary Sep.S. | 6 | D 6 |
| Holy Spirit Sep.S. | 31 | C 6 |
| Immaculate Conception Sep.S. | 16 | C 2 |
| Immaculate Heart of Mary Sep.S. | 25 | D 4 |
| James Cardinal McGuigan Sep.S | 20 | C 3 |
| James Culnan Sep.S. | 14 | A 2 |
| Jean Vanier Sep.S. | 27 | F 3 |
| John XXIII Sep.S. | 17 | C 4 |
| Josyf Cardinal Slipyj Sep.S. | 36 | D 5 |
| Loretto Abbey Sep.S. | 8 | F 4 |
| Loretto College ( South Campus ) | 4 | D 3 |
| Madonna Sep.S. ( Sec.) | 18 | D 4 |
| Marian Academy Sep.S. | 40 | E 3 |
| Marshall Mclauhan Sep. S. | 6 | E 3 |
| Mary Ward Sep.S. | 31 | D 1 |
| Mary Ward Sep.S. ( South Campus ) | 31 | D 2 |
| Michael Power / St.Joseph Sep.S. | 24 | A 3 |
| Mother Cabrini Sep.S. | 36 | B 4 |
| Mother Teresa Sep.S. | 41 | F 5 |
| Msgr De-Charbonnel Sep.S. ( Fr.) | 10 | F 2 |

| SEPARATE SCHOOLS | MAP NO | MAP AREA |
|---|---|---|
| Msgr Fraser College /ET Campus | 24 | A 3 |
| Msgr Fraser College /Parkdale Camp. | 14 | D 5 |
| Msgr Fraser College /Malvern Campus | 39 | C 2 |
| Msgr Fraser College /SC.Campus | 25 | F 2 |
| Msgr Fraser College /Toronto Campus | 5 | A 4 |
| Msgr John Corrigan Sep.S. | 40 | D 1 |
| Msgr Percy Johnson Sep.S. | 38 | F 2 |
| Nativity of Our Lord | 36 | C 6 |
| Neil McNeil Sep.S. | 25 | A 5 |
| Notre Dame Sep.S. | 15 | E 5 |
| Our Lady Fatima Sep.S. | 27 | A 6 |
| Our Lady of Assumption Sep.S. | 6 | C 1 |
| Our Lady of Good Council Sep.S. | 31 | A 3 |
| Our Lady of Grace Sep.S. | 41 | A 3 |
| Our Lady of Guadalupe Sep.S. | 21 | B 4 |
| Our Lady of Lourdes Sep.S. | 5 | B 4 |
| Our Lady of Mount Carmel Sep.S. | 21 | F 3 |
| Our Lady of Peace Sep.S. | 34 | F 2 |
| Our Lady of Perpetual Help Sep.S. | 5 | B 1 |
| Our Lady of Sorrows Sep.S. | 24 | C 3 |
| Our Lady of Victory Sep.S. | 16 | A-B 4 |
| Our Lady of Wisdom Sep.S. | 29 | B 3 |
| Pope John Paul the Second Sep.S. | 49 | A 3 |
| Pope Paul Sep.S. | 14 | E 1 |
| Precious Blood Sep.S. | 27 | A-B 1-2 |
| Prince of Peace Sep.S. | 41 | A 1 |
| Regina Mundi Sep.S. | 16 | F 1 |
| Regina Pacis Sep.S. | 30 | F 3 |
| Richard W Scott Sep.S. | 14 | F 1 |
| Sacre,-Coeur Sep.S. ( Fr.) | 5 | B 4 |
| Sacred Heart Sep.S. | 41 | F 5 |
| Sainte-Madeleine Sep.S. ( Fr.) | 19 | F 3 |
| Sainte-Marguerite- d'Youville ( Fr.) | 24 | D 4 |
| Saint-Jean-de-Lalande Sep.S. | 41 | B 4 |
| Saint-Noel-Chabanel Sep.S. ( Fr.) | 18 | B 3 |
| Santa Maria Sep.S. | 16 | B-C 5 |
| Senator O'Connor College | 19 | E 5 |
| Senhor Santo Cristo Sep.S. | 4 | B 6 |
| St Agatha Sep.S. | 37 | B 6 |
| St Agnes Sep.S. | 11 | C 1 |
| St Aidan Sep.S. | 31 | C 4 |
| St Albert Sep.S. | 27 | E 2 |
| St Aloysius Sep.S. | 15 | B 3 |
| St Alphonsus Sep.S. | 6 | B 6 |
| St Ambrose Sep.S. | 32 | C 2 |
| St Andrew Sep.S. | 30 | A 3 |
| St Angela Sep.S. | 40 | E 1 |
| St Ann Sep.S. | 5 | D 6 |
| St Anselm Sep.S. | 7 | D 4 |
| St Anthony Sep.S. | 4 | A 3 |
| St Antoine Daniel Sep.S. | 10 | E 3 |
| St Augustine of Canterbury Sep.S. | 30 | F 2 |
| St Barbara Sep.S. | 39 | D 6 |
| St Barnabas Sep.S. | 41 | E 6 |
| St Bartholomew Sep.S. | 31 | F 6 |
| St Basil Sep. S. (Sec.South Campus) | 28 | D 3 |
| St Basil The Great College | 30 | D 6 |
| St Bede Cath. Sep.S. | 51 | B 4 |
| St Benedict Sep.S. | 40 | F 6 |
| St Bernadette Cath. Sch. | 15 | E 3 |
| St Bernard Sep.S. | 14 | A 1 |
| St Bonaventure Sep.S. | 7 | F 1 |
| St Boniface Sep.S. | 37 | C 4 |
| St Brendan Sep.S. | 49 | E 5 |
| St Brigid Sep.S. | 15 | C 3 |

| SEPARATE SCHOOLS | MAP NO | MAP AREA |
|---|---|---|
| St Bruno Sep.S. | 4 | B 2 |
| St Camillo de Lellis Sep.S. | 30 | F 6 |
| St Catherine Sep.S. | 19 | E 6 |
| St Cecilia Sep.S. | 14 | B 2 |
| St Charles Garnier Sep.S. | 20 | A 3 |
| St Charles Sep.S. | 6 | A 1 |
| St Clare Sep.S. | 6 | A 6 |
| St Clement Sep.S. | 34 | B 4 |
| St Columba Sep. Sch. | 51 | A 5-6 |
| St Cyprian Cath. Sch. | 31 | A 3 |
| St Cyril Sep.S. | 10 | F 4 |
| St David Sep.S. | 4 | B 5 |
| St Demetrius Sep.S. | 26 | D 3 |
| St Denis Sep.S. | 15 | E 6 |
| St Dorothy Sep.S. | 40 | E 4 |
| St Dustan Sep.S. | 25 | A 3 |
| St Edmund Campion Sep.S. | 39 | E 2 |
| St Edward Sep.S. | 10 | E 6 |
| St Elizabeth Sep.S. | 34 | D 3-4 |
| St Elizabeth Seton Sep.S. | 39 | B-C 1 |
| St Eugene Sep.S. | 26 | C 2 |
| St Fidelis Sep.S. | 18 | C 5 |
| St Florence Sep.S. | 49 | A 1 |
| St Francis de Sales Sep.S. | 30 | F 4 |
| St Francis of Assisi Sep.S. | 4 | C 5 |
| St Francis Xavier Sep.S. | 18 | C 6 |
| St Gabriel Lalemant Sep.S. | 41 | E 4 |
| St Gabriel Sep.S. | 11 | C 6 |
| St Gaspar Sep.S. | 30 | C 1 |
| St Gerald Sep.S. | 21 | F 6 |
| St Gerard Majella Sep.S. | 28 | F 3 |
| St Gregory Sep.S. | 24 | F 6 |
| St Helen Sep.S. | 14 | F 5 |
| St Henry Sep.S. | 31 | B 1 |
| St Ignatius of Loyola Sep.S. | 41 | A 4-5 |
| St Isaac Jogues Sep.S. | 19 | F 3 |
| St James Sep.S. | 24 | F 1 |
| St Jane Frances Sep.S. | 20 | A 5-6 |
| St Jean de Brebeuf Sep.S. | 49 | D 2 |
| St Jerome Sep.S. | 20 | C 6 |
| St Joachim Sep.S. | 25 | C 1 |
| St John Bosco Sep.S. | 16 | F 4 |
| St John Elem. Sch. | 28 | E 5 |
| St John Fisher Sep.S. | 31 | A-B 4 |
| St John the Evangelist Elem. Sch. | 28 | D 6 |
| St John Vianney Sep.S. | 30 | C 5 |
| St Josaphat Cath. Sch. | 14 | E 3 |
| St Joseph's College | 4 | F 4 |
| St Joseph Elem. Sch. | 14 | E 2 |
| St Josephs Morrow Park Sep.S. | 11 | D 2 |
| St Jude Sep.S. | 30 | D 5 |
| St Kevin Sep.S. | 29 | A 5 |
| St Lawrence Sep.S. | 29 | D 6 |
| St Leo Sep.S. | 22 | D 3 |
| St Leonard Sep.S. | 21 | A 3 |
| St Louis Sep.S. | 22 | D 1 |
| St Lucy Sep.S. | 4 | C 4 |
| St Luigi Elem. Sep.S. | 14 | E 3 |
| St Luke Sep.S. | 4 | B 5 |
| St Malachy Sep.S. | 47 | C 2 |
| St Marcellus Sep.S. | 36 | F 3 |
| St Margaret Sep.S. | 8 | D 4 |
| St Marguerite Bourgeoys Sep.S. | 31 | F 3 |
| St Maria Goretti Sep.S. | 27 | E 4 |
| St Mark Sep.S. | 24 | E 5 |
| St Martha Sep.S. | 18 | B 1 |
| St Martin De Pores Sep.S. | 47 | A 1 |
| St Martin Sep.S. | 5 | C 5 |
| St Mary of the Angels Sep.S. | 4 | A 2 |
| St Mary Sec. Sep.S. | 4 | A 4 |
| St Mary Sep.S. | 2 | C 1 |
| St Matthew Sep.S. | 16 | D 5 |
| St Matthias Sep.S. | 21 | B 4 |
| St Maurice Sep.S. | 28 | A 5 |
| St Maximillian Kolbe Sep.S. | 31 | C 2 |
| St Michael Choir Sep.S. ( Elm./Sec.) | 5 | A 6 |
| St Michael Sep.S. | 3 | B 2 |
| St Monica Sep.S. | 7 | A 3 |
| St Nicholas of Bari Sep.S. | 16 | E 5 |

| SEPARATE/ PRIVATE SCHOOLS | MAP NO | MAP AREA |
|---|---|---|
| St Nicholas Sep.S. | 37 | B 2 |
| St Nobert Sep.S. | 18 | F 3 |
| St Paschal Baylon Sep.S. | 10 | E 1 |
| St Patrick Sep.S. | 15 | A 4 |
| St Paul Sep.S. | 3 | C 1 |
| St Peter Sep.S. | 4 | C 3 |
| St Philip Neri Sep.S. | 28 | F 4 |
| St Pius X Sep.S. | 14 | A 3 |
| St Raphael Sep.S. | 18 | C 3 |
| St Raymond Sep.S. | 4 | B 3 |
| St Rene Goupil Sep.S. | 31 | F 2 |
| St Richard Sep.S. | 39 | B 5 |
| St Rita Sep.S. | 14 | D 2 |
| St Robert Sep.S. | 8 | B 1 |
| St Roch Sep.S. | 30 | C 3 |
| St Rose of Lima Sep.S. | 39 | B 6 |
| St Sebastian Sep.S. | 14 | F 3 |
| St Simon Sep.S. | 28 | D 3 |
| St Stephen Sep.S. | 28 | B 2 |
| St Sylvester Sep.S. | 31 | D 3 |
| St Teresa Sep.S. | 22 | B 5 |
| St Theresa Shrine Sep.S. | 25 | F 2 |
| St Thomas Aquinas Sep.S. | 6 | A 4 |
| St Thomas More Sep.S. | 39 | D 3 |
| St Timothy Sep.S. | 21 | B 6 |
| St Ursula Sep.S. | 37 | F 3 |
| St Veronica Sep.S. | 14 | F 5 |
| St Victor Sep.S. | 39 | A 4 |
| St Vincent de Paul Sep.S. | 14 | D 5 |
| St Wilfrid Sep.S. | 20 | B 4 |
| St William Sep.S. | 5 | F 5 |
| St. Conrad Sep. S. | 18 | B 3 |
| St.Dominic Savio Sep.S. | 49 | E 3 |
| Stella Maris Sep.S. | 16 | F 6 |
| Sts Cosmas and Damian Sep.S. | 6 | B 2 |
| The Divine Infant Sep.S. | 41 | B 2 |
| Transfiguration Sep.S. | 36 | F 1 |
| Venerable John Merlini Sep.S. | 30 | B 2 |

| PRIVATE SCHOOLS | MAP NO | MAP AREA |
|---|---|---|
| Arrowsmith - Cohen Sch. | 4 | F 3 |
| Associated Hebrew Sch. of Toronto | 10 | D 3 |
| Associated Hebrew Sch./J.H.S. | 8 | C 4 |
| Bais Yaakov Elementary Sch. | 6 | D 1 |
| Bayview Glen Jr. Sch. | 9 | D 5 |
| Beth Jacob Private Sch. | 8 | D 6 |
| Bialik Hebrew Day Sch. | 6 | C 2 |
| Bishop Strachan Sch., The | 6 | E 5 |
| Bleiweiss Centre for Learning | 7 | A 3 |
| Bnei Akiva Pvt. Sch. | 8 | B 2 |
| Branksome Hall | 5 | A 3 |
| Cambridge Int'l College of Canada | 22 | B 2 |
| Community Hebrew Academy | 10 | A-B 5 |
| Crawford Adventist Academy | 10 | C 4 |
| Crescent School, The | 9 | D 5-6 |
| Crestwood Private Sch. | 9 | D 6 |
| Danforth College | 15 | C 4 |
| De La Salle College | 4 | E 1 |
| Dominion College | 24 | F 1 |
| Dunblaine Sch., The | 8 | E 4 |
| E.L.L. Eng.as a Living Language Sch. | 4 | D 2 |
| Eitz Chaim Day Sch. | 10 | D 2 |
| Ellesmere Montessori Sch. | 29 | B 4 |
| Great Lakes College of Toronto | 14 | D 3 |
| Guildwood Village Montessori Sch. | 39 | E 4 |
| Havergal College | 6 | E 1 |
| High Park Montessori Sch. | 14 | E 4 |
| Holy Cross American Sch. | 19 | F 6 |
| Centre Ltd. | 34 | F 4 |
| John Martin College | 37 | B 5 |
| Kingsley Primary Sch. | 26 | A 4 |
| Kohai Educational Centre | 7 | A 3 |
| International Language | | |

| PARKS/ARENAS | MAP NO | MAP AREA |
|---|---|---|
| Denison Armory . . . . . . . . . . .8 | A-B | 4 |
| Downsview Dells Park . . . .18 | A-B | 2 |
| E.T. Seton Park . . . . . . . .17 | A-B | 3-6 |
| Earl Bales Park . . . . . . . . . . .8 | D | 1-2 |
| East Don Parkland . . . . . .11 | D-F | 4-5 |
| East Point Park . . . . . . . .47 | C-E | 3 |
| Edwards Garden . . . . . . . . . .7 | F | 1 |
| Fleetwood Park . . . . . . . .34 | A | 3 |
| G. Ross Lord Park . . . . . .10 | A-C | 1-3 |
| Garnetwood Park . . . . . . .34 | A | 2 |
| Glen Rough Park . . . . . . .49 | E-F | 1-3 |
| High Park . . . . . . . . . . . .14 | B-C | 4-6 |
| Humber Bay Park East/West .22 | E-F | 2-3 |
| James Garden . . . . . . . . .26 | D | 5 |
| Kings Mill Park . . . . . . . .24 | E | 3-4 |
| L'Amoreaux Park . . . . . . .31 | D | 3-4 |
| Marie Curtis Park . . . . . . .32 | B-C | 5-6 |
| Metropolitan Toronto Zoo . .51 | B-C | 4-6 |
| Milliken Park . . . . . . . . . .41 | B | 1 |
| Morningside Park . . . . . . .39 | E-F | 3-6 |
| Rowntree Mill Park . . . . . .30 | A-C | 1-5 |
| Scarborough Bluffs | | |
| West Park . . . . . . . . . .25 | F | 2-3 |
| Steeles District Park . . . . .31 | D | 2 |
| Summerlea Park . . . . . . . .28 | B-C | 1 |
| Sunnybrook Park . . . . . . . .7 | E-F | 2-3 |
| Taylor Creek Park . . . . . .15 | A-F | 1-3 |
| West Dean Park . . . . . . . .36 | D-E | 4-6 |

### ARENAS

| ARENAS | MAP NO | MAP AREA |
|---|---|---|
| Agincourt Rec. Ctr., Scarborough | | |
| 31 Glen Watford Dr. . . . . . .31 | F | 6 |
| Air Canada Ctr., Toronto | | |
| 40 Bay St . . . . . . . . . . . . . .2 | F | 2 |
| Albion Arena, Etobicoke | | |
| 1501 Albion Rd . . . . . . . . . .40 | F | 3 |
| Amesbury Arena, North York | | |
| 155 Culford Rd . . . . . . . . . .16 | C | 1 |
| Baycrest Arena, North York | | |
| 160 Neptune Dr . . . . . . . . . .8 | B | 4 |
| Bayview Arena, North York | | |
| 3230 Bayview Av . . . . . . . .11 | C | 3 |
| Beatrice, North York | | |
| York Univ. Ice Garden . . . . .20 | B | 1 |
| Centennial Arena, Etobicoke | | |
| 56 Centennial Park Rd . . . . .36 | B | 5 |
| Centennial Community Ctr., Scarborough | | |
| 1967 Ellesmere Rd . . . . . . .39 | C | 4 |
| Chesswood Arenas, North York | | |
| 000 Chesswood Dr. . . . . . .20 | E | 5 |
| Chris Tonks, York | | |
| 2801 Eglinton W . . . . . . . .16 | C | 4 |
| Commander Park Arena, Scarborough | | |
| 140 Commander Blvd . . . . .41 | A | 5 |
| Cummer Park Arena, North York | | |
| 6000 Leslie St . . . . . . . . . .11 | F | 2 |
| De LaSalle Arena, Toronto | | |
| De LaSalle College . . . . . . .4 | F | 1 |
| Don Mills Arena, North York | | |
| 1030 Don Mills Rd. . . . . . .17 | B | 1 |
| Downsview Arena, North York | | |
| 1633 Wilson Av . . . . . . . . .28 | F | 4 |
| East York Memorial Arena, East York | | |
| 888 Cosburn Av . . . . . . . .15 | C | 2 |
| Etobicoke Central Arena, Etobicoke | | |
| 50 Montgomery Rd . . . . . . .24 | B | 3 |
| Fenside Arena, North York | | |
| 30 Slidell Cr . . . . . . . . . . . .19 | E | 3 |
| Flemingdon Arena, North York | | |
| 165 Grenoble Dr . . . . . . . .17 | C | 4 |
| Forest Hill Memorial Arena, Toronto | | |
| 340 Chaplin Cr . . . . . . . . . .6 | D | 3 |
| George Bell Arena, Toronto | | |
| 215 Ryding Av . . . . . . . . . .14 | B | 1 |
| Gord & Irene Risk, North York | | |
| 2650 Finch W . . . . . . . . . .30 | B | 4 |
| Goulding Arena, North York | | |
| 45 Goulding Av . . . . . . . . .10 | F | 2 |
| Grandravine Arena, North York | | |
| 23 Grandravine Dr . . . . . . .20 | C | 5 |
| Habitant Arena, North York | | |
| 3383 Weston Rd . . . . . . . . .30 | D | 4 |

| ARENAS | MAP NO | MAP AREA |
|---|---|---|
| Heron Park, Scarborough | | |
| 4285 Lawrence Ave. E. . . . .47 | B | 1 |
| Ice Sport Scarborough, Scarborough | | |
| 159 Dynamic Dr. . . . . . . . .41 | C | 1 |
| Ice Sports Etobicoke, Etobicoke | | |
| 120 Martin Grove Rd . . . . .38 | E | 4 |
| John Booth Memorial, North York | | |
| 230 Gosford Blvd . . . . . . . .20 | A | 2 |
| Lakeshore Lions Arena, Etobicoke | | |
| 300 Birmingham St . . . . . . .32 | F | 4 |
| Lambton, York | | |
| 4100 Dundas W . . . . . . . . .26 | E | 6 |
| Leaside Gardens, East York | | |
| 1073 Millwood Rd . . . . . . . .32 | E | 5 |
| Long Branch Centennial Arena, Etobicoke | | |
| 75 Arcadian Circle . . . . . . .32 | E | 5 |
| Malvern Rec. Ctr., Scarborough | | |
| 30 Sewells Rd . . . . . . . . . .41 | F | 5 |
| Maple Leaf Gardens, Toronto | | |
| 60 Carlton St . . . . . . . . . . . .5 | A | 5 |
| McCormick Rec. Ctr. & Arena, Toronto | | |
| 179 Brock Av . . . . . . . . . . .14 | F | 5 |
| McGregor Park Arena, Scarborough | | |
| 2231 Lawrence Ave. E. . . . .27 | D | 1 |
| Mid-Scarborough Community Ctr., Scarborough | | |
| 2467 Eglinton Ave. E. . . . . .27 | E | 1 |
| Mimico Arena, Etobicoke | | |
| 31 Drummond St . . . . . . . .22 | C | 3 |
| Mitchell Field Arena, North York | | |
| 89 Church Av . . . . . . . . . .11 | A | 4 |
| Moss Park, Toronto | | |
| 140 Sherbourne . . . . . . . . . .5 | B | 6 |
| North T Memorial Gardens, Toronto | | |
| 174 Orchard View Blvd . . . . .6 | F | 3 |
| North York Centennial Arena, North York | | |
| 580 Finch Av W . . . . . . . . .10 | B | 3 |
| Oriole Arena, North York | | |
| 2975 Don Mills Rd . . . . . . .21 | B | 5 |
| Patrick Johnson Arena, Toronto | | |
| Upper Canada College . . . . .6 | E | 5 |
| Phil White, York | | |
| 443 Arlington Av. . . . . . . . . .6 | B | 5 |
| Pine Point Arena, Etobicoke | | |
| 15 Grierson Rd . . . . . . . . . .28 | C | 4 |
| Pleasantview Arena, North York | | |
| 545 Van Home . . . . . . . . . .21 | C | 5 |
| Rinx Arena, The, North York | | |
| 65 Orfus Rd. . . . . . . . . . . .18 | E | 5 |
| Roding, North York | | |
| 600 Roding . . . . . . . . . . . .18 | B | 3 |
| Scarborough Arena Gardens, Scarborough | | |
| 75 Birchmount Rd . . . . . . . .25 | C | 4 |
| Scarborough Village, Scarborough | | |
| 3600 Kingston Rd . . . . . . . .37 | D | 4 |
| Seneca Sports Ctr., North York | | |
| Seneca College . . . . . . . . .21 | C | 3 |
| St. Michael's Arena, Toronto | | |
| St. Michael's College . . . . . .6 | C | 6 |
| Stephen Leacock Community Ctr., Scarborough | | |
| 2500 Birchmount Rd . . . . . .31 | C | 6 |
| Ted Reeve Arena, Toronto | | |
| 175 Main St . . . . . . . . . . . .15 | E | 4 |
| Varsity Arena, Toronto | | |
| 275 Bloor W . . . . . . . . . . . . .4 | E | 4 |
| Victoria Village, North York | | |
| 190 Bermondsey . . . . . . . .17 | E | 3 |
| Weston, York | | |
| 2125 Lawrence Ave. W. . . .26 | E | 1 |
| Westwood Arenas, Etobicoke | | |
| 90 Woodbine Downs | | |
| (Humber College) . . . . . .40 | C | 3 |
| William H Bolton, Toronto | | |
| 40 Rossmore Rd . . . . . . . . .4 | C | 3 |
| York Mills, North York | | |
| 2539 Bayview Av . . . . . . . . .9 | D | 4 |

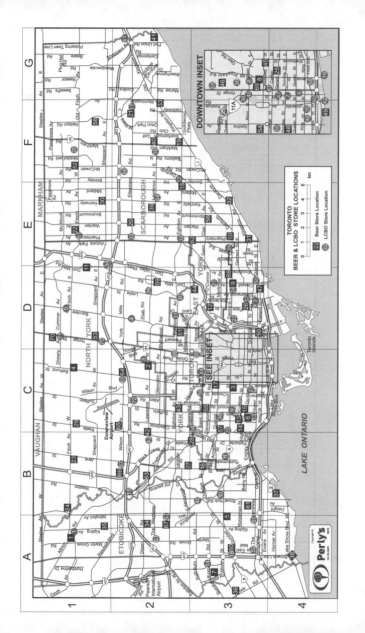

## BEER STORES HOURS OF OPERATION CODE TABLE

|  |  |  |
|---|---|---|
| A | Mon-Wed | 10:00 - 8:00 |
| | Thurs-Fri | 10:00 - 9:00 |
| | Sat | 9:30 - 9:00 |
| B | Mon-Fri | 9:30 - 9:00 |
| | Sat | 9:30 - 6:00 |
| C | Mon-Sat | 9:00 - 9:00 |
| D | Mon-Sat | 9:00 - 9:00 |
| E | Mon-Fri | 10:00 - 9:00 |
| | Sat | 9:00 - 9:00 |
| F | Mon-Thurs | 10:00 - 10:00 |
| | Fri | 10:00 - 11:00 |
| | Sat | 9:30 - 11:00 |
| G | Mon-Thurs | 9:00 - 10:00 |
| | Fri | 9:00 - 11:00 |
| | Sat | 9:00 - 10:00 |
| H | Mon-Fri | 9:00 - 10:00 |
| | Sat | 9:00 - 6:00 |
| I | Mon-Fri | 9:00 - 9:00 |
| | Sat | 9:00 - 6:00 |
| J | Mon-Thurs | 9:00 - 10:00 |
| | Fri-Sat | 9:30 - 11:00 |
| K | Mon-Fri | 9:00 - 9:00 |
| L | Mon-Wed | 9:00 - 6:00 |
| | Thurs-Fri | 9:00 - 9:00 |
| | Sat | 9:30 - 10:00 |
| M | Mon-Fri | 9:00 - 9:00 |
| | Sat | 9:30 - 6:00 |
| N | Mon-Wed | 9:00 - 7:00 |
| | Thurs-Fri | 9:00 - 9:00 |
| | Sat | 9:00 - 6:00 |

**Sunday Hours**
11:00 - 6:00
** 11:00 - 5:00
*** 12:00 - 5:00
Hours are subject to change

### Beer Stores — Addresses

| # | Address | Hrs | Map Ref |
|---|---|---|---|
| 1 | 1530 Albion Rd** | D | A 1 |
| 2 | 1580 Avenue Rd | A | C 2 |
| 3 | 452 Bathurst St | E | C 3 |
| 4 | 4905 Bathurst St | A | C 1 |
| 5 | 3429 Bloor St W | A | A 3 |
| 6 | 65 Brock Ave | C | C 3 |
| 7 | 666 Burnhamthorpe Av | A | A 2 |
| 8 | 5177 Church St | D | G 3 |
| 9 | 3177 Danforth Ave | F | E 3 |
| 10 | 3130 Danforth Ave | F | F 3 |
| 11 | 13078 Don Mills Rd* | B | D 1 |
| 12 | 2380 Don Mills Rd | A | D 3 |
| 13 | 3904 Dufferin St | A | D 3 |
| 14 | 2135 Dundas St W | A | C 3 |
| 15 | 3205 Dundas St W | E | A 3 |
| 16 | 3524 Dundas St W | A | A 3 |
| 17 | 1500 Dupont St | A | C 3 |
| 18 | 2727 Eglinton Ave E | F | E 2 |
| 19 | 3205 Eglinton Ave E | F | F 2 |
| 20 | 40 Ellesmere | A | A 2 |
| 21 | 2866 Ellesmere Rd | H | E 2 |
| 22 | 2005 Finch Ave W | I | B 1 |
| 23 | 2568 Finch Ave E | A | B 1 |
| 24 | 227 Gerrard St E | A | D 3 |
| 25 | 26800 Woodbine Ave | N | G 3 |
| 26 | 27839 Jane St | | |
| 27 | 28515 Keele St | D | |
| 28 | 29385 Keele St | E | |
| 29 | 30 360 Kennedy Rd | A | |
| 30 | 31 1089 Kingston Rd | M | |
| 31 | 32 2229 Kingston Rd | A | |
| 33 | 33 4455 Kingston Rd | A | |
| 34 | 34 1735 Kipling Ave | A | |
| 35 | 35 2251 Kipling Ave | M | |
| 36 | 36 Dixie Rd | | |
| 37 | 37 2458 Lakeshore Blvd W | A | |
| 38 | 38 3580 Lakeshore Blvd W | A | |
| 39 | 39 2300 Lawrence Ave E | A | |
| 40 | 40 3561 Lawrence Ave E | | |
| 41 | 41 1544 Lawrence Ave W | K | |
| 42 | 42 1301 Lawrence Ave W | A | |
| 43 | 43 529 Oakwood Ave | M | |
| 44 | 44 45 Overlea Blvd | A | |

## THE BEER STORE — Addresses

| Address | Hrs | Map Ref |
|---|---|---|
| 45 534 Parliament St | A | D 1 |
| 45 10 Price St | A | C 2 |
| 47 1285 Queen St W | E | C 3 |
| 48 614 Queen St W | A | A 3 |
| 49 350 Queens Quay W | A | A 3 |
| 50 28 River St | C | C 3 |
| 51 609 Roehampton Av | D | G 3 |
| 52 1001 Sandhurst Cir. | D | G 3 |
| 53 179 Sheppard Ave | F | E 3 |
| 54 720 Spadina Ave | A | F 3 |
| 55 1083 St. Clair Ave W | B | D 1 |
| 56 3431 St. Clair Ave W | A | D 3 |
| 57 323 Symington Ave | E | C 3 |
| 58 31 Tapscott Rd | A | C 2 |
| 59 49 The Donway W | A | B 3 |
| 60 10 The East Mall Cr | I | B 2 |
| 61 78 The Queensway | F | C 3 |
| 62 1437 Victoria Pk | E | E 2 |
| 63 2061 Wilson Ave | H | E 2 |
| 64 322 Wilson Ave | A | A 2 |
| 65 1010 Wilson Ave | I | B 1 |
| 66 1718 Wilson Ave | B | B 1 |
| 67 250 Wilson Ave | A | D 3 |
| 68 1270 Woodbine Ave | D | G 4 |
| 69 709 Yonge St* | A | B 3 |
| 70 6212 Yonge St | A | D 3 |

**The Beer Store**

## LCBO RETAIL STORES HOURS OF OPERATION CODE TABLE

|  |  |  |
|---|---|---|
| A | Mon-Sat | 9:00 - 9:00 |
| B | Mon-Thurs,Sat | 8:00 - 10:00 |
| | Fri | 8:00 - 11:00 |
| C | Mon-Sat | 8:00 - 11:00 |
| D | Mon-Fri | 9:00 - 9:00 |
| | Sat | 9:00 - 6:00 |
| E | Mon-Fri | 9:30 - 6:00 |
| | Sat | 9:00 - 6:00 |
| F | Mon-Fri | 9:00 - 6:00 |
| | Sat | 9:30 - 6:00 |
| G | Mon-Fri | 9:00 - 6:00 |
| | Sat-Sun | Closed |
| H | Mon-Wed,Fri-Sat | 9:30 - 6:00 |
| | Thurs | 9:30 - 8:00 |
| I | Mon-Fri | 9:00 - 6:00 |
| | Thurs-Sat | 9:30 - 6:00 |
| J | Mon-Sat | 9:00 - 9:00 |
| K | Mon-wed,Sat | 9:30 - 6:00 |
| | Thurs-Fri | 9:30 - 8:00 |
| L | Mon-Fri | 9:00 - 9:00 |
| | Sat | 9:00 - 6:00 |
| M | Mon-Fri | 9:00 - 9:00 |
| | Sat | 9:30 - 6:00 |
| N | Mon-Fri | 9:00 - 9:00 |
| | Sat | 9:00 - 6:00 |
| O | Mon-Fri | 9:00 - 6:00 |
| | San | 9:00 - 6:00 |
| P | Mon-Fri | 9:00 - 6:00 |
| | Sat | 9:00 - 6:00 |
| Q | Mon-wed,Sat | 9:30 - 6:00 |
| R | Mon-Sat | 9:00 - 9:00 |
| S | Mon-Sat | 9:00 - 9:00 |
| | Sat | 9:30 - 6:00 |
| T | Mon-Fri | 9:00 - 9:00 |
| U | Mon-Fri | 9:00 - 6:00 |
| | Thurs-Fri | 9:00 - 6:00 |
| V | Mon-wed | 9:00 - 7:00 |
| | Thurs-Fri | 9:00 - 9:00 |
| | San | 9:00 - 6:00 |
| W | Mon-Sat | 11:00 - 7:00 |
| X | Mon-Fri | 9:00 - 9:30 |
| Y | Mon-Thurs | 9:00 - 10:00 |
| | Fri-Sat | 9:00 - 11:00 |
| Z | Mon-Sat | 9:00 - 11:00 |

**Sunday Hours 11:00 - 6:00**
* Closed on Sun
** 11:00 - 5:00
*** 12:00 - 5:00
Hours are subject to change

### LCBO Retail Stores — Addresses

| # | Address | Hrs | Map Ref |
|---|---|---|---|
| 1 | 1530 Albion Rd*** | E | A 1 |
| 2 | Atrium on Bay, 595 Bay St** | D | G 4 |
| 3 | 1717 Avenue Rd | N | C 2 |
| 4 | 2512 Bayview Av | U | D 2 |
| 5 | Bayview, 2901 Bayview Av | Z | D 1 |
| 6 | The Bay, 176 Yonge St | S | G 4 |
| 7 | Baseba ... | A | D 2 |
| 8 | 345 Bloor St. E. | A | D 3 |
| 9 | 879 Bloor St W | A | C 3 |
| 10 | 2948 Bloor St W | A | A 3 |
| 11 | Bloor Vill., 2180 Bloor St W | A | B 3 |
| 12 | 2510 Brimley Rd | A | F 2 |
| 13 | 1311 Brock Av | Y | C 3 |
| 14 | 4368 Burnhamthorpe Rd | X | C 2 |
| 15 | B.Y.O. 2625D Weston Rd | N | B 2 |
| 16 | Cedarbrae, 3441 Lawrence Av | A | F 2 |
| 17 | Centenary, 2868 Ellesmere Av | F | F 2 |
| 18 | Cloverdale, 250 The East Mall | C | G 4 |
| 19 | 2 Cooper St | N | F 1 |
| 20 | Coventry, 1001 Sandhurst Cir | A | F 1 |
| 21 | Diablo, 2185 Avenue | T | X 2 |
| 22 | Crossways, 2340 Dundas St W | X | D 3 |
| 23 | 3213 Danforth Av | Y | E 3 |
| 24 | 1145 Danforth Av | A | D 3 |
| 25 | 3111 Danforth Avenue | Y | E 3 |
| 26 | 49 The Donway W | A | D 2 |
| 27 | 3230 Dundas St W | L | F 3 |
| 28 | 2520 Dundas St W | A | X 3 |
| 29 | 198 Dupont St | D | D 2 |
| 30 | East York Ctr, 45 Overlea Blvd** | A | D 2 |
| 31 | 812 Eglinton Av E | P | E 2 |
| 32 | Eglinton Sq., 130 Market Ct* | Y | E 1 |
| 33 | 335 Ellesmere Rd | E | F 1 |
| 34 | Fairview M., 1800 Sheppard E** | A | F 4 |
| 35 | First Canadian Place* | A | C 3 |
| 36 | Galleria Ctr, 1245 Dupont St | T | D 3 |
| 37 | 932 Gerrard St E | H | G 3 |
| 38 | 36 Hazelton La., 87 Avenue Rd*** | V | G 3 |
| 39 | Hudson Bay Centre, 20 Bloor St W | A | A 4 |
| 40 | Humbertown Pl., 259 The Kingsway | A | B 4 |
| 41 | 4541 Kingston Rd | A | A 2 |
| 42 | 42762 Lakeshore Blvd W | B | C 3 |
| 43 | 1405 Lawrence Blvd, North Park Pl | | |
| 44 | Loblaws, 396 St. Clair Av W | | |

### LCBO Retail Stores — Addresses (continued)

| # | Address | Hrs | Map Ref |
|---|---|---|---|
| 45 | Manulife Ctr, 55 Bloor St W**** | W | G 3 |
| 46 | Metro Hall, 200 Wellington St W | G | F 4 |
| 47 | 512 Parliament St | N | C 2 |
| 48 | Pearson Int'l Airport, Terminal 1 | M | A 2 |
| 49 | Pearson Int'l Airport, Terminal 2 | M | A 2 |
| 50 | 1650 Queen St E | A | D 3 |
| 51 | 1090 The Queensway | Y | A 3 |
| 52 | 1750 The Queensway | A | A 3 |
| 53 | Richview Sq., Pl, 250 Wincott Drive | A | A 3 |
| 54 | 475 Rogers Rd | A | C 3 |
| 55 | 337 Spadina Av | A | D 3 |
| 56 | Scarborough, 300 Borough Dr*** | A | F 2 |
| 57 | Sheridan Mall, 1618 Wilson Av | A | B 2 |
| 58 | St. Lawrence Market, 87 Front St E | N | C 1 |
| 59 | 908 St. Clair Av W | X | C 3 |
| 60 | Union Station | E | G 4 |
| 61 | Village Sq., 2946 Finch Av. E | A | E 1 |
| 62 | 25 The West Mall Door No. 3 | C | G 4 |
| 63 | 415 The Westway | A | A 3 |
| 64 | White Shields Pl, 2300 Lawrence Av | A | A 3 |
| 65 | 381 Wilson Av | K | R 2 |
| 66 | Yonge Eglinton Ctr, 2300 Yonge St* | A | G 3 |
| 67 | 545 Yonge St | Z | G 3 |
| 68 | 1121 Yonge St | A | C 3 |
| 69 | 1493 Yonge St | Y | E 3 |
| 70 | 4763 Yonge St | O | D 1 |
| 71 | 1595 Yonge St | X | F 3 |
| 72 | Yorkdale Shopping Centre | J | C 2 |

# NOTES

# NOTES

# NOTES

# NOTES